CIMA C
*Learning*

Relevant fo
Computer-

# C4 —
## of Bu
## Econ

## CIMA C
# Business Accounting

## Steve Adams
## Paul Periton

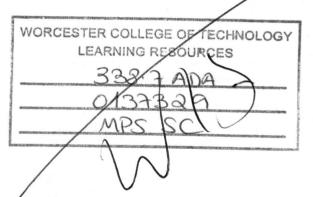

**ELSEVIER**

AMSTERDAM   BOSTON   HEIDELBERG   LONDON   NEW YORK   OXFORD
PARIS   SAN DIEGO   SAN FRANCISCO   SIN

D1382258

0137329

CIMA Publishing is an imprint of Elsevier
Linacre House, Jordan Hill, Oxford OX2 8DP, UK
30 Corporate Drive, Suite 400, Burlington, MA 01803, USA

First edition 2008

**British Library Cataloguing in Publication Data**
A catalogue record for this book is available from the British Library

**Library of Congress Cataloguing in Publication Data**
A catalogue record for this book is available from the Library of Congress

978-1-85617-721-4

For information on all CIMA publications
visit our website at www.elsevierdirect.com

Typeset by Macmillan Publishing Solutions
(www.macmillansolutions.com)

Printed and bound in Italy

09  10  11     11  10  9  8  7  6  5  4  3  2  1

Working together to grow
libraries in developing countries

www.elsevier.com | www.bookaid.org | www.sabre.org

ELSEVIER    BOOK AID International    Sabre Foundation

# Contents

## 3 The Financial System

## 4 The Macroeconomic Context of Business: The Domestic Economy

# The CIMA *Learning System*

## Acknowledgements

Every effort has been made to contact the holders of copyright material, but if any here have been inadvertently overlooked the publishers will be pleased to make the necessary arrangements at the first opportunity.

## How to use your CIMA *Learning System*

This *Fundamentals of Business Economics* has been devised as a resource for students attempting to pass their CIMA computer-based assessments, and provides:

- a detailed explanation of all syllabus areas;
- extensive 'practical' materials, including readings from relevant journals;
- generous question practice, together with full solutions;
- an exam preparation section, complete with exam standard questions and solutions.

This Learning System has been designed with the needs of home-study and distance-learning candidates in mind. Such students require very full coverage of the syllabus topics, and also the facility to undertake extensive question practice. However, the Learning System is also ideal for fully taught courses.

The main body of the text is divided into a number of chapters, each of which is organised on the following pattern:

- *Detailed learning outcomes.* This is expected after your studies of the chapter are complete. You should assimilate these before beginning detailed work on the chapter, so that you can appreciate where your studies are leading.
- *Step-by-step topic coverage.* This is the heart of each chapter, containing detailed explanatory text supported where appropriate by worked examples and exercises. You should work carefully through this section, ensuring that you understand the material being explained and can tackle the examples and exercises successfully. Remember that in many cases knowledge is cumulative; if you fail to digest earlier material thoroughly, you may struggle to understand later chapters.
- *Readings and activities.* Most chapters are illustrated by more practical elements, such as relevant journal articles or other readings, together with comments and questions designed to stimulate discussion.
- *Question practice.* The test of how well you have learned the material is your ability to tackle exam standard questions. Make a serious attempt at producing your own answers,

but at this stage don't be too concerned about attempting the questions in exam conditions. In particular, it is more important to absorb the material thoroughly by completing a full solution than to observe the time limits that would apply in the actual exam.

- *Solutions.* Avoid the temptation merely to 'audit' the solutions provided. It is an illusion to think that this provides the same benefits as you would gain from a serious attempt of your own. However, if you are struggling to get started on a question you should read the introductory guidance provided at the beginning of the solution, and then make your own attempt before referring back to the full solution.

Having worked through the chapters you are ready to begin your final preparations for the examination. The final section of this CIMA *Learning System* provides you with the guidance you need. It includes the following features:

- A brief guide to revision technique.
- Guidance on how to tackle the assessment itself.
- A table mapping revision questions to the syllabus learning outcomes allowing you to quickly identify questions by subject area.
- Revision questions are of exam standard and should be tackled in exam conditions, especially as regards the time allocation.
- Solutions to the revision questions, As before, indicate the length and the quality of solution that would be expected of a well-prepared candidate.
- Mock Assessments – you should plan to attempt these just before the date of the real exam. By this stage your revision should be complete and you should be able to attempt the mock paper in exam conditions.

If you work conscientiously through this CIMA *Learning System* according to the guidelines above you will be giving yourself an excellent chance of exam success. Good luck with your studies!

## Guide to the Icons used within this Text

Key term or definition

Equation to learn

Exam tip or topic likely to appear in the exam

Exercise

Question

Solution

Comment or Note

## Study technique

Passing exams is partly a matter of intellectual ability, but however accomplished you are in that respect you can improve your chances significantly by the use of appropriate study and revision techniques. In this section we briefly outline some tips for effective study during the earlier stages of your approach to the exam. Later in the text we mention some techniques that you will find useful at the revision stage.

## Planning

To begin with, formal planning is essential to get the best return from the time you spend studying. Estimate how much time in total you are going to need for each subject that you face. Remember that you need to allow time for revision as well as for initial study of the material. The amount of notional study time for any subject is the minimum estimated time that students will need to achieve the specified learning outcomes set out earlier in this chapter. This time includes all appropriate learning activities, for example face-to-face tuition, private study, directed home study, learning in the workplace, revision time and so on. You may find it helpful to read *Better exam results* by Sam Malone, CIMA Publishing, ISBN: 075066357X. This book will provide you with proven study techniques. Chapter by chapter it covers the building blocks of successful learning and examination techniques.

The notional study time for Foundation level *Fundamentals of Business Economics* is 130 hours. Note that the standard amount of notional learning hours attributed to one full-time academic year of approximately 30 weeks is 1,200 hours.

By way of example, the notional study time might be made up as follows:

|  | Hours |
|---|---|
| Face-to-face study: up to | 40 |
| Personal study: up to | 65 |
| 'Other' study, e.g. learning in the workplace, revision, etc.: up to | 25 |
|  | 130 |

Note that all study and learning-time recommendations should be used only as a guideline and are intended as minimum amounts. The amount of time recommended for face-to-face tuition, personal study and/or additional learning will vary according to the type of course undertaken, prior learning of the student and the pace at which different students learn.

Now split your total time requirement over the weeks between now and the examination. This will give you an idea of how much time you need to devote to study each week. Remember to allow for holidays or other periods during which you will not be able to study (e.g. because of seasonal workloads).

With your study material before you, decide which chapters you are going to study in each week, and which weeks you will devote to revision and final question practice.

Prepare a written schedule summarising the above and stick to it!

The amount of space allocated to a topic in the study material is not a very good guide as to how long it will take you. Some topics require large numbers of diagrams and/or tables and thus occupy a larger proportion of the text than their weighting in the syllabus. The weighting of topics in the syllabus is the best guide as to how long you should spend on it.

It is essential to know your syllabus. As your course progresses, you will become more familiar with how long it takes to cover topics in sufficient depth. Your timetable may need to be adapted to allocate enough time for the whole syllabus.

## Tips for effective studying

(1)   Aim to find a quiet and undisturbed location for your study, and plan as far as possible to use the same period of time each day. Getting into a routine helps to avoid wasting time. Make sure that you have all the materials you need before you begin so as to minimise interruptions.

(2)   Store all your materials in one place, so that you do not waste time searching for items around the house. If you have to pack everything away after each study period, keep them in a box, or even a suitcase, which will not be disturbed until the next time.

(3)   Limit distractions. To make the most effective use of your study periods you should be able to apply total concentration, so turn off the TV, set your phones to message mode, and put up your 'do not disturb' sign.

(4)   Your timetable will tell you which topic to study. However, before diving in and becoming engrossed in the finer points, make sure you have an overall picture of all the areas that need to be covered by the end of that session. After an hour, allow yourself a short break and move away from your books. With experience, you will learn to assess the pace you need to work at. You should also allow enough time to read relevant articles from newspapers and journals, which will supplement your knowledge and demonstrate a wider perspective.

(5)   Work carefully through a chapter, making notes as you go. When you have covered a suitable amount of material, vary the pattern by attempting a practice question. Preparing an answer plan is a good habit to get into, while you are both studying and revising, and also in the examination room. It helps to impose a structure on your solutions, and avoids rambling. When you have finished your attempt, make notes of any mistakes you made, or any areas that you failed to cover or covered only simpily.

(6)   Make notes as you study, and discover the techniques that work best for you. Your notes may be in the form of lists, bullet points, diagrams, summaries, 'mind maps' or the written word, but remember that you will need to refer back to them at a later date, so they must be intelligible. If you are on a taught course, make sure you highlight any issues you would like to follow up with your lecturer.

(7)   Organise your paperwork. There are now numerous paper storage systems available to ensure that all your notes, calculations and articles can be effectively filed and easily retrieved later.

## Computer-Based Assessments

CIMA has introduced computer-based assessments (CBAs) for all subjects at Certificate level. The website says:

Objective questions are used. The most common type is 'multiple choice', where you have to choose the correct answer from a list of possible answers, but there are a variety of other objective question types that can be used within the system. These include true/false questions, matching pairs of text and graphic, sequencing and ranking, labelling diagrams and single and multiple numeric entry.

Candidates answer the questions by either pointing and clicking the mouse, moving objects around the screen, typing numbers, or a combination of these responses. Try the online demo at www.cimaglobal.com to see how the technology works.

The CBA system can ensure that a wide range of the syllabus is assessed, as a pre-determined number of questions from each syllabus area (dependent upon the syllabus weighting for that particular area) are selected in each assessment.

In every chapter of this learning system we have introduced these types of questions but obviously we have to label answers A, B, C and so on rather than using click boxes. For convenience we have retained quite a lot of questions where an initial scenario leads to a number of sub-questions. There will be questions of this type in the CBA but they will rarely have more than three sub-questions. In all such cases, examiners will ensure that the answer to one part does not hinge upon a prior answer.

There are two types of questions which were previously involved in objective testing in paper-based exams and which are not at present possible in a CBA. The actual drawing of graphs and charts is not yet possible. Equally, there will be no questions calling for comments to be written by students. Charts and interpretations remain on many syllabi and will be examined at Certificate level but using other methods.

For further CBA practice, CIMA Publishing has produced CIMA Interactive CD-ROMs for all certificate level subjects. These products will be available at www.cimapublishing.com.

## Fundamentals of Business Economics and Computer-Based Assessments

The examination for *Fundamentals of Business Economics* is a 2-hour computer-based assessments comprising 75 compulsory questions, with one or more parts. Single part questions are generally worth 1–2 marks each, but two and three part questions may be worth 4 or 6 marks. There will be no choice and all questions should be attempted if time permits. CIMA are continuously developing the question styles within the CBA system and you are advised to try the online website demo, to both gain familiarity with assessment software and examine the latest style of questions being used.

### Additional Reading

J. Sloman, *Economics and the Business Environment* 2nd ed. (Pearson Education, 2007).

## Fundamentals of Business Economics Syllabus

### Syllabus outline

The syllabus comprises:

Topic and Study Weighting
A   The Goals and Decisions of Organisations – 20%
B   The Market System and the Competitive Process – 30%
C   The Financial System – 20%
D   The Macroeconomic Context of Business – 30%

## Learning aims

This syllabus aims to test students ability to:

- distinguish the differing goals of organisations and identify how these differing goals affect the decisions made by managers;
- illustrate how market economies function and identify the reasons for, and impacts of, government involvement in economic activities;
- identify the role of financial institutions and markets in the provision of short- and long-term finance to individuals, businesses and governmental organizations;
- identify how macroeconomic variables and government economic policies affect the organization.

# Learning outcomes and indicative syllabus content

## A The Goals and Decisions of Organisations – 20%

### Learning outcomes

On completion of their studies students should be able to:

- distinguish the goals of profit-seeking organisations, not-for-profit organisations and governmental organisations;
- compute the point of profit maximisation for a single product firm in the short run;
- distinguish the likely behaviour of a firm's unit costs in the short run and long run;
- illustrate the effects of long-run cost behaviour on prices, the size of the organisation and the number of competitors in the industry;
- illustrate shareholder wealth, the variables affecting shareholder wealth and its application in management decision-making;
- identify stakeholders and their likely impact on the goals of not-for-profit organisations and the decisions of the management of not-for-profit organisations;
- distinguish between the potential objectives of management and those of shareholders, and the effects of this principal–agent problem on decisions concerning price, output and growth of the firm.
- describe the main mechanisms to improve corporate governance in profit-seeking organisations.

### Indicative syllabus content

- The forms of ownership of organisations by which we mean public, private and mutual, and their goals.
- Graphical treatment of short-run cost and revenue behaviour as output increases (revenue and cost curves) and identification of point of short-run profit maximisation using graphical techniques and from data.
- Long-run cost behaviour and the impact of economies and diseconomies of scale.
- Concept of returns to shareholder investment in the short run (ROCE and EPS) and long run (NPV of free cash flows) leading to the need for firms to provide rates of return to shareholders at least equal to the firm's cost of capital.

- Calculation of impact on the value of shares of a change to a company's forecast cash flows or required rate. (*Note:* Calculations required will be either perpetual annuity valuations with constant annual free cash flows, or NPV calculations with variable cash flows over three years.)
- Types of not-for-profit organisations (NPOs) and the status of economic considerations as constraints rather than primary objectives in the long run.
- Role of stakeholders in setting goals and influencing decisions in not-for-profit organisations (NPOs) and potential ways of resolving differing stakeholder demands.
- The principal–agent problem, its likely effect on decision-making in profit-seeking and NPO organisations, and the concepts of scrutiny and corporate governance.

# B  The Market System and the Competitive Process – 30%

## Learning outcomes

On completion of their studies students should be able to:

- identify the equilibrium price in a product or factor markets likely to result from specified changes in conditions of demand or supply;
- calculate the price elasticity of demand and the price elasticity of supply;
- identify the effects of price elasticity of demand on a firm's revenues following a change in prices.
- describe market concentration and the factors giving rise to differing levels of concentration between markets;
- describe market failures, their effects on prices, efficiency of market operation and economic welfare and the likely responses of government to these;
- distinguish the nature of competition in different market structures; identify the impacts of the different forms of competition on prices and profitability.

## Indicative syllabus content

- The price mechanism: determinants of supply and demand and their interaction to form and change equilibrium price.
- The price elasticity of demand and its effect on firms' revenues and pricing decisions.
- The price elasticity of supply and its impact on prices, supply and buyers' expenditure.
- Business integration: mergers, vertical integration and conglomerates.
- Calculation of market concentration and its impact on efficiency, innovation and competitive behaviour.
- Impact of monopolies and collusive practices on prices and output and role of competition policy in regulating this.
- Factors causing instability of prices in primary goods markets (i.e. periodic and short-run inelasticity of supply, the cobweb or hog cycle) and the implications of this for producer incomes, industry stability and supply and government policies to combat this (e.g. deficiency payments, set-aside, subsidies).
- Impact of minimum price (minimum wages) and maximum price policies in goods and factor markets.

- Positive and negative externalities in goods markets and government policies to deal with these (including indirect taxes, subsidies, polluter pays policies and regulation).
- Public assurance of access to public goods, healthcare, education and housing.
- Public versus private provision of services (nationalisation, privatisation, contracting out, public private partnerships).

# C  The Financial System – 20%

## Learning outcomes

On completion of their studies students should be able to:

- identify the factors leading to liquidity surpluses and deficits in the short, medium and long run in households, firms and governments;
- explain the role of various financial assets, markets and institutions in assisting organisations to manage their liquidity position and to provide an economic return to holders of liquidity;
- identify the role of insurance markets in the facilitation of the economic transfer and bearing of risk for households, firms and governments;
- identify the role of the foreign exchange market and the factors influencing it, in setting exchange rates and in helping organisations finance international trade and investment;
- explain the role of national and international governmental organisations in regulating and influencing the financial system, and the likely impact of their policy instruments on businesses.

## Indicative syllabus content

- The causes of short-term, medium-term and long-term lack of synchronisation between payments and receipts in households (i.e. month-to-month cash flow, short-term saving and borrowing, and longer-term property purchases and pensions provision).
- The causes of short-term, medium-term and long-term lack of synchronisation between payments and receipts in firms (i.e. month-to-month cash flow management, finance of working capital and short-term assets and long-term permanent capital).
- The causes of short-term, medium-term and long-term lack of synchronisation between payments and receipts in governmental organisations (i.e. month-to-month cash flow management, finance of public projects and long-term management of the national debt).
- The principal contracts and assets issued by financial institutions and borrowers to attract liquidity in the short, medium and long term (e.g. credit agreements, mortgages, bills of exchange, bonds, certificates of deposit and equities).
- The roles and functions of financial intermediaries and the principal institutions and markets in the financial system.
- The influence of commercial banks on the supply of liquidity to the financial system through their activities in credit creation.
- Yield on financial instruments (i.e. bill rate, running yield on bonds, net dividend yield on equity), relation between rates, role of risk, the yield curve.
- Influence of central banks on yield rates through market activity and as providers of liquidity to the financial system.

- Principal insurance contracts available and basic operation of insurance markets including terminology (e.g. broking, underwriting, reinsurance).
- The role of foreign exchange markets in facilitating international trade and in determining the exchange rate.
- Effect of exchange rates on the international competitiveness of firms, including elementary foreign exchange translation calculations.
- Credit and foreign exchange risks of international trading firms and the use of letters of credit, export credit guarantees and exchange rate hedging to manage these risks.
- Influences on exchange rates: interest rates, inflation rates, trade balance, currency speculation.
- Governmental and international policies on exchange rates (i.e. exchange rate management, fixed and floating rate systems, single currency zones) and the implications of these policies for international business.

# D   The Macroeconomic Context of Business – 30%

## Learning outcomes

On completion of their studies students should be able to:

- explain macroeconomic phenomena, including growth, inflation, unemployment, demand management and supply-side policies;
- explain the main measures and indicators of a country's economic performance and the problems of using these to assess the wealth and commercial potential of a country;
- identify the stages of the trade cycle, its causes and consequences, and discuss the business impacts of potential policy responses of government to each stage;
- explain the main principles of public finance (i.e. deficit financing, forms of taxation) and macroeconomic policy;
- explain the concept of the balance of payments and its implications for business and for government policy;
- identify the main elements of national policy with respect to trade, including protectionism, trade agreements and trading blocks;
- identify the conditions and policies necessary for economic growth in traditional, industrial and post-industrial societies, and the potential consequences of such growth;
- explain the concept and consequences of globalisation for businesses and national economies;
- identify the major institutions promoting global trade and development, and their respective roles.

## Indicative syllabus content

- National Income Accounting identity and the three approaches to calculation and presentation of national income (Output, Expenditure and Income).
- Interpretation of national income accounting information for purposes of time series or cross-sectional evaluation of economic performance.
- The circular flow of income and the main injections and withdrawals.
- Illustration of changes to equilibrium level of national income using aggregate demand and supply analysis.

- Government macroeconomic policy goals (low unemployment, inflation, external equilibrium and growth) and the effects on business of the government's pursuit of these.
- Types and consequences of unemployment, inflation and balance of payments deficits.
- The trade cycle and the implications for unemployment, inflation and trade balance of each stage (recession, depression, recovery, boom).
- Government policy for each stage of the business cycle and the implications of each policy for business.
- The central government budget and forms of direct and indirect taxation. Incidence of taxation (progressive, regressive) and potential impact of high taxation on incentives and avoidance.
- Fiscal, monetary and supply-side policies, including relative merits of each.
- Layout of balance of payments accounts and the causes and effects of fundamental imbalances in the balance of payments.
- Arguments for and against free trade and policies to encourage free trade (e.g. bi-lateral trade agreements, multi-lateral agreements, free trade areas, economic communities and economic unions), and protectionist instruments (tariffs, quotas, administrative controls, embargoes).
- Principal institutions encouraging international trade (e.g. WTO/GATT, EU, G6) Nature of globalisation and factors driving it (e.g. improved communications, political realignments, growth of global industries and institutions, cost differentials).
- Impacts of globalisation (e.g. industrial relocation, emergence of growth markets, enhanced competition, cross-national business alliances and mergers, widening economic divisions between countries).
- Role of major institutions (e.g. World Bank, International Monetary Fund, European Bank) in fostering international development and economic stabilisation.

# 1

# The Goals and Decisions of Organisations

# The Goals and Decisions of Organisations

## LEARNING OUTCOMES

This chapter introduces some key concepts in the study of business economics. It begins with a discussion of the allocation of scarce resources and the ways in which this can be resolved.

It examines the goals of organisations with special reference to the quest for profits alongside an analysis of the cost structures of firms. It looks at the role of stakeholders paying particular attention to shareholders. Finally, it considers how stakeholders are involved in decision-making within organisations and the ways in which such governance can be improved.

After completing this chapter you should be able to:

▶ distinguish the goals of profit-seeking organisations, not-for-profit organisations and governmental organisations;

▶ compute the point of profit maximisation for a single product firm in the short run;

▶ distinguish the likely behaviour of a firm's unit costs in the short run and in the long run;

▶ illustrate the effects of long-run cost behaviour on prices, the size of the organisation and the number of competitors in the industry;

▶ illustrate shareholder wealth, the variables affecting shareholder wealth and its application in management decision-making;

▶ identify stakeholders and their likely impact on the goals of not-for-profit organisations and the decisions of the management of not-for-profit organisations;

▶ distinguish between the potential objectives of management and those of shareholders, and the effects of this principal–agent problem on decisions concerning price, output and growth of the firm;

▶ describe the main mechanisms to improve corporate governance in profit-seeking organisations.

## 1.1 Scarce resources

### 1.1.1 Scarcity

To Many people economics is about money. This is because money is used to value things. Most of the things are more accurately termed 'goods' and 'services' and they have a price, which shows what people are prepared to pay for the ownership of these goods and services.

- The price, or exchange value, of a good/service will usually reflect the *resources* which are combined to produce it. These resources, such as land and labour, also have a price and this is largely determined by demand and supply factors. For example, coloured pencils are cheap because wood is in plentiful supply but quill pens are more expensive as there is a limited supply of raw materials required to produce them.
- Thus, scarce resources usually command a high price.
- Sometimes, there are *competing ends* for which resources could be used. If these ends are many and varied in importance and the means of achieving them are limited, then there is an economic problem. For example, wood can be used for a variety of products ranging from furniture to tent pegs, and someone has to decide which end will be satisfied through production.

The decision regarding how to use the wood will need to take into account people's *wants*. If the demand for furniture is enormous and the demand for tent pegs is minuscule, it is likely that furniture will be produced.

Generally, there are insufficient resources available to produce all the goods and services which people want. This *relative scarcity* of resources means that a choice has to be made.

When a choice arises, an alternative has to be given up.

- Thus, a producer might have to choose between using wood for furniture or tent pegs, because his resources are limited.
- Similarly, a consumer may have a limited amount of income and thus has to choose between two alternative products; for example a painting or a new garden mower, both valued at £400.

The sacrifice, when a choice is made, is termed the opportunity cost because it is the alternative forgone. Usually, the *opportunity cost* has a monetary value. However, it could be a choice over the use of time, for example, write a chapter of a book or play 36 holes of golf!

- Choice arises because of relative scarcity.
- Opportunity cost is a measurement of the foregone alternative.

### 1.1.2 Production decisions

When allocating scarce resources between competing ends, several production decisions need to be made.

- For whom to produce?
  This decision will be determined by those with political power, and it therefore largely depends on the nature of the *political system* within which the economic system operates. For example, in a communist state, such as Cuba, the government dictates that production is organised for the equal benefit of all citizens. In contrast, in a liberal democracy with a capitalist-oriented economy, such as the United States, the driving force is profits.

Consequently, production will be directed towards those who can afford to purchase output as this will be the most profitable for the individuals and groups with control over resources.

- What to produce?
  In a market economy the goods and services produced will be those which generate the greatest profit. Thus the American economy might produce a wide range of ostentatious luxury services, such as drive-in funeral parlours for the busy bereaved, which can be bought by the affluent few. However, in economies where the profit motive is not dominant, for example Cuba, output will be more oriented towards producing basic merit goods, such as education to benefit all in society.
- How to produce?
  Resources need utilising in the most cost-efficient way. Businesses strive for the lowest unit cost in theory. They regularly appraise production methods and may vary the resource inputs in order to maximise output. This may mean the substitution of one resource for another, for example machines for people. Generally though, the resource of labour is kept as fully employed as possible in most economic systems for political as much as economic reasons.
- How to distribute?
  The goods and services which are produced need sharing so that consumption can take place and wants are fulfilled. In most systems, the distribution of most goods and services is by *price* – those who cannot afford to pay go without. The price may be set by the state, in the command economy, or by the independent business, in the free-market approach.
- In a market economy, production decisions are driven by the profit motive.

### 1.1.3    Factors of production

The economic resources which are used in tackling the economic problem are referred to as factors of production. These are usually classified as:

- *Land.* This is the term used to cover all *natural resources.* Although largely in limited supply it can be improved through technological advances, for example irrigation. The reward accruing to land in the production process is termed *rent.*
- *Labour.* This is a specific category of *human resource.* The quality of labour can be raised through education and training. The application of capital, through the use of machinery, will improve labour productivity. The reward of labour is termed *wages.*
- *Enterprise.* This is another human resource but refers to the role played by the organiser of production, including *risk.* In return for risk-taking, organising and decision taking, entrepreneurs receive *profit.*
- *Capital.* These are man-made resources. Capital may be *fixed,* for example a factory, or *working* capital, for example raw materials and work in progress. The reward accruing to capital in the production process is termed *interest.*

### 1.1.4    Production possibilities

The production possibilities for any economy can be shown in a simplified form by a production possibility frontier (PPF) curve. The axes on the graph represent the different types of goods that could be produced, such as capital goods (goods used to produce an output of other goods and services, e.g. a machine) and consumer goods.

THE GOALS AND DECISIONS OF ORGANISATIONS

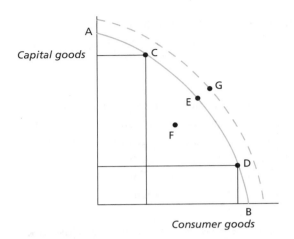

**Figure 1.1** Production possibility curve

The curve then shows the maximum of all the possible combinations of the two types of output that could be produced with the existing resources. It assumes an unchanging state of technology. In Figure 1.1, AB represents all the possible output combinations. Thus at point C, existing resources produce a large quantity of capital goods and a small quantity of consumer goods. Point D indicates the opposite combination.

The curve is normally drawn concave to the origin, thereby showing that some resources are better suited to the production of one good rather than another and vice versa.

- In this theory there is an optimum production point which lies along the PPF, for example, at point E. Here resources are fully utilised at existing prices.
- An economy operating within the PPF, for example at point F, typifies an economy operating within its potential. It is operating inefficiently and will be experiencing unemployment.
- An outward movement in the PPF, as indicated by the dotted line in Figure 1.1 and the point G, shows an increase in productive potential and the capacity for long-term economic growth.

## 1.1.5 The role of government

The ways in which the allocation decisions are made depends upon the *economic system* used to resolve the economic problem of scarcity. The economic system used depends on the political system in a country and the political views of the prevailing government.

Usually three main types of economic system are identified: *planned*, *market* and *mixed*.

The label 'planned' usually refers to an economy in which decisions as to resource allocation are made by a *centralised body*, rather than through the price mechanism. As the plans regarding production and distribution are determined by a powerful group who control the use of resources, the epithet *command* is also used to describe such an economy.

At the other extreme of the economic spectrum, an economy may be *free*. In such a system the resources are allocated through *market* price, with the individuals as producers and consumers making their own economic decisions.

Between these two extremes, *mixed* economies can be located. In a mixed economy, some resources are allocated in a planned way and others in the market way. Furthermore, the distribution of the production may be both controlled and subject to market forces, for example health provision by the state or by fee-paying.

This classification by *resource allocation* leads to the practical conclusion that *all economies are mixed but to varying degrees.* In the United States, there is a small but important state sector. In the former USSR, the bulk of resource allocation was determined by the state but now, in Russia and the other independent states, there is a large and rapidly growing market sector. Also, recent developments in China, which have seen an opening up of the economy to outsiders, confirm the trend towards the acceptance of a need for a market sector.

In mixed market economies, governments may wish to intervene in the economy in various ways.

- They may wish to influence the relative prices of goods and inputs, by taxing or subsidising them or by direct price controls.
- They can affect the pattern of production and consumption by direct provision, for example by defence and health, or by regulations prohibiting certain type of goods, such as illicit firearms or unsafe goods.
- They can influence relative incomes by the use of taxes and welfare payments.
- Finally, the government concerns itself with macroeconomic issues of unemployment, inflation, economic growth and the balance of payments.

The mixture in an economic system categorised by ownership is between a *public* sector and a *private* sector. The relative size of each sector is often determined by political considerations. However, the ultimate intention is to make the most efficient use of the resources available in order to improve the well-being of the society. This usually means improvements in the standard of living.

## 1.2 The business organisation

Businesses in the private sector aim to make profits, which can be distributed to their owners. However, in the public sector, firms often have different motivations. For example, British Universities seek to break even.

The aims and activities of firms may also be constrained in practice by factors such as:

- *The law.* The legal status of a firm affects its behaviour. A public company's line of business is determined by its Memorandum of Association. The responsibilities of public corporations have been specified in the Act which created them.
- *The nature of the business.* Certain enterprises have important social considerations. Thus, subsidies may be given to rural bus services to provide uneconomic services for passengers. On other occasions, subsidies may be given to promote environmentally friendly output, such as wind power. For some firms ethical considerations may be important, for example, confidentiality in private health firms. Other firms, such as airlines, must ensure that safety precedes profit. Consequently although profit-making may be the major driving force behind private firms, other secondary considerations may have an important role to play in the way they operate.
- *Human nature.* No two entrepreneurs or managers are the same. Thus, prediction about decision-making is difficult. Individuals have different values, morals and perceptions. Even if senior management is united on a course of action, this may be thwarted by the behaviour of other key people in an organisation.

### 1.2.1  Profit maximisation as an objective

The profit maximising assumption is based on two premises:

- First, that owners are in control of the everyday management of the firm;
- Secondly, that the motivation of owners is for the highest possible profit. This is considered a self-evident truth of human nature in that people prefer 'more to less'.

The case for profit maximising behaviour is undermined if either of these two premises fails to exist in the real world of business.

### 1.2.2  Principal–agent theory

The owners who control the dominant form of business organisation, the public limited company (PLC), are the shareholders. The people who run the PLC are normally the managers. This may lead to conflict of interest between the owners (shareholders) and the managers whenever the managers pursue goals which differ from those of the owners. This is referred to as a type of *principal–agent* problem.

- A principal–agent problem emerges when the shareholders (principals) contract a second party, the managers (agents), to carry out some tasks on their behalf. In the contract the principals offer their agents compensation in the form of salaries and wages.

  However, as the principals are divorced from the everyday running of the business, the agents may be able to act in their own interests. This independence of action may be due to their superior knowledge of the business and of managerial issues in general as well as their ability to disguise their actions from the principals.
- Thus the agents' goals may determine the objectives of the business. This observation has led to alternative theories of a firm's behaviour.

The principal–agent problem is discussed in more detail in Section 1.7.2.

### 1.2.3  Alternative theories of the firm

Though there are many variants on the alternative theories of the firm, the following indicate the main formats.

#### Managerial theories

These theories focus on management as the decision-maker with a maximising aim other than profit, but subject to a profit constraint. Baumol proposed a theory in which sales maximisation was the objective but a certain level of profits was necessary to keep shareholders happy. The underlying aims behind sales maximisation varied from the personal motive of higher salary through to the more laudable company objective of increased market share. Others have interpreted the latter as a profit-maximising goal, but in the long run.

#### Satisficing theories

These theories assume that management needs to achieve a satisfactory target for at least two major variables. Thus, Marris suggests an approach in which managers sought to satisfy certain goals of company growth and share price value. From the growth goal, management could gain the satisfactions of power, prestige and pay while a high share value would keep shareholders happy, reduce the threat of predatory stock market takeovers and enable the management to survive.

### Behavioural theories

These are somewhat similar to the satisficing theories but differ in that they perceive that the firm's objective is a compatible set of target figures for the major operating variables. The firm is recognised to be a coalition of various groups, each with its own objectives regarding output, sales, profit and so on. The decision-makers in the firm seek acceptable levels of attainment for each major variable. For example, a managerial approach seeking compatibility between various objectives might expand output and sales even though total profits fell as a result, provided that the profit level was acceptable. However, if the output target was incompatible with total profits it would be abandoned in favour of a more compatible level. Once compatible targets have been agreed, then pricing and output decisions would be made accordingly.

Despite all of the above theories, the ultimate goal of many managers is *survival*.

## 1.2.4   Not-for-profit theories of the firm

Most such organisations are found in the public sector. However, interestingly there are some private sector firms, notably charity shops, that seek to maximise their income. However, their 'profits' are termed 'surpluses' and are not subject to corporation tax, because of their tax-exempt status. Increasingly the profit motive, and professional management in accordance with commercial principles, has been inculcated into the operation of charities. For example, Oxfam employs specialists, in addition to unpaid volunteers, to run its retailing activities and is prepared to close down unviable shops. In the case of charities, profits are not the be-all and end-all of business because for them it is a means to an end, that is, the relief of suffering.

Public sector bodies, agencies and government departments are examples of not-for-profit organisations. The Conservative government decision in the 1980s to privatise some nationalised industries and hive off certain civil service functions to separate agencies was based on the assumption that only profit-driven organisations could be efficient. This was a very questionable assumption. Many local government services were also privatised and much public spending became cash flow/budget limited rather than open-ended. Although value for money and less waste were sought, in many practical cases such restrictions meant a poorer service.

Thus, one clear alternative motive to profit in the public sector is service. However, because the costs of providing the service have to be met out of the public purse, most organisations attempt to operate efficiently. This has meant the implementation of modern commercial practices, target-setting and certain minimum standards of work. For example, social workers have referral response rate targets which are monitored as part of a customer care policy. Similarly schools are set targets in respect of the percentage of their students who pass examinations.

Production by the state sometimes does not yield revenue. Merit goods, such as healthcare and education, are sold at zero price or heavily subsidised. They could earn large amounts of revenue, as shown by the fact that similar services provided privately are substantial profit-makers.

## 1.3  Profit maximisation calculation

The specific aim of profit-making is rather imprecise and subject to various interpretations. Thus, in theory, economists distinguish between different types of profit.

- *Normal profit.* The amount of profit needed to keep an entrepreneur in their present activity. It is the reward gained for skill in risk-bearing and organising the factors of production. For this reason, normal profit is treated as a cost of production and therefore included in total costs.
- *Abnormal profit.* Profits obtained above the normal profit. This is the excess when total revenue is greater than total costs. It could be the reward for successful innovation or the result of market imperfections. These could arise from shortages in an industry which enable a firm to raise prices and take extra profits. Whether these surplus profits remain in the long run depends on the nature of the industry and its market conditions. Generally, if entry barriers exist to prevent new firms joining an industry, then abnormal profits will be retained in the long run.

In order to be able to calculate the profit maximising position for a firm it is first necessary to define certain concepts.

- *Total revenue* is obtained by multiplying output sold by price.
- *Average revenue* is calculated by dividing total revenue by units sold. Average revenue and price are always the same.
- *Marginal revenue* is the change in total revenue resulting from the sale of one more unit of output. It thus represents incremental revenue.
- *Total cost* is the cost of all the resources needed to produce any particular level of output.
- *Average cost* is the total cost divided by the number of units of output produced.
- *Marginal cost* is the change in total cost resulting from the production of one more unit of output. It thus represents incremental cost.

The relationship between these concepts is shown in Table 1.1.

Profit maximisation will then occur when:

- Total revenue exceeds total cost by the greatest amount.
- Marginal cost equals marginal revenue and marginal cost is rising. Increasing output will be more profitable if marginal revenue exceeds marginal cost because each unit of extra output adds more to total revenue than to total cost. In Table 1.1, total profit is the same at output level 20 as at output level 30. However, as marginal revenue exceeds marginal cost between these levels of output *profit maximisation* will occur at output level 30, as only here does marginal revenue equal marginal cost and marginal cost is rising.

**Table 1.1**   Cost, Revenue and Profit

| Output Q | Average Revenue AR (Price) | Total Revenue TR | Marginal Revenue MR | Total Cost TC | Average Cost AC | Marginal Cost MC | Total Profit TP |
|---|---|---|---|---|---|---|---|
| 0 | 9 | 0 | – | 40 | – | – | −40 |
| 10 | 8 | 80 | 80 | 70 | 7 | 30 | 10 |
| 20 | 7 | 140 | 60 | 100 | 5 | 30 | 40 |
| 30 | 6 | 180 | 40 | 140 | 4.7 | 40 | 40 |
| 40 | 5 | 200 | 20 | 180 | 4.5 | 40 | 20 |
| 50 | 4 | 200 | 0 | 200 | 4 | 20 | 0 |

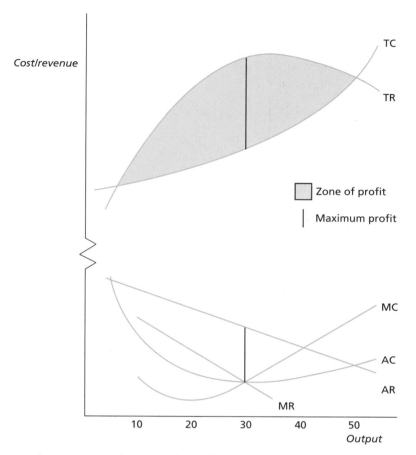

**Figure 1.2**  Profit maximisation

The same point of profit maximisation can be shown in diagrammatic form as in Figure 1.2. The top part of the figure shows total concepts while the lower part shows average and marginal concepts. It illustrates the link between the two. The shaded area represents the levels of output within which profits are made. The maximum profit is shown by the greatest difference between total revenue and total cost which is at output level 30. If the firm increased output above level 30 it would still be profitable because total revenue exceeds total costs, but would not be operating at the point of maximum profitability which is where marginal revenue equals marginal cost. Somewhere below output 10 and beyond output 50 losses are suffered.

- Breakeven for a firm occurs where average revenue equals average cost and total revenue equals total cost.

In Figure 1.2 this will occur at two points, somewhere below output level 10 and at output level 50. A firm will expand output beyond the first point as long as marginal revenue exceeds marginal cost. Beyond the second breakeven point at output level 50, marginal cost will be rising and exceeding marginal revenue so that losses are incurred.

To summarise the major points:

- Profit maximisation occurs when marginal revenue equals marginal cost.
- Total cost includes an element for normal profit.
- Breakeven profit occurs when total revenue equals total cost.

The amount of profit obtained and whether it is normal or abnormal depends upon:

- The market structure within which a firm operates.
- The time period involved.

Both of these points are considered later.

## 1.4 The theory of costs

### 1.4.1 Costs of production

These are the prices paid for the factors of production and the opportunity cost attributable to factors already owned. Costs are related to output over a period of time. For simplicity the term 'firm' will be used for a productive unit which sells its output at a price, irrespective of whether it is producing goods or services or whether it is in the public sector or the private sector of the economy.

#### Fixed and variable costs

- Fixed costs are costs which do not change with the level of production. For example, the rent of premises, the depreciation of a machine, the managing director's salary.
- Variable costs are costs which do change with the level of output. For example, more steel is needed for producing 1,000 cars than for making 10 cars. Variable costs arise from using inputs such as labour and raw materials. In practice there are costs such as sales expenses which are semi-variable, but the analysis is simplified by distinguishing only fixed and variable costs.

#### Short run

- The short run, in economics, is defined as a period of time in which at least one factor of production is fixed. Thus it is not a time period which can be measured in days or months.
- This fixed-factor definition means that the level of production in the short run can be increased only by adding more long-run variable factors to the fixed factor.

#### Long run

- In the long run, all factors are considered to be variable. However, it is assumed that the quality of the factors stays constant.
- In the very long run the assumption of fixed technology is removed.
- Consequently, advances in technology can lead to improvements in the productivity of factors of production.

#### Average costs and marginal costs

If fixed costs and variable costs are added they give the total cost of production at different levels of output. The average cost is calculated by dividing the total costs by output.

When average cost is at its minimum, a firm is operating most efficiently. This optimum output point is that of technical efficiency. In Figure 1.3, this is where the marginal cost curve intersects the average cost curve. This is always at the bottom point of the AC curve.

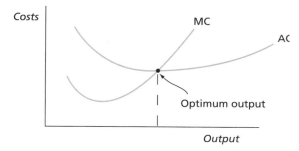

**Figure 1.3** The relationship of AC to MC in the short run

**Table 1.2** Costs

| Output (units) | Fixed costs | Variable costs | TC | AC | MC |
|---|---|---|---|---|---|
| 1 | 30 | 10 | 40 | 40 | 40 |
| 2 | 30 | 40 | 70 | 35 | 30 |
| 3 | 30 | 60 | 90 | 30 | 20 |
| 4 | 30 | 70 | 100 | 25 | 10 |
| 5 | 30 | 120 | 150 | 30 | 50 |
| 6 | 30 | 180 | 210 | 35 | 60 |
| 7 | 30 | 250 | 280 | 40 | 70 |

Thus the marginal cost of producing different levels of output is crucial information for a firm. When considering the best level of output, producers need to know the incremental changes in costs when output is varied. Marginal cost is the *extra* cost of increasing output by one unit. Table 1.2 illustrates the various costs which have been defined and shows how they are related.

- If average cost is decreasing then marginal cost will be below average cost, for example, outputs 1–4.
- If average cost is increasing then marginal cost will be above average cost, for example, outputs 5–6.
- If average cost is constant then marginal cost will also be constant.

Generally, marginal cost falls and rises more rapidly than average cost.

## 1.4.2 Short-run production – diminishing marginal returns

The theory of diminishing marginal returns explains why, eventually, in the short run average cost starts to rise. This is illustrated in the 'U'-shaped MC curve in Figure 1.3. In Table 1.3, labour is being employed to raise output, but it becomes less productive after the fourth worker is recruited. Marginal output starts to fall, ultimately being negative.

The explanation for the eventual rising average cost is as follows.

- When a firm increases output in the short run it adds variable inputs, such as labour, to a fixed factor, such as land. Initially total output rises rapidly and the average cost of production falls.

**Table 1.3**  Negative marginal output

| Number of workers | Total output | Average output | Marginal output |
|---|---|---|---|
| 0 | 0 | 0 | 0 |
| 1 | 20 | 20 | 20 |
| 2 | 44 | 22 | 24 |
| 3 | 75 | 25 | 31 |
| 4 | 108 | 27 | 33 |
| 5 | 130 | 26 | 22 |
| 6 | 132 | 22 | 2 |
| 7 | 119 | 17 | −13 |

- This is because of greater specialisation in the use of variable factors and the elimination of under-utilisation in their use. The result is rising productivity and hence reduced average costs. In Tables 1.2 and 1.3, this is shown over the range of outputs 1–4.
- However, there are limits to the process of specialisation, and eventually extra units of variable factors produce diminishing additions to output. To raise output by a given amount thus requires much greater additional inputs of variable factors and thus average costs rise. For example, if land is the fixed factor and more labour is applied to it, eventually efficiency will be limited as workers get in one another's way.
- This causes the marginal cost of production to rise and average output to fall, as shown for outputs 5–7.

Furthermore, if extra pay is given to attract the extra labour needed to increase output, the marginal costs rise steeply. This happens because the extra pay over the previous wage is given to all of the workers, not just the additional new recruit. Thus, production in the short run is characterised by *diminishing returns* and *rising average costs* eventually. These are different sides of the same coin, given our assumptions about the standard quality of the factors of production.

## U-shaped average cost curve

As production increases, total fixed costs remain unchanged in the short run. However, because they are spread over more units of output, average fixed costs fall, as in Figure 1.4.

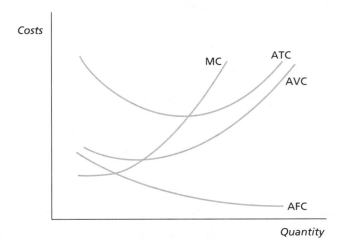

**Figure 1.4**  U-shaped cost curves

Variable costs will change with output. They are, therefore, marginal costs and the marginal cost curve will cut both the AVC and ATC curve at its lowest point. When AVC is added to AFC one gets ATC. Note that as AFC gets less, the gap between AVC and ATC narrows.

### 1.4.3  Long-run production – variable returns to scale

In the long run, because all factors of production are variable a firm can change its scale of production significantly. It could, for example, build a new factory and recruit more labour. The returns from such investment will vary, according to the efficiency shown.

There are three different possibilities:

- *increasing* returns to scale, that is, a given percentage increase in inputs will lead to a higher percentage increase in output;
- *constant* returns to scale, that is, a given percentage increase in inputs will create the same percentage increase in output;
- *decreasing* returns to scale, that is, a given percentage increase in inputs will cause a smaller percentage increase in output.

Clearly a firm seeks the first. If it is achieved we can say that *economies of scale* have occurred. These will be explained later. Conversely, if decreasing returns accrue then *diseconomies of scale* are operating.

### Long-run average costs

The implication of the variable returns to scale is that in the long run average costs will also be variable. Since there are no fixed factors, there are no long-run fixed costs. The three possible shapes of long-run average cost are shown in Figure 1.5. Clearly, $LRAC_1$ would be a situation of increasing returns to scale and falling average cost.

However, it is usually assumed that the long-run average cost curve will be *saucer-shaped*, as in Figure 1.6. Also, that it is composed of a series of different short-run average cost curves. Each short-run average cost curve shows a different scale of production, and once diminishing returns start, the firm varies its factors, thereby moving to a new short-run curve. Between outputs 0 and A economies of scale will occur as output increases and so

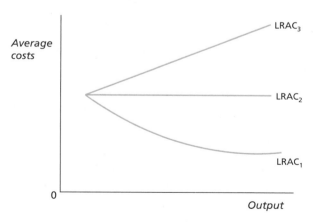

**Figure 1.5**  Long-run average cost curves

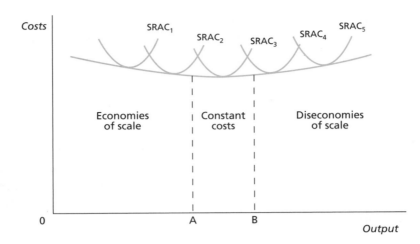

**Figure 1.6** 'Normal' long-run AC curve

average costs fall. From A to B there are constant costs (and constant returns) but after B diseconomies of scale result. If the firm realises the latter, then in theory it could cut back production or seek a more efficient combination of its factors of production.

The following table summarises what can happen in the long run:

| Variable returns in scale | Increase in inputs (%) | Increase in output (%) | Change in average cost |
|---|---|---|---|
| Increasing | Given | Bigger | Fall, i.e. economies of scale |
| Constant | Given | Same | Same, i.e. constant |
| Decreasing | Given | Smaller | Rise, i.e. diseconomies of scale |

### 1.4.4 Economies of scale

The advantages of producing on a large scale are known as the *economies of scale*. Generally, by producing in large quantities, the average cost per unit can be reduced because fixed costs are spread over more units.

It is useful at this point to make a distinction between increased production and increased productivity. Increased production occurs when more is produced, but this may be because more inputs are applied and it does not mean greater efficiency. However, higher productivity means more produced per person, and that *is* more efficiency. It is interesting to note that Britain experienced increased productivity in the 1980s in many industries at a time of falling production, as a result of the rapid shedding of labour and the slower fall in output. In absolute terms, Britain's productivity is low compared to other developed countries, especially the United States where productivity is 18 per cent above that in the United Kingdom.

When the advantages of expanding the scale of operation accrue to just one firm, these economies are termed *internal*. They can be obtained in one plant, belonging to a firm, or across the whole company. The main internal economies are as follows:

- *Technical economies.* These relate to the scale of the production and are usually obtained in one plant. Large-scale operations may make greater use of advanced machinery. Some machines are only worth using beyond a minimum level of output which may be beyond the capacity of a small firm, for example, robots used in car assembly. Such equipment may facilitate the division of labour. In addition, more resources can be devoted to research in large firms, because the cost is borne over more units of output, and this may lead to further technical improvements and subsequent cost reductions, for the whole company.

- *Financial economies.* It is usually easier for large firms with household names to borrow money from commercial banks and raise funds on the Stock Exchange. Similarly, their loans and overdrafts will probably be charged at lower interest rates because of their reputation and assets.
- *Trading economies.* Large firms may be able to secure advantages both when buying inputs and selling their outputs. They could employ specialist buyers and, through the quantity of their purchases, gain significant discounts from their suppliers.

    Similarly, bulk selling enables a large firm to make savings in distribution costs, the time and cost of salespeople and advertising expenses.

    These savings are more marked when many products are sold together in related markets. Thus, one big advantage of Nestlé's takeover of Rowntree Mackintosh was that the goods of each could be marketed together, with little extra total cost, thereby reducing the distribution costs of each product sold.

    If a large firm produces several products in different markets, then one failure is unlikely to cause the closure of the whole conglomerate. Thus, trading risks can be spread when a wide range of products are sold.
- *Managerial economies.* These are the many administrative gains which can be achieved when the scale of production grows. The need for management and supervision does not increase at the same rate as output. Specialists can be employed and their talents can be fully utilised in personnel, production, selling, accountancy and so on. Such organisational benefits may lower the indirect costs of production and lead to the efficient use of labour resources.

However, it is possible for general advantages to be obtained by all of the firms in an industry, and these are classed as *external economies of scale*. Most of these occur when an industry is heavily concentrated in one area. The area may develop a reputation for success, for example, computers and electronics in Silicon Valley in California. There may be a pool of skilled labour which is available, and this may lower training costs for a firm. Specialised training may be provided locally in accordance with the industry's needs. This might be provided by a training board to which firms contribute to gain access to the available expertise. Furthermore, a localised industry may attract to it specialist suppliers of raw materials, components and services, who gain from a large market and achieve their own economies of scale, which are passed on through lower input prices. Occasionally, firms in an industry share their research and development facilities, because each firm individually could not bear the overheads involved but can fund a joint enterprise.

## 1.4.5 Diseconomies of scale

These exist when the average cost rises with increased production. If they are specific to one firm they are categorised as internal.

- *Technical diseconomies.* The optimum technical size of plant may create large administrative overheads in its operation, thereby raising TAC, even though the production cost is lowered.

- *Trading diseconomies.* With large-scale production, products may become standardised. This lack of individualism may reduce consumer choice and lead to lower sales. In addition, it may be difficult to quickly adapt mass-produced goods to changing market trends. Marks & Spencer plc have experienced this problem in recent years.
- *Managerial diseconomies.* As the chain of command becomes longer in an expanding hierarchy (when productive capacity grows), senior management may become too remote and lose control. This may lead to cross-inefficiency (complacency) in middle management and shop floor hostility. A concomitant of this is the generally poor state of labour relations in large organisations, which are more prone to industrial stoppages than small firms. This is partly because the trade unions are better organised. Other administrative weaknesses faced by increasingly large organisations are the prevalence of red tape and the conflict between departmental managers who have different objectives and priorities.

However, there may also be general disadvantages which afflict all firms as the scale of the industry grows. The main external diseconomy is technical. If a resource is overutilised then shortages may arise. A shortage of labour might lead to higher wages in order to attract new recruits, while a shortage of raw materials might lower output. Both changes would raise the average cost of production.

### 1.4.6 Short-run and long-run production decisions

The distinction between fixed costs and variable costs is important in deciding whether firms should cease production. The firm is obliged to cover its fixed costs whether it undertakes production or not. For example, even when the firm produces no output it still incurs costs such as insurance charges, depreciation on assets, mortgage repayments, rent on premises and so on. However, variable costs are incurred only when the firm undertakes production. For example, when the firm produces no output it incurs no costs from purchasing raw materials or charges for power to drive the machinery and so on. Once a firm has incurred fixed costs, its decision about whether to continue producing is, therefore, determined by whether its total revenue (the amount it earns from production) is sufficient to cover its total variable costs. Therefore, we must consider the circumstances in which the firm will be prepared to produce in the short run when fixed costs exist, and the circumstances in which it is prepared to produce in the long run when there are no fixed costs.

In the short run, fixed costs are the same whether or not the firm undertakes production. Variable costs are, however, avoidable if the firm chooses not to start production.

- If total revenue is greater than total variable costs, then the firm should continue production as it is making a contribution to covering its fixed costs.
- If total revenue just covers total variable costs then the firm is neither better off nor worse off if it continues in production. It normally would continue production in the hope that future revenues will improve.
- If total revenue is less than total variable costs, then the firm should cease production. In this situation, the firm's total loss is equal to its unavoidable fixed costs, compared with a loss equal to the deficit incurred by the variable costs plus the fixed costs if it undertakes production.
- As average revenue is the same as price, a firm will undertake production in the short run if the price at which their product sold is at least equal to the variable cost of production.

However in the long run, a firm must cover all its costs as it cannot sustain losses indefinitely. In the long run, all costs become variable.

- In the long run, a firm will only continue in production if the price at which their product is sold at least equals the average total cost of production.
- Hence, to reiterate, in the short run average revenue must cover average variable costs, whereas in the long run average revenue must cover average total costs.

### 1.4.7 Economists' and Accountants' understanding of costs

- An accountant will view the cost of producing a product in terms of its historical cost. This means the actual amount paid to factors of production to make the product.
- An economist will view the cost of a product in terms of its opportunity cost. This means the cost is reckoned in terms of the foregone revenue which would have been earned if the factors of production had been put to their next best alternative use. An example will make this distinction clear.

---

### Example 1.A

Suppose that a self-employed trader sells goods worth £500,000. His/her accounts are set out in Table 1.4.

**Table 1.4** Self-employed trader

|  | £ | £ |
| --- | --- | --- |
| Sales |  | 500,000 |
| Materials | 250,000 |  |
| Labour | 150,000 |  |
| Depreciation | 40,000 |  |
| Other expenses | 20,000 | (460,000) |
| Gross profit |  | 40,000 |

In accounting terms his profit would be £40,000.

Suppose, however, that the premises used for the business could be put to alternative use and earn a rent of £10,000. The capital needed in the business could have been invested and earned £15,000 in interest. Finally the trader's own labour could have earned income in other employment, earning £35,000. The change in the profit/loss account can be seen in Table 1.5.

**Table 1.5** Self-employed trader

|  | £ |
| --- | --- |
| Sales less historic costs | 40,000 |
| Opportunity costs | (60,000) |
| Gross loss | (20,000) |

From the economist's perspective the trader has now made a loss. When opportunity costs are considered, the trader should take the decision to put his assets to alternative uses and employ his own labour another way.

The economist is concerned with the allocation of resources whereas the accountant views historic revenue and costs.

---

## Exercise 1.1

Answer the following questions based on the preceding information. You can check your answers below.

1. What is the definition of fixed costs?
2. In what time period are all factors of production variable?
3. What is technical efficiency?
4. Why do diminishing returns occur in the short run?
5. Define constant returns to scale.
6. Using the data in Table 1.2, calculate average fixed cost and average variable cost. Plot these on a graph with the average total cost and briefly explain the result.
7. When should a business cease production in the short run?
8. What costs need to be covered in the long run?
9. Distinguish between internal and external economies of scale.
10. Give two examples of diseconomies of scale.

## Solutions

1. Fixed costs are those which do not change with the level of production.
2. All factors of production are variable in the long run and in the very long run.
3. Technical efficiency is the point where average cost is at its lowest.
4. Diminishing returns occur in the short run because one factor of production is fixed. Thus, output can be raised only by adding more units of a variable factor. This adds progressively smaller amounts of extra output and leads to increases in average cost.
5. Constant returns to scale means that for a given percentage increase in inputs there is the same percentage increase in output (and thus no change in average cost).
6. Costs:

| Output | AFC | AVC | ATC |
|--------|-----|-----|-----|
| 1 | 30 | 10 | 40 |
| 2 | 15 | 20 | 35 |
| 3 | 10 | 20 | 30 |
| 4 | 7.5 | 17.5 | 25 |
| 5 | 6 | 24 | 30 |
| 6 | 5 | 30 | 35 |
| 7 | 4.3 | 35.7 | 40 |

Graph:

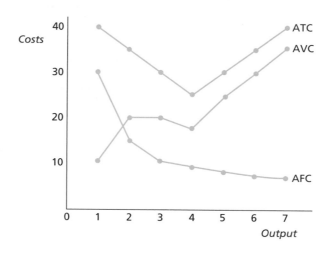

ATC is made up of AFC and AVC. AFC continues to decline as output increases but AVC declines between output 3 and 4 before rising due to the onset of diminishing returns. As a consequence, ATC rises after output 4 as the continued decrease in AFC is not sufficient to counter the rise in AVC.

7. When revenue falls below variable costs, as continued production only increases the total losses being made.

8. In the long run all costs become variable. Therefore, all costs must be covered. This will mean average revenue covering average total costs.

9. Internal economies are achieved by one firm within its own operations, whereas external economies are advantages available to most firms from the operation of the whole industry.

10. Administrative duplication and conflict of objectives between different departments in a large organisation.

## 1.5 Shareholder wealth

Businesses may be regarded as a combination of factors of production with the purpose of creating value added. Each of the factors of production receives a reward for its contribution to this process.

- Labour is paid wages and salaries.
- Land is paid rent.
- Capital is paid interest.
- Entrepreneurship is paid profits.

In practice, the distinction between providers of these factors of production may become blurred. Some employees may provide some aspects of entrepreneurship in the business, and shareholders may provide capital as much as undertaking the entrepreneurial function accepting risk. Nonetheless, the providers of capital and entrepreneurship are in a special position. The shareholders in a business are the legal owners of that business.

If one assumes that the owners of the business have ultimate control over its activity, one could assume that the ultimate objective of a profit-seeking business is to reward its shareholders who have invested capital into the business and are seeking a return on that investment. Thus the objective of a business might be seen as attempting to maximise *shareholder wealth*.

Shareholder wealth has two main aspects. Shareholders are interested in:

1. the performance of the business in terms of its ability to generate the *profits* which accrue to shareholders;
2. the *value of the shares* in the business to the investors.

There is series of accounting ratios which can be used to assess the performance of a business in relation to the interest of the shareholders. These ratios provide information that makes possible:

- an assessment of the financial performance of the business over time;
- a comparison of the performance of one business with another;
- an assessment of the attractiveness, or otherwise, of investing in the business.

### 1.5.1 Short-term measures of financial performance

It is quite possible that financial performance of a business in the short run could be different to its performance in the long run. Thus measures are needed both of short-run and long-run financial performance.

Two standard measures of short-run performance are:

1. the rate of *return on capital employed*;
2. *earnings per share*.

### Rate of return on capital employed (ROCE)

To assess the financial performance of companies and make comparisons over time and between companies, some measure of the return to the capital employed must be made. The standard way of measuring this is by calculating the productivity of the capital employed by the business: the *rate of return on capital employed*. This compares:

- profits earned before interest and tax are paid: in effect a measure of the ability of the organisation to generate net income;
- the value of capital employed averaged out between the beginning and the end of the year.

ROCE is expressed as a percentage and is measured as:

$$\pi \qquad \text{ROCE} = \frac{\text{profit before interest and tax}}{\text{average capital employed}} \times 100$$

Another useful measure of the return to shareholders' capital is:
Return on net assets which is measured as:

$$\text{Return on net assets} = \frac{\text{operating profit (before interest and tax)}}{\text{Total assets minus current liabilities}} \times 100$$

The higher the figure for ROCE or the return on net assets is, the more profitable the company is.

## *Earnings per share (EPS)*

Measures of the productivity of capital employed (ROCE) is a measure of the company's ability to generate earnings from its capital. However, potential shareholders are also interested in how much return they will get from investing in that company. In this case the potential investor would need to take into account the price they would have to pay to acquire the shares. Thus in this case, a comparison must be made between:

- *earnings per share;*
- *the market price of shares.*

EPS is measured by calculating profits minus tax, interest payments and payments of dividends on preference shares, and comparing this with the number of ordinary shares that have been issued.

EPS is expressed as a monetary value and is measured as:

$$\pi \qquad EPS = \frac{\text{profits after interest, preference share dividends and tax}}{\text{number of ordinary shares issued}}$$

Of course this figure only gives the earnings per share that each owner of ordinary shares might expect to receive. To calculate a rate of return for the shareholder, the price that the potential shareholder has to pay to acquire a share must be taken into account. This is done in the calculation of the *earnings yield.* This is calculated by comparing the earnings per share with the market price of the share.

The earnings yield is expressed as a percentage and is measured as:

$$\pi \qquad \text{Earnings yield} = \frac{\text{earnings per share}}{\text{market price of the share}} \times 100$$

Earnings yield may vary a great deal between companies. The earnings yield depends on the market price of the shares and this in turn reflects the expectations of investors about the company's current and future prospects and the general level of stock market prices. For example:

- a low earnings yield might indicate that investors are confident that the company will generate higher earnings in the future and the buying of shares will boost the market price and reduce the earnings yield;
- a high earnings yield might be typical of companies operating in more risky business areas and the higher yield reflects this perceived risk.

A further measure of the performance of the business is the *price earnings ratio* (P/E ratio). This also compares the earnings per share with the market price of the share but shows the number of years that it would take to recoup, via dividend payments, the investment in ordinary shares.

The price earnings ratio is expressed as a number of years and is measured as:

$$\pi \qquad P/E \text{ ratio} = \frac{\text{current market price of the share}}{\text{EPS at last publication of results}}$$

The P/E ratio effectively measures how many years it would take for earnings to be equal to the price of buying the share.

- A very low P/E ratio would suggest a high return to the investment in the shares.
- A very high P/E ratio might suggest a risky investment because it would currently take many years to cover the cost of acquiring the share.

P/E ratios should be viewed with some care, however the direction and rate of change in the P/E ratio might be a better indicator of the longer-term health of the company than the absolute value of the P/E ratio at any one time. Thus changes in the P/E ratio might be used to take a more dynamic view of the progress of the business over time.

## 1.5.2 Long-term measures of financial performance

In addition to measuring current financial performance, companies also need to be able to measure longer-term performance, in particular, in relation to investment. In this case it is important that a business can be sure that returns to shareholders are at least equal to the cost of acquiring the capital required to produce a long-term flow of earnings.

In making these sorts of assessment several problems arise:

- establishing the cost of capital to finance the investment project;
- estimating the flow of income derived from the capital investment over the whole life of the investment;
- valuing the flow of income.

The last problem arises because clearly income at some future date is worth less than the same amount of income now. We know that this is the case since everyone who lends money to another expects to be compensated when repayment is made at some future date: this compensation takes the form of interest. Calculating the difference in value of income generated at different time periods in the future is known as the problem of *discounting*.

The objective of these calculations is to measure the *discounted cash flow* (DCF) that would be generated by the project.

- The future flow of income must be *discounted*; that is future income flows must be calculated as a reduced value to reflect the lower current valuation of income in the future compared to the valuation of income in the present.
- This is done by applying *a discount rate* to that stream of income.
- The normal presumption is that the discount rate to be used is the current *rate of interest* since it is assumed that this in turn reflects savers' and investors' time preferences.

Thus it is necessary to apply a rate of interest as the discount rate to the future stream of earnings. Of course the present value of that stream of earnings will depend on which rate of interest is chosen to discount the stream of earnings.

- A high rate of interest implies a very low valuation of future income compared to the present.
- A low rate of interest implies a much less low valuation of future income compared to the present.

Which rate of discount should be used? After all, at any one time there will be a range of market interest rates reflecting different types of lending and borrowing and different types of lenders and borrowers. The appropriate rate to be used by a business should be the *average cost of capital* to the company. Although there are some problems in identifying this, in principle it can done.

Once the interest rate or discount rate has been applied to the stream of earnings, the resulting calculation is the *discounted cash flow* (DCF).

The DCF is measured by applying the discount rate. Since there is a compounding effect with interest this must be reflected in the calculation. The appropriate calculation is that the value of $1 of income received at a future date is:

$$\text{Discounted value} = \frac{Y_t}{(1 + r)^t}$$

where Y is the earnings in year t
r is the rate of discount

Thus if an income stream of $1,000 a year is expected, and a discount rate of 10 per cent is to be applied, the calculation for each year is:

| Year 1 | Year 2 | Year 3 | Year 4 |
|---|---|---|---|
| $\dfrac{\$1{,}000}{1.1}$ | $\dfrac{\$1{,}000}{(1.1)^2}$ | $\dfrac{\$1{,}000}{(1.1)^3}$ | $\dfrac{\$1{,}000}{(1.1)^4}$ |
| = $909 | $826 | $751 | $683 |

The discount factor can also be derived from the 'present value tables' which are provided by CIMA. This only requires reading off the discount factor from the appropriate number of years and the discount rate to be used.

 Thus the application of the discount factor gives a DCF. The final task is to calculate the *net present value* of the project. This can be done in two ways.

- The capital cost of the project can be subtracted from the DCF. In the example given, the sum of the discounted cash flow is $3,169. If the capital cost of the project was $3,000 then the NPV is $169.
- The capital cost of the project can be included in the calculation of the DCF. Thus the capital cost of $3,000 would be included as a *negative* cash flow in Year 0. As the outlay is assumed to take place at the very start of the project, no discounting is needed as the discount factor applied is effectively 1.

Either approach will produce the same answer for the NPV of the project. Once the NPV has been calculated, the value of the project to the company and the impact it would have on shareholder value can be determined.

- If the NPV is positive it indicates that the project is profitable and would increase shareholder wealth and should therefore be undertaken.
- If the NPV is negative it indicates that the project is not profitable and would decrease shareholder wealth and should therefore not be undertaken.

Calculations of NPV can also be used to rank alternative investment projects or alternative technologies. As it measures cash flow and takes into account the time taken for the cash flow to materialize, it is the best measure of the long-term impact on shareholder wealth of the decisions made by the company.

### 1.5.3 Share values

For shareholders there are two important elements to their return from investing in a company:

1. the flow of *dividends* from the ownership of the shares;
2. change in *the value (price) of the shares*.

Of course these two are not unrelated since:

- the return that a stream of dividends represents depends on the market price of the share paid by the investor (i.e. earnings yield);
- the current and expected stream of profits and dividends will affect the value of shares.

Many variables will affect the value of shares. These tend to fall into two groups:

1. factors *external* to the business which may affect a wide range of shares: the onset of a recession would tend to depress share values in general as would a rise in interest rates;
2. factors *internal* to the business that might affect the future flow of profits such as the failure of a new product, an expected decline in sales or a significant rise in costs.

In the latter case the impact on the share price would follow from the expected change in the flow of cash, and in principle, this effect could be calculated. Using the *net present value* method outlined above, the effect of an expected fall in the flow of profits might be calculated. In the example given the effect of an expected fall in profits in the fourth year from $1,000 to $500 could be calculated, thus:

| Year 1 | Year 2 | Year 3 | Year 4 |
|--------|--------|--------|--------|
| $\dfrac{\$1{,}000}{1.1}$ | $\dfrac{\$1{,}000}{(1.1)^2}$ | $\dfrac{\$1{,}000}{(1.1)^3}$ | $\dfrac{\$500}{(1.1)^4}$ |
| $= \$909$ | $\$826$ | $\$751$ | $\$342$ |

Thus the DCF is reduced from $3,169 to £2,828 – fall of 10.76 per cent and one would expect this to be reflected in share values.

## 1.6 Not-for-profit organisations

### 1.6.1 Types of not-for-profit organisations

Not all organisations, even business organisations, are profit-making organisations. A whole range of not-for-profit organisations exist. Some of the most important are:

- charities
- voluntary organizations
- clubs
- mutual societies
- public sector organizations
- QUANGOs (quasi autonomous non-governmental organisations).

Although these organisation are not profit-orientated as with most business organisations, they have some characteristics in common with them. These include:

- they *use resources* (factors of production) in order to produce some good or service;
- in turn, the use of resources implies a *flow of expenditure* to finance those resources and other operating costs;
- the existence of a flow of expenditure requires a *flow of income* to finance that expenditure;
- the flow of *income* is derived from sales of services or goods to its customers, clients or members.

Thus, although not-for-profit organisations are not profit-making they have some things in common with profit-seeking organisations. Indeed, some of these organisations can be very big businesses. Examples include mutual building societies in the United Kingdom and some Savings and Loans Companies in the United States. In the United Kingdom, the John Lewis organisation owns an extensive chain of department stores and supermarkets. However, it is a partnership rather than a shareholder-owned business. Virtually all universities are not-for-profit organisations yet they have very large flows of income and expenditure and employ large numbers of people. Thus there are important economic constraints on these organisations. These business organisations need to:

- Avoid making a financial loss: profits are not made but operating surpluses or deficits will occur and these are carried over into future years. Continued deficits would lead to serious financial problems and eventually the closure of the organisation.
- Be efficiently managed to ensure that the organisation achieves its objectives and ensures financial stability. Even if the organisation is not aiming to make profits, it needs to use its physical and financial resources in an efficient manner.
- Choose investment projects carefully so that they contribute to the achievement of the objectives of the business in an efficient manner.

Overall, the not-for-profit organisation must be managed so that it is *effective*; that is, it achieves its objectives in an efficient manner and cost-effective manner. Thus there are important economic constraints operating on not-for-profit organisations.

Thus much of the management activity in not-for-profit organisations is similar to that which occurs in profit-seeking businesses. Similar decisions have to be made concerning:

- types of product and service to be produced
- which markets to be emphasised
- the level of output to be produced
- the prices to be charged for the product or services
- choice of production methods and technologies
- investment decisions
- sources of finance.

However, for profit-making organisations the objectives of the business are clear: in principle the core objective is the maximisation of shareholders' wealth. For not-for-profit organisations the problem is the absence of shareholders. It is therefore not clear on whose behalf the organisation should function. What should the management of a not-for-profit organisation aim to maximise? This question can only be answered by reference to the concept of *stakeholders*.

THE GOALS AND DECISIONS OF ORGANISATIONS

## 1.6.2 Stakeholders

### Stakeholders: interest and influence

The stakeholders in a business may be defined as:

> *those persons and organisations that have an interest in the strategy and behaviour of the organization*

All business organisations have stakeholders. For the typical business the most important stake holders are:

- Shareholders
- Customers
- suppliers
- employees including senior management
- the providers of finance
- relevant regulatory and statutory bodies
- the local community.

For some very large businesses, stakeholders may also include the national community since their actions may have national or even international effects. Some companies in the oil industry, the aviation industry and in the financial services industry may have this feature. For not-for-profit organisations, the absence of shareholders means that the interests of the other stakeholders become more important in influencing the strategy and behaviour of the organisation.

How do stakeholders influence the activities of the not-for-profit organisation? This depends first of all on two important variables:

- stakeholder *interest*
- stakeholder *influence*.

Stakeholder interest refers to the strength of the stakeholders' interest in the organisation. How much effort will the stakeholder put into influencing the organisation? This degree of interest and the willingness to attempt to affect the organisation will vary from one stakeholder to another.

- Customer interest may vary: single customers buying the occasional low price service will have low interest, but a major and regular customer (e.g. a government buying military equipment from an arms producer) would have a high level of interest.
- Employees are likely to have high interest as stakeholders as their working life, income and financial futures will be affected by the behaviour of the organisation.
- Local communities may have high or low interest depending on the potential impact and the importance of the activity on the local community. The local community will have high stakeholder interest in a big local employer or a company whose activities have a big impact on the local environment.

Stakeholder *influence* refers to the degree to which an individual stakeholder or group of stakeholders can exert influence over the organisation. Thus the concern here is not the level of interest that the stakeholder has, but the ability of the stakeholder to affect the behaviour of the organisation. Again, the influence of stakeholders will vary:

- Stakeholders inside the organisation, such as employees and management, will have more influence than stakeholders outside of the organisation such as the local community.

- Stakeholders who are important to the organisation, such as its major customers, will have more influence than those who are less important. Less important stakeholder might be suppliers for whom there are lots of alternatives for the organisation to use.
- Groups of stakeholders with common interests ('coalitions') will have more influence than single stakeholders. For an organisation which is the major employer in a locality, the interests of that local community and of the employees would be similar.

Ultimately the influence of stakeholders will vary greatly from one organisation to another. In some cases coalitions of external stakeholders may have considerable effect on organisations; in other cases external stakeholders may be weak and divided. Real problems may arise for organisations if they are faced with competing groups of influential stakeholders with different views of how the organisation should operate. In this case, *conflict* between stakeholders may generate very real problems for the management of organisations.

## Stakeholders in not-for-profit organisations

Who are likely to be the important stakeholders in not-for-profit organisations? In most profit-seeking companies one would expect shareholders and their representatives – the chairman, chief executive and the board of directors – to have both interest and influence. However, not-for-profit organisations do not have shareholders. Who then are the important stakeholders in these organisations? There is no simple answer to this question as there is such a wide variety of not-for-profit organisations.

- In government-owned organisations, the government itself or the civil service administering such organisations may have a great deal of power.
- For charities, the donors, especially if they are large donors, as the principal source of income for the organisation may be powerful stakeholders.
- In all not-for-profit organisations, the employees, especially the management, are likely to be powerful stakeholders.

How do stakeholders affect the management of not-for-profit organisations? Again the effect will vary a great deal from one organisation to another, but the effect of stakeholders will be felt in several ways. Stakeholders may affect:

- the overall *goals and objectives* of the organisation. Since profit cannot be the main objective, there is more scope for debate about the goals and objectives of the organisation;
- the *strategy* of the organisation in attempting to reach those objectives. Since profit is not the main objective, different strategies cannot be judged by reference to their contribution to profits. Concepts of efficiency and effectiveness might be more appropriate in these circumstances but problems still remain. Business strategies have implications other than those for efficiency and effectiveness; there may, for example, be ethical issues with different stakeholders holding different views about those issues;
- the *organisation and management* of the organisation. There clearly exist different possible management style and structures, and stakeholders – especially employees and management – will have views about which are most appropriate for the organisation and personal preferences.

All this leads to the possibility of *conflict between* the various stakeholders in organisations. This will occur in profit-seeking organisations, but may be muted given the overall objective of maximising shareholder value. The problem might be more serious in not-or-profit organisations given the absence of a strong stakeholder with a single primary objective.

The existence of differing demands from various stakeholders presents serious problems for the organisation; the determination of business strategy and its implementation becomes much more difficult. How might stakeholder conflicts in not-for-profit organisations be resolved?

There are broadly three approaches to conflicts in stakeholder interest.

1. Developing a consensus around the aims and objectives of the senior management of the organisation – in effect getting other stakeholders to accept the appropriateness of the core objectives of the business. This is sometimes related to the notion of developing *strong cultures* in businesses whereby there is common acceptance of the company's aims. The problem here is how to deal with stakeholders who are external to the company.

2. The *dominant coalition* of stakeholder will impose their views about the aims and objectives of the business. It is likely that the dominant coalition will include the senior management and they might impose systems and controls to ensure this. Indeed, an informal condition of employment in the business might be acceptance of those particular stakeholder interests.

3. The business may recognise the existence of different stakeholders and acknowledge that they have differing but legitimate interests which ought to be met. This view suggest that it is possible to incorporate these differing interests without damage to the core objectives of the organisation. For example, meeting employees aspirations for good working conditions and financial rewards, through performance pay schemes, might lead to higher productivity thus contributing to the success of the organisation. Likewise, meeting the aspirations of suppliers and customers might lead to confidence, flexibility and loyalty in these relationships.

Nonetheless, it remains the case that if there are irreconcilable differences in the aims and objectives of different stakeholders, the task of the senior management in a business will be to identify priorities and devise management system and processes to place those at the core of the business.

## 1.7  Corporate governance

### 1.7.1  Why does corporate governance matter?

The final issue discussed in this chapter is that of corporate governance. Corporate governance is:

*the systems by which companies and other organisations are directed and controlled.*

Thus corporate governance is concerned with how power is used to direct the operations and behaviour of organisations. In the case of companies this power, and indeed this responsibility, rests with boards of directors. The role of shareholders in companies is to:

- appoint the directors of the company
- appoint the auditors for the company
- assure themselves that the system of governance is appropriate and effective.

Thus the board of directors has powers delegated to it from the shareholders. The main responsibilities of the board of directors of a company are:

- to determine the broad long-term aims of the company; that is, to determine the broad business strategy of the company.
- to provide a focus of leadership in the pursuit of the strategic goals that it has set;
- to supervise the management of the company and to monitor the performance of the company in relation to the strategic aims of the company;
- to report to shareholders on the performance of the company.

The board of directors are collectively responsible to the shareholders who may determine policy at a general meeting of all shareholders. In addition, the board must operate within a particular set of laws and regulations that specify the roles and duties of directors.

In recent years in the United Kingdom and in other countries there has been a concern that the processes of corporate governance have not been working as well as they ought. This concern has arisen partly out of a series of scandals concerning some of the biggest and most well-known business companies. Box 1.1 outlines some examples of these. While there is no reason to suppose that problems were necessarily widespread in business, there was a concern that corporate governance needed attention.

---

### Box 1.1 Problems with corporate governance: the United Kingdom

In recent years there have been many scandals concerning some major companies. In the United Kingdom among the more notable have been the cases of Robert Maxwell who was found to have used employees pensions funds to finance the Mirror Group business for which he was responsible and the Guinness company where some directors were found guilty of falsifying the company's accounts. Perhaps the most famous case is that of the US company, Enron. This company, operating in the US energy market, grew very rapidly and regularly reported strong income and profit growth. However through the use of subsidiaries the company was hiding its debts and exaggerating its financial strength. The Company eventually collapsed and filed for bankruptcy. Even the company's auditors were found to have behaved illegally.

---

### 1.7.2 The principal-agent problem

The origins of this governance problem lies in what is known as agency theory or the *principal–agent* problem. In any organisation there are:

- *principals*: in the case of companies the principals are the legal owners of the organisation – the shareholders;
- *agents*: those appointed by the principals to act on their behalf such as the board of directors and senior managers in a company.

The principal–agent problem is not confined to business and companies, it affects all organisations.

- In the case of public sector industries, the principal is the legal owner, that is the state represented by the government, and the agents are the senior managers placed in charge of the industries.
- The issue may arise for individuals. If an individual wishes to buy a house he or she may well appoint a lawyer to conduct the legal aspects of the transactions. Here the house buyer is the principal, and the lawyer is the agent.

The problem posed by agency theory is how can the principal ensure that the agent will behave in such a way as to achieve the aims and intentions of the principal? There is clearly the possibility of conflict in that the agent may act to achieve a set of objectives reflecting their self interest and objectives rather than those of the principals. In companies the board of directors and/or senior management may pursue objectives that are not the same as those of the shareholders. In effect, the shareholders may lose control of the companies they legally own.

This loss of control by shareholders over their companies is called the *divorce of control from ownership*. How might this loss of control occur?

- organisations may become *too large* for shareholders to effectively control;
- organisations may become *too complex* for shareholders to effectively control; this complexity may be in technologically, commercially or structurally;
- individual shareholders may lose control especially where they only own a small number of shares or where they own shares in many companies because they lack the time or incentive to exert their control.

Indeed, it is because of these sorts of problems that shareholders face that they appoint agents to act for them in the company. The problem is less acute for institutional shareholders such as pension funds. Because they have large shareholdings and have time and expertise they find it rather easier to ensure that directors and managers comply with their overall wishes. Nonetheless, shareholders still need to create mechanisms to encourage directors and managers to act in a way that promotes shareholder interest. Since shareholders are primarily interested in the flow of dividends and the share price, it is possible to devise incentive schemes to encourage directors to emphasise the pursuit of profits. Examples include:

- renumeration and bonuses related to the profit performance of the company;
- share distribution schemes to encourage directors and managers to aim for a higher share price for the company;
- bonuses related to variables that will indirectly contribute to the maximisation of shareholders wealth such as sales growth or market share.

Even here, however, there is some disquiet. The incentive schemes are often designed by the directors and renumeration committees that in turn often reflect the interests of directors in general. There is thus a feeling that the schemes provide targets that are too easy to achieve and bonuses that are often only very loosely linked to the achievement of those targets. Even worse the bonus system may lead to serious problems. The crisis in the financial systems of many countries in 2008 was partly ascribed to the bonus system. It was claimed that directors and senior managers in banks and other financial institutions adopted excessively risky business policies in the pursuit of generous short-term bonuses at the expense of longer-term financial stability. The result was a wave of banking collapses that was only stemmed by massive government intervention and support. Thus the problem of the agents in a company pursuing a different set of objectives from those of the principals remains.

What sort of objectives might directors and senior managers in companies pursue? It is likely that their objectives will be more complex than those of the shareholders. In the first place, management will face pressures from a wide range of stakeholders, not just the shareholders. Moreover, management will have its own aims and objectives which may differ in important ways from those of the shareholders. Box 1.2 illustrates the nature of this problem in the United Sates.

How might the aims and objectives of management differ from those of shareholders?

- Management will have to balance the interests of different stakeholders in the company. Since these stakeholders have a variety of objectives, profit is unlikely to be the sole aim of management.
- Management may have objectives of its own. These may include:

    salaries
    non-salary benefits ('perks')
    power
    status and prestige
    safety and security
    a 'quiet life'.

The problem with these is that they *may conflict* with the objectives of profitability. For example, many of the management's objectives, such as salary, power and prestige, may be related more strongly to the *size* of the company (sales, market share, number of employees) than to the underlying *profitability* of the company (return on capital employed). Box 1.2 illustrates the nature of this problem in the United Kingdom and Section 1.2.3 discusses some alternative theories of the firm based on the idea that companies reflect managers and not owners objectives.

---

### Box 1.2   Bonuses become the norm for bosses

Only four chief executives in the FTSE 100 went without a bonus last year, as companies increasingly rely on the extra payments to reward their top executives.

The bonuses are more often paid in cash and shares tied to the company's performance than options and long-term incentives. According to a report published today by PricewaterhouseCoopers, they are the one part of executives' pay packages that most effectively motivate them.

PwC argues that traditional compensation can provide 'outstanding rewards' for outstanding performance, but gives rise to anomalies where performance is anything less than stellar. 'Our research shows that commonly used packages are often not hugely successful at aligning pay with how well CEOs perform for shareholders over a sustained period. At the same time, some plans are just too complex, meaning that they can be severely undervalued by executives and, in our experience, often discounted altogether. In many cases, they are not effective in encouraging executives to perform better.'

*Source*: Fiona Walsh: *The Guardian*, August 21st 2006

Thus management may have a complex set of objectives. Nonetheless, it is likely that the profitability of the company will remain an important, indeed probably the most important objective. If a company has a poor profitability performance then the board of directors and senior managers may face:

- smaller bonuses and performance related pay
- the possibility of dismissal by shareholders
- the threat of takeovers if the company share price falls significantly.

Thus the relationship between shareholders (the 'principals') and boards of directors ('the agents') is complex one and might differ from company to company. Nonetheless, the belief that there are problems in the process of corporate governance has prompted attempts in many countries at reform of this relationship.

### 1.7.3 The reform of corporate governance in the United Kingdom

In the United Kingdom, concern over corporate governance led to the establishment in 1991 of the *Cadbury Committee*. The task of this committee was to review the process of corporate governance in the United Kingdom and to try and identify what it regarded as the best features of the system. The intention was that it would be recommended that these best features should become standard practice. The main recommendations of the committee were:

- the board of directors should meet on a *regular basis* and that active *responsibilities* at board level should be spread over the board and not concentrated in a few hands; in particular, the roles of *chairperson* and *chief executive* should be kept separate;
- directors should have *limited contracts* (3 years) and all director reward and *payments should be publicly disclosed*;
- there should be three *sub-committees* of the board: an *audit* committee, a *nominations* (to the board) committee and a *renumerations* (of board members) committee;
- greater use should be made of *non-executive directors* with no direct financial interest in the company in order to provide some independence within the board especially on the board's sub committees;
- the annual accounts should contain a statement, approved by the auditors, that the business is financially sound and is a *going concern*.

Since the Cadbury Committee's report, its recommendations have effectively become the standard procedure for larger companies and especially those publicly quoted on the London Stock Exchange. Since the work of the Cadbury Committee, the issue of corporate governance has been the subject of further reports.

- The *Greenbury Report* (1995) looked at the issue of director's pay.
- The *Nolan Committee* (1995) looked at governance issue in the public sector.
- The *Hempel Committee* (1998) reviewed corporate governance issues.
- The *Higgs Report* (2003) reviewed issues relating to the membership of boards of directors including age, gender and skills and abilities.

The outcome of this work is the creation of the *Combined Code* which specifies what the various groups and committees have come to believe represents 'best practice' in corporate governance and what be seen as a model for companies to adopt. The main features of this model are:

- *separation of powers* especially in relation to roles of the chairman and the chief executive;
- *board membership* to include an appropriate balance especially in relation to executive and non-executive directors;
- the adoption of the principles of *transparency, openness* and *fairness*;
- to adopt an approach which reflects the interest of all *stakeholders*;
- to ensure that the board of directors are fully *accountable*;
- detailed disclosure and reporting requirements;
- remuneration committees to determine the pay of directors;
- nomination committees to oversee appointments to the board;
- arrangements for organising the Annual General Meeting (AGM).

 ## Exercise 1.2

Answer the following questions based on the preceding information. You can check your answers below.

1. What does ROCE mean and what does it measure?
2. What does the term *discounting* mean?
3. How is the net present value (NPV) of an investment project calculated?
4. If the rate of interest used as the discount rate in the calculation of the NPV of a project rose, would the NPV rise or fall?
5. Identify four different types of not-for-profit organisations.
6. Explain what is meant by the term *stakeholders*.
7. Identify five stakeholders for a typical business.
8. Explain what is meant by the *principal–agent* problem.
9. Give two reasons why shareholders may lose control of the company they own.
10. What is meant by the term *corporate governance*?

 ## Solutions

1. ROCE is the *rate of return on capital employed* and is a measure of the flow of profits compared to the capital employed in the business. It is thus a measure of the profitability of that capital.
2. Discounting is the process by which future streams of income can be given a present value; that is the value is reduced to take account of the factor that income in the future is valued less highly that income now. This gives the *discounted cash flow*.
3. The NPV of a project is calculated by adding together the discounted cash flow for each of the years of the lifetime of the investment project and subtracting from this the initial capital cost of the project.
4. The value of the NVP would fall since a rise in the discount rate would mean giving lower valuations to future streams of income.
5. Not-for-profit organisations include state-owned (public sector) activities, mutual societies, charities, private clubs, QUANGOs and voluntary organisations.
6. Stakeholders are those persons and organisations that have an interest in the strategy, aims and behaviour of the organisation.
7. Stakeholders may include: shareholders, management, employees, suppliers, customers, the suppliers of financial services, the local community.

8. The principal–agent problem arises when principals (such as shareholders) appoint some agents (such as directors) to act on their behalf (running a company) and cannot be sure that those agents will always act so as to promote the interest of the principals.

9. *There may a divorce of ownership from control* because:
   - companies may become too big for shareholders to effectively control
   - companies may become too complex for shareholders to control
   - individual shareholders may lack the power, knowledge, interest or time to control the companies they own.

10. The term *corporate governance* refers to the systems by which companies and other organisations are directed and controlled. For Plc companies this means the role of the Board of Directors and its relationship to the shareholders.

## 1.8 Chapter summary

On completing this chapter you should have acquired a good grasp of some of the important economic concepts related to the nature, aims and structure of organisations. In particular this chapter has:

- described the different forms of ownership of organisations;
- explained the way in which costs in a business behave in the short and long run and how this relates to the point of profit maximisation;
- demonstrated the importance of economies of scale in affecting the competitive process and the structure of an industry;
- discussed the concept of shareholder value and explained the various short- and longer-term measures of returns to shareholders;
- discussed the way in share values might be affected by a variety of factors, especially the expected flow of profits;
- described various not-for-profit organisations and their objectives;
- discussed the role of stakeholders in not-for-profit organisations and their impact on business objectives;
- outlined the principal–agent problem and the impact this has on corporate governance.

The next chapter in the text deals with the market environment within which organisations function and the processes of competition in markets. Chapter 3 looks specially at the financial environment for organisations and the services provided by the financial sector. The last two chapters discuss the wider macroeconomic environment within which all businesses function.

# Revision Questions

1

You should use these questions for practice and revision for the content of this chapter.

 **Question 1** Multiple-choice selection

**1.1** In economics, 'the central economic problem' means that:

    (A) consumers do not have as much money as they would wish.
    (B) there will always be a certain level of unemployment.
    (C) resources are not always allocated in an optimum way.
    (D) output is restricted to the limited availability of resources.

**1.2** Which *one* of the following best describes the opportunity cost to society of building a new school?

    (A) the increased taxation to pay for the school.
    (B) the money that was spent on building the school.
    (C) the other goods that could have been produced with the resources used to build the school.
    (D) the running cost of the school when it is opened.

**1.3** The opportunity cost of constructing a road is:

    (A) the money spent on the construction of the road.
    (B) the value of the goods and services that could otherwise have been produced with the resources used to build the road.
    (C) the cost of the traffic congestion caused during the construction of the road.
    (D) the value of goods that could have been produced with the labour employed in the construction of the road.

**1.4** In a market economy, the allocation of resources between different productive activities is determined mainly by:

    (A) the decisions of the government.
    (B) the wealth of entrepreneurs.
    (C) the pattern of consumer expenditure.
    (D) the supply of factors of production.

**1.5**   Which of the following would cause the production possibility frontier for an economy to shift outwards?

   (i)   A reduction in the level of unemployment.
   (ii)  A rise in the rate of investment.
   (iii) A fall in the price of one factor of production.
   (iv)  A rise in output per worker.

   (A) (i) and (ii) only.
   (B) (i), (ii) and (iii) only.
   (C) (i), (iii) and (iv) only.
   (D) (ii) and (iv) only.

**1.6**   In a market economy, the price system provides all of the following except which one?

   (A) Signals to consumers.
   (B) Incentives to producers.
   (C) A means of allocating scarce resources.
   (D) A store of value.

**1.7**   The 'law of diminishing returns' can apply to a business only when:

   (A) all factors of production can be varied.
   (B) at least one factor of production is fixed.
   (C) all factors of production are fixed.
   (D) capital used in production is fixed.

**1.8**   Which of the following is *not* a source of economies of scale?

   (A) The introduction of specalist capital equipment.
   (B) Bulk-buying.
   (C) The employment of specialist managers.
   (D) Cost savings resulting from new production techniques.

**1.9**   Discounting a future stream of income means:

   (A) taking into account possible future falls in the stream of income.
   (B) ignoring yearly fluctuations in income and taking the average.
   (C) reducing the present value of future income streams because future income is worth less than current income.
   (D) reducing the present value of future income streams to take account of the effect of inflation.

**1.10**   Which one of the following would *not* be a stakeholder for a mutual society?

   (A) shareholders.
   (B) customers.
   (C) employees.
   (D) managers.

# Question 2

A company is planning to invest in a new project. The information about this project is as follows.

| | | | |
|---|---|---|---|
| Capital cost of the project | $20,000 | | |
| Expected life of the project | 3 years | | |
| Scrap value of investment at end | $5,000 | | |
| Expected net income streams | Year 1 | $10,000 | |
| | Year 2 | $10,000 | |
| | Year 3 | $10,000 | |

You are required to:

(a)  Calculate the net present value of the project assuming a discount rate of 10%.

**(2 marks)**

(b)  Calculate the net present value of the project assuming that the income stream in the third year is reduced to $7,000. **(2 marks)**

(c)  Calculate the net present value of the project assuming the original income streams but a discount rate of 5%. **(2 marks)**

(d)  State whether each of the following would be likely to make the project more or less profitable:

(i)  a rise in interest rates                                  more profitable/less profitable

**(1 mark)**

(ii)  a fall in labour costs for the company           more profitable/less profitable

**(1 mark)**

(iii)  an expected fall in the value of scrap machinery      more profitable/less profitable

**(1 mark)**

(iv)  a higher than expected sales volume from the new project

more profitable/less profitable

**(1 mark)**

**(Total marks = 10)**

# Solutions to Revision Questions

The answers to the multiple-choice questions given below indicate the single correct answer for each question. The multiple-choice questions used in examinations are a form of objective testing. There is only one correct answer and this is not subject to differences of opinion among economists. The task of the candidate is to identify the one correct answer.

## ✔ Solution 1

**1.1** Solution: (D)

The central economic problem refers to the scarcity of resources relative to human wants. A refers to money rather than real resources and B refers to a real problem but one which, if solved, would still leave resources relatively scarce. This is also true of C; even if resources were optimally allocated, they would still be scarce.

**1.2** Solution: (C)

Opportunity cost refers to the opportunity to produce other goods and services which are forgone when those resources are used for a particular purpose. A and B refer to financial considerations rather than real resources and D refers to the opportunity cost of running the school, not of building it.

**1.3** Solution: (B)

A refers to the financial implications of road building and D refers to only one of the real resources involved. Congestion, mentioned in C, is a real cost, but does refer to the cost of the road itself.

**1.4** Solution: (C)

In a market economy, producers in the search of profits must respond to consumer demand. Thus the allocation of resources reflects consumer preferences as expressed in their expenditure. Governments play some role in resource allocation, but in market economies this is limited. D refers to the availability of resources not their allocation between different uses.

**1.5** Solution: (D)

The possibility production frontier shows maximum output given the total resources available and their productivity. Thus (ii) (more resources) and (iv) (higher productivity) would have this effect. A fall in unemployment (i) would move the economy closer to its frontier but would not lead to any shift in the frontier. A change in factor prices (iii) would have no effect on the real resources available.

**1.6** Solution: (D)

Prices are signals to both consumers and producers which influence their buying and producing decisions and in this way help to allocate resources between different goods and services. However, prices do not act as a store of value; this is a function of money.

**1.7** Solution: (B)

The law of diminishing returns states that if more units of a variable factor are added to a fixed factor, the increment in output will eventually decline. Responses (A) and (C) are therefore incorrect. Response (D) is also incorrect, since the law applies for any fixed factor, not only capital.

**1.8** Solution: (D)

Economies of scale are the cost savings resulting from any activity or process which is made possible by increasing the scale of output. This applies to responses (A), (B) and (C), since these are made possible as the size of businesses increases. Response (D), however, is incorrect since it refers to technical change, and this would reduce costs for all producers, large and small.

**1.9** Solution: (C)

Responses (A) and (B) are concerned with the absolute value of income streams and not discounting those streams. Response (C) is correct since discounting is done because future income is worth less now even in the absence of inflation. Response (D) is concerned with the effects of inflation.

**1.10** Solution: (A)

Response (A) is the correct answer as a mutual society does not have shareholders but is owned collectively by its customers, for example a mutual building society is owned by its depositors.

## ✅ Solution 2

(a) The net present value will be: $8,625

For Year 1 the discounted income stream is $\dfrac{\$10,000}{(1.1)} = \$9,090.91$

For Year 2 the discounted income stream is $\dfrac{\$10,000}{(1.21)} = \$8,264.46$

For Year 3 the discounted income stream is $\dfrac{\$10,000 + \$5,000}{(1.331)} = \$11,269.72$

The NPV is thus ($9,090.91 + $8,264.46 + $11,269.72) minus the initial capital cost of $20,000 = $8,625

(b)   The NPV would be: $6,371

For Year 3 the discounted income stream is   $\dfrac{\$7,000+\$5,000}{(1.331)} = \$9,015.77$

The DCF is thus reduced to $26,371 and the NPV is reduced to $6,371.

(c)   In this case the NPV would be $11,552

For Year 1 the discounted income stream is   $\dfrac{\$10,000}{(1.05)} = \$9,523.81$

For Year 2 the discounted income stream is   $\dfrac{\$10,000}{(1.1025)} = \$9,070.29$

For Year 3 the discounted income stream is   $\dfrac{\$10,000+\$5,000}{(1.1576)} = \$12,957.84$

The NPV is thus ($9,523.81 + $9,070.29 + $12,957.84) minus the initial capital cost of $20,000 = $11,552.

(d)   (i)   *less profitable* as a higher interest rate would increase the cost of capital and raise the discount rate to be used.
   (ii)   *more profitable* as lower labour cost would raise the net income stream from the project.
   (iii)   *less profitable* as this would reduce the scrap value of the investment at the end of its life.
   (iv)   *more profitable* as this would raise revenue and it would be expected to raise the net income stream from the project.

# 2

# The Market System and the Competitive Process

# The Market System and the Competitive Process

2

## LEARNING OUTCOMES

This chapter seeks to explain the way in which a competitive market works. The roles of the consumer and firm are examined. The impact of consumer behaviour, both individually and collectively, on demand allows the introduction of concepts such as elasticity. The idea of time periods is featured as the theory of supply is developed. Demand and supply are then put together to show how market prices are determined. The concept of market equilibrium is developed.

The different forms of market structure are identified and explained. The effect these structures have on price and output determination are outlined with their consequent impact for allocative and technical efficiency.

Finally, instances of market failure are considered. The implications these have for the operation of the market are outlined. The case for a public sector and intervention by government is described along with some of the forms such intervention can take.

On completion of their studies students should be able to:

- identify the equilibrium price in product or factor markets likely to result from specified changes in conditions of demand or supply;

- calculate the price elasticity of demand and the price elasticity of supply;

- identify the effects of price elasticity of demand on a firm's revenues following a change in prices;

- describe market concentration and the factors giving rise to differing levels of concentration between markets;

- describe market failures, their effects on prices, efficiency of market operation and economic welfare, and the likely responses of government to these;

- distinguish the nature of competition in different market structures;

- identify the impacts of the different forms of competition on prices and profitability.

## 2.1 Consumer behaviour and demand

### 2.1.1 Individual demand

Individual demand shows how much of a good or service someone intends to buy at different prices. This demand needs to be effective in that it is backed by available money, rather than just a general desire without the necessary financial backing. When considering demand at a price, we assume that the conditions of demand (i.e. other variables) are held constant.

- Demand tends to be higher at a low price and lower at a high price for most goods and services.
- When the demand for a good or service changes in response to a change in its price, the change is referred to as:.
  - an *expansion* in demand as demand rises when the price falls;
  - a *contraction* in demand as demand falls when the price rises.
- Thus in Figure 2.1 the downward-sloping demand curve D illustrates a normal downward-sloping demand curve and movements along this curve as the price changes would be called a contraction in demand (price is rising) or an expansion in demand (price is falling).
- For *normal* goods, the lower the price, the higher will be its demand. This is the result of two processes.
  - There is a *substitution effect*. This is where a consumer buys more of one good and less of another because of relative price changes. Thus if two goods are substitutes, a fall in the price of the first will lead consumers to switch some demand to the lower-price good, substituting the first good for the second.
  - There is a *income effect*. This is where a change in the price of good affects the purchasing power of the consumers' income (a change in their real income). If the price of a good falls, the consumer experiences a rise in their real income and, as a result, tends to buy more of all normal goods and services.
- In most cases the income effect is relatively weak. However, if expenditure on the good is a large proportion of consumer income, e.g. in the case of house purchase the effect will be relatively large.
- There are also *inferior* goods. In these cases, a rise in income leads to a lower demand for the product as consumers, now being richer, substitute better quality and preferred goods and services for the original ('inferior') good or service. An example of this is public transport. Here, as incomes rise, the demand for public transport falls as consumers substitute private transport such as cars.

## 2.1.2 Market demand

Market demand shows the total amount of effective demand from all the consumers in a market. It is an *aggregate*, like the supply curve for an industry. *Market demand* is usually shortened to demand and represented by a straight-line curve on a graph. The demand

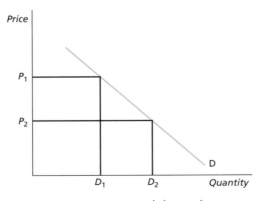

**Figure 2.1** A normal demand curve

curve for most normal goods is negatively inclined sloping downwards from right to left for reasons explained in the previous section.

### 2.1.3 Elasticity of demand

Elasticity, generally, refers to the relationship between two variables and measures the responsiveness of one (dependent) variable to a change in another (independent) variable: There are several types which are useful to economists.

#### Price elasticity of demand

This concept explains the relationship between *changes* in quantity demand and *changes* in price.

- Price elasticity of demand explains the responsiveness of demand to changes in price.
- The co-efficient of price elasticity of demand (PED) is calculated by:

$$\pi \quad \frac{\text{Percentage change in quantity demanded}}{\text{Percentage change in price}}$$

The formula can be applied either at one point (point elasticity) or over the whole curve (arc elasticity).

The *coefficient of elasticity* calculations for normal goods give a negative result because price and quantity demanded are inversely related. A summary of price elasticity is given below:

| Description of curve's elasticity | Coefficient value | Actual examples |
|---|---|---|
| Perfectly inelastic | 0 (zero) | — |
| Relatively inelastic | Between 0 and 1 | Tea, salt |
| Unit elasticity | 1 | — |
| Relatively elastic | Between 1 and ∞ | cameras, air travel |
| Perfectly elastic | ∞ (infinity) | — |

Generally, if the demand curve is fairly steep, a large change in price will cause only a relatively small change in demand, indicating an *inelastic* demand curve. It is often wrongly assumed that two demand curves with the same shape will have the same elasticity coefficient. The coefficients for the same range of $D_1$ and $D_2$ in Figure 2.2 are calculated for a price fall (triangle *c*).

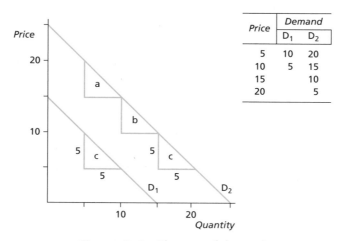

| Price | Demand | |
|---|---|---|
| | $D_1$ | $D_2$ |
| 5 | 10 | 20 |
| 10 | 5 | 15 |
| 15 | | 10 |
| 20 | | 5 |

**Figure 2.2**  Elasticity of demand

For $D_1$ (triangle $c$) the quantity demanded increases from 5 to 10 $\left(\text{i.e.} = +\frac{5}{5}\right)$ as the price falls from 10 to 5 $\left(\text{i.e.} -\frac{1}{2}\right)$. Elasticity is therefore calculated as $\frac{5}{5} \div \left(-\frac{1}{2}\right) = -2$.

In contrast, $D_2$ (triangle $c$) shows that quantity demanded increased from 15 to 20 $\left(\text{i.e.} +\frac{1}{3}\right)$ when the price fell from 10 to 5 $\left(\text{i.e.} -\frac{1}{2}\right)$. Elasticity is therefore calculated as $\frac{1}{3} \div \left(-\frac{1}{2}\right) = -\frac{2}{3}$.

This demonstrates the importance of the position of the demand curve. Generally, a curve further from the origin will tend to be less elastic, as shown above.

The numerical value of the elasticity coefficient also varies according to:

- whether a price fall or price rise is calculated. In Figure 2.2, $D_2$ elasticity $= -\frac{2}{3}$ when price fell from 10p to 5p. However, a price rise of 5p to 10p gives $-\frac{1}{4}\left(\text{i.e.} -\frac{1}{4} \div 1\right)$. This occurs because elasticity shows relative percentage changes and the base from which the calculations are made differs.
- which part of the demand curve is selected. Elasticity varies from point to point on a straight-line demand curve (but not on a rectangular hyperbola). As calculation moves down a linear curve from top left to bottom right the elasticity value falls, that is, the curve becomes relatively more inelastic. In Figure 2.2 the price elasticity of demand for a price fall of 5p on $D_2$ at $a = -4\left(\text{i.e.} 1 \div \left(-\frac{1}{4}\right)\right)$, whereas at $b$ it is $-\frac{3}{2}\left(\text{i.e.} \frac{1}{2} \div \left(-\frac{1}{3}\right)\right)$ and at $c$, $-\frac{2}{3}\left(\text{i.e.} -\frac{1}{2} \div \left(\frac{1}{2}\right)\right)$.

The elasticity can also be calculated by examining *total revenue*. This method is most useful to business people.

- If total revenue increases following a price cut, then demand is price elastic.
- If total revenue increases following a price rise, then demand is price inelastic.

Conversely, if total revenue falls after a price cut, then the demand is inelastic; and after a price rise it is elastic. If total revenue remains unchanged, then the demand is of unitary elasticity.

There are several factors which determine the price elasticity of demand:

- *Income.* Where a good constitutes a small proportion of consumers' income spent, then a small price change will be unlikely to have much impact. Therefore, the demand for unimportant items such as shoe polish, matches and pencils is likely to be very inelastic. Conversely, the demand for quality clothing will probably be elastic.
- *Substitutes.* If there are close and available substitutes for a product, then an increase in its price is likely to cause a much greater fall in the quantity demanded as consumers buy suitable alternatives. Thus, the demand for a specific variety box of chocolates may be fairly elastic because there are many competing brands in the market. In contrast, the demand for a unique product such as the *Timeform Racehorses Annual* for racing enthusiasts will tend to be inelastic.
- *Necessities.* The demand for vital goods such as sugar, milk and bread tends to be stable and inelastic; conversely luxury items such as foreign skiing holidays are likely to be fairly elastic in demand. It is interesting to note that improvements in living standards push certain commodities such as televisions from the luxury to the necessity category.

However, with luxuries the income elasticity of demand (see below) is more significant than the price elasticity of demand.

- *Habit.* When goods are purchased automatically, without customers perhaps being fully aware of their price, for example, newspapers, the demand is inelastic. This also applies to addictive products such as cigarettes, cocaine and heroin.
- *Time.* In the short run, consumers may be ignorant of possible alternative goods in many markets, so they may continue to buy certain goods when their prices rise. Such inelasticity may be lessened in the long run as consumers acquire greater knowledge of markets.
- *Definition of market.* If a market is defined widely (e.g. food), there are likely to be fewer alternatives and so demand will tend to be inelastic. In contrast, if a market is specified narrowly (e.g. orange drinks) there will probably be many brands available, thereby creating elasticity in the demand for these brands.

## Income elasticity of demand

Income elasticity of demand explains the responsiveness of demand to changes in income.

When income rises, people not only increase their demand for existing goods but also start to demand other goods, which they previously could not afford. These goods may be luxuries (e.g. yachts) or better quality normal goods (e.g. organic vegetables). The purchase of such goods may be to the detriment of other goods (e.g. frozen chickens) which then become inferior goods.

The income elasticity of demand (YED) is calculated by the formula:

 $$\frac{\text{Percentage change in quantity demanded}}{\text{Percentage change in income}}$$

If an increase in income of 10 per cent causes a 20 per cent increase in the demand for vegetarian food, then its income elasticity is $2\left(\frac{20}{10}\right)$.

A summary of income elasticity is given below:

| Description of income elasticity | Value | Type of good | Examples |
|---|---|---|---|
| Negative | — | Inferior | Matches |
| Zero to inelastic | 0–1 | Basic necessities | Bread, toothpaste |
| Positive (elastic) | +1 | Superior | Restaurant meals |

Income elasticity can be identified by market research using representative samples and by examining the household expenditure survey statistics published by the government. The evidence collected can be used by a business to plan its production and company strategy. Thus, the British Match Corporation diversified from its main product, matches, into a range of other wood-based products because it recognised matches as an inferior good (even though it is price inelastic).

### Cross-elasticity of demand

Cross elasticity of demand measures the responsiveness of the quantity demanded for one good to a price change in another. It shows the relationship between two goods. It will indicate whether the two goods are substitutes, complements or unrelated.

Cross elasticity of demand is calculated by the formula:

$$\frac{\text{Percentage change in quantity demanded of good A}}{\text{Percentage change in price of good B}}$$

For example, if the price of muesli falls by 10 per cent and the quantity of cornflakes bought falls by 20 per cent, then the cross-elasticity is $+2\left(\frac{-20}{-10}\right)$. Generally a positive sign indicates that the two goods are substitutes and the size of the number shows the strength of the relationship. High statistics indicate strong relationships, and low ones suggest a weak one. A negative sign for cross elasticity of demand indicates that the two goods are complements, that is they are used in conjunction with each other. A summary of cross-elasticity is given below:

| Description of cross-elasticity | Value | Example |
| --- | --- | --- |
| Complements | – | Bread and butter |
| Substitutes | + | Apples and oranges |
| Close substitutes | +high | Worcester apples and Granny Smith apples |
| Unrelated products | 0 | Apples and cars |

The interpretation of data on cross-elasticity is difficult because the impact of just one variable on another cannot be isolated in the real world. For example, a business person cannot be sure that the increase in demand for their product is solely caused by the pricing behaviour of their rivals, as other factors such as changes in income and tastes may also have been influential. Such factors are considered in the next section.

### 2.1.4 Conditions of demand

Individual and market demand consider exclusively the influence of price on the quantity demanded, assuming other factors to be constant. These factors, termed the conditions of demand, will now be considered, with price held constant.

- Any change in one or more of the conditions of demand will create *shifts in the demand curve* itself.
- If the shift in the demand curve is outward, to the right, such a shift is called a *increase in demand*.
- If the shift in the demand curve is inward, to the left, such a shift is called a *decrease in demand*.

It is important to distinguish such *increases* and *decreases* in demand that result from a shift in the demand curve as a whole from *expansions* and *contractions* in demand that result from price changes leading to movements along the demand curve itself. The differences are illustrated in Figure 2.3.

The main conditions of demand are as follows:

- *Income.* Changes in income often affect demand, as the income elasticity section illustrated. *Lower direct taxes* raise disposable incomes and, other things being equal, make

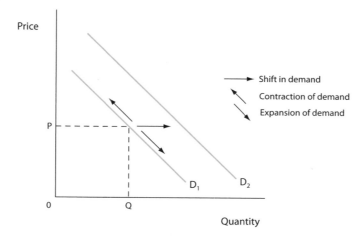

**Figure 2.3**    A change in quantity demanded and a shift in demand

consumers better off. This might cause less demand for necessities and more demand for luxuries. In recent years improvements in the standard of living have led to greater spending on services and leisure activities. A redistribution of income via more progressive and less regressive taxation might have a similar effect. Furthermore, if average wage increases exceed the rate of inflation, consumers will become better off in real terms and thus have greater flexibility and scope in the use of their income.

- *Tastes.* Tastes, in particular fashions, change frequently and it may make the demand for certain goods volatile. For instance, the demand for jeans had rapidly risen with greater female independence and individualism. Similarly, concern about health and the greater awareness of the causes of senile illness have increased the demand for brown bread and vegetable oil at the expense of white bread and animal fats. Tastes, of course, can be manipulated by advertising and producers to try to 'create' markets, particularly for ostentatious goods, for example, air conditioners which our ancestors survived perfectly well without. Some goods are in seasonal demand (e.g. cooked meat) even though they are available all year round, because tastes change (i.e. more salads are consumed in the summer).

- *The prices of other goods.* Goods may be unrelated, or they may be complements or substitutes. The former have no effect but the latter two are significant. If goods are in joint demand (i.e. complements such as cars and tyres) a change in the price of one will affect the other also. Therefore, if the price of cars falls, there is likely to be an increase in demand for tyres. Where goods are substitutes (e.g. Quality Street chocolates and Roses chocolates), a rise in the price of one will cause an increase in demand for the other (and thus the demand curve will shift to the right). Sometimes, technological breakthroughs mean that new products come into the market. For instance, the advent of ink cartridge pens reduced the demand for fountain pens, because the former became a cheaper (and less messy) substitute.

- *Population.* An *increase* in population creates a larger market for most goods, thereby shifting demand outwards. For instance, an influx of immigrant workers will raise the demand for most essential goods. Changes in population distribution will also affect demand patterns. If the proportion of old people relative to young people increases, then the demand for products such as false teeth, wheelchairs and old people's homes will increase to the detriment of gripe water, nappies and cots.

In the analysis of how the demand and supply model works, the distinctions between *increase / decrease* in demand and *expansion / contraction* in demand are very important. Remember:

- If a *price change* occurs, there will be a *movement along the demand curve* and the result will be either an *expansion* or a *contraction* in demand;
- If the *conditions of demand* change, there will be a *shift in the demand curve* and the result will be either an *increase* or a *decrease* in demand.

 **Exercise 2.1**

Answer the following questions based on the preceding information. You can check your answers below.

1. Describe the shape of a typical demand curve.
2. What are 'inferior' goods?
3. What is the price elasticity of demand?
4. The price of a good falls by 10 per cent but the quantity demanded increases from 100 to 120 units. Calculate the price elasticity of demand.
5. List four factors that influence price elasticity of demand.
6. How would you classify a good with a high positive income elasticity?
7. What value would you expect from a cross-elasticity calculation where the two goods are complements?
8. What is the difference between a shift in demand and an expansion of demand?

 **Solutions**

1. Downward sloping from top left to bottom right is the shape of a typical demand curve.
2. Inferior goods are goods for which the demand decreases as income rises. Thus a rise in income would lead the demand curve to shift to the left as opposed to the right for normal goods.
3. Price elasticity of demand shows the responsiveness of demand to a change in price.
4. The price elasticity of demand is $-2$ (i.e. $+20\%/-10\%$). The demand for the good is therefore price elastic.
5. Income, substitutes, necessities, time, definition of the market.
6. A superior good has a high positive income elasticity of demand, for example, luxury services.
7. A negative $(-)$ value.
8. A shift in demand occurs when the conditions of demand change, whereas an expansion of demand is the result of a fall in price.

## 2.2 Supply and market

### 2.2.1 The supply curve of a firm

The supply curve of a firm is underpinned by the desire to make profit. It demonstrates what a firm will provide to the market at certain prices. Usually it is assumed that suppliers are *profit maximisers* and produce where *marginal cost* equals *marginal revenue*. What a firm will supply onto a market will be affected by the average cost of production. This will vary between the short run and the long run.

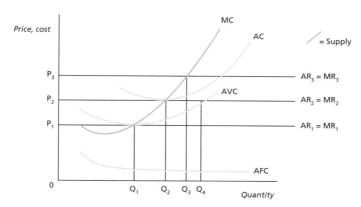

**Figure 2.4** Short-run supply curve based on marginal cost

### Short run

(a) The shape of the supply curve depends upon which theory of the firm is applied. In the traditional theory, where average cost (AC) includes normal profit, the AC curve is U-shaped in the short run with marginal cost (MC) rising more steeply than AC. Assuming one selling price for all firms (perfect competition – see later), the firm's average revenue (AR) and marginal revenue (MR) will be identical. Thus the firm will supply output where MC = MR in order to maximise profit.

- This is illustrated in Figure 2.4. If the market price rises, then it is assumed that the firm has the capacity (or stocks) to increase its sales output.
- In these conditions, the *marginal cost curve* becomes the firm's *supply curve*. Thus, at price $P_1$ the firm supplies $Q_1$ output because MC = $MR_1$. When price rises to $P_2$ and $P_3$, then output is also increased to $Q_2$ and $Q_3$ respectively. The firm is also prepared to supply at prices above $P_3$ where MC = MR.

However, there is a minimum level below which a firm will not supply. In the short run it will continue to supply even when making a loss, as long as the firm covers all its *variable costs*. At $P_2$ and $Q_4$ the supplier's average revenue will be less than its average cost (loss) but greater than its average *variable costs*. This means that a loss is made but some of the fixed costs are paid for. A complete shut-down would be financially worse because there would be no sales income to pay for any of the fixed costs. At price $P_1$, average revenue ($AR_1$) just equals average variable costs at $Q_1$ and so output will not be supplied onto the market below $P_1$. Thus the firm's supply curve equals the marginal cost above the average variable cost curve.

(b) The new theories of the firm incorporate the cost-plus pricing approach. In this, a firm adds a profit margin to its average cost, which has been calculated for a planned level of output, to establish a selling price. This approach, which seems to accord with practice, gives a horizontal supply curve. Supply is made elastic at a market price ($P_1$), which is determined for the whole industry.

The minimum and maximum levels of output occur where AR crosses the AC curve. A profit maximizing or loss minimizing firm will supply only where AR exceeds AC, that is, between $Q_1$ and $Q_2$ in Figure 2.5. Below output $Q_1$ and above $Q_2$ losses progressively increase, at price $P_1$.

Changes in the market price (we are still assuming perfect competition) will lead to changes in output. A higher price such as $P_2$ will lead to a new lower minimum level of supply $Q_3$ and a new higher maximum output $Q_4$.

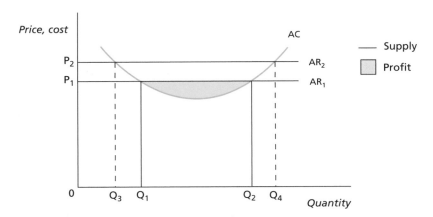

**Figure 2.5** Short-run supply curves based on cost-plus pricing

### Long run

(a) In the traditional theory, the marginal cost curve also becomes the supply curve in the long run. However, it will not necessarily be upward sloping because AC (and thus MC) can be increasing, constant or decreasing in the long run. The AC was increasing in the short run because of diminishing returns caused by the fixed factor assumption. This assumption is relaxed in the long run and so MC (and thus supply) could be downward-sloping left to right (if economies of scale occur), constant or upward-sloping (diseconomies). In the long run all costs of production, not just variable costs, need to be covered, because there is no fixed factor.

(b) The full-cost pricing theory still retains a horizontal supply curve in the long run. It will be at a higher or lower level than in the short run depending on whether or not economies or diseconomies of scale are obtained. There will also be minimum and maximum output levels where AC = AR.

The behaviour of suppliers will also be determined by changes in demand and the nature of the markets within which they trade. These factors are considered in more detail later.

- In the short run under conditions of perfect competition, the supply curve of the firm is its marginal cost curve
- In the short run a firm must cover its variable costs if it is to continue in production
- In the long run, when all costs become variable, the firm must cover all its costs to remain in production

### 2.2.2 The supply curve of an industry

Assuming that all the firms in an industry are identical, a market supply curve is composed of all the supply curves of the individual producers in the industry added together. The industry supply curve is an aggregate, which shows what producers are willing to offer for sale at any given price. In Table 2.1, the supply schedules of three firms are combined to show the industry supply at each price.

Thus, the supply curve of an industry is similar to that of its individual component firms but at a higher level.

**Table 2.1**  Supply schedules

| | Quantity supplied | | | |
|---|---|---|---|---|
| **Price** | **Firm A** | **Firm B** | **Firm C** | **Industry** |
| 0 | 0 | 0 | 0 | 0 |
| 1 | 10 | 15 | 20 | 45 |
| 2 | 20 | 30 | 25 | 75 |
| 3 | 30 | 45 | 30 | 105 |
| 4 | 40 | 60 | 35 | 135 |
| 5 | 50 | 75 | 40 | 165 |

## 2.2.3  The elasticity of supply

The elasticity of supply is calculated by the formula:

$$\frac{\text{Percentage change in quantity supplied}}{\text{Percentage change in price}}$$

A normal supply curve will always slope upwards from left to right indicating that suppliers are willing to supply more the higher is the price. Thus a price rise will lead to an *expansion* in supply and a price fall will lead to a *contraction* in supply. Therefore, the value of the price elasticity of supply (PES) is always negative.

- If a change in price induces a *larger proportionate* change in the quantity supplied, the price elasticity of supply will have a value of more than 1 and supply is said to be *price elastic*.
- If a change in price induces a *smaller proportionate* change in the quantity supplied, the price elasticity of supply will have a value of less than 1 and supply is said to be *price inelastic*.
- If a change in price induces an *equally proportionate* change in the quantity supplied, the price elasticity of supply will have a value of 1 and supply is  said to have *unit elasticity*.

If the supply curves are drawn as straight lines then the points of intersection with the price and quantity axis indicate their elasticity. This is shown in Figure 2.6.

In addition, a supply curve parallel to the output axis indicates perfect elasticity, while a supply curve parallel to the price axis demonstrates perfect inelasticity.

There are several factors which affect the elasticity of supply:

- *Time.* Supply tends to be more elastic in the long run. Production plans can be varied and firms can react to price changes. In some industries, notably agriculture, supply is fixed in the short run and thus perfectly inelastic. However, in manufacturing, supply is more adaptable.
- *Factors of production.* Supply can be quickly changed (elastic) if there are available factors, such as trained labour, unused productive capacity and plentiful raw materials, with which output can be raised. Although one firm may be able to expand production in the short run, a whole industry may not, so there could be a divergence between a firm's elasticity and that of the industry as a whole.
- *Stock levels.* If there are extensive stocks of finished products warehoused, then these can be released onto the market, making supply relatively elastic. Stock levels tend to be higher when business people are optimistic and interest rates are low.
- *Number of firms in the industry.* Supply will tend to be more elastic if there are many firms in the industry, because there is a greater chance of some having the available factors and high stock. Also, it is possible that industries with no entry barriers or import restrictions could expand supply quickly as new firms enter the industry in response to higher prices.

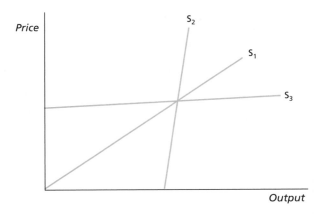

**Figure 2.6** Supply elasticity

$S_1$ intersects the origin and shows unit elasticity.
$S_2$ intersects the output axis and shows inelastic supply.
$S_3$ intersects the price axis and shows elastic supply.

### 2.2.4 Shifts in supply

The analysis so far has just considered the response of suppliers to differing prices. It has assumed that the conditions of supply which determine the costs of production are held constant. In this section, price is assumed to be unchanged and the conditions of supply are varied. These variations cause shifts in the supply curve.

#### An upward shift of supply

This means that the cost of supply has increased. At existing prices less will now be supplied, as shown on the upward-sloping, elastic supply curve in Figure 2.7. At price $P$, the quantity supplied falls from $Q$ to $Q_1$ as the supply curve shifts from $S_2$ to $S_1$.

This results from:

- *Higher production costs.* In the traditional theory of the firm this means higher marginal costs, resulting from increased average costs. In the new theory of the firm it may mean a higher average cost of production or a higher profit margin or a combination of the two. To keep matters simple we will assume unchanged profit margins.

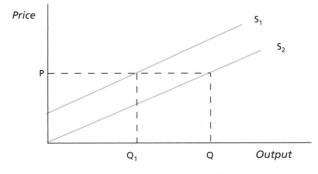

**Figure 2.7** Shifts in supply

The costs of production may increase because the factors of production become expensive. Thus conditions such as higher wage costs per unit, higher input prices and increased interest rates will lead to reductions in supply.

- *Indirect taxes.* The imposition of an indirect tax, or a higher rate charged, or lower sub-sidies all make supply at existing prices less profitable. A tax means that the profit margin (or normal profit) is lowered directly and the costs of production are raised indirectly (because of the extra administrative costs). The impact of taxation is demonstrated in Chapter 3.

### A downward shift of supply

In Figure 2.7, a shift in the supply curve from $S_1$ to $S_2$ illustrates an increase in supply with more being supplied at each price, showing that the cost of production has fallen or lower profits are being taken. Lower unit costs may arise from:

- technological innovations, for example, the advance of microchip technology lowered the cost of computers and led to large increases in supply;
- more efficient use of existing factors of production, for example, introduction of a shift system of working might mean fuller use of productive capacity, leading to lower unit costs. Improvements in productivity may be secured by maintaining output but with fewer workers;
- lower input prices, such as, cheaper raw material imports and lower-priced components could bring down production costs.

## Exercise 2.2

Answer the following questions based on the preceding information. You can check your answer below.

1. Describe the shape of the short-run supply curve.
2. What is the shape of the supply curve called?
3. Which factors affect the elasticity of supply?
4. What effect will higher wages have on the supply curve?

## Solutions

1. The short-run supply curve is a straight line from bottom left to top right.
2. The short-run supply curve is the marginal cost curve in the traditional theory of the firm. With cost-plus pricing, the supply curve is the price (average revenue) line.
3. The elasticity of supply is determined by time, the factors of production, stock levels and the number of firms in the industry.
4. Higher wages will cause the supply curve to shift upwards and parallel to the original supply.

# 2.3 Prices

## 2.3.1 Definitions and terms

Price is the money paid by the purchaser of a good or service, for example, the £8 entry fee to the cinema. In economics, we are mainly concerned with the prices of new goods, rather than secondhand ones. This market price is made up of the costs of production in the traditional theory of the firm or costs plus a profit mark-up in other approaches to pricing. The price reflects the *economic cost*, which represents the total sacrifice made in making one good rather than another.

Occasionally the price does not exactly represent the costs. If the price is higher than the costs this could be because of government-imposed taxation. For example, the actual cost of making cigarettes is about 40 per cent of the sale price, because of excise duty and VAT which are imposed.

In contrast, the provision of a *subsidy* can bring about an artificially low price. Subsidies are less common, and there are few remaining examples. Many medicines and pills bought via prescription charges are subsidised in Britain's NHS.

- *Transfer price* – an internal price set for sale within a multinational organisation, so that profit is made in the country with lowest taxes.
- *Value* – this is a subjective term and appears in many phrases concerned with prices.
- *Market value* – the exchange value which is determined by supply and demand forces. This term is used by economists to mean the same thing as market prices.
- *Nominal value or price* – the market price at any given time.
- *Relative value or price* – the market price of a good or service relative to some other. Thus the relative value or price of electronic goods has fallen in recent years relative to the values or prices of other goods.
- *Real value (or price)* – since inflation raises all prices, the nominal price or value of a good may rise but its real value (after making allowance for inflation) may not have. Thus the real value of wages may fall if nominal wage rises are less than the rate of inflation.

## 2.3.2 The price mechanism

The main characteristic of any market is price. It enables a market to operate. The price charged for a good or service conveys information to buyers and sellers. This information may modify their behaviour and change the nature of the market.

Figure 2.8 shows the *intended demand* and *planned supply* at a set of prices. It is only at price $P$ where demand and supply are the same. If the demand of consumers and the supply plans of sellers correspond, then the market is deemed to be in *equilibrium*. Only at output $Q$ and price $P$ are the plans of both sellers and buyers realised. Thus $Q$ in the *equilibrium quantity* and $P$ is the *equilibrium price* in this market.

There is only one equilibrium position in a market. At this point, there is no tendency for change in the market, because the plans of both buyers and sellers are satisfied. At prices and outputs other than the equilibrium ($P$, $Q$) either demand or supply aspirations could be fulfilled but not both simultaneously.

- For instance at price $P_1$, consumers only want $Q_1$ output but producers are making $Q_2$ output available. There is a surplus, the excess supply being $Q_1 Q_2$ output. Assuming the conditions of demand and supply remain unchanged, it is likely that the buyers and

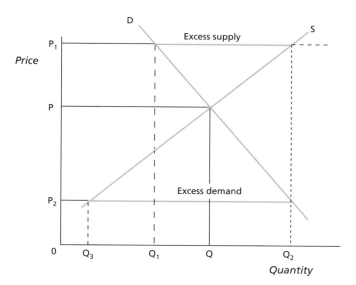

**Figure 2.8** Price mechanism and equilibrium

sellers will reassess their intentions. For instance, firms may not want unsold stocks of goods (because of the financial costs which result) and so may be prepared to accept lower prices than $P_1$ for their goods. This reduction in price will lead to a *contraction* in supply and an *expansion* in demand until *equilibrium* is reached at price $P$.

- Conversely, at a price of $P_2$, the quantity demanded, $Q_2$, will exceed the quantity supplied, $Q_3$. There will be a shortage ($Q_2 - Q_3$), demonstrating the *excess demand*. This excess demand will lead to a rise in the market price, and demand will *contract* and supply will *expand* until *equilibrium* is reached at price $P$.

As well as signalling information in a market, price acts as a *stimulant*. The price information may provide incentives for buyers and sellers. For instance, a price rise may encourage firms to shift resources into one industry in order to obtain a better reward for their use.

- In Figure 2.9, the equilibrium is disturbed when the conditions of demand change. Consumers' tastes have moved positively in favour of the good and a new curve $D_1$ shows customers' intentions.
- Supply is initially $Q$, at the equilibrium, and it is momentarily fixed, so the market price is bid up to $P_1$.
- However, producers will respond to this stimulus by expanding the quantity supplied, perhaps by running down their stocks.
- This expansion in supply to $Q_2$ reduces some of the shortage, bringing price down to $P_2$, a new equilibrium position, which is above the old equilibrium $P$.

The longer-term effects of these changes in the market depend upon the reactions of the consumers and producers. The consumers may adjust their marginal utilities (or preferences) and producers may reconsider their production plans. The impact of the latter on supply depends upon the length of the production period. Generally the longer the production period, and the more inelastic the supply is, the more unstable price will tend to be.

The short-run and long-run equilibrium positions vary between the different types of market. The number and independence of the suppliers and the ease of entry to, and exit

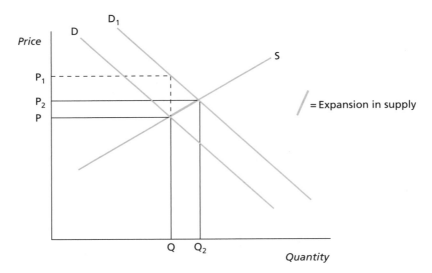

**Figure 2.9** Old and new equilibrium position

from, a market have a crucial bearing on price determination. These factors are considered in more detail in Sections 2.5 and 2.6.

- Price acts as a signal to sellers on what to produce.
- Price rises, with all other market conditions unchanged, will act as a stimulus to extra supply.
- Equilibrium price is where the plans of both buyers and sellers are satisfied.

---

**Box 2.1  Paying for Roads?**

Britain moved a step closer towards the introduction of road pricing yesterday when the government announced it had chosen seven local authorities to run pilot schemes aimed at tackling local traffic congestion in their areas. Transport secretary Alistair Darling told the CBI conference road congestion was one of the biggest threats to economic expansion over the next 10 to 15 years. The government he said was adding new capacity where it was needed and changing the ways roads were managed. But while he acknowledged such measures would make a difference, he warned that without radical measures congestion would get worse.

A CBI survey published yesterday showed business is increasingly concerned about the impact of congested roads and rail hold-ups which it is estimated costs British business about £20 b in a year.

*Source*: Mark Milner, *The Guardian*, November 29th 2005

---

### 2.3.3  Prices and resource allocation

In a free market economy the prices of demand and supply combine to solve the problem of resource allocation. Prices will act as a means for consumers to signal to the market what it is that they wish to buy. Prices will indicate to producers where their factors of production will be most profitably utilised. If demand increases for a particular product then, other than in the case of perfectly elastic supply, price will rise. This will offer profitable opportunities for producers who will move extra resources into this line of production thereby expanding supply. If price falls because of a reduction in demand, producers will transfer resources to other lines of production where profitable opportunities are greater. Thus consumers and producers pursuing their own self-interest ensure efficient resource allocation in a competitive market economy.

Resources are allocated in a competitive market economy according to enlightened self-interest.

### 2.3.4  Agricultural prices

These are focused upon and sometimes regulated because of the natural instability in supply. Changes in supply can occur due to natural events such as harvest failure. The cobweb theory shows the instability to which agricultural prices are subject. This involves large fluctuations in the prices of foodstuffs and in the incomes of farmers, both of which governments believe to be economically and politically undesirable.

Price fluctuations may also be caused by demand factors. For instance, industrial demand for raw materials varies erratically, depending on consumer demand for the final product, stock levels and the interest and exchange rate cost of holding materials ready for use. It is usually in the primary goods sector, particularly agriculture and raw materials, where price is most unstable. While price changes generally may have beneficial dynamic effects, frequent and large price variations can be harmful. They can create uncertainty, which is bad for trade, and convey misleading information, which might cause market failures. Thus, governments may intervene in the market and adjust prices in certain circumstances.

- Instability in the prices of primary products occurs due to inelastic supply in the short run.
- Rapid changes in demand for primary products when matched by inelastic supply causes erratic movements in prices and in the incomes of producers.

### Cobweb theorem

The instability of price is demonstrated by the cobweb theorem, which is illustrated in Figure 2.10. This theory was originally used to explain the fluctuations in pig prices in the United States. At the initial equilibrium (*P*, *Q*) pig farmers felt that the market price was

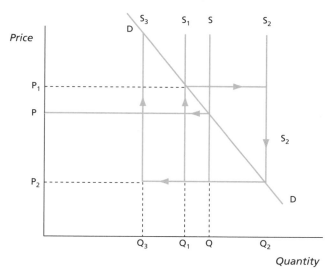

**Figure 2.10**  Price instability – the cobweb theorem

too low, so they transferred resources to other activities. This action lowered the following year's supply to $S_1$; but the ensuing shortage raised prices to $P_1$. This price rise acted as a stimulant and so in the following year more pigs were raised ($S_2$). However, this increase in supply glutted the market, leading to a dramatic price fall to $P_2$. Thus, a high price was followed by a high supply and therefore a low price (and then a low supply . . .).

To prevent such price fluctuation for primary products, such as cocoa, tin, etc., *buffer stock systems* have been developed by the world's main suppliers. They form cartels to regulate prices, which fluctuate within fairly narrow ranges. The bigger stockholders buy surpluses if a large supply threatens to push prices through the floor. Alternatively, they sell stocks if shortages threaten to force prices above the ceiling. Apart from providing fairly constant prices for buyers, the policy also maintains fairly stable incomes for producers.

### The Common Agricultural Policy

As members of the European Union, Britain participates in the Common Agricultural Policy (CAP). This is a buffer stock system combined with an external tariff. This tariff protects European suppliers from foreign competition. The European Union sets target prices for foodstuffs and buys stocks at intervention prices if target prices are not achieved.

The intervention price ($P_I$) is usually above the (world) market price ($P_M$) with the result that excess quantities are supplied ($Q_1 Q_3$). These are the famous butter mountains and wine lakes. Thus a stable and high price is sustained to the benefit of European farmers. A tariff, equivalent to $P_M P_T$, is placed on imports to further protect domestic suppliers, (Figure 2.11).

However, consumers pay a price ($P_I$) above the market price ($P_M$). This entails a loss of consumer surplus. The EU stores the surplus quantity of food. Even if a bad harvest shifts supply to $S_1$, then the same price is received by farmers (although their income falls as quantity is lowered); but the Community does not have the costs of storage. The increase in farm efficiency and high intervention prices led to growing stocks in the 1980s. Thus, in the case of butter, milk quotas were introduced in an attempt to limit the excess supply and reduce the costs and waste of intervention. It went further in the 1990s by bringing in *set-aside* conditions.

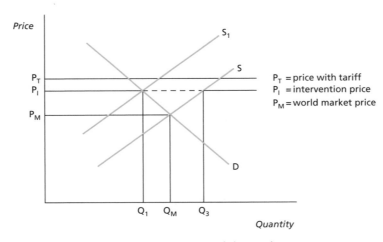

**Figure 2.11** Price stability and CAP

**Exercise 2.3**

Answer the following questions based on the preceding information. You can check your answers below.

1. What is the difference between a 'real' price and a 'nominal' price?
2. When does excess supply occur?
3. What mainly causes the price instability of agricultural goods?
4. How can producers attempt to overcome the problems that the cobweb theory illustrates?
5. What does the operation of the CAP and similar schemes tend to cause?

 **Solutions**

1. A 'real' price allows for inflation whereas a 'nominal' price is the present face value.
2. Excess supply occurs when the amount supplied is greater than the amount demanded at a given price, that is when the price is above the equilibrium level.
3. The price instability of agricultural goods is caused by wide variations in the supply, which is naturally inelastic in the short run.
4. Producers can overcome the fluctuations in agricultural goods prices by price-fixing within a narrow range. This requires them to co-operate through a cartel and storing surplus stocks, which are then released on to the market if there is insufficiency.
5. The operation of the CAP causes higher prices, excess supplies and storage costs, but it does stabilise farm prices.

### 2.3.5 Interference with market prices

There may be occasions when the equilibrium price established by the market forces of demand and supply may not be the most desirable price. The market price might be too low, as in the case of the wage rate, to enable workers to have an acceptable standard of living. Alternatively the market price might be too high, as in the case of the housing rent, to provide affordable accommodation for people. With such cases the government might wish to set prices above or below the market equilibrium price.

#### Minimum price

If the government sets a minimum price above the equilibrium price (often called a price floor), there will be a surplus of supply created. In Figure 2.12 this surplus is $Q_1 Q_2$. If this minimum price was applied in the labour market it would be known as a minimum wage and the surplus would be the equivalent of unemployment.

The problem with price floors is that they cause surpluses of products which have to be stored or destroyed, or unemployment which would be a waste of a factor of production. Another way of looking at the same problem is to state that it leads to a misallocation of resources both in the product and/or the factor market which causes lower economic growth. There also may be the temptation for firms to attempt to ignore the price floor, for example, by informal arrangements with workers, which would lead to a further waste of resources in implementing such arrangements as well as raising issues of fair treatment for the workers involved.

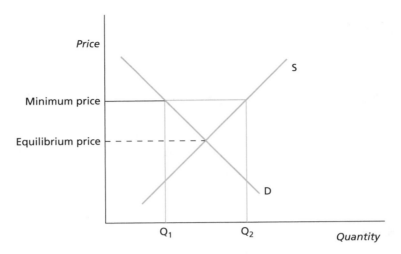

**Figure 2.12** Minimum price/wage

Government-imposed minimum prices cause:

- Excess supply
- Misallocation of resources
- Waste of resources.

## Maximum price

If the government sets a maximum price below the equilibrium price (often called a price ceiling), there will be a shortage of supply created. In Figure 2.13 this shortage is $Q_1 Q_2$.

If the shortages of supply persist then problems can arise. The limited supply has to be allocated by some means other than by price. This can be done by queuing, by rationing or by some form of favouritism, for example, by giving preference to regular customers. The difficulty with any of these alternative mechanisms is that they can be considered arbitrary and unfair by those who fail to secure the product. A consequence of the shortage can be the emergence of black markets. This is where buyers and sellers agree upon an illegal price which is higher than that which has been officially sanctioned at the maximum price.

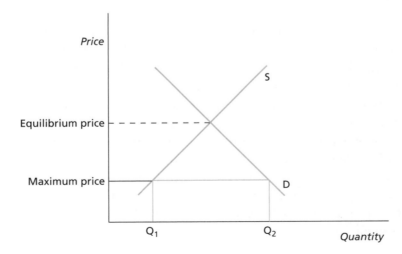

**Figure 2.13** Maximum price

Maximum prices can also lead to a misallocation of resources. Producers will reduce output of those products subject to price controls as these products are now relatively less profitable than those products where no price controls exist. In the housing market this may lead to fewer apartments for rent as landowners develop office blocks rather than residential houses. Alternatively the quality of the product may be allowed to drop as a way of reducing costs when profits are constrained by price controls. This failure to maintain property can mean that apartments fall into disrepair.

Government-imposed maximum prices cause:

- Shortages of supply
- Arbitrary ways of allocating a product
- Misallocation of resources.

## 2.4  Large-scale production

### 2.4.1  The growth of firms

Firms grow through internal expansion and integration. A firm may expand by producing and selling more of its existing products or by extending its range of products. Thus, the general retailer Boots started off as Jesse Boot's, a Nottingham chemists shop. Such successful firms have often developed through enterprising management, which has utilised a willing workforce, unused capacity and available finance.

Integration occurs when firms join together, by either merger or takeover. A *merger* is an amalgamation of at least two firms into one organisation, for example, Astra Zeneca. It is usual for shareholders in the old firm to exchange their old shares for shares in the new firm in agreed proportions.

The Competition Commission investigates mergers and recommends a decision to the Trade and Industry Secretary. For example, in 1998 it recommended that Bass be allowed to buy Carlsberg-Tetley for £200 m, provided that it then sold 1,900 pubs. However, trade minister Margaret Beckett blocked the bid and overturned the MMC ruling because of Bass's 'significant increase' in market power as a producer and wholesaler of beer.

A *takeover* differs from a merger in that the initiative for acquisition comes from the offering company and the board of the target company is *opposed* to, or not fully in favour of, the bid. In March 2000, the Royal Bank of Scotland made a hostile bid for (and took over) Nat West. With mergers there is usually willing co-operation between the two firms. Takeovers are financed either with cash and/or an offer in shares in the acquiring companies, with maybe a cash adjustment. The price offered is nearly always higher than the current Stock Exchange valuation. The Stock Exchange has a Takeover Panel which vets the procedures to ensure fair and equal treatment for all the shareholders of the target company.

The general objective of mergers and takeovers is to increase profits, usually in the short run, and earnings per share. This has been criticised as short sighted as it may reduce longer-term product development and market development.

There are three main types of integration: horizontal, vertical and diversification.

### Horizontal integration

Firms in the *same industry* and at the *same stage of production* join together. Horizontal integration is common in manufacturing industries such as brewing, for instance Scottish and

Newcastle Breweries took over many regional breweries in the United Kingdom in the 1980s and 1990s and then merged with Courage Brewery in 1995.

The reasons for such integration include:

- *To obtain the benefits of economies of scale.* A big retailer will have much more buying power than two smaller retailers and so will be able to lower their input costs. The increased financial muscle enables the large retailer to negotiate better terms with their suppliers. In manufacturing industry, horizontal integration was justified in the 1960s as a 'synergy' between companies on the basis of '2 + 2 = 5'. However, in some cases it was unsuccessful when rationalisation was slow. A notable example of failure was when Asda and MFI demerged.
- *To increase market share.* If a takeover reduces competition, the acquiring company can probably raise its market share. In retailing, mergers usually mean more outlets through which to sell the products of the two companies. Outside retailing, horizontal mergers have declined since the 1970s, partly because of the legislation on monopolies.
- *To fight off imports.* This defensive motive was behind the proposed GEC–Plessey merger (which the Department of Trade supported but the Ministry of Defence opposed in evidence to the Monopolies Commission), as they competed in an electronics industry which the Americans and Japanese were infiltrating from their dominant international positions.
- *To pool technology.* The wasteful duplication of research facilities can be avoided and the beneficial sharing of technical 'know-how' can be developed when manufacturers integrate, for example, Renault–Nissan.

### Vertical integration

Vertical growth occurs when one firm moves into another stage of production, which might otherwise be independent, in the same industry. This integration may be *backwards* towards the source of supply, for example, Ross Foods, which sells frozen food, purchasing its own fleet of trawlers; or *forwards* when the producer buys out stages nearer the market, for example, Ross Foods purchasing a retail outlet. The reasons for vertical integration include:

- *The elimination of transaction costs.* This will increase cost efficiency between the various stages of production, by reducing delivery costs and eliminating the profits of middlemen. This partly explains the mergers in the brewing industry.
- *Increasing entry barriers.* By gaining more control over supplies and/or sales, it will become more difficult for new competitors to enter the market.
- *Securing supplies.* By controlling its own sources of supply as a result of backward integration, a firm can achieve more flexible production. For instance a brewer experiencing increased demand could readily use his own lorry fleet to collect hops from stock and thereby temporarily raise production levels.
- *Improving the distribution network* with better market access. Forward integration into marketing enables a firm to control the conditions under which its goods are sold. For instance, a brewer can dictate pricing, advertising and display of his beer to a 'tied' public house.
- *Gaining economies of scale*;                  these benefits are common
- *making better use of existing technology.*  to vertical and horizontal integration.

### Diversification

This occurs when one firm expands into an industry with which it was previously unconnected, for example, Virgin records into travel. Some mergers are classed as *lateral* where the goods being newly produced by the expanding firm have a close link with their main products, for example, cars and lorries.

However, increasingly integration creates *conglomerates,* that is, groups of companies pursuing different activities in different industries. The mergers of the 1980s led to many of Britain's most successful enterprises, for example, Hanson Trust, becoming *financial holding companies*, rather than integrated producers of goods and services. These organisations sell off the inadequate parts of underperforming companies and develop those with potential. The conglomerates thus behave like investment bankers.

The reasons, other than short-term profit motives, for diversifications are:

- *To minimise risks.* If its main line is subject to trade fluctuations or going out of fashion, a firm may diversify into an expanding area to protect itself, for example, British American Tobacco purchasing Eagle Star. Such takeovers seek financial security, and higher corporate growth;
- *To make full use of expertise.* Dynamic management can use the expertise residing in a company in seemingly unconnected areas. Thus Centrica, initially a company selling gas, took over the AA, a motoring organisation, so as to fully utilise its large customer data base and sell a greater range of products.
- *To achieve economies of scale.* Particularly in *administration*. Thus a merger might lead to the fuller utilisation of, and greater return from, departments such as data processing, accounts and exports.

However, mergers are not always successful. Sometimes diseconomies of scale occur when merged managements experience personality clashes and become divided. Rationalisation does not always lead to lower cost production and may alienate customers and workers. The same is true of takeovers which lead to asset stripping and to less production and redundancies. Indeed, some have argued that the costs to society outweigh the private gains; thus the proponents of a merger should have to 'prove' its virtue rather than the critics have to demonstrate its 'guilt' (against the public interest) as happens now.

In 1995, the phrase *'vertical disintegration'* entered the dictionary. This explains the hiving off by a company of many of its service sectors or product centres, often to management buyouts, in order to reduce costs and concentrate on its core business. Such a policy is not quite the same as a *demerger*, where a firm sells off a brand (or brands) to an existing large company. The latter is often a rival and thus augments its market share. In 1995, Forte sold its chain of Little Chefs, Travelodges and Welcome Breaks to Whitbread, which already owned Beefeaters, Travel Inns, Brewers Fayres and Pizza Huts.

## 2.4.2 Market concentration

The growth of firms has increasingly led to greater domination of individual markets by few firms. This is referred to as *market concentration* and describes the extent to which the largest firms in an industry control their output, sales and employment. Concentration ratios can take two forms.

- Market and seller concentration
  This measures the share of production, sales or employment of the largest few firms in an industry or market. Often a five-firm concentration ratio is used. Traditionally, manufacturing industries are the most concentrated. In 2004 the United Kingdom had five-firm concentration ratios of over 85 per cent in car, cement, steel and tobacco production. There is also increasing concentration in service industries such as accountancy,

advertising, banking and food retailing. The growth in five-firm concentration ratios is driven by the desire to exploit economies of scale.

- High concentration ratios
  There are associated with a high degree of market or monopoly power by the largest firms in an industry or market sector.
  Sometimes concentration ratios overstate the extent of market power in an industry held by the leading five firms. This occurs when there is a significant amount of competition from imports. However, concentration ratios may also understate the true level of market power held by the leading five firms where local or regional monopolies exist, as in the case of supermarkets.
- Aggregate concentration ratio
  This measures the share of total production or employment contributed by the largest firms in the whole economy. The oldest concentration ratio used in the United Kingdom is the 100-firm ratio used in manufacturing. This measures the share of the largest 100 private firms in total manufacturing net output. This ratio rose from 14.8 per cent in 1900 to 41.7 per cent in 1975 but fell back to 32 per cent in 2001.
- Increases in firm size implicit in the rise in concentration ratios have occurred more by takeovers and mergers than by internal growth of the leading firms. We will examine the effect on market competition and structures later in Section 2.5.

An example of high market concentration in the retail industry is illustrated in Box 2.2.

---

**Box 2.2   Where to avoid Tesco**

Tesco is now the dominant supermarket in 81 of Britain's 121 postcode areas – up from 67 a year ago.

The rapidly increasing power of the Tesco empire is revealed in a report by retail consultants CACI, which also shows that Tesco holds second place in 24 of the remaining 40 postcode districts and is almost neck and neck with the number 2 supermarket in 4 of the remaining 16.

The retailing juggernaut, which now has a market share only slightly less than Asda and Sainsbury's added together, last week reported half-year profits of more than £1 b for the first time. The retailer is central to a Competition Commission inquiry into the power of supermarkets.

The researchers say that there are six United Kingdom postcode areas where Tesco accounts for more than 50 per cent of grocery spending. Wal-Mart owned Asda's highest market share is 38 per cent, in Wigan, while Sainsbury's is most dominant in south-west London, where it accounts for 36 per cent of shopping.

*Source*: Julia Finch: *The Guardian*, October 11th 2006

---

## 2.5   Market structures

### 2.5.1   Markets in economies

The word 'market' is used in many contexts. In economic theory a market is where *goods and services are bought and sold*, although it may not be an actual place. For instance, foreign currencies are bought and sold through international telephone deals and telex transfers between bank accounts. The buyers and sellers must be in *contact* and in modern societies the exchange is via the medium of *money*. The traders involved are willingly participating in the exchange and usually require information on the *prices* of the goods/services involved.

Most markets in practice are unorganised and decentralised. Governments may influence markets generally through legal constraints but they do not decide how much is traded. This is usually determined by price, which acts as a signal and as an incentive.

There are many markets in all types of modern economy, ranging from large-scale and official, for example, the Stock Exchange, to small and illegal, like a drug addict buying heroin from a street pusher. Some markets are very specialised, for example, the copper exchange on the London Metal Exchange. Markets tend to be dynamic, expanding and becoming more sophisticated to meet particular needs. Thus, not only can major commodities be bought and sold at prevailing prices (spot market), they can also be purchased now for an agreed price to be supplied at a future date. Such a *futures* market meets industry's need to plan future production.

Markets are also *segmented*. They can be divided by:

- *Geography*. The market for primary products may be international, national, regional or local depending on the suppliers and customers involved.
- *Time*. Demand and supply conditions can change, particularly when services are sold. For instance, travel on the railways may be cheaper from Monday to Thursday (than on Friday) for the same service. Such price discrimination between off-peak and peak times makes the market less homogeneous.
- *Customer type*. Suppliers may discriminate between their customers. For instance, large regular customers may get preferential quantity discounts off the listed prices, which other consumers pay.

Economic analysis needs to simplify the understanding of all these diverse markets. Thus we shall consider the *product* or *goods markets*. These markets refer to newly produced goods and services, and avoid the pricing of secondhand goods.

## 2.5.2　Forms of market structure

The purpose of this section is briefly to describe the main characteristics and assumptions which define each form of market. The detailed operation of each form is considered in the next section.

There are two extreme and largely theoretical forms of market: *perfect competition* and *monopoly*, which are polar opposites. In between, under the broad heading of imperfect competition, there are three other structures which have more grounding in reality. These are *monopolistic competition, oligopoly* and *duopoly*. All of these market structures are defined largely in terms of the number of suppliers in the market (Figure 2.14).

### Perfect competition

This structure describes an imaginary situation whose characteristics are as follows:

- *Many buyers and sellers*, so no one individual, can influence price by their actions. Buyers and sellers can trade as much as they want at the ruling market price, which is determined by the interaction of market demand and supply.

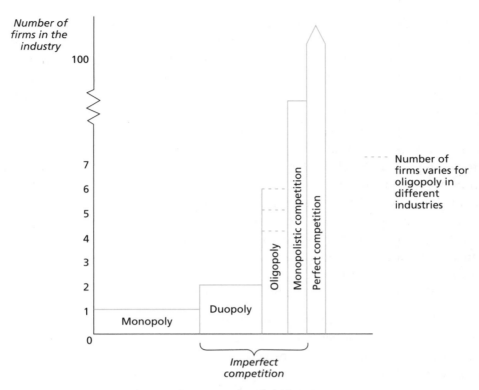

**Figure 2.14** Forms of market structure

- Buyers and sellers are *rational* economic beings. This translates into firms being profit maximisers.
- Buyers and sellers have *perfect information* about the product.
- The product is *homogeneous.* Hence there is no brand differentiation.
- There are *no entry barriers.* Buyers and sellers are free to enter and leave the market and there is no government interference in the market.
- *Perfect mobility* exists in the market both for products and factors of production.
- *Normal profits* are earned in the long run as any abnormal profits/losses are removed by competitive forces.

In reality, perfect markets rarely exist. An approximation is the Stock Exchange or local farmers' markets.

## Monopoly

This term is subject to two interpretations. First, in *theory*, it denotes a market in which there is one supplier and many consumers. Thus in a pure monopoly the firm is the industry, and thereby controls market supply. It can either fix price and let demand determine the amount supplied, or fix supply and let demand determine the market price.

Second, in *practice* British legislation identifies a firm in the private sector as holding a monopoly if its market share exceeds 25 per cent. As we shall see, this definition includes duopolists and oligopolists.

In a capitalist economy, a monopolist would be a profit maximiser. However, in a planned economy it is unlikely that state monopolies would have such a goal. In the United Kingdom mixed economy the previously nationalised industries operated like monopolies and sought large profits, for example, gas and electricity. Although facing competition from one another in the market for energy, each had a monopoly in its own fuel since there were entry barriers which limited the ability of new firms to enter the market. However, the law creating the sole supplier rights of such public monopolies is not sacrosanct. The government sets price controls on their operation and opened them up to competition and eventual full privatisation.

## Imperfect competition

Between perfect competition and monopoly, several forms of market exist, exhibiting some of the characteristics of the two extreme structures.

*Monopolistic competition.*
This is characterised by:

- Large number of producers who supply similar but not homogeneous products.
- Products are differentiated in style, image and price.
- There is not one prevailing market price. Firms may compete on price to try and gain market share at the expense of rivals.
- Consumers lack perfect knowledge but have a choice of products. This choice may be extended if new firms enter the industry perhaps attracted by the prospect of abnormal profits.
- There are no entry barriers; new firms can enter the industry and existing firms can leave at little cost.

*Oligopoly.*
This is characterised by:

- A few large firms with a high concentration ratio.
- There is a substantial non-price competition, for example, by advertising. Firms often produce several branded goods in the same market. Hence products are not homogeneous.
- The behaviour of firms is often dependent on their rivals' actions and hence the market has a degree of uncertainty about it. A firm is not certain how rivals will respond to action initiated by itself. Consequently, there is *interdependence* in decision making.
- Price stability is often associated with oligopolistic behaviour as firms choose not to raise or lower prices as they cannot be sure how rival firms will react to any such price changes.
- Consumers in oligopolistic markets lack detailed market information and are susceptible to the market strategies of the suppliers.
- New firms are unlikely to enter an oligopoly. The entrenched dominance often involving economies of scale enable them to fight off new competition. However, advances in technology and the financial power of transnational corporations mean that existing oligopolies can be challenged today.

In a *competitive oligopoly*, the features of monopolistic competition apply. However, the large firms in an oligopoly may *collude together*; oligopolists may raise the *total profits* which can be made in the industry and thereby increase their own profits. In contrast, cut-throat competition renders profit-making more difficult. But such price fixing and market sharing is illegal in virtually all countries, and such activities would be investigated by the competition authorities. However, it could be argued that consumers may benefit from an oligopoly through a wide range of branded goods, price stability and after-sales servicing. In addition if price stability facilitates accurate forward planning by producers, then consumers might gain from better products and lower costs of production in the long run.

*Duopoly.*

This market is characterised by:

- Two, usually large, firms dominate.
- Each producer has some control over price and output, but most consider the possible reactions of the competitor firm. Duopolists, like oligopolists, can act competitively or collusively.
- Extensive non-price competition exists.

### 2.5.3 Efficiency

This much-used (and -abused) term has various adjectives applied to it in economics. However, it is possible to discern two general meanings and associate descriptors with each aspect of economic performance.

- *Technical efficiency* – production at the lowest cost. This is usually used to describe the efficiency of a firm in the production of a good. An extension of this idea to the whole economy is *productive efficiency*, which is maximised when an economic system operates at the limit of the production frontier. This general meaning tries to relate inputs to output.
- *Allocative efficiency* – the best use of resources to produce goods and services which people want. The idea is to maximise the welfare of consumers. When each market in an economy operates so as to maximise consumer satisfaction, there is said to be *economic efficiency.* This general meaning relates the use of resources to consumer satisfaction.

The issue is further complicated by *time.* The most efficient firm at one point in time may not be so at a later date. For example the relative technical efficiency of one firm may change over time as a result of investment. For the whole economy, this would be shown by an outward movement of a production possibility curve. Similarly, people's preferences for goods may change and so utilities alter, thereby affecting allocative efficiency.

The result of such changes is that identification of productive and economic efficiency for the whole economy at a macro level is impossible. Thus, it makes more sense to concentrate on considering technical and allocative efficiency in markets in a micro analysis.

### Spotting efficiency

*Technical* efficiency is shown when a firm (or industry) produces at the lowest point on its average cost curve, that is, where MC crosses AC.

*Allocative* efficiency occurs when the price charged to the consumer equals the marginal cost of its supply, that is, $P = MC$. This indicates that the value to the consumer equals the cost of production to the supplier. The price paid indicates the utility gained by the consumer and this satisfaction is represented by the demand curve. Conversely, the marginal cost of the unit of output is shown by the supply curve. Thus, allocative efficiency occurs where *demand equals supply.* This explanation of allocative efficiency makes a significant simplifying assumption. This is that the cost of the output is the cost to society. In practice, it is the cost to the firm, which is a private cost and not necessarily the total cost to society. This latter includes externalities which may occur from production but are not included in the cost. For example, if the price of a packet of 20 cigarettes is £4.00p, the full cost including the indirect effects of extra healthcare, etc., might be £4.50.

# Exercise 2.4

Answer the following questions based on the preceding information. You can check your answers below.

1. What is a market?
2. What are the main assumptions of perfect competition?
3. In a monopoly, if a firm fixes the price, what determines the amount supplied?
4. Imperfect competition can be divided into three submarkets. What are they?
5. What is allocative efficiency?

 # Solutions

1. A market is where goods and services are bought and sold.
2. The assumptions of perfect competition are:
   - many buyers and sellers;
   - homogeneous product;
   - perfect information;
   - freedom of entry and exit.
3. Demand for the product.
4. Imperfect competition can be subdivided into monopolistic competition, oligopoly and duopoly.
5. Allocative efficiency refers to the best use of resources producing goods and services which people want. At the level of an individual firm, it occurs when the prices charged equal the marginal costs of production. In theory, it occurs only in perfect competition in the long run (when only normal profit is made). See Figure 2.17.

## 2.6   Price and output determination

For each of the market forms previously described, we will now look at how price and output decisions arise.

### 2.6.1   Perfect competition

In this market, individual buyers and sellers believe that their own behaviour has no influence on market price. As explained earlier, the goods are homogeneous, there is perfect knowledge of market conditions and there are no entry or exit barriers. These conditions ensure that all firms charge the same price for their product as is seen in Figure 2.15.

The firm in perfect competition is thus a price taker, which accepts a market price which is beyond its control.

- If the firm charged a higher price than $P$ it would lose all its customers, who would act rationally and buy the identical good from another supplier at a lower price.
- Conversely, there is no point selling at a lower price because the firm can sell all of its output at the market price and thereby gain higher profits.

Consequently, the demand curve for the individual firm is perfectly elastic at the price $P$. This horizontal demand curve is also the average revenue curve, because all units are sold at the same price, and the marginal revenue curve, because each additional unit of output sold brings in the same amount of extra revenue ($0P$).

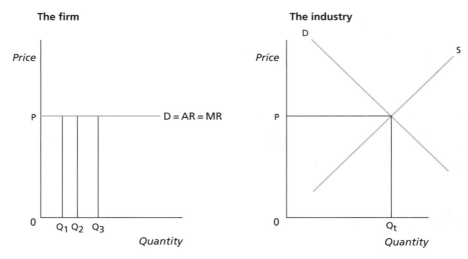

**Figure 2.15** The firm and the industry in perfect competition

The demand curve facing the industry as a whole is a normal downward-sloping demand curve. Similarly, market supply is shown in the traditional way. However, the amount supplied onto the market by an individual firm will be a very small proportion of the total quantity (given the basic assumptions). Whether it is $Q_1$, $Q_2$, $Q_3$ or any other level of output depends on the costs of production. Assuming that the firm is a profit maximiser, it will produce where marginal cost equals marginal revenue. Figure 2.16 shows the cost curves and the derivation of the short-run equilibrium.

Figure 2.16 shows that at the market price of $P$, the individual firm would wish to maximise profits by producing the level of output where marginal cost (MC) equals marginal revenue (MR), that is output level $Q$. At this level of output, average revenue ($P$) exceeds average cost ($C$) and so abnormal profits are made. The firm's total revenue is $PEQ0$ and its abnormal profits equal $PEFC$. It is worth noting that these abnormal profits do not equate with technical efficiency, as this would be achieved at output $X$, where AC is at its minimum.

## Profits

However, in perfect competition these abnormal profits occur only in the short run. It is assumed in the long run that firms can enter the industry. In the above case the market price

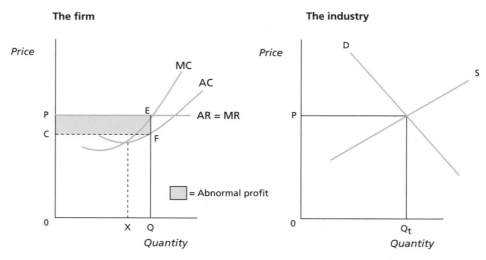

**Figure 2.16** Short-run equilibrium with abnormal profits

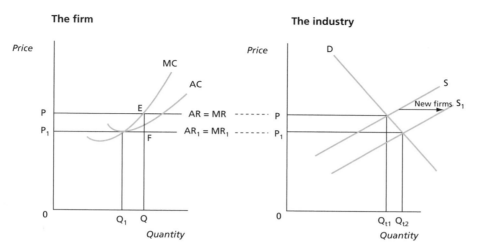

**Figure 2.17**    Long-run equilibrium with normal profits

signals abnormal profits and gives an incentive to firms to transfer resources to this industry. The advent of many new producers leads to an increase in supply from S to $S_1$ (see Figure 2.17).

The extra supply causes a fall in market price to $P_1$ and shifts the firm's demand curve downwards accordingly. If we assume that the firm's costs are unchanged, then at price $P_1$, MC = $MR_1$ and profit is maximised. At this output $Q_1$, only normal profit is made. Also, the firm is operating at its most *cost-effective* point (minimum AC) and the market is cleared with no wastage of resources. For such reasons, long-run equilibrium in perfect competition is lauded as a desirable model for an economy.

### Entry and exit

(i) *Long run*. Whenever price is between $P$ and $P_1$, new firms will enter the industry to secure a share of the abnormal profits. Conversely, at prices below $P_1$ firms will exit from the industry because of losses, thereby reducing supply and making the market price move upwards. At the long-run equilibrium there will be sufficient (normal) profit to keep existing firms in the industry and insufficient (as no abnormal) profit to attract new entrants.

(ii) *Short run*. A firm may not shut down production, even if it is making a loss. As long as a firm receives enough revenue to cover its variable costs, it will continue production. The reason for this is that it has to pay fixed costs anyway and any excess revenue over the variable costs can offset some of the fixed costs, thereby reducing losses. The firm's short-run supply curve is thus the part of the marginal cost curve above the average variable cost curve. (In the long run, the firm's supply curve is that portion above the AC.)

### Efficiency

The long-run equilibrium position in perfect competition is unique in that *price equals marginal cost*. This is significant because it gives *allocative efficiency*. If consumers take price as their measure of the value of a good and marginal cost measures the cost of attracting resources from alternative uses, then the price of the last unit of output is equal to its opportunity cost of production. Furthermore, as already indicated, these resources are being used to maximum technical efficiency because the firm is producing at the point of minimum average cost.

- Under perfect competition the firm is a price taker
- The demand curve for the film is horizontal so that the price equals AR which is the same as MR
- Competition ensures only normal profits are earned in the long run
- Long run equilibrium position ensures allocative efficiency as price equals MC and technical efficiency as the output level is where AC is minimised.

### 2.6.2 Monopoly

In theory, a (pure) monopoly is where one firm is the whole industry. It can be a *price maker* (and thus quantity taker) or a *quantity setter* (and price taker). The monopolist cannot fix both price and quantity because it cannot control market demand.

Unlike in perfect competition, the firm's average revenue does not necessarily equal its marginal revenue. In a monopoly, the firm, being the industry, faces a downward sloping demand curve. Thus, to sell more, a monopolist may have to lower his price. This means that marginal revenue will be less than average revenue. For any given price, average revenue is twice marginal revenue (assuming straight-line average revenue curves). Total revenue is maximised when marginal revenue is zero, that is, at $Q_2$ on Figure 2.18. This is because, beyond $Q_2$, MR becomes negative and thus reduces TR.

#### Profits

The price-fixing monopolist will have the usual U-shaped cost curves in the short run (because of the fixed factor assumption). Production will be at $Q_1$ assuming the monopolist is a profit maximiser and produces where MC = MR. The price will be *P*, exceeding average cost (*C*) by *PC*, and so *abnormal profits* are made.

These profits remain in the long run, because of the entry barriers. It is also possible that in the long run a monopolist's costs may fall (although they could rise or be constant, as the fixed factor assumption is removed) and this could raise profits even further. Similarly, if demand becomes more inelastic then profits may increase as any rise in price produces a smaller proportionate change in quantity demanded, thereby raising total revenue.

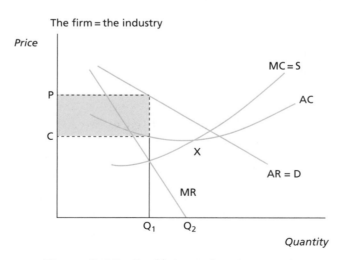

**Figure 2.18** Equilibrium in (pure) monopoly

### Exit/entry

As explained earlier, the definition of monopoly means that new firms cannot enter the industry. Thus, there is no need to distinguish between short-run and long-run equilibrium. Furthermore, it means that abnormal profits are not competed away since monopolists maintain *entry barriers*.

In practice, a firm may have monopoly power even if there are other firms in the industry. An effective monopoly must be able to exclude potential rivals from the market by creating and maintaining entry barriers.

- *Legal barriers.* Public corporations may be given a monopoly by statute when they are created, for example, public utilities. This prevents wasteful duplication. Patent law also creates a monopoly of sixteen years for new inventions.
- *Geographical barriers.* Markets in different parts of the United Kingdom may be separate and different firms may be sole producers in each region. Transport costs may act as a barrier to access. For instance, the village store may have a local monopoly.
- *Economies of scale.* These may give an established firm both cost and technical advantages over potential entrants. High fixed costs of production may deter competitors and keep one firm with a monopoly.
- *Exclusive controls.* A monopolist might have total control over the necessary raw materials for production. For instance, the control of British Telecom over the telephone network in the UK initially made competition from new entrants to the United Kingdom telephone markets more difficult. Similarly, the control over market outlets until recently allowed breweries to have a local monopoly for their beer in tied public houses.
- *Cartel agreements.* An effective monopoly can exist when firms in an industry agree to co-operate rather than compete. Such collusion may be in the form of either *price fixing* or *market sharing*. In Germany sixty-two companies in the ready-mixed concrete industry were fined DM320 million in 2000 for operating a quota cartel, while six leading accountancy firms in Italy were heavily fined in the same year for a price-fixing arrangement. Market sharing is rather more acceptable in smaller markets, such as milk and newspaper deliveries in rural areas.

### Efficiency

In a monopoly there is neither allocative nor technical efficiency. As Figure 2.18 shows, price is higher than marginal cost (at $Q_1$) and the firm is not producing at the lowest average cost (point X).

- A monopolist has a downward sloping demand curve
- A monopolist can fix price or quantity but not both
- Abnormal profits exist in the long run due to barriers to entry

## 2.6.3  Imperfect competition

In each of the three market structures which follow, the firm is a *price searcher*. Its behaviour is to seek a price which will maximise profits, given the conditions in the market. The traditional theory of the firm still has MC = MR as the key decision rule for production, although in practice cost-plus pricing is probably more realistic.

### Monopolistic competition

This type of market includes features of both perfect competition and monopoly. There are no entry barriers, which is similar to perfect competition. However, each firm has influence over the price of its output, as in monopoly, because the products are differentiated, by style, packaging, brand names and advertising. The newspaper industry is a good example of such a market. Therefore, each firm faces a normal downward sloping demand curve for its product, and so marginal revenue is less than average revenue.

The short-run equilibrium position for a firm in monopolistic competition is very similar to that of a (pure) monopolist. The only difference is that the average revenue (demand) curve is likely to be more elastic. This happens because of the competitive features of the market, when the consumer has a choice between differentiated products and is subject to persuasive advertising.

Nevertheless in the *short run*, firms in monopolistic competition may earn *abnormal profits*, as shown in Figure 2.19. However, these profits attract new entrants and so in the long run they are competed away. The competitive rivalry causes the loss of some of the firm's customers, but not all of them because brand loyalties exist. These loyalties may be genuinely held because of a product's peculiar satisfaction for a consumer or they may be spuriously created by advertised images. The loss of customers is shown by the leftward shift in the demand curve and the resultant absence of abnormal profit in Figure 2.20. Thus, a firm in monopolistic competition makes only normal profit in the long run.

Although the features of monopolistic competition make it more realistic than perfect competition, the implications for the allocation of resources are undesirable for society in two ways:

- There is no allocative efficiency because price does not equal marginal cost. Price is greater than marginal cost at the equilibrium and so if output were expanded some people could be made better off without others suffering:
- There is no technical efficiency because the average cost ($P_1$) of the equilibrium output ($Q_1$) is greater than the lowest point of average cost ($X$).

This suggests as in Figure 2.20, that the firm has excess capacity in the long run as well as not operating at technical efficiency.

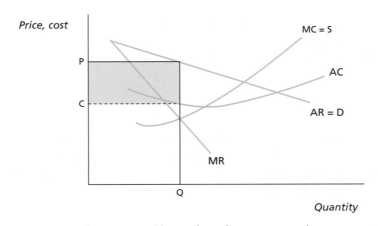

**Figure 2.19**  Short-run equilibrium for a firm in monopolistic competition

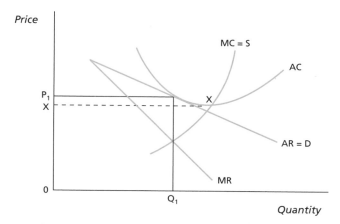

**Figure 2.20**  Long-run equilibrium for a firm in monopolistic competition

## Oligopoly

In the oligopolistic market structure a few large firms dominate the market, for example Lloyds TSB, HSBC, Barclays and RBS in retail banking and Tesco, Asda, Sainsburys and Morrisons in supermarkets. There is *price* and *non-price competition* between firms, with pricing behaviour being partly determined by how a firm expects its rivals to react. Thus, there is much uncertainty in oligopolistic markets, and greater *interdependence* between firms than in other market structures.

There are four strategies which an oligopolist firm might adopt:

- *co-operate* with the other large firms. In such a *collusive oligopoly*, a common policy is agreed on pricing and market sharing and joint profit maximisation is the objective. The market structure then resembles the *monopoly* model. However, this may not be possible in practice because of restrictive practices legislation. This is considered under competition policy later in this chapter.
- *make their own decisions* and ignore their rivals. A firm could estimate its demand (average revenue) curve and set a price. The effect of this depends upon other prevailing prices for what are broadly similar goods/services, and how the rivals react. A higher price may lower sales and lead to a fall in market share if rivals do nothing. A lower price may increase sales if rivals do nothing but lead to lower profits (as demand tends to be inelastic). If rivals follow suit when the firm initiates a price rise, it becomes the *market leader*. This position is akin to that of a monopolist, who can make price changes with impunity. If rivals copy a price cut, there may *be price warfare*. Each firm is seeking to maintain its market share and protect its profits. The price cuts will benefit the consumer, as may some of the non-price competition.
- *become a price follower* by awaiting the action of the price leader. (This strategy makes the firm a *price taker*.)
- *do nothing*. A firm may feel that any change in its price would be disadvantageous because it faces a kinked demand curve. An increase in price above *P* will lead to a large drop in revenue, as consumers now buy relatively cheaper alternatives. Conversely, a fall in price below *P* creates a large fall in revenue, as existing consumers pay less for each unit of output. Thus the curve is relatively elastic above the fulcrum point and relatively inelastic below that point as in Figure 2.21(a).

This kinked demand curve is derived from two separate demand curves, being composed of the upper part of $D_1$ and the lower part of $D_2$. As the demand curve

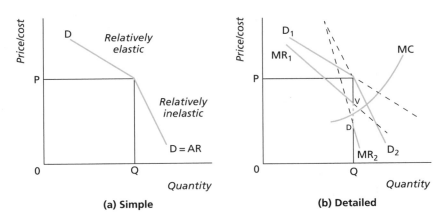

**Figure 2.21** An oligopolist's kinked demand curve

equals the average revenue curve, that too is obviously kinked. However, the composite marginal revenue curve (the top of $MR_1$ and bottom of $MR_2$) displays a vertical discontinuity, along the section parallel to the price axis, between points V and D. This reinforces a tendency towards price stability because there is a series of points where $MC = MR$. In the detailed diagram (Figure 2.21(b)) MC crosses MR in the section VD. However, MC could shift upward towards V and downwards towards D and still equal MR at this output level and price. Thus, costs can rise or fall within the range VD without causing a profit-maximizing oligopolist to change either price or output. This is unique to oligopoly.

Although some of the above strategies lead to price instability, most create *price stability*. In addition, *non-price competition* gives suppliers a chance to influence demand and ultimately profits, without having to change price. The non-price competition can be through special offers, persuasive advertising, extended guarantees, elaborate packaging, free competitions and after-sales service. The intention is either to make demand for their good *more inelastic* or to *shift demand* to the right by securing a positive increase in taste and fashion.

Another strategy to maintain abnormal profits is to operate *entry barriers*, similar to those used by monopolists. In addition, firms could operate as *cartels* and fix prices and/or market shares.

Given all the caveats regarding oligopolistic behaviour, it is impossible to outline a single set of rules for the equilibrium of either the firm or the industry. There is clearly great uncertainty and an incentive for oligopolists to collude in order to maximise joint profit. Such behaviour tips oligopoly towards the monopoly model and relative price stability. However, occasionally there is fierce price competition and regularly there is active non-price competition, as is evident in petrol retailing, supermarkets and the market for car insurance. Unfortunately, none of the theory explains how a firm selects a price in the first place in an oligopolistic market.

- Oligopoly is characterised by uncertainty in the pricing decisions
- Non-price competition occurs

## Duopoly

In such a market, there is *pure conflict* where the gains of one firm become the losses of the other firm, assuming a constant size of market. Game theory can be applied to this market structure but only with difficulty. Like oligopoly, we assume rational behaviour within

|  |  | Company B's strategies | | |
|---|---|---|---|---|
|  |  | 4 | 5 | 6 |
| Company A's strategies | 1 | 65 | 50 | 55 |
|  | 2 | 55 | 50 | 45 |
|  | 3 | 60 | 45 | 55 |

**Figure 2.22**  Company A's market share (%) – game theory

the context of the uncertainty, conflict and interdependence which exist. Assume that companies A and B share the market for sugar. Company A considers three possible strategies designed to maximise its market share:

- extensive advertising;
- new brands;
- price cuts.

Figure 2.22 shows the percentage market share that A can expect if B realises what is happening and counters the strategy in some way. For instance, if A undertakes extensive advertising (strategy 1) B's best counter would be strategy 5, which keeps the market shares at 50 per cent each. A must assume that B will try to minimise the impact of A's strategy and find the most effective counter. Clearly, strategies 2 and 3 are inferior to strategy 1 because the worst scenario for each gives A only 45 per cent of the market. In this example, A might deploy strategy 1 because at worst it maintains 50 per cent of the market, which it already held, and could achieve 65 per cent if B selects the 'wrong' counter-strategy.

## 2.6.4  Price discrimination

A monopolist may be able to *subdivide one market* into two or more sectors, and then price discriminate between different customers, although selling the same product. There are several ways to discriminate:

- by **time** – a golf club will charge non-members a higher green fee to play at weekends than during the week;
- by **customer** – a golf club will charge non-members playing with a member less than non-members would otherwise pay;
- by **income** – a hairdresser may charge a pensioner less than a breadwinner because the former has a lower income;
- by **place** – a hairdresser may charge extra for providing the service at the customer's home, as opposed to what would be charged at the salon.

These pricing strategies are likely to be successful if several conditions are fulfilled:

- at least *two distinct markets* with no *seepage* between them so that a higher price can be charged in one of the markets. If there was seepage then enterprising consumers could buy the good in the lower-priced market and then resell it in the other market, perhaps undercutting the discriminating monopolist;
- a *market imperfection*, such as transport costs, which gives the supplier a monopoly and thus keeps out competitors who might undercut him in his high-price market;
- *differing demand elasticities* so that the monopolist can gain extra profit from his price discrimination.

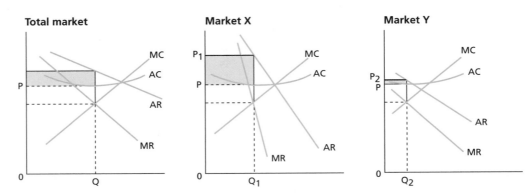

**Figure 2.23** Price discrimination

The diagrams in Figure 2.23 illustrate the theoretical basis of price discrimination. The total market shows the aggregate AR and MR and the profit maximising output of $0Q$. The price in each market is determined by the intersection of the aggregate marginal cost curve and the specific marginal revenue curve. In market X the price charged is $P_1$, which is higher than $P_2$ in market Y. $P_1$ is higher because the demand in market X is more price inelastic than in market Y. Assuming that the costs are similar for each market, the supplier will make more profit in market X than in market Y. The total output of this monopolist is $0Q$, which equals $0Q_1$ plus $0Q_2$. The monopolist increases abnormal profit by selling more in the market where demand is most inelastic (i.e. market X).

---

### Box 2.3   Contestable markets

This is a relatively new theory which accentuates the importance of *entry* and *exit* costs into a market. A contestable market is one in which entry is relatively easy, and so is exit. The latter is possible because there are low fixed costs. In practice, this means that start-up costs are low and so firms can *'hit and run'* – that is, enter the market, take a share of the (excessive) profits and then leave the industry fairly pain-lessly. Existing firms in the market have no market power to deny new entrants and live in a very competitive environment.

A good example of a contestable market is coach travel since privatisation. The capital costs of entry are low (i.e. buying secondhand buses), the best routes can be cream-skimmed and once (or if) sales begin to diminish, the operator can sell up and leave the industry (i.e. sell secondhand buses).

---

### 2.6.5   Perfect competition versus monopoly

In the long run in perfect competition technical and allocative efficiency are both achieved. Long-run equilibrium is obtained at lowest AC, where price equals mar-ginal cost. In contrast the long-run monopoly equilibrium is not at lowest AC and has price above marginal cost. In Figure 2.24 we assume the monopoly firm and the per-fectly competitive firm have the same AC and MC curves. The monopolist faces a downward sloping demand curve $AR_M$ and produces $Q_M$ at $P_M$ (where MC = MR) making abnormal profits ($P_M$YVX). The firm in perfect competition faces a horizontal

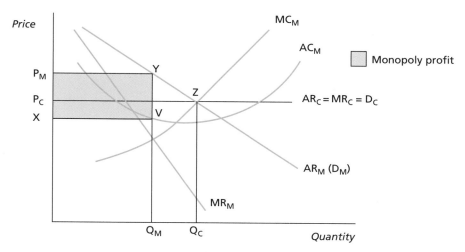

**Figure 2.24**  Perfect competition and monopoly

demand curve ($AR_C = MR_C = D_C$) and produces $Q_C$ at $P_C$. At point Z, $MC_C$ will equate with $MR_C$. Thus, the effect of a monopoly seems to be *lower output* ($Q_M - Q_C$) and *higher prices* ($P_M - P_C$), which means a welfare loss to consumers.

Despite monopoly being inferior to perfect competition in respect of both technical and allocative efficiency, a case of monopoly can be justified on three grounds:

- it may be public utility (such as water supply) where there exists a *natural monopoly* in that the structure of costs indicates that a monopoly is the most cost-effective way of supplying the service;
- there may be significant *economies of scale* and therefore the monopolist may be able to produce a larger output and charge a lower price than if the industry comprised a large number of small firms;
- abnormal profits earned may be used to finance future investment or extensive research and development, thus providing customers with newer and cheaper products in the future.

However the case against monopoly is powerful.

- It is allocatively inefficient as it produces less at higher prices than under perfect competition.
- It produces welfare losses for society as there is a divergence between public interest and the self-interest of the monopolist.
- It has less incentive to innovate because it can keep abnormal profits in the long run.
- It may restrict choice by eliminating uneconomic brands, indulging in price discrimination and using predatory pricing to keep out potential competitors.

## Exercise 2.5

Answer the following questions based on the preceding information. You can check your answers below.

1. Why does an individual firm face a perfectly elastic demand at one price in perfect competition?
2. What happens to abnormal profits in the long run in perfect competition?

3. In the short run, why might a firm in perfect competition continue production even though it is making a loss?
4. In which market is the firm a price maker?
5. What happens to abnormal profits in the long run in a monopoly?
6. Suggest three entry barriers in a monopoly.
7. Can a firm in monopolistic competition make abnormal profits?
8. Describe the demand curve in a competitive oligopoly.
9. What is the main type of competition in an oligopoly?
10. What does 'price discrimination' mean?
11. What is the aim of price discrimination?
12. Give two reasons to justify monopolies.

## ☑ Solutions

1. An individual firm faces a perfectly elastic demand at one price in perfect competition because it is just one small supplier of a small share of a large market. As its product is homogeneous, a price rise will lead to no sales, because consumers will buy other products in the market.
2. Abnormal profits totally disappear in the long run in perfect competition.
3. A firm will continue production in the short run in perfect competition as long as it is covering all of its variable costs. This is because it has to pay fixed costs even if there is no production.
4. A firm is a price maker in monopoly.
5. Abnormal profits can be maintained in the long run in monopoly.
6. Entry barriers to monopoly include legal restraints, geographical barriers, economies of scale and exclusive controls.
7. A firm in monopolistic competition can earn abnormal profits in the short run but not in the long run.
8. In a competitive oligopoly, the demand curve is kinked.
9. In oligopoly, the competition is through non-price factors.
10. Price discrimination means selling the same product/service in different markets at varying prices.
11. The aim of price discrimination is to maximise profits.
12. Monopolies can achieve economies of scale and thereby lower prices, and they may use abnormal profits to fund investment or R and D.

## 2.7 The public sector

### 2.7.1 Definition

The public sector contains a range of businesses *sponsored* by the government, and often run by officials who are *accountable* (often very indirectly) to elected politicians. The main organisations are shown in Figure 2.25.

During the 1980s, the public sector shrank as a result of privatisation, both through the sale of state assets and the hiving-off of public services to other agencies. Local authorities were forced to offer some services for tender (e.g. school meals) while others were taken away (e.g. transport). Government departments became subject to market criteria in their operations, while new QUANGOs with commercial ethics and private

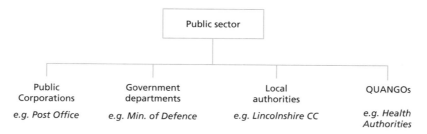

**Figure 2.25** Public sector organizations

sector business personnel were encouraged, for example, London Docklands Development Corporation.

## 2.7.2 Public corporations/nationalised industries

These are state-owned organisations (public corporations and nationalised industries are virtually synonymous except in legal terms) created by Acts of Parliament and given specific responsibilities. They are mainly associated with the Labour government of 1945–51. Their assets are publicly owned but they are not usually required to make a profit. A minister exercises general control and is responsible to Parliament. However, the day-to-day management is by a *board* appointed by the minister.

### Arguments for nationalisation

- *Low costs* may be obtained through economies of scale, and the avoidance of waste and duplication. These points were particularly true of 'natural' monopolies such as gas, water and other public utilities.
- *Sufficient capital* available for investment, because of government support. This was particularly true for aircraft and shipbuilding, which were belatedly nationalised by Labour in 1976.
- *Provides uneconomic services* for consumers. This argument places social benefit above private profit and is the justification for keeping small railway stations open.
- *Allows strategic control* over key resources. This was an important factor in the immediate postwar period but is less so today, as privatisations of steel and electricity indicate.
- *Protects employment* and minimises social costs. The keeping open of 'uneconomic pits' could be justified on this argument, because of the opportunity cost to the local communities based on coal mines (and steel plant) closures. Not only did closure mean lost output, it also meant extra public spending on unemployment benefit and the intangible social costs of 'loss of community', increased marital stress, higher crime, etc.
- *Gives a fairer distribution of wealth* whereby the surpluses could be used for the benefit of society rather than profits being expropriated by capitalist owners. This argument also justified high wages and job security for public employees, as well as more sympathetic management.

### Pricing

(a) *Commercial principles*. Nationalised industries are monopolies. If they operate like private-sector monopolies then they can make abnormal profits by producing where MC = MR (see Figure 2.18). However, because of public service obligations this has

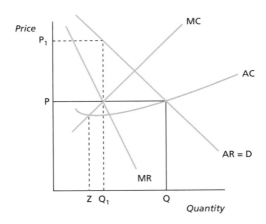

**Figure 2.26**   Breakeven pricing

rarely happened. As shown earlier such a monopoly is not technically or allocatively efficient. Since 1979 the government has moved nationalised industries in this direction through setting them stiffer financial targets and by requiring managers to be more commercially focused.

An alternative approach, which was tried in the 1960s and 1970s, was *breakeven*, or meeting certain financial obligations.

Breakeven occurs where total cost equals total revenue, which is also where AC = AR. However, as shown in Figure 2.26, such a policy is both allocatively and technically inefficient. The price charged, $P$, does not equal MC and so it is allocatively inefficient. Furthermore, the quantity produced, $Q$, is above the optimum output level ($Z$). However, breakeven policy does lead to greater output and lower prices than that achieved at the point of profit maximisation, $P_1Q_1$.

(b) *Marginal cost pricing*. This policy will maximise allocative efficiency (as price equals MC) but it could lead to losses if, at the point of pricing, marginal cost is below average cost. Furthermore it does not produce the technically most efficient output because the quantity produced is not at the minimum point of AC.

(c) *Price discrimination*. A nationalised industry as a monopolist can discriminate to increase its profits/minimise its losses. Thus when the railways in the United Kingdom were a nationalised industry, British Rail at peak travel times and on popular routes loaded the price because demand is highly inelastic, for example, Friday travel and London commuters. This was explained earlier.

### 2.7.3   Privatisation

There were two main strands to privatisation:

- *Sale of state assets*, either whole industries (e.g. gas) or firms (e.g. Jaguar to Ford Motors) or parts of local authorities (e.g. council houses). This is denationalisation.
- *Introduction of competition* into areas previously monopolised by state suppliers, deregulation of various industries (e.g. bus travel) and compulsory competitive tendering (e.g. local authority refuse collection services).

Whole industries have been privatised in the United Kingdom, for example British Telecom (BT) in the 1980s and British Rail in the 1990s.

### Arguments for privatisation

- *Improved 'efficiency'* in sleepy state monopolies. Overmanning and wasteful investment had occurred because of demoralised management (and frequently changed government objectives) and immunity to takeover. Thus it was claimed that the fear of takeover in the private sector and competition would lead to *innovation* in the search for profit, for example, use of minibuses after the deregulation of bus services. These pressures would also give managers an incentive to minimise costs and shake out unproductive labour, which might have been featherbedded in the public sector, for instance, BT axed 15,000 jobs in 1993.
- *Wider share ownership.* It is argued that if employees become shareholders they work harder and strike less, thereby engendering economic gains to firms. Furthermore, the increase in the number of adults with shares (7 per cent in 1979 to 25 per cent in 1992) will create empathy with the private profit motive and better understanding of business problems.
- *Improved quality* will result because privatised concerns will have to compete to survive and be responsive to consumer complaints. Long-distance bus travel has seen significant price cutting and better quality coaches.
- *Greater economic freedom* will occur because the privatised companies will not be subject to the 'dead hand' of state control. For example, nationalised industry chairmen were sometimes pressured by government ministers to make decisions for political reasons, for example, hold prices steady during a period of incomes policy. Market forces should have more influence.
- *Will provide funds for the Treasury.* This reason brought a record £7.1 billion in 1988–99 into the Exchequer. It allowed a reduction in the public sector borrowing requirement and tax cutting which was part of the government's overall economic strategy.

### Criticisms of privatisation

- *Fewer services and higher prices* – for example, rural transport.
- *Private monopolies* have been created. For instance BT had 70 per cent of the domestic market in the 1990s and faced only limited competition. Thus there were few pressures to reduce costs and it was able to raise prices and make over £1 billion profits annually.
- *Quality of service has diminished*, particularly where local authority functions have been contracted out, for instance, costs have been saved by reducing staff, paying lower wages and reducing what was provided, like schools cleaned less frequently. The gains in technical efficiency as cost per unit has fallen is thus an illusion as quality of service has simultaneously declined.
- *Asset sales were underpriced* (to attract buyers) and this created big capital gains for private investors. One estimate of the underpricing of Railtrack shares at the time they were sold was £2 billion.
- *Only the profitable parts of the public sector are sold off,* which means that there is less public income in the future to contribute to government spending.
- The sale of shares to overseas buyers means that *other governments can influence the decisions of British firms* and dividend payments go abroad, thereby weakening the balance of payments.
- *Markets have been 'cream-skimmed'* as, with deregulation, the most profitable parts have been supplied and the loss-making elements ignored. The previous tendency of state enterprises to cross-subsidise has disappeared. A good example of this was BT's attempt to remove rural telephones until partly prevented from doing so by the regulator responsible for the industry.

- Top executives of privatised companies have paid themselves *large salaries and generous share* options, while simultaneously preaching wage restraint to their trade unionists. This seems most unfair and hardly likely to induce high productivity and employee commitment.
- Competition has not been enhanced.

### Pricing

As many privatised companies are now private monopolies, they would be expected to conform to profit maximisation principles. Indeed, in most cases they have. However, this does not create technical or allocative efficiency. As the model for such efficiency is perfect competition, the government has tried to create competition. For example, when electricity was privatised, the power generation was split between National Power and Powergen. However, this was rather artificial and still only gave a duopoly. A major problem for the government of creating competition has been that it makes the nationalised industry to be sold less likely to be profitable and thereby depresses the share price, and so raises less money than required. It was for that reason that Mercury was not allowed to become a big competitor against BT while it was being privatised.

A different approach has been to impose *price limits* on privatised monopolies. For example electricity had a *price formula*:

$$\text{RPI} - X + Y$$

where RPI is the change in retail prices index; $X$ is a percentage deduction (designed to squeeze costs); and $Y$ is a percentage addition (for costs which cannot be passed on).

The regulator for BT has renegotiated its maximum prices. For a period in the 1990s, BT price changes were based on (RPI–7.5 per cent) which in practice meant price cuts. Clearly, such intervention undermines the rationale for privatisation and implies that allocative efficiency is not being pursued, although technical efficiencies are probably being achieved.

### 2.7.4 Public–private partnerships

Public-private partnerships (PPP), of which the best known example is the private finance initiative (PFI), describes any private sector involvement in public services including the transfer of council homes to housing associations using private loans, and contracting out services like rubbish collection to private companies. The PFI refers to a strictly defined legal contract for private consortiums, usually involving large construction firms, to design, build, finance and manage a new public project, typically a school or hospital, over a 30-year period. The building is not publicly owned but leased by a public authority.

The perceived advantages of the PFI are:

- Finances public projects without the need for government to borrow funds or raise taxes.
- Risk is transferred to the private provider. If the private consortium misses performance targets, it will be paid less.
- Introduces private sector qualities such as efficiency and innovation into the public sector, thereby, raising the quality of provision.

Critics of PFI, however, point out:

- The methods of financing used to make public projects more expensive. The Edinburgh Royal Infirmary cost £180 million to build but will cost £900 million over its 30-year contract. This includes the operating costs but, as government has access to cheap funds, it would still have been cheaper to build and manage using traditional public sector funding.
- There is also a question mark over how much risk is genuinely transferred to the private sector given the government's record of bailing out private companies managing troubled public services.
- Efficiency savings have been made at the expense of quality deterioration in the service, for example hospital cleaning.

However it will take a much longer period of time, when the first PFI contracts have been completed, before the real costs and benefits of this form of PPP can be judged.

## 2.7.5 Externalities

An externality occurs when the costs or benefits of an economic action are not borne or received by the instigator. Externalities are, therefore, the spill-over effects of production and consumption which affect society as a whole rather than just the individual producers or consumers.

- Externalities created by nationalised industries can be good and bad. For example, the railways may be beneficial by relieving roads of congestion and maintaining communications for isolated communities, but may be detrimental in terms of noise and air pollution.
- The pricing policies considered so far have been based purely on social costs. If any pricing policy was to maximise net social benefit (or minimise net social cost) then costs would need to include such externalities.
- Calculate *social marginal costs.* These would indicate the true cost to society of production which could be matched with marginal revenue to give a socially beneficial optimum level of production. However externalities are very difficult to calculate as they are not always attributable, for example noise, and their impact is not universally identical.
- Use *indirect taxes and subsidies.* Where private costs of production are below social costs, an indirect tax could be imposed so that price is raised to reflect the true social costs of production. Taxes on alcohol and tobacco can be justified on these grounds. Subsidies to home owners to install roof insulation will reduce energy consumption and help conserve a scarce resource for wider social benefit.
- Extend *private property rights* so that those suffering negative externalities can charge the polluters for the harm they are causing. If the right level of charges are made then this should result in a socially efficient level of production being achieved. Emission charges on firms discharging waste are an example of this approach.
- *Regulations.* A government can set maximum permitted levels of emission or minimum levels of environmental quality. The European Union has over 200 pieces of legislation covering environmental controls. Fines can be imposed on firms contravening these limits.
- *Tradable permits.* A maximum permitted level of emission is set for a given pollutant, for example carbon emissions, and a firm or a country is given a permit to emit up to this amount. If it emits less than this amount, it is given a credit for the difference, which it

can sell to enable the buyer to go above its permitted level. Thus the overall level of emissions is set by a government or regulatory body, whereas their distribution is determined by the market.

Despite the many measures to deal with externalities, the issue of achieving the socially optimal level of production remains unresolved. Problems of calculating externalities and the correct level of taxation; issues of avoidance and enforcement; administrative costs can all mean that market failure and how to deal with it has yet to find an optimum solution.

### 2.7.6  Public and merit goods

These are provided by the government because the free market underproduces them. *Public goods* are products such as *defence* where one person's consumption does not diminish someone else's (*non-rivalry*) and that person cannot stop someone else benefiting from it (*non-exclusivity*). This enables free-riders to take advantage and so the person would not be prepared to pay for the service. Hence the government provides defence at *zero price* but taxpayers fund the service.

As the government is providing public goods on a nationwide basis, it can benefit from *economies of scale*. This could lower costs and the industry would strive for technical efficiency. There is no *allocative efficiency* because consumers do not have a choice – the services, such as police, prisons, fire, are provided whether they like it or not. However, a consumer who seeks more protection could buy additions in the marketplace, like burglar alarms, underground concrete bunkers, security men, etc.

*Merit goods* are goods which it is generally agreed should be made available to all irrespective of whether everyone can afford to pay for them. They are different from public goods in that their under-provision results from ignorance, lack of information and (perhaps) irrationality. Some consumers possess the means and the willingness to buy merit goods, such as education and healthcare. Government provision is made in the interests of the general well-being of the nation. However, the private sector provides alternatives, although these are often seen as 'different', or even superior goods/services, for example, private school education, private health schemes.

In the case of state-provided merit goods, economies of scale could be achieved and technical efficiency sought. The cost of education per student is about three times cheaper in the state sector than in the private sector. However, it is rather difficult to maximise technical efficiency as shown by the failure to close small local hospitals and village schools. Ironically, the support for these threatened organisations comes from local users, thereby indicating that consumer needs are being met. Also, they are making a rational choice because a local service is better than a more distant (alternative) one in terms of time and travel cost. Free marketeers would thus point to the folly of zero pricing, which negates allocative efficiency.

 ## Exercise 2.6

Answer the following questions based on the preceding information. You can check your answers below.

1. What caused the shrinkage of the public sector in the 1980s?
2. Give three arguments for nationalisation.
3. What is marginal cost pricing?

4. What were three reasons for privatisation?
5. How do merit goods differ from public goods?

## ☑ Solutions

1. The public sector shrank in the 1980s because of privatisation.
2. Nationalisation can be justified because it provides low costs of production, uneconomic services which otherwise might not exist and strategic control over key resources.
3. Marginal cost pricing means that price is determined by the interactions of supply and demand. In diagrammatic form, that is where marginal cost (i.e. S) equals average revenue (i.e. D).
4. Three reasons for privatisation are funds for the Treasury, greater economic freedom for producers and improved efficiency within the organisation.
5. Public goods are freely provided by the government as there is non-rivalry and non-exclusivity in their use. Merit goods are provided by the government as it is believed they should be made available to all irrespective of the ability to pay.

## 2.8 Regulation

### 2.8.1 Competition policy

There are two aspects to this which involve government regulation:

(i) *Consideration of mergers* which might create monopolies. These are generally undesirable, as explained earlier, because they lead to allocative inefficiency.

(ii) *Investigation of restrictive trade practices* which reduce competition within a market and undermine consumer sovereignty. As markets have become more heavily concentrated among fewer firms and competition has become more imperfect, so more controls have been applied to restrictive trade practices and pricing. The economic justifications for such a policy are fairly clear. Collusion by suppliers and the operation of cartels usually lead to higher prices and/or monopoly profits and possibly lower output. These in turn reduce the consumer surplus and thereby reduce *consumer sovereignty* (but increase producer sovereignty). Furthermore, they are a diminution in allocative efficiency. However, it must be remembered that extra profits may lead to investment in research, which could eventually benefit consumers via new products.

Various legislation established the basis for competition policy in the United Kingdom. The most recent major legislation has been as follows:

- *Competition Act 1980.* Established a new 'competition reference' procedure, with the Director General, Office of Fair Trading (OFT) investigating anti-competitive activities, which might restrict, distort or prevent competition. The Director General can either negotiate a voluntary undertaking with a firm to drop the activity within two months or refer an activity to the Monopolies and Mergers Commission (MMC) replaced by the Competition Commission (CC) in 1999 within 6 months. If the MMC decides that the activity is 'against the public interest' then the Department of Trade can prohibit it. In addition, the Department of Trade can refer nationalised industries and other bodies to the MMC for examination of their efficiency, costs and service.

- *Companies Act 1989.* Requires companies planning to merge to notify the Office of Fair Trading in advance of their intentions. Companies have to provide details of the proposed merger. If no merger reference to the MMC/CC is made within twenty days then the merger can go ahead. Rather than refer the merger to the MMC/CC, the Secretary of State can ask the companies involved to sell off some of their assets in order to decrease their market power resulting from the merger.
- *Competition Act 1998.* This came into force on 1 March 2000. It seeks to reform and strengthen United Kingdom competition law by introducing prohibitions of anticompetitive agreements and abuses of a dominant position. These prohibitions are modelled on Articles 81 and 82 of the EC Treaty.
- *Enterprise Act 2002.* The competition and consumer provisions of this act came into force in summer 2003. The Act establishes the OFT as a corporate body with independent board members. This replaces the former statutory office of the Director of Fair Trading. The Act builds on the Competition Act of 1998 and also introduces new provisions relating to criminalisation of cartels, disqualification of directors for breaches of competition law and super-complaints. The latter enables certain designated bodies, for example the National Consumer Council, to have enhanced status in drawing to the attention of the OFT any anti-competitive behaviour.

Up to the Competition Act 1998 the legislation has presumed that restraints on competition should be permitted unless found to be against the public interest. Since 1998 the presumption of legislation is that any anti-competitive arrangements are against the public interest and will be outlawed.

Since 1946, the British government has been increasingly involved in vetting the operation of markets in the United Kingdom. The approach has been *discretionary* and *pragmatic*. Each case has been judged on its merits, although increasingly general guidelines and supervisory institutions have been created. Critics of this approach argue that it has been inconsistent, weak and ineffective in dealing with mergers, monopoly power and exploitative pricing. America has much tougher legislation which can break up monopolies (i.e. trust-busting). It is the American approach that current legislation seeks to mimic.

## 2.8.2 The work of the MMC/CC

The Monopolies and Restrictive Practices Commission was established by the Monopolies and Restrictive Practices (Inquiry and Control) Act 1948. The Commission ceased to be responsible for restrictive practices in 1956. These were handled by the DGFT and the Restrictive Practices Court. The title of Monopolies and Mergers Commission (MMC) came from the Fair Trading Act 1973 (the 'FTA').

The *Competition Commission* (CC) is a public body established by the Competition Act 1998. It replaced the Monopolies and Mergers Commission (MMC) on 1 April 1999.

The Commission has two sides to its work: a reporting side which has taken on the former MMC role; and an appeals side which will hear appeals against decisions made under the prohibition provisions of the new Competition Act 1998.

The CC investigates situations where one firm controls at least one-quarter of the market, and mergers involving worldwide assets exceeding £70 million. However, firms are not automatically investigated as it depends on a reference from the Director General. Investigations are carried out by experts, within a limited time. However, critics feel that too long is often taken over this work. The CC reports to the Minister, who may implement its recommendations, ignore them or do something to the contrary.

The CC seeks to promote competition and stresses the need to extend consumer sovereignty, efficiency and enterprise. It opposes most entry barriers, vertical integration and aggressive competition. However, it recognises the benefits which large-scale enterprises enjoy from economies of scale and accepts that abnormal profits may be a justifiable reward for research and development and the risks associated with innovation. Usually, the government complies with the spirit of a CC report, although occasionally recommendations have been ignored and public criticism has resulted. Sanctions have been imposed only rarely, for example, Hoffman LaRoche was ordered to repay £3 million to the National Health Service. Proposed mergers have been stopped, for instance, Imperial Tobacco (makers of Golden Wonder crisps) and Smiths Crisps because of the monopoly power which would have resulted. In September 2003 the Trade and Industry Secretary accepted the conclusion of the CC that the proposed acquisition of Safeway by Asda, Sainsbury's and Tesco would operate against the public interest and should be prohibited. The proposed acquisition of Safeway by Morrisons would be allowed to proceed, subject to Morrisons agreeing to sell 53 stores in areas where local competition concerns would arise as a result of the acquisition. By this outcome a fourth major firm would be established in the United Kingdom supermarket sector thereby enhancing competition.

However, not all eligible mergers are investigated by the MMC/CC. On average about five out of 150 were referred by the Office of Fair Trading (OFT) and the Board of Trade to the MMC for consideration. Although it could be argued that the OFT's guidance to firms deters unacceptable mergers from being attempted, the procedure can lead to apparent anomalies and bias. For instance, in 1985 Imperial Tobacco's bid for United Biscuits was remitted ( because it would give 45 per cent of the total snacks market to them and create a virtual duopoly with Nabisco holding another 45 per cent) but Hanson Trust's hostile bid for Imperial was allowed. The latter did not raise any competition worries, although it promised the creation of a giant conglomerate.

Since 1980 the role of the MMC/CC has changed. The Conservative government's Competition Act gave it the power to make efficiency audits of public sector enterprises. By the end of 1984, fifteen references had been made and reports published on eleven. In every instance, the MMC made recommendations as to how the state concern could improve its performance. While praising the Civil Aviation Authority's standard of service and safety (1983), the MMC found forty-nine ways in which performance could be improved, largely by making more effective use of manpower.

With privatisation MMC investigations were less necessary, as each industry's regulator (see later) undertakes a watchdog role and reports annually. Interestingly, the conflict between British Gas and OFGAS led to an investigation by the MMC in 1993. This recommended ending the British Gas monopoly of supply to domestic users by 31 March 1997 and to all consumers by 2002. It also suggested, again subject to the Trade Secretary's approval, splitting British Gas into two separate companies, one covering transportation and storage assets and the other being responsible for sales of gas and appliances to industrial, commercial and domestic consumers.

In 1997, the MMC arbitrated between the regulator and Transco and British Gas, but largely supported OFGAS's recommendations over transport prices. It proposed a 21 per cent first-year cut, followed by RPI minus 2 per cent over the next four years.

Improved efficiency can result from MMC proposals. For example, the Post Office Letter Service made £23 million annual savings by implementing MMC recommendations.

The weakness of the MMC and its reliance on ministerial support to drive through its recommendations was epitomised by the brewing industry fiasco. The government accepted the MMC recommendations in 1990 then gradually retreated on most of the issues, in the face of the brewers' intransigence, over the next three years.

The 1998 Competition Act established the Competition Commission in April 1999. The 1998 Act made the prohibition of abuse of a dominant market position the principal tool for dealing with anti-competitive conduct by monopolies. These prohibitions will be enforced primarily by the Director General of Fair Trading who can impose fines of up to 10 per cent of United Kingdom turnover. The CC has taken on the investigating functions of the MMC but will also hear appeals against the Director General's decisions.

In August 2008, the CC provisionally found that there were competition problems arising from BAA's dominant position as owner of seven UK airports with adverse consequences for passengers and airlines. The CC's proposed remedy in respect of BAA was to order it to sell two of its London airports and either Glasgow or Edinburgh airport in Scotland.

### 2.8.3 Restrictive practices

The Restrictive Trade Practices (RTP) Court considers *registered agreements* under which at least two persons support restrictions relating to the price of goods, the conditions, quantities, processes or areas and persons supplied. It operates on the principle of guilty until proven innocent, assuming that restrictive practices are against the public interest. The court could uphold the agreements or have them banned. Originally, there were eight defences (nicknamed 'gateways') which could be legitimately used to justify the restrictive practice. In addition, the benefits to the consumer needed to outweigh the costs of the practice. Gradually, investigations have been widened as more trading activities have been seen to offend against the public interest.

However, there are major differences of opinion over the precise nature of 'the public interest' and which actions promote or undermine the public interest. The 1983 RTP Court report on the Association of British Travel Agents' (ABTA) stabiliser illustrates these issues.

- The stabiliser was an agreement between tour operators and retail travel agents which was aimed at limiting destructive competition and protecting consumers against the effects of bankruptcies.
- This agreement restricted price competition between tour oper-ators within the season and thereby reduced the possibility of financial collapse.
- This kept prices higher but consumers benefited from a stable market in which there was less risk of tour operators going bankrupt.

The RTP Court decided that price agreements between tour operators and resale price maintenance between travel agents should be abandoned. This helped the consumer through price competition in the short term. However, if the long-run effects of competition were fewer operators and agents (with larger market shares) and some dramatic failures, then certain unlucky consumers would suffer immediately and most might lose out as the market became oligopolised.

ABTA also operated an entry barrier – *exclusive dealing*, where ABTA operators sold tours only through ABTA agents, who in turn only sold ABTA tours. The objective of this restrictive practice was to enforce default rules and maintain a quality service, thereby minimizing company failures and ultimately benefiting the consumer. The RTP Court accepted that this was in 'the public interest', although a few minor limitations, such as the requirement that travel premises should house two ABTA-trained staff, were outlawed.

Undoubtedly, many restrictive practices still exist, but in secret. The Office of Fair Trading regularly discovers anti-competitive behaviour, particularly when frustrated retailers are threatened by manufacturers that their supplies of products will be curtailed if they continue to sell them at cut prices or as loss leaders (against the maker's wishes). This suggests that competitive policy in the area of restrictive trade practices needed to be strengthened.

In response to this the government has placed 'fostering competition' at the centre of its policy towards business.

- The 1998 Competition Act, which came into effect on 1 March 2000, outlaws any agreements, business practice and conduct which have a damaging effect on competition in the United Kingdom.
- Such prohibition applies to both informal and formal arrangements whether or not they are set out in writing. These include agreements to fix prices; to limit production and technical development; to share markets; and to make contracts subject to unrelated conditions.
- Equally the prohibition covers the abuse by one or more undertakings of a dominant position in a market. Examples of abuse of a dominant position include unfair pricing, limiting production and attaching unrelated supplementary conditions to contracts.
- Although there are exemptions from the Act, the emphasis increasingly is being placed on the assumption that any restriction of competition is undesirable.

The Act gives the Director General wide-ranging powers to investigate infringements of the prohibitions. Where an undertaking is found to have breached any prohibition, the Director General may order it to terminate or amend the offending agreement. Undertakings may be liable to a financial penalty of up to 10 per cent of their turnover in the United Kingdom. However, smaller firms will be immune from financial penalties unless they are involved in price fixing.

In 2003 Argos and Littlewoods were fined £22 million by the OFT for fixing the price of toys and games together with Hasbro in breach of the Competition Act 1998. Similarly ten businesses including Manchester United, were fined a total of £18.6 million in October 2003 for fixing the price of Umbro replica football kits in breach of the competition Act 1998.

### 2.8.4   The European Commission

The Commission of the European Union can use its powers, directly derived from the Treaty of Rome, to control the behaviour of monopolists and to increase the degree of competition across the European Union. It has long had powers, similar to those now adopted by the United Kingdom in the 1998 Competition Act, to prohibit price fixing, market sharing and production limitations. In this context they do not allow 'dual pricing'.

This is a system whereby exports to other EU countries are not allowed to be charged at different prices. For instance, Distillers sold whisky at higher prices in France and tried to restrict British buyers from purchasing the whisky more cheaply in England for resale at lower prices in France. The European Court adjudged that Distillers was distorting competition by trying to prevent its dual pricing being undermined.

The European Union also agreed in 1989 to cross-border merger regulations. There were three criteria for judging such mergers.

- First, the merging companies needed to have a combined world turnover of over 5 billion ECU.
- Second, the companies involved in the merger must have a turnover in the EU of at least 250 million ECU each.
- Third, if two-thirds of the business of the companies in the merger is within one country of the European Union, the merger would fall within national rather than EU regulations.

Proposed mergers must be notified to the Commission of the European Union and will be judged against any potential abuse of a dominant position. Decisions regarding the merger will be made within five months of notification. Finally, to enhance competition the European Union does not allow government subsidies to industries or firms which will distort competition. In this respect Ryanair faced regulatory pressure from the European Commission to repay financial support it received from the Wallonia region in Belgium in establishing its operations at Brussels–Charleroi airport.

---

### Box 2.4   Hotel prices in Paris

Anyone willing to fork out 14,000 euros for a Paris hotel room is unlikely to lose much sleep over the claim that that they may have paid marginally over the odds. But lesser mortals learned yesterday that six super-deluxe hotels in the French capital were guilty of regularly exchanging confidential price information. In other words, operating a cartel.

France's competition watchdog on Monday imposed fines ranging from 55,000 euros to 248,000 euros on half-dozen obscenely opulent and staggeringly expensive hotels known as the Palaces of Paris: the Bristol, Crillon, George V, Meurice, Plaza Athenee, and Ritz.

The watchdog report said the six hotels were a distinct, "oligopolistic" market and the exchange of information would falsify competition. It said representatives of the hotels met regularly and exchanged mails frequently. Among evidence was a 2001 email sent by a George V manager to his rivals. Attached was a table detailing the hotel's occupancy rates and average room price. According to the report, the average price of a room in the six hotels 1999 and 2001 was 700 euros a night while an average suite cost 6,000 euros.

*Source*: *The Guardian*, November 30th 2005

---

### 2.8.5   Specific industry regulators

As privatisation of large nationalised industries usually transformed public monopolies into private monopolies, the government accepted the need to create *regulatory watchdogs*. These bodies, such as the Office of Telecommunications (OFTEL) to supervise British Telecom, were performing a role which government departments did formerly. They were created in the 1980s as privatisation grew, and operated independently of any other investigatory body, such as the MMC. For example, British Gas was privatised in 1986 and then investigated by the MMC in 1988 and again in 1993. This latter report resulted from the long-running dispute between British Gas and OFGAS, its regulator.

On 28 December 2003 the Office of Communications (OFCOM) was established. It is now the regulator for the media and telecommunications industries and replaces five other regularity bodies including OFTEL. OFCOM will regulate standards of taste and decency on all TV and radio channels. It will licence commercial TV and radio. It will also oversee the telecommunications industry, where OFTEL was seen to have performed poorly particularly in relation to the regulation of BT and the deregulation of directory inquiries.

The role of specific industry regulators (SIRs) is essentially twofold.

- First, when large state monopolies were privatised, they lacked effective competition.
- SIRs can introduce an element of competition by setting price caps and performance standards. In this way consumers can share in the benefits of competitive behaviour even if competition does not actually exist in the market.
- Second, SIRs can speed up the introduction of competition in such markets by reducing barriers to entry for new firms.

The SIRs have enjoyed some success in limiting price rises and in getting some price reductions and freezes (e.g. British Gas 1992–93) and ending anti-competitive practices (e.g. BT preventing new telephone companies, such as Cable and Wireless, having access to its network). The regulators have also made recommendations to change the structure of their industry to improve competition, e.g. OFGAS's call to split British Gas into twelve regional distributional companies. As a result of more effective competition, the share of their respective markets for BT and British Gas have fallen considerably since privatisation.

##  Exercise 2.7

Answer the following questions based on the preceding information. You can check your answers below.

1. What is the main weakness of the Monopolies and Mergers Commission/Competition Commission?
2. Name one gateway (defence) against the charge of restrictive practice?
3. What do the regulatory watchdogs supervise?

##  Solutions

1. The main weakness of the MMC/CC is that it can only recommend changes, and ministers have often ignored its proposals, for example, the brewers.
2. There are many defences to the charge of restrictive practice, but the main one is 'public interest'.
3. The main regulatory watchdogs are OFWAT, OFGAS, OFTEL, OFFER, OFLOT and OFRAIL, and they supervise recently privatised former nationalised industries.

## 2.9 Chapter summary

This chapter has dealt with the way in which the individual markets which make up the economy function. The primary model is that of market price determined by the interaction of supply and demand. However the exact mechanisms by which this occurs varies from market to market and from industry to industry. Thus price and output determination under different market structures, including the public sector, were investigated. In particular, the chapter considered:

- The factors influencing individual and market demand;
- The importance of the price, income and cross-elasticity of demand;
- The factors influencing the structure and elasticity of supply;
- Price determination and equilibrium in the market;
- The growth of large-scale production;
- Price and output determination, and the competitive process in competitive, oligopolistic and monopoly-dominated markets;
- Government policy towards market failure and competition including public sector activities, regulation and competition policy.

The analysis in this chapter will equip you to understand the workings of particular markets and the issues of policy related to them. However, the economy as a whole may function differently from individual markets. The behaviour of the economy as a whole is the subject of macroeconomics, and is the subject matter of the next chapter.

# Revision Questions

2

This section of the chapter contains examination-standard questions drawn from past CIMA examinations. You should use these for practice and revision. As in the previous chapter, the multiple-choice questions have only one correct answer and this answer is not subject to debate by economists. This section also contains data response questions. Again there is only one correct answer to each of the elements of these questions.

 **Question 1** Multiple-choice selection

**1.1** A business, currently selling 10,000 units of its product per month, plans to reduce the retail price from £1 to £0.90. It knows from previous experience that the price elasticity of demand for this product is (−)1.5. Assuming no other changes, the sales the business can now expect each month will be:

(A) 8,500
(B) 10,500
(C) 11,000
(D) 11,500

**1.2** If the demand for a good *is price elastic*, a fall in its price will lead to:

(i) a rise in sales.
(ii) a fall in sales.
(iii) a rise in total expenditure on the good.
(iv) a fall in total expenditure on the good.

(A) (i) and (iii) only.
(B) (i) and (iv) only.
(C) (ii) and (iii) only.
(D) (ii) and (iv) only.

**1.3** Which one of the following would *not* lead to a shift in the demand curve for overseas holidays?

(A) An advertising campaign by holiday-tour operators.
(B) A fall in the disposable income of consumers.
(C) A rise in the price of domestic holidays.
(D) A rise in the exchange rate for the domestic currency.

**1.4** Which of the following is *not* normally a characteristic of an oligopolistic market?

   (A) Heavy expenditure on advertising.
   (B) Abnormal profits in the long run.
   (C) Barriers to the entry of new firms.
   (D) A preference for price competition.

**1.5** Which one of the following would *not* act as a barrier to the entry of new firms into an industry?

   (A) Perfect consumer knowledge.
   (B) Economies of scale.
   (C) High fixed costs of production.
   (D) Brand loyalty.

**1.6** Which one of the following is *not* a valid economic reason for producing a good or service in the public sector?

   (A) The good is a basic commodity consumed by everyone.
   (B) It is a public good.
   (C) There is a natural monopoly in the production of the good.
   (D) It is a merit good.

**1.7** Which one of the following is *not* a feature of an industry operating under conditions of monopolistic competition?

   (A) There is product differentiation.
   (B) Producers operate at below full capacity output.
   (C) Firms maximise profits where marginal cost equals marginal revenue.
   (D) There is one dominant producer.

**1.8** Which of the following statements about a policy of privatising a public sector industry are *true*?

   (i) It will permit economies of scale.
   (ii) It is a means of widening share ownership.
   (iii) The industry would become more responsive to the profit motive.
   (iv) It is a source of funds for the government.

   (A) (i) and (ii) only.
   (B) (i), (ii) and (iii) only.
   (C) (i) and (iii) only.
   (D) (ii), (iii) and (iv) only.

## ? Question 2

The following data refer to the United Kingdom economy:
   *Estimates of **price** elasticities of demand for goods and services*

| Broad category | | Narrow category | |
|---|---|---|---|
| Fuel & light | −0.47 | Dairy produce | −0.05 |
| Food | −0.52 | Bread & cereals | −0.22 |
| Alcohol | −0.83 | Entertainment | −1.40 |
| Durable goods | −0.89 | Travel abroad | −1.63 |
| Services | −1.02 | Catering | −2.61 |

*Estimates of **income** elasticities of demand for goods and services*

| Broad category | | Narrow category | |
|---|---|---|---|
| Fuel & light | 0.30 | Coal | −2.02 |
| Food | 0.45 | Bread & cereals | −0.50 |
| Alcohol | 1.14 | Vegetables | 0.87 |
| Durable goods | 1.47 | Travel abroad | 1.14 |
| Services | 1.75 | Wines & spirits | 2.60 |

## Requirements

Using *both* your knowledge of economic theory *and* the data above:

(a) From the data state whether the following goods have 'price elastic demand' or 'price inelastic demand'

  (i) Fuel and light.
  (ii) Services.
  (iii) Catering. **(3 marks)**

(b) Which of the following statements best describes the concept of 'income elasticity of demand'?

  (i) The extent to which the demand for goods and services changes in response to a change in income.
  (ii) The impact on consumer income of a change in the price of goods and services.
  (iii) The extent to which the demand for a good or service rises when consumer incomes rise. **(1 mark)**

(c) State whether each of the following are true or false:

  (i) In a recession, the demand for goods which have high income elasticities of demand will fall the most.
  (ii) If an indirect tax is placed on a good with a high price elasticity of demand, the main burden of the tax will fall on the producer.
  (iii) Inferior goods are those good with a price elasticity of less than −1.
  (iv) A price elasticity with a negative value shows that the good in question has a very low price elasticity.
  (v) If the demand for a good has a very low price elasticity of demand, an increase in the supply of the good will lead to a steep fall in its price.
  (vi) If a good or service has a negative income elasticity of demand, the demand for it will rise when incomes rise but at a less rapid rate. **(6 marks)**
  **(Total marks = 10)**

**Question 3**

The following data refer to the costs of a firm and the demand for its product:

| Quantity sold | Price £ | Total cost £ |
|---|---|---|
| 1 | 34 | 12 |
| 2 | 30 | 20 |
| 3 | 27 | 34 |
| 4 | 25 | 53 |
| 5 | 23 | 75 |
| 6 | 21 | 102 |
| 7 | 19 | 131 |

**Requirements**

Using *both* your knowledge of economic theory *and* the data above:

(a) State which are the correct values for the following:

    (i) Marginal cost at output level 3. Is it £14, £7 or £11.33?
    (ii) Marginal revenue at output level 4. Is it £2, £19 or £25?
    (iii) Average cost at output level 5. Is it £15, £22, or £75?
    (iv) The profit maximizing level of output. Is it 4, 5 or 6?
    (v) The price elasticity of demand for a fall in price from £25 to £23. Is it $-3.125$, $-2$ or $-0.5$? **(5 marks)**

(b) State whether each of the following would lead to a high or a low price elasticity of demand for the good or have no effect on price elasticity.

    (i) The existence of many substitutes.
    (ii) A low proportion of income spent on the good.
    (iii) A long time period under consideration.
    (iv) Effective differentiation of the good by strong advertising.
    (v) A high indirect tax placed on the good. **(5 marks)**

**(Total marks = 10)**

 **Question 4**

The following passage is based on a newspaper article:

British cod – the staple of fish and chips – is on the verge of becoming an endangered species, according to the Worldwide Fund for Nature (WWF), the conservation group. It stressed that the crisis in the fishing industry was due to poor management and to over-fishing. The total weight of cod caught in the North Sea had halved since the 1960s. Similar falls in catches had occurred for other types of fish.

The WWF proposes the establishment of fishing free zones to protect areas where young fish grow and develop. The WWF said that such a strategy would lead to increased fish stocks and a larger fishing catch for fisherman within five years. However, the problem may become less urgent as consumer demand for this type of fish may decline in the long run. Higher prices themselves may discourage consumers and some observers believe that for many consumers fish and chips may be an inferior good and, in many cases, faces a growing number of alternatives.

## Requirements

Using *both* your knowledge of economic theory *and* material contained in the above passage:

(a) State whether each of the following would lead to a shift in the demand curve for fish or a movement along the demand curve for fish.

   (i) An increase in the number of substitutes for fish.
   (ii) A rise in the price of fish.
   (iii) An outward shift in the supply curve of fish.
   (iv) A rise in income of fish consumers.            **(4 marks)**

(b) State whether each of the following is *true* or *false*.

   (i) If the demand for fish is very price elastic a fall in supply will raise prices a great deal.           **(1 mark)**
   (ii) If the supply of fish is price inelastic, a reduction in supply will have a smaller effect on price than if the supply were price elastic.      **(1 mark)**
   (iii) Price changes affect demand by leading to a shift in the demand curve for the product.           **(1 mark)**
   (iv) Effective advertising might raise sales by shifting the demand curve to the right.
           **(1 mark)**
   (v) If the demand for fish was perfectly price inelastic, a change in income would have no effect on demand.        **(1 mark)**
   (vi) The longer the time period considered, the greater becomes the price elasticity of demand for goods.        **(1 mark)**

**(Total marks = 10)**

# Solutions to Revision Questions

The answers given for the data response questions are what might reasonably be expected of a candidate in an examination in order to achieve a good pass mark. You should also pay particular attention to the extracts from examiners' reports indicating what were the common errors in answering these questions.

##  Solution 1

**1.1**  Solution: (D)

$$PED = \frac{Percentage\ change\ in\ demand}{Percentage\ change\ in\ price}$$

A value of $(-)1.5$ implies that a 10 per cent price cut will raise demand and sales by 15 per cent, that is, from 10,000 per month to 11,500 per month.

**1.2**  Solution: (A)

If the demand for a good is price elastic, the demand for it will change more than proportionately to the change in price. Thus a price fall will raise sales and will increase total expenditure on the good.

**1.3**  Solution: D

Responses (A), (B) and (C) all involve changes in the conditions of demand and hence would lead to a shift in the demand curve. However, response (D) involves a change in the price of the holiday (a rise in the exchange rate would reduce the price of the holiday), and thus demand would rise as a result of a movement along the demand curve.

**1.4**  Solution: D

A typical feature of oligopoly is the desire to avoid price cutting, because other firms will react with similar price cuts. The preference in oligopolistic markets is for non-price competition.

**1.5**  Solution: A

Perfect information for consumers would provide them with information about new entrants into the industry as well as about existing producers. This would remove a barrier to entry. The other responses all represent significant difficulties for new entrants and thus act as barriers to entry.

**1.6** Solution: A

Because a commodity is consumed by everyone (e.g. food), it does not follow that it has any special features such that it cannot be produced efficiently in a competitive market in the private sector. All other responses are valid reasons why a good or service should be produced wholly, or partly, in the public sector.

**1.7** Solution: D

Monopolistic competition is a situation where a market has many suppliers producing similar, but differentiated goods. A typical result is that no firm has a share of the market large enough to produce at the optimum level. Response (C) applies to all markets including monopolistic competition. Response (D) is the correct response since this refers to a monopoly market.

**1.8** Solution: D

Privatisation does not produce larger firms and often leads to smaller firms when public sector monopolies are broken up into smaller companies (e.g. railways) on privatisation. Thus the privatisation process cannot increase the scope for economies of scale. All the other responses are valid reasons for privatisation.

## ✓ Solution 2

(a) (i) price inelastic demand
   (ii) price elastic demand
   (iii) price elastic demand

(b) Statement (i)
(c) (i) True
   (ii) True
   (iii) False
   (iv) False
   (v) True
   (vi) False

## ✓ Solution 3

(a) (i) £14
   (ii) £19
   (iii) £15
   (iv) Output level 4
   (v) − 3.125

(b) (i) high elasticity
   (ii) low elasticity
   (iii) high elasticity
   (iv) low elasticity
   (v) no effect

**Solution 4**

(a) (i) a shift of the demand curve.
 (ii) a movement along the demand curve.
 (iii) a movement along the demand curve.
 (iv) a shift of the demand curve.

(b) (i) *False*; price will rise much more if demand is price inelastic.
 (ii) *True*; because supply is inelastic, the reduction in supply is mitigated as is the effect on price.
 (iii) *False*; price changes lead to movements along the demand curve.
 (iv) *True*; advertising may get consumers to buy more at every price.
 (v) *False*; a change in income would lead to a shift in the demand curve.
 (vi) *True*; the longer the time period, the easier it is to find substitutes.

# The Financial System

# The Financial
# System

3

## LEARNING OUTCOMES

In earlier chapters you will have learned about some of the important ideas and principles in microeconomics – that part of economics concerned with the way in which economic agents, such as consumers and businesses organisations, function in particular markets. This chapter introduces you to the financial system which is concerned with the role of financial organisations and instruments in meeting the various financial needs of individuals and businesses. After completing this chapter you should be able to:

▸ identify the factors leading to liquidity surpluses and deficits in the short, medium and long run in households, firms and governments.

▸ explain the role of various financial assets, markets and institutions in assisting organisations to manage their liquidity position and to provide an economic return to holders of liquidity;

▸ identify the role of insurance markets in facilitation of the economic transfer and bearing of risks for households, firms and governments;

▸ explain the role of national and international government organisations in regulating and influencing the financial system, and the likely impact of their policy instruments on businesses.

## 3.1  The financial needs of individuals and organisations

One of the common features of all economies is the existence of money. Moreover, all economies have organisations whose principal activities are related to the management of money and various other financial instruments: in effect there exists something called a *financial system*. In order to understand the role and nature of the financial system it is helpful to understand the nature of money itself.

### 3.1.1   Functions and qualities of money

#### Functions of money

Modern economies are totally dependent upon money in its many various forms. Money facilitates trading, both domestically and internationally, and overcomes the weaknesses of barter, which limited primitive societies. Money is any asset that is acceptable to its users in fulfilling the main functions of money in an economic system. The different forms of money – gold, notes, coin, bank accounts – that are used today confirm the oft-made remark that 'money is what money does'. Thus as long as something is acceptable and enables the performance of certain functions, it can be regarded as money.

There are four main functions of money.

1. *A medium of exchange.* The existence of money means that buyers and sellers can meet and trade, without the problems associated with barter.
   - Without money, trade was limited because some goods were indivisible, a rate of exchange might be disputed and the wants and needs of the buyer needed to match identically with the needs and wants of the seller.
   - With money, small quantities can be purchased, prices are largely fixed at the point of sale, and buyers and sellers do not need to reciprocate.
2. *A store of value.* When people receive money they may not spend it all on consumption.
   - Thus money needs to be capable of storage until required for consumption while simultaneously maintaining its value during the saving period.
   - If there is inflation, the value of savings held in money form or denominated in money terms will lose value; money will not be performing this function very well and the desire to save may be reduced.
3. *A unit of account.* In this role, money allows goods to be compared in a common denomination which people understand – namely money.
   - The prices of goods and services reflect their scarcity values and costs of production and enable consumers to make rational judgements.
   - Thus money enables people to establish relative values.
4. *A standard of deferred payment.* This means the ability to determine the value of future payments in contracts specifying prices and payments measured in money terms.

The issue of 'what is money?' has led to much discussion among economists and to various definitions and measures of money in the economy. If something performs the above functions and is acceptable to people it will be used as 'money'.

In order to fulfill the functions of money, an asset must have certain characteristics.

#### Qualities of money

In order to fulfill all of the functions of money, a financial asset should have the following characteristics:

- *Acceptability.* All participants in a transaction must be willing to accept money in exchange for real goods and services in order to fulfill the function of acting as a medium of exchange.
- *Durability.* It is important, especially with cash, that money does not physically deteriorate, especially if the money is used as means of storing value over time.
- *Stable value.* The purchasing power of money must be stable otherwise money cannot act as a store of value or a standard of deferred payment.
- *Portable and divisible.* Money needs to be convenient for small transactions and easily transported.

The overall quality which money derives from these features is *liquidity*: the ability to turn a financial asset into a form – effectively cash, that can be used as a medium of exchange – the primary function of money.

This raises the question of what should, and what should not, be classified as money.

- Cash clearly meets all of the above requirements.
- Both bank and building society accounts which give customers (fairly) immediate access to their money also meet these requirements and are included in most measures of the total of money in the economy. These accounts give their holders liquidity, the vital characteristic of money. They also perform the storage function.
- However, credit cards which are treated as 'money' by their users and enable customers to buy goods are really only money substitutes. This is because they do not perform the storage function.

The obvious problem in modern economics with the necessary qualities of money is the requirement for a *stable value*. This is only possible in the absence of inflation – the process by which the general price level rises over time. Indeed, the clearest definition of inflation is a *decline in the purchasing power of money*. If the purchasing power of money were to decline rapidly, for example, in periods of hyper-inflation such as occurred in Germany in the early 1920s and is currently occurring in Zimbabwe, money cannot fulfill its function as a store of value or standard of deferred payment and this in turn makes it less and less acceptable as a medium of exchange. Thus inflation, especially if it is rapid, will damage all forms of money and damage the workings of financial institutions.

## Money and inflation

There is a variety of measures of inflation all of which are designed to give some indication of the rate of change in the general price level. These include:

- *consumer price indices* which attempt to measure the rate of change in consumer prices;
- GDP (*gross domestic product*) *deflators* which attempt to measure the rate of change of all prices in the economy;
- *special price indices* which attempt to measure the rate of change in prices of a selected range of goods or services, or prices faced by a particular part of the economy, such as producer price indices, factor gate price indices, pensioner consumer price indices, export and import price indices.

These indices are all constructed in much the same way and involve:

- identifying a *base year* from which price changes are measured;
- selecting the *range of goods and services* whose prices are to be monitored;
- *weighting* each of the goods and services included according to their relative importance in expenditure.

The rate of inflation, or indeed the rate of *disinflation* where prices are falling, can be derived by comparing the index for one period, usually a year, with another.

The most commonly used price indices are for consumer goods. Prior to 2004 the United Kingdom used a retail price index (RPI) as the principal measure of inflation. From 2004 the United Kingdom has used a new measure of inflation, the consumer price index. This excludes mortgage payments and is consistent with the measure of inflation used in the rest of the European Union. Table 3.1 shows the United Kingdom consumer price index for the years 2000 to 2008 and the annual rate of inflation that it reveals.

**Table 3.1**  Inflation in the UK

|  | Consumer price index (2005 = 100) | Annual rate of inflation (annual % change) |
|---|---|---|
| 2000 | 93.3 | 0.8 |
| 2001 | 94.9 | 1.7 |
| 2002 | 95.5 | 0.6 |
| 2003 | 96.5 | 1.1 |
| 2004 | 98.1 | 1.6 |
| 2005 | 100.0 | 2.0 |
| 2006 | 102.5 | 2.5 |
| 2007 | 105.0 | 2.4 |
| 2008 | 109.0 | 3.8 |

*Source*: ONS

## 3.1.2   Payments and receipts

Money is the crucial element in the move from a barter economy to a market economy and the benefits of specialisation and the division of labour. But money also introduces another feature of market economies: the separation of income from expenditure. In a barter economy income, that is output, and expenditure such as consumption are conducted in the same household and, for the large part, is simultaneous. Money makes it possible for the earning of income and its expenditure to be separated in time and space. In modern economies, it is possible for individuals and organisations to have a flow of income and a flow of expenditure which, in any one period of time, are not equal. This is made possible by money and other financial assets and by the services of financial institutions. In particular, in any one period of time there will be individuals and organisations:

- whose *income exceeds their expenditure* and may be defined as net *savers*;
- whose *expenditure exceeds their income* and may be defined as net *borrowers*.

The main function of financial institutions is to provide an efficient link between net savers and net borrowers and to provide a range of financial instruments which are effective in moving the surplus money of net savers to the net borrowers in forms that are most appropriate to their needs.

- This function is known as *financial intermediation*.
- The financial organisations which undertake it, such as banks, are known *financial intermediaries*.

This problem, the lack of synchronisation between payments and receipts, has a variety of origins and affects individuals, businesses and governments.

### Individuals

The lack of synchronisation in payments and receipts for individuals can occur in the short, medium and long term.

### Short term

Household income comes in a variety of forms. The main ones being:

- wages and salaries
- income from investments, property and savings
- social security and pension payments.

The common feature of these is that the flow of such income tends to be regular, but not continuous. Typically wages and salaries are paid monthly (and bonuses annually) as are social security and pension payments. Income from investments may be monthly, but are more commonly bi-annually or annually.

Consumption expenditure, however, is typically more or less continuous and irregular. Most households spend some money every day but rarely exactly the same amount. Thus there is a lack of synchronisation in the flow of receipts (income) and payments (expenditure). Some payments may match receipts, for example monthly direct debits and monthly salaries but this relates only to certain types of expenditure.

Households can deal with this lack of synchronization in a variety of ways. Households can:

- retain *a stock of cash* to meet day-to-day expenditure;
- use *credit* such as credit cards and overdrafts facilities;
- *save* in periods when receipts exceed payments to finance periods when the reverse happens.

In all of these cases, households use the services of financial intermediaries: bank accounts, credit cards and overdrafts.

### Medium term

Such a lack of synchronization in receipts and payments for households can also occur in the medium term and arise out of the infrequent purchase of expensive items such as consumer durables, including cars and some services such as holidays and medical bills. Again these expenditure flows are unrelated to the flow of income. The solutions for households are broadly twofold:

- to *save* over a period of time prior to the purchase;
- to *borrow* and repay over a period of time.

Again both of these require appropriate financial instruments; in the first case efficient means of saving such as deposit accounts, and in the second case, cost effective means of borrowing, including bank loans and consumer credit. These facilities are provided by financial intermediaries.

### Long term

Over the whole lifetime of the household, one would expect that household income (receipts) and household expenditure (payments) would match. But even in the long term there may be a mismatch between payments and receipts. This arises from the very long-term nature of some income and spending decisions. Examples of this include:

- long-term purchase of assets, for example housing property;
- long-term savings for pensions.

These require very long-term financial instruments with life spans of decades. It is also important that such instruments are efficient as these savings and expenditures are very large in relation to household income. Thus a range of different types of mortgages have been developed to meet the needs of house buyers and if some of these turn out to less efficient than expected, this can become a serious problem for households. The recent difficulties experienced with some endowment mortgages in the United Kingdom illustrates this issue.

### Business

As with individuals, businesses will find that flows of payments and flows of receipts rarely match. This is often referred to as the cash flow problem and can occur in short, medium and long run.

### Short run

All business have day-to-day costs to meet. For most payments for wages and salaries and for the regular flow of physical inputs such as energy, raw materials and components represent the biggest item in these payments. In effect, businesses need *working* capital. However, the receipts for the business come mainly from sales revenue and these may not follow the same pattern of costs. For businesses then the solutions to this cash flow problem are:

- retaining a large stock of cash to meet periods of low or delayed income;
- access to credit, for example trade credit of various kinds to pay for physical inputs;
- access to overdraft facilities with their banks.

Of course when receipts are lower than payments businesses need access to credit and overdraft facilities, but when the reverse happens secure, and preferably profitable, savings instruments are required.

### Medium term

Cash flow issues might arise in the medium term for businesses. Examples where this may arise include:

- sales revenue is received long after the first costs are incurred such as in building and construction activity, shipbuilding and aerospace;
- where contracts specify part payments long before delivery;
- reorganisation costs are incurred before benefits from lower costs or increased revenues are achieved.

Businesses thus require medium-term finance, typically 2–3 years, to meet these medium-term financial problems.

### Long term

Most long-term financing problems in business arise out of their investment activities. This may take a variety of forms:

- investment in physical capital
- investment in long-term Research and Development programmes (R&D)
- take-overs and mergers of existing businesses.

These activities may involve very large capital outlays with the prospect of increased incomes delayed well into the future. Businesses thus need long-term finance and have three main options:

- the use of *internally generated funds*
- *equity capital* through the issue of shares
- *debt capital* including mortgages, bank borrowing and bonds.

In the latter two cases, businesses need access to the capital market as sources of funds for long-term investment.

## Government

The government may have some income from profitable state industries or charges made to consumers for state-provided services, but the vast bulk of its income comes from taxation. The main sources of taxation revenue are:

* a range of *indirect taxes* (sales taxes) such as value added tax and excise duties on alcohol, petrol and tobacco products;
* *direct taxes* on individuals most importantly income tax and social security taxes;
* *direct taxes* on business organisations such as corporation tax.

Some of these flows of taxation revenue are quite regular, such as income tax paid through the pay-as-you-earn system in the United Kingdom, but many are not. The flow of receipts from corporation tax, for example, can be very uneven with significant payments towards the end of the tax year. This, as with households, implies a problem of synchronisation of payments and receipts.

### Short term

In the short term, governments must finance their day-to-day activities such as:

* payments of wages and salaries to government employees;
* payment of social security and state pensions to the unemployed and the retired;
* payments to providers of goods and services to enable the day-to-day running of the government activities.

Most of these payments are spread over the financial year and are relatively stable from one month to another. It is therefore difficult to match tax revenue to the payments made for these items. Thus the government, like households, needs short-term financial facilities so that it can meet its day-to-day running expenses. The credit and savings needs of government in this respect are often met by the central bank, one of whose functions is to act as banker to the government and to manage the government's finances.

### Medium term

Governments also have medium-term financial commitments that largely arise from investment activities in the public sector. Governments engage in investment when they finance such as:

* school and hospital building;
* construction projects for the economic infrastructure, for example motorway and railway construction;
* loans to private sector activities to help finance investment by those organisations; this typically occurs in high technology and risky activities such as aerospace.

These expenditures are not likely to be evenly spread over the years. Indeed, governments may deliberately concentrate such expenditures in some years rather than other as part of a fiscal policy designed to manage the trade cycle. In this case, government will raise such expenditure in recessions exactly when receipts from taxation are likely to be low as consumer incomes and spending fall. Thus governments may run *budget deficits* which have to be financed by borrowing from the private sector.

*Long term*

Since it is possible for governments to be net savers or net borrowers over very long periods of time, they may need of the services of financial intermediaries over that period. It is more likely that governments will be net long-term borrowers:

- governments often take responsibility for financing very long-term investment projects in the development of the infrastructure of the economy, for example nuclear power and telecommunications, and given that these are investments, not current consumption, borrowing is an acceptable means of finance for these projects;
- governments can continue to borrow in the very long run as long as there is sufficient taxation income to finance the subsequent debt.

Even if governments do not engage in additional long-term borrowing, all have debts accumulated from the past – the national debt. This must be managed as there is no real possibility of repaying it. Thus governments need the services of financial intermediaries to manage and renew this debt.

 ## Exercise 3.1

Answer the following questions based on the preceding information. You can check your answers below.

1. What are the four main functions of money?
2. How does the consumer price index differ from the GDP deflator?
3. Explain why there is a problem of synchronisation in monetary flows.
4. What is meant by *financial intermediation?*
5. What are the three main types of long-term funding for businesses?
6. What is the national debt?

 ## Solutions

1. The main functions of money are to act as:
   - a medium of exchange
   - a store of value
   - a unit of account
   - a standard of deferred payment.
2. The consumer price index is a measure of change in the prices of goods and services bought by consumers; the GDP deflator is a measure of change in the prices of all goods and services including those bought by businesses.
3. The lack of synchronisation arises because the flows of payments for goods and services will not be exactly matched in time by the flow of receipts. Thus individuals and organisations will sometimes have payments exceeding receipts and sometimes receipts exceeding payments. Some means of financing these deficits and surpluses is therefore required.
4. *Financial intermediation* is the process of bringing together those organisations and individuals with surplus funds ('savers') and those with deficits ('borrowers'). This function is provided by financial intermediaries such as banks.

5. The three main sources of long-term funding for businesses are:
   1. internally generated funds
   2. equity capital (issuing shares)
   3. debt capital (borrowing).
6. The national debt is the accumulated sum of previous borrowing undertaken by the government to finance its budget deficits in the past.

## 3.2 The organisations of the financial system

### 3.2.1 Financial intermediaries

#### Financial intermediaries: functions

Financial intermediaries are organisations which enable money to be transferred from savers to borrowers. They channel funds into places where the 'best' return can be made and given financial advice to customers. In addition, they facilitate the spreading of risks and the acquisition of liquidity. The main functions of financial intermediaries are as follows.

#### Channeling funds

The primary function of financial intermediaries is to provide an efficient means of channeling funds from net savers to net borrowers. This removes the need for individual savers and borrowers to make bilateral arrangements. Moreover financial intermediaries, in providing this link between savers and borrowers also:

- provide efficient and cost-effective sources of funds for net borrowers;
- safe and profitable (that is earning interest) assets for savers.

In addition, these organisations provide a range of services for their customers who hold accounts with them, including money transfer facilities, safe and convenient keeping of liquid assets, foreign exchange and financial advice.

#### Maturity transformation

A major reason why bilateral agreements between individual savers and borrowers is difficult is because of differing time preferences. Typically,

- lenders wish to retain a degree of liquidity in their assets and are not prepared to lend for very long periods;
- whereas borrowers often wish to borrow for very long periods especially for long-term financing.

Financial intermediaries are able to perform *maturity transformation*: they provide liquid short-term assets for savers and long-term liabilities for borrowers. An example of this is the role of banks and building societies in the housing market where deposits from millions of customers are accepted on relatively short term, often instant access, and money is lent for very long periods – up to 30 years, in the form of mortgages for house buyers.

#### Risk transformation

A similar function fulfilled by financial intermediaries is that of *risk transformation*. For an individual saver, lending to one borrower might entail an unacceptable risk of nonpayment of the debt. However a financial intermediary, by borrowing from large number of savers and lending to large number of borrowers, can effectively spread the risk and reduce the risk to any one saver close to zero.

## Financial intermediaries: institutions

The financial intermediaries can be classified into three principal groups:

- banks
- other authorised institutions
- non-bank financial intermediaries.

All of these institutions are formally or informally supervised by the central bank – for example in the United Kingdom, the Bank of England; and in the USA, the Federal Reserve Board.

### Banks

There are two main types of bank in operation:

- *retail* banks
- *wholesale* banks.

Retail banks are familiar to most people in the form of 'high street' banks, such as Barclays and HSBC. Their principal activity is in accepting retail deposits, granting retail loans and providing payments and money transfer facilities through the cheque and debit card systems. The main customers of these banks are individual households and businesses. Box 3.1 describes the evolution of banks in the United Kingdom.

---

### Box 3.1   Banks in the United Kingdom

Before the 1979 Banking Act, any organisation could call itself a 'bank' and accept deposits from the public and then lend money. The crash of several 'fringe banks' in 1975 and the subsequent 'lifeboat' action of the Bank of England to prevent a collapse of confidence pushed the government into legislation. The main purpose of the new Bank of England supervisory scheme is to protect depositors. Thus, no one can accept deposits from the public without express authorisation from the Bank of England.

The 1979 and 1987 Banking Acts introduced definitions of 'banks' and 'authorised institutions'. The title 'bank' is reserved for institutions with not less than £5 m paid-up equity capital, and Bank of England authorisation. To be authorised, a bank or other institution needs to pass a number of financial tests and to satisfy the Bank of England about the quality and honesty of their management. Once authorised, an institution is also subject to continuous monitoring. The elite among these banks are the clearing banks. They are members of the Bankers Clearing House. They are often termed 'retail banks' because of their direct relationship with their customers and their High Street premises. Nearly all of the commercial banks are public limited companies, part of whose profits are remitted to shareholders.

---

The retail or commercial banks' main activities are as follows.

### Safeguarding money

Customers' deposits are kept in deposit and current accounts.

- *Deposit* (*time*) accounts are operated for savers who receive interest for storing their money at the bank. The rate of interest received varies with movements in the bank's base rate. If interest rates in the money market rise, then bank base rate is increased so depositors receive more interest on their deposits.

- *Current* (*sight*) accounts do not usually gain significant amounts of interest, although they do provide the holder with a chequebook facility. Customers can settle debts by writing cheques or by using debit cards, and also withdraw cash on demand (i.e. no charges) in current accounts while the customer stays in credit.
- The distinction between deposit and current accounts is becoming less clear cut, as banks devise new financial instruments. For example, high interest cheque accounts continue the traditional features of deposit and current accounts and were invented to attract specific customers.

### Transferring money

Banks move cash between their branches when required. In operating the cheque clearing system they transfer money between accounts within a branch, between different branches and between different banks.

- Each clearing bank has an account at the central bank. In effect, every time one of a bank's customers writes a cheque, which is presented at another bank, the payer's bank has its account at the central bank debited. Conversely, the recipient's bank has its account credited. In practice, at daily clearing, each bank totals up its accounts with every other bank and the net amount owed (or gained) is deducted from (or credited to) its account.
- This is a money transmission service. It is also undertaken by the use of direct debits, standing orders and credit transfers.

### Lending money

When goldsmiths realised that only a small proportion of their gold deposits was required daily, they decided to put the gold to work by lending and charging interest. The banks perform a similar profit-earning function by providing loans and overdrafts to customers. Generally the rates of interest charged to businesses are less than those levied on personal borrowing. Such loans generally take two forms:

- When a customer has a current account, he or she might seek an *overdraft*. Usually, overdrafts are for short periods of time, allowing customers to write cheques to a value greater than the funds in the current account. Interest is charged on a daily basis on the actual amount by which the customer is overdrawn. This tends to be a cheaper form of borrowing, if prior authority is given by the bank. Overdrafts are more informal and more flexible than loans, although penalty rates of interest may be charged for unauthorised borrowing.
- *Loans.* These tend to be for larger amounts and over longer periods of time. They are often tied to particular purchases and are repaid over longer periods of time.

### Facilitating trade

Modern banks provide numerous services which facilitate easier trading. The accepting of commercial bills and the provision of foreign exchange make international trade smoother in operation. Similarly the development of advisory services for small firms, the participation in loan guarantee schemes and the giving of financial advice and market information encourage domestic trade.

In addition to retail banks there are also wholesale banks. These are also known as investment or secondary banks. The most common of these banks are:

- merchant banks such as Morgan Grenfell;
- overseas banks operating in countries other than their home country.

Merchant banks are banking brokers who bring together the lenders and borrowers of large sums of money, for example business companies. Merchant banks:

- Operate in a high-risk area and deal in very large deposits and loans primarily from industry and commerce. They often borrow from each other on what is known as the *inter-bank market.*
- Advise companies on money management.
- Negotiate bills of exchange. A bill of exchange is a trading contract, usually for three months, upon which a trader can usually get credit.
- Underwrite the launching of new shares, for example Lazard Bros. organised the privatisation of Britoil in 1985.
- Supervise company takeovers on the stock market.
- As accepting houses, they guarantee commercial bills for companies.

They are thus wholesalers of money in the system.

Also, overseas banks now operate in most financial centres and their banking activity is mainly related to:

- financing international trade
- international capital movements
- international currency transactions.

In practice the distinction between retail and wholesale banks has become less clear in recent years. Many banks which previously operated only as retail banks have taken on many of the functions of wholesale banks, especially in relational to international transactions. They have often achieved this by setting up or acquiring specialist subsidiary companies.

Discount houses are another type of unofficial bank, which are unique to Britain. These nine institutions operate in the money market by borrowing from the commercial banks for a short period (which may be as little as overnight) and lending for up to three months. They make a profit on the difference between the interest rate paid and charged.

### Non-bank financial intermediaries

These institutions are not officially authorised by the Bank of England, although they are informally watched. However, they often perform banking tasks and since financial deregulation in the 1980s they have competed with banks for business. The best-known type of non-bank in the United Kingdom is the building society. Some are owned by their members ('mutual' building societies), others by shareholders. They tend to 'borrow short' and 'lend long' (via mortgages), profiting from interest-rate differentials and fulfilling the function of *maturity transformation.*

Since the 1980s, building societies have became more independent and competitive. No longer are society interest rates kept in harmony by the Building Societies Association, so there is more competition between them. In addition, competition with banks and other authorised institutions has increased, particularly in home loans and high-interest, instant-access accounts. However, building societies are still constrained by the requirement that they can lend only a maximum of 5 per cent of their assets for personal finance. Many building societies have become banks in recent years.

Another trend has been the growth of financial conglomerates. Formerly financial institutions tended to specialise, for example building societies and mortgages. Now they are branching out into non-traditional lines of business and offering mortgages. The diversification has also brought estate agents, unit trusts and big High Street retailers into financial intermediaries. In the mid-1990s, several building societies decided to 'go public' and become banks. The process takes a while, such that it was not until 1997 that the Halifax, Woolwich and Alliance & Leicester emerged on to the stock market. Thus the distinction between banks and building societies is now blurred and institutions providing the entire range of financial services are dominating the financial system.

Many other financial institutions exist, mostly providing specialist financial services. The most important of these are:

- *Investment and unit trusts* which accept savings by selling shares and invest these savings, mainly in company shares;
- *Pension funds* which accept savings from their customers, both individuals and companies, normally on an ongoing basis, to invest and to provide retirement pensions for their customers;
- *Insurance companies* which invest their premium income in a range of assets but mainly long term such as shares and property.
- *Finance companies* which provide medium-term credit for business and individual customers. Others act as leasing companies (leasing out capital equipment to businesses) and factoring companies (providing funds for businesses using their creditors as collateral).

---

### Box 3.2   Crisis in the Banking System

In the autumn of 2008 the banking systems of many countries entered an unprecedented crisis. The origins of the problem lay in the US sub-prime mortgage market. These mortgages had been granted to low-income borrowers on a large scale and then packaged as bundles of securities sold on to many financial institutions. When these mortgages failed, many banks were left holding near worthless assets. This capital loss, combined with a growing lack of confidence among depositors following some bank failure such as Northern Rock in the UK (see box 3.3), led to a chronic lack of credit in the financial system. This was reflected in the virtual seizing up of the inter-bank loan market where interest rates on lending between banks (e.g. Libor) went to previously unknown levels. There was a real possibility that some major banks would collapse. As a result governments had to intervene. In the UK this involved the central bank making very large sums of credit available to banks (acting as 'lender of the last resort') and the government putting significant sums of capital into many banks in return for preference shares. In effect, a significant element of the banking system was part nationalised.

---

## 3.2.2   The central bank

All countries have a central bank: in the United Kingdom, the Bank of England; in the USA, the Federal Reserve Board; in the eurozone, the European Central Bank and in Japan, the Bank of Japan. These are normally government-owned organisations. Although the functions of central banks vary a little from country to country, there are some common functions of these organisations.

The main functions of central banks are as follows.

### Banker to the banks

All commercial banks keep accounts at the central bank. These accounts:

- act as a liquid reserve for the commercial banks; thus acting as lender of the last resort;
- facilitate transfers from one bank to another arising out of the cheque clearing system.

In most countries these accounts are compulsory and must be equal to a minimum percentage of the commercial banks liabilities.

### Banker to the government

The central bank provides a range of banking services for the government and for government departments:

- accounts of government departments are held at the central bank and used in the same way as bank accounts in commercial banks; thus taxation revenue is paid into, and government expenditure paid out of these accounts;
- debt management which involves organising the raising of new borrowing for government when they run budget deficits, redeeming old debts when they run budget surpluses and managing the national debt.
- the central bank operates monetary policy on behalf of the government and is largely concerned with managing the supply of money in the economy, rates of interest and the rate of exchange for the currency.
- it manages the country's reserves of foreign currency; in the United Kingdom this is done through the Exchange and Equalization account which may be used to buy and sell sterling on the foreign exchange market in order to smooth out excessive fluctuations in the value of sterling.

### Note issue

The central bank has the sole right of note issue in an economy. These notes are liabilities on the central banks balance sheet and the matching assets are largely government securities. Paper currency is no longer backed by gold.

### Supervision of the banking system

The central bank normally has the duty of supervising the financial system and ensuring that the banks in the system meet the requirements laid down for them. These normally concern:

- *Capital adequacy.* To ensure that banks have sufficient capital to meet problems arising from business losses or loss of value in their assets, for example losses arising from bad debts.
- *Liquidity.* To ensure banks can meet the normal day-to-day requirements of their customers for cash.

In order to support the banking system should problem of liquidity arise, the central bank also acts as *lender of the last resort.* In this role the central bank will be willing to rediscount bills or buy bank government stock ('repos') thus providing cash for the banking system.

### Box 3.3   The Bank of England and Northern Rock

In the autumn of 2007 the UK based building society Northern Rock faced major problems in raising the funds it needed to continue its business. This was the result of a shortage of credit in the inter-bank market where financial institutions lend to each other. The result was a growing fear that Northern Rock would collapse because of a shortage of liquidity. This fear led to customers withdrawing deposits and a classic 'run on the bank' ensued. In these circumstances the Bank of England stepped in and loaned up to £25 billion to Northern Rock albeit a rate of interest higher than prevailing market levels. In effect the Bank of England had acted as 'lender of the last resort'.

In December 2007 central banks in Europe, the UK and the USA made a coordinated move to provide up to $100 billion of credit for the banking system in response to the continuing shortage of credit in the inter-bank market. This was acting as 'lender of the last resort' on a grand scale.

In the autumn of 2008 the condition of the banking system worsened considerably. Central banks were faced with a major banking crisis (the 'credit crunch'). As a result central banks had to undertake much more drastic action; enormous amounts of liquidity were made available as loans to banks and government money was injected into many banks to provide them with additional capital.

## 3.2.3   Financial markets

Financial institutions operate in a range of financial markets. The most important of these are:

- money markets
- capital markets
- international markets.

### Money markets

In most economies, the financial markets are dominated by the *money market*. It is here that banks, companies, local authorities and the government operate via the discount houses in buying and selling short-term debt. The discount houses are described as market makers in bills. This is because they will buy (or sell) treasury and commercial bills to enable holders to transform their assets into liquidity (or their cash into paper financial assets).

One important element of this function is the obligation of the discount houses to purchase each week the full issue of treasury bills. These are issued in order to make up the difference between government expenditure and reserves. Other buyers may purchase most of the treasury bills but the discount houses guarantee to make good any shortfall in demand.

- The price which the discount house pays reflects the market rate of interest.
- A high bid price makes a low rate of interest, because the difference between the price paid and the maturity value (usually three months later) is effectively the interest paid on the loan.
- For example, a bill bought for £4,900 is redeemed for £5,000 after three months. Thus £100 profit is made on an outlay of £4,900 over three months, approximately 8.2 per cent per annum.

The main commercial bill is a bill of exchange.

- When a financial intermediary accepts a bill of exchange it is effectively loaning money to a private trader upon promise of a refund by another trader.
- The bill is a contract between the two traders, with the buyer promising to pay a sum of money in return for goods on a certain date to the seller.
- The seller may sell the bill or cash to a financial intermediary who will discount it. A bank will discount the bill by paying less than the face value, knowing that it will receive the full value at a later date. The difference between the two sums of money is the interest.

These treasury and commercial bills are also often resold before maturity, again facilitating liquidity for the seller. The discount houses, in turn, raise their funds by borrowing 'money at call' from the banks, at very low rates of interest. They make a profit by charging slightly higher rates of interest when buying bills.

The 1970s and 1980s saw enormous financial innovation and the creation of new markets. These are known as *parallel money markets*. A key characteristic is that transactions are mainly between financial intermediaries, firms and local authorities but not the government. Secondary markets were developed in:

- bank liabilities, such as *certificates of deposit*
- and in bank assets, such as *resaleable bank loans.*

Such markets as the inter-bank market evolved to enable banks to accommodate fluctuations in customers' transactions by making loans to one another. With the increase in financial deregulation since the mid-1980s, new parallel markets in local authority debt, inter-company deposits and finance house borrowing have also sprung up.

### Capital markets

Capital markets provide long term finance for business and government and are discussed under 3.3.3 and 3.3.4.

### Foreign exchange markets

International markets are in broadly two groups.

1. the foreign exchange market
2. international capital markets.

Foreign exchange markets are concerned with the purchase and sale of foreign exchange. This is primarily for three reasons:

1. the finance of international trade;
2. companies holding and managing a portfolio of currencies as part of their financial asset management function;
3. financial institutions dealing in foreign exchange to on behalf of their customers and in order to benefit from changes in exchange rates.

International capital markets have greatly expanded since the 1950s. This has been the result of:

- the progressive abolition of exchange controls limiting the flow of capital in and out of economies;
- growth of *multinational companies* (MNCs) who often do not use capital markets in the 'home' country; by borrowing abroad in different currencies, MNCs can shop around for favourable terms and also avoid any domestic government credit restraints.

The funds available on international capital markets fall into three broad categories:

1. short-term capital (*Eurocurrency*) borrowed mainly for the purposes of working capital;
2. medium-term capital (*Eurocredit*) borrowed for working capital and investment purposes;
3. long-term capital (*Eurobonds*) borrowed for investment purposes and for financing mergers and acquisitions. Eurobonds are bonds issued by very large companies, banks, governments and supranational institutions, such as the European Commission, to raise long-term finance (typically five years and over). These bonds are denominated in a currency other than that of the borrower, although often US dollars are used. The bonds are bought and traded by investment institutions and banks.

The international capital market is useful not only for business borrowers. It is also used for government borrowers (e.g. United Kingdom local government authorities) and provides a market for lending funds for businesses with surplus cash. Thus the market performs a useful international element to the financial asset management function of commercial enterprises.

Although these international markets operate in many financial centres they are dominated by Europe and the USA, and especially London. The term 'euromarket' had its origins in the 1970s. International trading expanded and this led to new foreign currency markets, such as the Eurodollar market. In this market, dollar balances earned by European exporters (to the USA) were held in European banks earning interest on favourable terms because they are offshore (held outside the country of origin and not subject to central bank control).

## 3.3 The credit creation process

### 3.3.1 The credit multiplier

Banks create credit as a way of making profit. They are able to do this because not all of the cash that is deposited at a bank will be regularly withdrawn. Furthermore, when a bank lends money to a borrower, some of that money may be deposited back in the bank by another customer who deals with the borrower. This provides more cash reserves. In practice, the banks have discovered that at most 10 per cent of the deposited cash will be withdrawn, thereby leaving the remainder for loans and/or investment. This percentage is known as the cash ratio.

The use of the cash ratio makes possible the multiple creation of credit by banks. In the simple example given in Figure 3.1, the following sequence occurs.

- The bank opens with 'A' deposit of £1,000 on day 1.
- On day 2 the bank manager decides, on the basis of the 10 per cent cash ratio, to make a loan to business woman 'B' of £900.

| | Liabilities | | Assets | |
|---|---|---|---|---|
| Day one | Deposit | A – 1,000 | Cash | 1,000 |
| Day two | Deposit | A – 1,000 | Cash | 100 |
| | | | B-loan | 900 |
| Day three | Deposit | A – 1,000 | Cash | 500 |
| | | C – 400 | B-loan | 900 |
| Day four | Deposit | A – 1,000 | Cash | 140 |
| | | C – 400 | B-loan | 900 |
| | | | Investment | 360 |

**Figure 3.1** The credit multiplier

- In the course of their business dealing, 'B' pays £400 to 'C', who banks at the same bank.
- When 'C' pays in £400 on day 3, this raises the cash at the bank to £500 and total liabilities (deposit accounts) to £1,400.
- These liabilities only necessitate £140 in cash (i.e. 10 per cent ratio) which means that the bank can put the 'excess' cash of £360 to work. This is done on day 4 when investments to that account are made. This broadens the bank's asset structure.
- Alternatively, the bank could have lent the £360 to another customer seeking a loan.

The process of credit creation can continue as long as the ratio of cash/liquid assets to total deposits is maintained. The term 'deposit multiplier' (or credit multiplier) denotes the amount by which total deposits can increase as a result of the bank acquiring additional cash. This amount equals the reciprocal of the cash ratio:

$$\text{Change in total deposits} = \frac{1}{\text{cash ratio}} \times \text{the initial cash deposit}$$

Hence a cash ratio of 10% gives a balance sheet multiplier of 10: the total increase in the money supply is ten times the initial cash deposit. The credit multiplier (the amount by which credit expands in the economy) is, strictly speaking, the balance sheet multiplier $-1$, since 10% of the rise in the balance sheet consists of the initial cash deposit rather than created credit.

Thus banks can create credit on the basis of the cash and near cash liquid assets they hold. However, in practice their ability to do so may be limited by external factors such as:

### The behaviour of other banks

- If one bank has a lower cash ratio than its rivals, at each daily clearing of cheques it will face net indebtedness (i.e. there will be more money owed to other banks as a result of its customers' written cheques than received from cheques drawn on the accounts of other banks).
- This will reduce its balance at the central bank, which is treated as part of its cash base, and force a contraction of credit.
- If such action is not undertaken, the bank will eventually not be able to repay depositors who seek cash. This would undermine public confidence.

### The actions of the central bank

This can have an effect in two ways:

1. If the central bank sells bills or bonds to a bank's customers, it may reduce the bank's cash base and thus a bank's capacity to create credit. This happens because a bank's cash base includes its balance at the central bank and this will be reduced when the customer's cheques to buy the bills are drawn on the bank.
2. if the central bank forces up interest rates, it may reduce the demand for credit (because this action makes credit more expensive) and so a bank may not have sufficient customers seeking credit.

### The behaviour of other financial institutions

As institutional investors, such as insurance companies, save money in competing financial institutions, interest-rate differentials are very significant for them. Thus, if one bank raises its interest rates to attract custom, then this might limit another institution's capacity to create credit when it loses the deposits of an institutional investor.

### *Recent changes*

The model of credit creation given above is the traditional one. However, since the deregulation process started in the 1980s, financial systems have developed and changed. This has involved the development of new financial instruments and new banking practices. These changes have included:

- the adoption of new financial practices;
- the high level of investments as opposed to credit advances shown by financial firms;
- the growth of international trade and finance;
- libertarian economic attitudes leading to financial deregulation;
- technological innovations that integrated markets, for example electronic money transmission.

These developments have led banks into liability management and international credit, rather than just asset management and domestic credit as outlined earlier. The changes have also brought new credit creators into the fray.

Banks were faced with a falling (retail) deposit base in the 1980s and so have increased their reliance on wholesale funding. Thus cash deposits by customers only account for about 30 per cent of total liabilities. This undermines the relationship between customers' deposits (liabilities) and the cash base when considering credit creation.

This dependence on wholesale markets as source of funds was at the heart of the banking crisis in 2008. The rapid contraction of wholesale and inter-bank markets followed a loss of confidence in banks and building societies and reflected a growing desire of banks to retain funds that they might otherwise have lent to other financial institutions. Thus banks and other financial institutions found themselves chronically short of funds. This resulted in a considerable contraction in bank lending, especially for house purchase and to small businesses. This, in turn, was the major factor behind the recession which affected virtually all developed economies in 2008–2009.

In addition, distinctions are fading between the activities of financial institutions.

- Traditional lines of demarcation have been eroded between banks and building societies, while some mergers have created financial conglomerates offering a wide variety of financial services.
- Not only have non-bank institutions, such as building societies, engaged in credit creation but also non-financial bodies, such as large companies, for example high-street retailers.

Furthermore, the international dimension has developed rapidly, with the creation of Euronote facilities and swap activities, as corporate borrowers search worldwide for funding. These facilities have enabled British firms to borrow large sums abroad to finance activities in Britain. Credit has become internationally mobile, as financial innovators package domestic debts (e.g. cars, mortgages) into instruments marketable on world markets.

## 3.3.2 Financial instruments: assets and liabilities

All financial instruments are both assets to lenders and liabilities to borrowers. In the case of retail banks, all deposits are banks' liabilities because a bank has to provide money if a customer seeks a withdrawal. The bank's assets are the ways in which the bank has used the deposits.

THE FINANCIAL SYSTEM

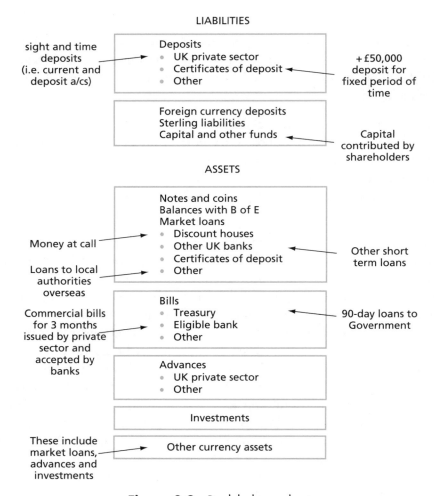

**Figure 3.2** Bank balance sheet

The bank balance sheet shows the portfolio of assets which the bank holds. These range from:

- the cash on the premises, which is extremely liquid but not profitable,
- through to advances which may be very difficult to repossess but yield high returns (Figure 3.2).

Prudent banks, and other financial institutions, arrange, and regularly rearrange, their asset structure to meet these contrasting objectives of *liquidity* and *profitability*.

- In general, the most profitable assets are the least liquid. For example, advances to the private sector may earn in excess of 20 per cent interest but they often cannot very quickly be called in.
- It is also true that the most liquid assets, such as notes and coin, are the least profitable. Not only do they not earn interest but also they incur financial costs in being handled and guarded. However, they do act as a buffer in case there is a run on the bank.

Banks also see *security*. Some of the assets, for example treasury bills, have government backing, which is reassuring for the banks. However, many are risky and collateral may be sought from customers. It is interesting that in some cases a bank has been the one to 'pull the plug' on a risky business, such as a football club, because it was the major creditor.

Advances and investments are considered to be illiquid. They are difficult to redeem quickly and then sometimes only with a loss being incurred. For example, a sale of stock could raise cash but a capital loss may result because the sale occurs when the market is depressed.

Certificates of deposit (CD) which are paper assets issued by banks to depositors who are willing to leave their money on deposit for a specified period of time. The certificates are bought (and sold) by banks, thereby giving their original holders, firms, access to cash. This makes a CD liquid and it is also profitable to a bank, because it receives the interest due on the CD.

Foreign currencies also feature as assets and liabilities in the banks' balance sheets. Their increasing importance and size shows the international importance of British banking. As these currencies are held on the assets side as loans, advances and investments, they are lucrative but fairly illiquid, like their British counterparts.

The 'banks in the United Kingdom: consolidated balance sheet' is now shown in a rather different way (Figure 3.2).

### 3.3.3 Finance for business

As discussed in Section 3.1.2, there are financial problems for businesses when there is a lack of synchronisation in the flows of payments and receipts. The financial needs of business vary and take a variety of forms. In general their needs can be classified as:

- funds to finance day-to-day business including payments for wages and salaries, raw materials and components – *working capital*;
- funds to finance the purchase of new capital equipment or to finance acquisitions and mergers – *investment capital*;
- suitable instruments for investing any surplus funds as part of the *asset management function*.

In acquiring funds to finance their activities, businesses have a large range of different types of financial instruments from which to choose. But in making the choice, businesses will follow a general rule that the instrument should be appropriate to the use to which the funds are to be put. Thus:

- short-term instruments should be chosen to finance the short-term needs of *working capital*;
- long-term instruments should be chosen to finance the long-term needs of *investment*.

With the investment of surplus funds a similar rule is generally adopted and the instrument chosen will be balanced between profitability and the needs to match the term of the instrument to the period during which the funds will not be needed.

In most economies and for most businesses, the bulk of the financial needs of those businesses are met by internally generated funds. For the rest of their financial needs, businesses can employ a range of financial instruments. The most important of these are:

### Short- and medium-term instruments

These are typically acquired from the money markets. The most important are:

- short-term bank loans and overdrafts, the latter are expensive and avoided if possible;
- bills of exchange, these are typically of 3–6 months duration are sold with a promise to repay at that date;

- commercial paper which are debt securities issued by the largest companies;
- trade credit which allows business to delay payment for raw materials, components, business services, etc.
- leasing and hire purchase.

Financial intermediaries have thus built up a wide range of instruments to meet the short- and medium-term financial needs of business. However, there has been a persistent complaint in many countries over recent years that the system has been poor at meeting the financial needs of small and newly established businesses. This explains the growth various government measures designed specifically to help the small business sector.

### Long-term instruments

In meeting their long-term financial needs, businesses have a broad choice between two forms of long-term finance:

- *equity* finance
- *debt* finance.

Equity finance is available to limited liability companies through the issue of shares. For publicly quoted companies, additional shares ('rights issues') can be issued via the Stock Market. This is discussed in the next section.

The alternative is long-term borrowing. This might be done by long-term commercial paper for the largest firms. Funds may also be raised by forms of Preference Shares on which fixed rates of interest are paid and mortgaged.

Although there is a wide choice of instruments for larger firms, especially those quoted on the stock market, there have been problems in many economies for small and new businesses. A persistent complaint has been the difficulty that small firms face in acquiring the finance they need from the financial system. In response many governments have created a series of initiative designed to meet the specific financing needs of small firms. Box 3.3 identifies some of the initiatives undertaken in the United Kingdom.

---

### Box 3.4  The Finance of Small Firms

In the United Kingdom, a range of measures have been introduced to meet the financial needs of small companies. These include:

*The Small Firms Loan Guarantee Scheme* by which the government guarantees loans from banks to small firms.

*Regional venture Capital Funds* which are public/private partnerships supported by the Department of Trade and Industry to encourage equity investment in small companies.

*Phoenix Fund* to support small businesses in disadvantaged urban areas.

*Enterprise Investment Scheme* to encourage equity investment in small and unquoted companies.

*Alternative Investment Market* (AIM) which enables small and middling companies to obtain equity capital on the London stock market.

In addition, the government has granted a series of tax concessions to help small companies. This includes lower rates of corporation tax for small companies.

## 3.3.4 The stock market

In the United Kingdom this encompasses several markets:

- the equities/securities market where ordinary shares, preference shares and debentures are traded;
- the AIM where smaller companies gain access to capital, under less stringent and less costly entry procedures;
- government bonds/gilts market where government sells short (up to 5 years) medium (5–15 years), long (over 15 years) and undated stock.

The phrase 'capital instruments' refers to the means (e.g. shares, bonds, etc.) by which organisations raise finance.

In October 1986 the 'Big Bang' occurred and the United Kingdom Stock Exchange radically changed. Its central function as a market for the purchase and sale of secondhand securities remained but its operations and procedures were reformed.

- Previously, an individual bought shares through a stockbroker.
- The broker acted as an adviser and an agent for his client (who was charged a commission) and bought shares from a stockjobber.
- The jobber was a dealer in securities who was willing to buy and sell at a price and hold on to unrequired shares. He did not deal with the general public.
- This system of single capacity was ended in October 1986 and the broker and jobbing functions were merged. The new dealer, of which there are about 200, has become known as a market-maker.

### Equity market

Transactions in company securities are the most numerous but average only £15,000 per transaction. These can be subdivided into equities (ordinary shares) and loan capital securities.

- Equities bestow full voting rights on the shareholder and an entitlement to dividends, once the preference shareholders and the holders of loan capital have been paid out.
- Preference shareholders receive a fixed dividend and get their capital repaid before ordinary shareholders if a company is wound up.
- Company bond sand debentures do not confer ownership rights but their holders receive a fixed rate of interest over a set period of time. In 1978 'traded options' were introduced, whereby an option holder can buy/sell a quantity of a company's shares at a fixed price on a specified date.

In 1985, convertible securities became prominent. They combine both debt and equity. The holder of the debt has the option of converting to equity, if desired. The securities market performs two main functions:

- It is a primary market for newly issued shares. Typically, a company's new shares are issued by an issuing house with the help and advice of a stockbroker. There are several possible methods of issuing new shares – by an offer for sale, by placing, by tender and by public issue: issuing a prospectus.
- In addition, existing companies wishing to raise capital may introduce a rights issue. This gives existing shareholders the right to subscribe cash for more shares in proportion to their existing shareholdings. The stockbroker's involvement is to obtain stock exchange approval for the issue, which a merchant bank usually undertakes.

- A secondary market exists for the buying and selling of existing shares. Although this does not contribute to economic production, it has some value. It raises the liquidity of company shares because buyers of new issues know that they can sell in the future. In addition, the worth of a company can be calculated from its share price.
- Furthermore, a company can raise further capital by an issue of extra shares more easily and cheaply if it has a high market share price. This was very clear in the stock market boom of 1986–87.

The stock market is usually given as an example of a perfectly competitive market because there are many buyers and sellers with excellent knowledge and rapid reactions to price changes. Share prices are published daily and they reflect demand changes. For instance market-makers will 'mark down' the prices of shares for which they have a plentiful supply.

However, in practice many non-economic factors affect share prices:

- *political factors* – wars, crises and elections tend to depress prices generally because of the uncertainty created;
- *the general mood of business* – optimism about the economy and government policy may stimulate confidence in share buying, thus raising share prices.

The price of a specific company share is more likely to be influenced by economic and commercial considerations directly relevant to that company.

- If a company reveals lower profits than expected, its share price might fall.
- Conversely, if a companies' prospects are enhanced by rumours, or announcements of a takeover, its share price will tend to rise.

In Figure 3.3, the demand for a company's shares has fallen to D1. It could be that the institutional investors, who typically hold about 70 per cent of equities, are concerned about the management, recent trading or lower than expected dividends and so switch to other equities. A similar fall in share price could result from an issue of new shares ($S_1$), without any change in demand.

### Alternative investment market (AIM)

In the United Kingdom there exists a market for shares in smaller companies. This was originally the Unlisted Securities Market (USM) set up in 1980. The purpose was to enable smaller companies raise sums up to £250,000 through share issues. The AIM which

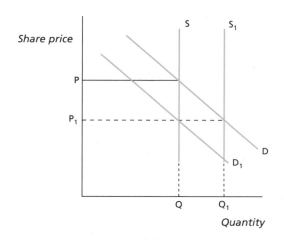

**Figure 3.3** A fall in share price

replaced the USM caters for smaller companies with none of the formal requirements regarding the age of the company and its market capitalisation for the main stock market.

## Government bond market

Government stocks, such as Gilt-edged stocks in the United Kingdom, are fewer in number than shares but marketed in greater volume, averaging £250,000 per transaction on long dated stock.

- The method of sale since 1979 has been by tender rather than at a fixed price (tap).
- However, the Bank of England usually sets the minimum tender price and when there is an excess demand all allotments are made at the lowest accepted price. These bonds are sold in £100 units, usually at a fixed interest rate.

There is a wide choice of interest payments and redemption dates to make bonds attractive to buyers. The main buyers are pension funds and life assurance companies who are attracted by a fixed certain income.

- As explained elsewhere the market price varies with the interest payment (called the 'coupon').
- For example, if interest rates are around 5 per cent then a bond with a £10 coupon will trade at around £200 (10/200 = 5 per cent). If interest rates then rise to 6 per cent, the bond price will move to £166 (10/166 = 6 per cent).

The supply of bonds is determined by the stock of bonds, which basically constitute the national debt. Public sector borrowing, which necessitates debt sales, will increase the supply of bonds.

## 3.3.5 Yields on assets and interest rates

The yield, or return, from an asset is calculated on the dividend relative to the market price. It is in effect a rate of interest and can be applied to most paper assets.

- Commonly, it is used to assess the return on dated government stock. The rate of return, or yield, varies with stocks of differing maturities. This happens partly because the dividend amount is fixed when the stock is sold.
- For example, at a time of relatively high inflation (e.g. 1990) the dividend would have to be high to attract investors. However, a stock sold four years later, with inflation at 2 per cent, might offer a lower dividend.

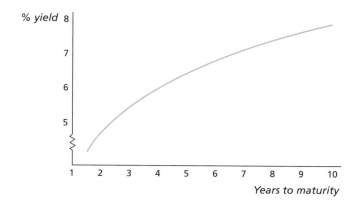

**Figure 3.4** A normal yield curve

As a stock nears maturity, its market price approaches its nominal price. Thus its yield falls. For example:

- a £100 stock carrying a dividend of £10, and with a market value of £90, gives a yield of 11 per cent (£10 divided by £90).
- as the stock approaches maturity, its market value approaches its nominal price (£100) and its yield becomes 10 per cent (£10 divided by £100).

Figure 3.4 shows a normal yield curve.

Yields rise when the prices of stocks fall. This could occur because market rates of interest on other substitutable assets are rising (i.e. their prices falling). These falling asset prices might result from:

- lower inflation
- increased supply of the assets
- lower company profits
- or financial pessimism.

In addition, because shares can be a substitute for stocks, a bullish share market could depress the price of stocks and so raise their yields. In January 2006 an example of the reverse happened. A sharp fall in share prices on the Tokyo stock market led to the following sequence of events in the United Kingdom.

- United Kingdom investors, fearing a similar fall in United Kingdom share prices, sold equity shares and bought government stock instead.
- The result was a steep rise in the price of United Kingdom government stock ('gilts').
- The rise in gilt prices produced a sharp fall in their yield significantly reducing likely incomes for large institutional investors with large gilt holdings.

The yield on equity is also important. In a perfectly efficient market, one would expect that the yield to an investor in bonds would be equal to the yield to an investor in equities. If this were not the case one would expect, other things being equal, that investors would sell the lower yielding assets in order to buy the higher yielding assets.

The yield on dividends is measured as:

$$\pi \quad \text{Dividend yield} = \frac{\text{dividend per ordinary share}}{\text{market price of the share}}$$

Thus if a company is paying 30 cents per ordinary share and each share has market price of $7.50 then the dividend yield would be:

$$\frac{30 \text{ cents}}{750 \text{ cents}} \times 100 = 4\%$$

Thus interest rates can affect the price of shares and their yields. If interest rates were to rise, the yield on bonds would also tend to rise. In an efficient market the following sequence would occur:

- investors would shift their portfolios towards bonds where yields are now rising and sell shares to do so;
- the sale of shares would reduce the prices of shares;
- the fall in the price of shares would raise the dividend yield (in the above example if the share price fell to $6.66, the yield would rise to 4.5 per cent).

The falling price of shares would raise the yield on those shares until an equilibrium was reached in which the yield on bonds and on shares was equalised. Thus changes in the rate of interest have important impacts on the prices and thus yields of shares and bonds.

## 3.3.6 Central banks and the rate of interest

### Money: demand and supply

In principle the rate of interest is the price of money (or more strictly, the price of liquidity). Therefore it should be determined, like any other price, by the interaction of the supply and demand for money.

### The supply of money

In order to establish what determines the supply of money, one needs to know what money is. The problem here is that range of financial assets can fulfill the function of money. Thus there is a long list of different measures of the supply of money in the economy; these range from very liquid assets, such as cash and current accounts, to a much broader notion of which assets should be regarded as money. The broad distinction here is between measures of:

- *narrow money* (or monetary bases) which includes cash in circulation;
- *broad money* which includes cash and current accounts but also deposit (time) accounts in retail and wholesale banking.

In the United Kingdom many of measures of money supply have been developed, from narrow money measures such as M0 and M2, to broader measures, such as M3 and M4.

In all cases, however, the total supply of money is linked to the amount of liquid assets that are present in the banking system. This is because it is the basis of these liquid assets, especially cash, that the banking system can create credit.

### The demand for money

The *demand for money* refers to the preference for holding the highly liquid asset of cash rather than holding other, less liquid but interest-bearing assets. For this reason the demand for money is sometimes referred to as 'liquidity preference'. Since holding cash means that interest is foregone, interest is clearly the price for holding that cash. Why should people and organisations wish to hold cash when it means foregoing the interest they could have earned?

In his 'liquidity preference' theory of the demand for money, the economist J.M. Keynes suggested that people and organisations have three general motives for holding money.

### Transactions Motive

As money is a medium of exchange giving liquidity, and people need to buy goods and services, clearly they require money for this purpose. Such money is usually held in cash and current accounts.

The demand for money for transactions purposes will be largely affected by the following.

- *The level of real income.* As living standards rise, expenditure rises and hence the demand for money to finance those transactions will increase. Thus the supply of money needs to be increased over time to match this rise in expenditure.
- *The rate of inflation.* In periods of inflation the demand for money for transactions purposes will increase, not because there is an increase in the real volume of expenditure, but because the total monetary value of those transactions has risen due to the rise in prices.

- *The frequency of wage and salary payments.* People paid monthly will probably have a higher average current account balance than those paid weekly.

### Precautionary Motive

As money acts as a store of value, people wish to keep it in order to meet unforeseen personal and financial contingencies.

- Such money tends to be held by individuals in bank and building society deposit accounts which are fairly accessible in an emergency.
- However, the expansion of private insurance, the wider provision of state benefits and the ease of transfer between deposit and current accounts have meant that people commit less income to saving for this purpose.
- It is unlikely that small increases in income affect the level of precautionary demand for money, although generally those on higher incomes tend to have higher savings balances.
- However, there is a clear link between precautionary savings and inflation. At times of rapid inflation, people tend to save more so as to maintain the real value of their money balances in case of emergency.

### Speculative Motive

As money gives immediate liquidity, some people wish to hold money in order to speculate with it.

- An individual may hold cash ready to undertake potentially profitable risks, varying from betting to the purchase of assets. The amount of money held for speculation is largely dependent on individual income levels.
- However, the main money speculators are financial institutions, rather than individuals. In 1990, over half of total M4 money in the United Kingdom was used for speculative purposes.
- Potential speculators are interested in the real rate of interest from asset buying. Thus their calculations take into account inflation. As a simple general rule, it is probably reasonable to say that the speculative demand for money is lowest at times of highest inflation, other things being equal. This is because money held ready for a suitable speculation is losing its value even more quickly at times of rapid inflation, and potential speculators recognise this real cost.
- Since there is an inverse relationship between interest rates and bond / share prices (see Section 3.3.5), the demand for money for speculative purposes is related to expectations about future movements in interest rates. If interest rates are expected to rise (fall) in the immediate future, investors will expect a fall (rise) in bond and share prices. In these circumstances they will wish to hold large (small) amounts of cash and relatively smaller (larger) amounts of bonds and shares.

### Monetary policy

From the foregoing discussion, it can be seen that interest rates might change if there is a change in the supply or demand for money. Changes in the demand for money are unlikely to be very large in the short run although there may be significant seasonal variations in the demand for money.

  The supply of money is different however since the supply of money is partly determined by the credit creation activities of the banks and a change in their policy and behaviour could affect the supply of money and hence the rate of interest. Moreover, since the ability of banks to create credit is constrained by the supply of cash and very liquid assets in the financial system, central banks may be able to influence the supply of money and interest rates by effecting changes in the amount of liquid asset in the financial system.

The central bank can alter interest rates by selling or buying bank ('redeeming') government stock. The central bank buys and sells treasury and commercial bills, and government bonds in the money market. This activity is known as 'open market operations'.

- If it seeks a multiple contraction of credit it will sell bills. The cheques paying for them will be drawn on the banks, whose deposits will fall and whose balances at the Bank of England will be lowered. Their cash base will be lowered and their potential to create credit will be limited.
- If it seeks a multiple expansion of credit it will buy bills. The result will be an increase in the commercial banks deposits at the central bank and thus their cash base will be increased and their ability to create credit will be raised.

When selling bills in an attempt to restrict credit, the central bank may find that, in practice the commercial banks can restore their cash base by reclaiming money at call from the discount houses (in the United Kingdom) and other financial organisations.

- The discount houses when they find themselves short of cash always sell bills to the Bank of England. Since 1981, the arrangement has been that they offer the bills to the bank at the prevailing market rate, which the bank can accept or reject.
- Thus, if the Bank of England wishes to see interest rates rise, it rejects the market rate offered by the discount houses and offers to buy at a new higher interest rate, thus penalising the discount houses.
- As the discount houses do not wish to make losses on their own loans they raise interest rates and the increase is thus transmitted through the money market.

Thus the central bank can either restrict the credit creating ability of banks by reducing the amount of cash in the financial system or it can force a rise in interest rates through the system. A similar outcome can be achieved by central bank operations in the market for government longer-term securities (in the United Kingdom, 'gilt-edged' securities). If the central bank:

- increases its sales of government bonds, the price will fall and the effective interest rate (the yield) will rise;
- decreases its sales of government bonds, the price will rise and the effective interest rate (the yield) will fall.

Box 3.5 outlines recent interest rate policy in the eurozone and debates about its impact on business.

In addition, the government and central bank might operate rather more directly on the ability of commercial banks to create credit through bank *assets ratios*. Banks are required to a proportion of their total assets in certain specified assets. The basic idea behind these ratios was to ensure *prudential standards of liquidity* but by varying these required ratios, the central banks could, in principle, affect the credit multiplier. In practice little sue is now made of this and most reliance is placed on open market operations and on interest rate policy.

In addition to the conduct of monetary policy central banks have an important role in supervision of the banking system.

### Box 3.5   Monetary policy in the UK

During the first half of 2008 the main concern of the Bank of England was the threat of rising inflation. The large rise in food and energy prices, especially the price of oil which rose to over $150 a barrel, was the main reason for a rise in rate of inflation which peaked at 5.2% in September. As a result the Bank kept interest rates at relatively high levels. Some members of the monetary policy committee voted for increases in rates despite the fears of one member, David Blanchflower, that the real threat was a collapse in house prices and a severe recession. By the autumn the threat of inflation had faded as food and energy prices fell, the price of oil to $40 a barrel in December, and the crisis in the banking system and the onset of a severe recession became the primary problems. The result was a rapid reversal of monetary policy. The Bank cut its interest rate by 0.5% in October, by 1.5% in November and by 1% in December. The result was the lowest Bank of England rate of interest for a generation. Given the severity of the financial and economic problems of the UK, most commentators expected further falls in 2009 with interest rates possibly going as low as 1%.

## Banking supervision

### Capital adequacy rules

Banks create credit for customers in order to make profits, by charging interest. However, not all recipients of credit repay the amount borrowed and so bad debts can arise. For example, in the late 1980s and early 1990s the four major British clearing banks wrote off billions of pounds of Third World debt from their balance sheets.

United Kingdom incorporated banks are watched over and advised by the Bank of England. There are certain rules and requirements which are imposed on banks; some of these are described below.

This problem of bad debt and the exposure of major banks throughout Europe precipitated the *Basle Agreement* 1988.

- This established a risk asset ratio relating a bank's capital to its assets and off balance sheet exposures.
- A minimum international standard capital adequacy ratio was set but an individual central bank was permitted to set higher levels if it wished.

The adequacy of a bank's capital is measured against the bank's risk assets, which are weighted by category. 'On balance sheet' items are weighted according to their location and any available collateral. For example, lending to a local authority attracts a 20 per cent weighting. 'Off balance sheet' items have a credit conversion factor applied to them, according to their perceived risk, to give them 'on balance sheet' equivalence. For example, a documentary credit is weighted at 20 per cent, indicating a low risk. This is because the the minimum capital requirement is calculated as follows:

| Liabilities | £ billion |
|---|---|
| Total sterling liabilities | 1,590 |
| (of which deposits) | (1,278) |
| Total foreign currency liabilities | 1,901 |
| Total liabilities | 3,491 |
| Assets | |
| Total sterling assets | 1,597 |
| (of which advances) | (988) |
| Total foreign currency assets | 1,894 |
| Total assets | 3,491 |

**Figure 3.5**   UK commercial banks consolidated balance sheet, January 2002
(*Source*: Bank of England)

Weighted risk asset $\times$ trigger ratio
The trigger ratio is the minimum for a bank's capital base to its weighted risk assets. The Basle Agreement sets this at 8 per cent minimum, but the Bank of England agrees a target ratio with each bank privately.

- The British clearers typically average 9 per cent. This means that to support £100 m of weighted risk assets, a bank requires £11 m minimum capital.
- At least half of the capital requirement must be shareholders' capital and accumulated profits, while the remainder will typically include loan stocks and general provisions against losses.

Thus, these rules attempt to ensure prudential lending by banks and consistency across the European banks. These risk asset ratios vary between banks largely because of the differing proportions of debt and equity in their capital base. The rules are an effective means of supervision by the central bank and cover:

- *Liquidity.* Banks need to hold money in cash to meet customer demand. Such cash flows can be profiled in advance and significant obligations identified.
- *Provisions.* The Bank of England encourages banks to make adequate provision for bad and doubtful debts. It has issued guidance enabling banks to 'score exposures' in less developed countries against a list of economic and financial factors. Also, under the 1987 Banking Act, banks have to report large exposures to a single customer and their exposures to individual sectors (e.g. property). In addition, a bank is not allowed to lend more than 10 per cent of its capital base to one single borrower.
- *Systems.* Each bank is obliged to report periodically on its procedures and controls. The Bank of England will examine a bank's methods for monitoring credit risk, its systems for recoverability, its arrears patterns and so on.
- *Personnel.* Directors, managers and large shareholders of banks have to satisfy the Bank of England that they are 'fit and proper' people for such positions. The Bank of England interprets this to mean people who are honest, competent, diligent and sound judges.

In addition, the reporting accountants of a bank have to regularly confirm that the central bank's guidelines have been observed. They also submit the necessary statistical returns which will be key data in the central banks' monitoring.

In 2008 the role of UK authorities in supervising the banking system came under severe scrutiny. The collapse of Northern Rock in 2007 was followed by a series of bank crises which led to the forced mergers of some banks and the need for enormous financial support from the Government and the Bank of England for many others. Similar problems and responses occurred in many other countries, particularly the United States. As a result, the banking supervision roles of the authorities and the nature of the regulation of the banking system they sought to enforce became the subject of considerable debate. Tighter supervision and much greater regulation of the banking system were expected to be the outcome of that debate.

 **Exercise 3.2**

1. What is a cash ratio?
2. What is the relationship between liquidity and profitability of banks assets?
3. How could a central bank reduce the supply of credit in the financial system?
4. How could a central bank reduce the demand for credit in the financial system?
5. What are the three motives for demanding money (liquidity)?
6. What are capital adequacy rules?

 **Solutions**

1. The amount of cash kept by banks in readiness to pay withdrawals as a proportion of their total assets.
2. The most liquid assets, for example cash, are the least profitable; and the least liquid assets, for example advances and loans to customers, are the most profitable.
3. The central bank would need to reduce the liquidity of the financial system as this is the basis upon which credit is created. It can do this by selling government stocks to financial institutions.
4. The central bank could raise interest rates as interest is the price of credit and a higher price will reduce demand.
5. The three motives for demanding money are:

   (i) the transactions motive
   (ii) the precautionary motive
   (iii) the speculative motive.

   Together they make up the demand for money, also known as liquidity preference.
6. Capital adequacy rules attempt to ensure that banks have sufficient capital to cover potential bad debts on risk assets.

## 3.4   The insurance market

All businesses face two types of risk:

1. general commercial risks which may affect their performance and profitability, including business confidence, consumer confidence, the demand for their product and broad economic conditions;
2. specific risks such as the loss of capital equipment and premises due to fire or accident or the risk of accidents to employees.

In the first case these risks are undertaken by *entrepreneurs* or by business organisations taking on the entrepreneurial function. The reward for accepting these risks is *profit*. It is not possible to insure against these sort of risks. However, in the latter case, risks are insurable because:

- it is very unlikely that an event or process could affect most businesses in the same way at the same time;
- therefore a probability of the risk occurring can be predicted and a premium can be calculated.

In many cases, businesses have little choice about taking out insurance for they may be required to do so by law. In the United Kingdom, businesses must take out insurance against accidents and ill health to their employees under the Employers' Liability Regulations.

### 3.4.1 Types of insurance

Insurance is a means of providing a degree of protection, for individuals or for businesses, against the financial consequences of range of risks including theft, or accidental damage to property, and death or injury.

Insurable risks fall into two categories:

1. risks of events that *may* occur ('insurance')
2. risks of events that *will* occur ('assurance').

For a typical business, the general risks which they may wish to insure against include:

- fire
- theft
- employers liability
- public liability
- consequential loss
- credit (bad debts)
- engineering/marine/motor.
- sickness and critical illness of employees

Indeed, in the United Kingdom businesses *must*, by law, take out insurance for employers liability, motor insurance, some forms of engineering insurance for some types of dangerous machinery and insurance to cover contractual obligations (e.g. when the business stores or transports other peoples' property).

In order to acquire insurance, a business can:

- approach insurance companies directly. These may be general insurance companies providing insurance against a range of risks or they may be companies specialising in one particular form of insurance.
- work through an intermediary known as an *insurance broker*. Brokers will seek an insurance company that can provide the business with the most appropriate policy for their needs. Lloyds of London is one of the most well known and biggest institutions acting as an intermediary between customers and the groups of individuals who provide the insurance cover.

THE FINANCIAL SYSTEM

### 3.4.2 The providers of insurance

Most insurance cover is provided by insurance companies. These companies can operate successfully by pooling the risks involved amongst a large number of policyholders. Given the large numbers the company can calculate the risks involved and thus calculate a premium to be charged. The task of calculating risks is a specialised one undertaken by *actuaries*. Thus the insurance company has two sources of income:

1. the premium income itself;
2. the income generated from that part of the premium income which can be invested by the company.

In this process, the insurance industry is undertaken the functions of:

- *Underwriting.* Here the financial institution is accepting the financial risk involved in the particular insurance transaction in return for an agreed payment (the 'premium'). Thus insurance companies underwrite range of insurance risks and will pay out compensation when there are genuine claims on the insurance policy.
- *Reinsurance.* Some individual risks may be very large. This would be the case when insuring ships and aircraft. In these cases insurance providers might wish to spread the risks via reinsurance. It does so by sharing the premium with other companies in relation to the share of the risk underwritten by each company.

In addition to these providers of standard insurance services, businesses can also use the *futures market* to provide cover against certain types of financial risk. An example of a futures market is the *London International Financial Futures and Options Exchange* (LIFFE). These markets provide a form of insurance cover for businesses where:

- the organisation is faced with a fixed financial commitment sometime in the future, such as the requirement to pay a fixed sum in a foreign currency to an overseas supplier.
- the organisation may be vulnerable to a range of financial risks arising out of price changes in the period between signing the contract and the date of payment, such as fluctuations in exchange rates.

Thus a business might be able to buy some foreign exchange at a fixed rate of exchange to be delivered at some specified point in the future in order to meet a contractual financial obligation.

### 3.5 Chapter summary

This chapter has discussed various roles, functions and features of the financial system. It has developed the following main sets of related ideas and principles.

- The problem of lack of synchronisation in payments and receipts for individuals, businesses and governments and how this problem may rise in the short, medium and long run.
- The role of financial institutions acting as financial intermediaries. Financial intermediation is the process of bringing together those individuals and organisations that have financial surpluses and deficits thus providing a means of dealing with the lack of financial synchronisation.

- The principal services and contracts provided by financial institutions to meet the financial needs of businesses and governments.
- The process of credit creation in the financial system and the importance of various interest rates.
- The role of the central bank in influencing the supply of credit and the rate of interest and its task of overseeing the work of the financial system.
- The importance of insurance for businesses and the different services provided by insurance companies.

All individuals and organisations function within a monetary environment and so the services provided by financial institutions and the efficiency and effectiveness of that provision is a crucial factor in business operation.

# Revision Questions

This section contains examination-standard questions and solutions relevant to the content of Chapter 3. You should use these questions for examination practice and revision.

## Question 1

**1.1** Which is the best description of the supply of money in an economy?

(A) Notes and coins issued by the central bank.
(B) Money created by the commercial banks.
(C) Coins, notes and bank deposits.
(D) All items of legal tender.

**1.2** The essential condition for an asset to act as money is that it is:

(A) Legal tender.
(B) Generally acceptable.
(C) Backed by gold or foreign exchange.
(D) A physical commodity.

**1.3** Which of the following are the likely consequences of a fall in interest rates?

(i) A rise in the demand for consumer goods.
(ii) A fall in investment.
(iii) A fall in government spending.
(iv) A rise in the demand for housing.

(A) (i) and (ii) only.
(B) (i), (ii) and (iii) only.
(C) (i), (iii) and (iv) only.
(D) (ii), (iii) and (iv) only.

**1.4** Which one of the following is not part of the transactions demand for money?

(A) Cash held to pay weekly supermarket bills.
(B) Money in the bank to meet a banks' direct debit for telephone bills.
(C) Money in a bank account held to pay for an annual holiday.
(D) Money kept in a current account to meet unforeseen bills.

**1.5** Which of the following would be expected to lead to a rise in share prices on a stock market?

(A) A fall in interest rates.
(B) A rise in the rate of inflation.
(C) A fall in share prices in other stock markets.
(D) An expected fall in company profits.

**1.6** Reinsurance is best defined as:

(A) A business renewing its insurance cover each year.
(B) A business increasing its level of insurance to meet new needs.
(C) An insurance broker finding a suitable insurance policy for a client.
(D) An insurance company sharing a particular insurance risk with other companies.

**1.7** Which one of the following could a business not insure itself against?

(A) Financial consequences of bad debts.
(B) Falling sales in the onset of a recession.
(C) Claims for damages by customers injured by faulty products of the business.
(D) Theft of the businesses property by an employee.

**1.8** A $100 stock with market price of $80 and a dividend of $5 will generate a yield of:

(A) 5%
(B) 8%
(C) 6.25%
(D) 12.5%

## ? Question 2

The following financial data refer to an economy for the period 2001–2006.

|  | 2001 | 2002 | 2003 | 2004 | 2005 | 2006 |
|---|---|---|---|---|---|---|
| **Interest rates** | | | | | | |
| Bank base rate (%) | 8.5 | 7.0 | 5.5 | 6.8 | 5.8 | 6.0 |
| Instant-access account deposit rate (%) | 6.3 | 4.9 | 3.8 | 4.2 | 2.8 | 2.3 |
| 90-day-access account deposit rate (%) | 8.8 | 6.2 | 4.5 | 4.9 | 3.9 | 3.9 |
| Mortgage rate | 11.0 | 9.4 | 7.7 | 8.4 | 7.0 | 7.4 |
| **Share prices** | | | | | | |
| Stock market index | 2521 | 2900 | 2919 | 2314 | 3711 | 4710 |
| **Inflation** | | | | | | |
| Percentage rise in consumer prices | 4.0 | 1.6 | 2.3 | 3.5 | 2.7 | 2.7 |

## Requirements

Using *both* your knowledge of economic theory and material contained in the table:

(a) With respect to the data given:

    (i)   using the bank base rate calculate the real rate of interest for 2003;

    (ii)  calculate the real mortgage rate of interest for 2004;

    (iii) state whether real share prices rose or fell between 2002 and 2003.    **(3 marks)**

(b) State whether each of the following are true or false.

    (i)   Rising real interest rates will encourage savings and investment.

    (ii)  Interest rates will only affect business investment if that investment is financed by borrowing.

    (iii) Rising interest rates in a country tend to raise the exchange rate for that country's currency.

    (iv) Producers of consumer durable goods are more sensitive to changes in interest rates than supermarkets.

    (v)  Central banks cannot increase the money supply and raise interest rates at the same time.    **(5 marks)**

(c) State whether the effect of a rise in interest rates will be to

    (i)   increase or decrease government spending;

    (ii)  reflate or deflate the economy.    **(2 marks)**

**(Total marks = 10)**

# Solutions to Revision Questions

3

## ✔ Solution 1

**1.1** Solution: (C)

The question concerns an economic definition of money. D refers to the legal definition. A and B are insufficient, since they refer to either cash or credit, but not to both.

**1.2** Solution: (B)

The most important function of money is to act as a medium of exchange; for this the essential condition is that it should be generally acceptable. Provided that it is acceptable, it does not need to be legal tender, or to be backed by gold or foreign exchange. Neither does it need to be a physical commodity; most money consists of entries in bank accounts.

**1.3** Solution: (C)

A fall in interest rates will encourage investment, not a fall. Lower interest rates reduce government expenditure on servicing the national debt, and will encourage consumers to take on more credit, including borrowing for house purchase. Thus C is the correct solution.

**1.4** Solution: (D)

Money held to meet unforeseen circumstances is called the precautionary motive, so D is the correct response. All the others are monies cash or assets in bank accounts to meet known items of expenditure and hence are for the transactions motive.

**1.5** Solution: (A)

A fall in company profits would clearly discourage the purchase of shares and so share prices would fall. Since stock markets are linked, a fall in one market tends to lead to a fall in share prices in other markets. A rise in inflation would lead to some business pessimism and might be expected to lead to a rise in interest rates. However, since share prices and interest rates move in opposite directions, A is the correct solution.

**1.6** Solution: (D)

Reinsurance concerns the way in which insurance companies handle large risks not with the activities of companies seeking insurance. Thus an insurance company, faced

**153**

THE FINANCIAL SYSTEM

with a large potential risk, may share the risk and the insurance premium with other insurance companies.

**1.7** Solution: (B)

All of the others are risks which can be calculated by insurance companies and will affect only a predictable number of businesses in any one period. However with a recession it would be difficult to predict and to estimate what proportion of falling sales were the result of the recession. Moreover this would affect most businesses at the same time. Thus no insurance company will insure such a risk and hence B is the correct solution.

**1.8** Solution: (C)

The yield of an asset is the relationship between the income derived from it and the price that has to be paid to acquire it. In this case the market price is $80 and the income gained is $5. The yield in percentage terms is $5 divided by $80 × 100. This is 6.25%

 **Solution 2**

(a)  (i)  3.2%
     (ii)  4.9%
     (iii)  fell

(b)  (i)  *False*. High interest rates encourage savings but discourage business investment.
     (ii)  *False*. A rise in interest rates raises the opportunity cost of using internal funds to finance investment.
     (iii)  *True*. Higher interest rates encourage capital inflows which increase the demand for the currency.
     (iv)  *True*. Consumer durables are often bought on credit.
     (v)  *True*. If the supply of money increases, its price, the rate of interest, will go down.

(c) A rise in interest rate would:
    (i)  *raise* government spending as the cost of financing government debt would increase.
    (ii)  *deflate* the economy since it would discourage expenditure.

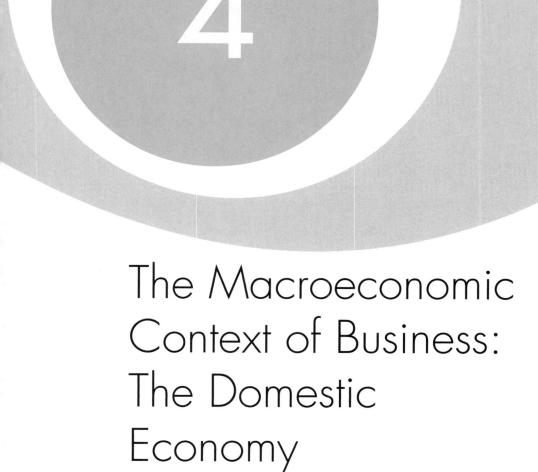

# 4

# The Macroeconomic Context of Business: The Domestic Economy

# The Macroeconomic Context of Business: The Domestic Economy

4

## 4.1  The economy as a whole

### 4.1.1  National income

So far the discussion of economic processes has concentrated on elements of the economy such as business organisations, markets and the financial system. It is now necessary to look at the economy as a whole, as a system. This makes it possible to answer some important questions including:

- How large is the economy?
- How fast is the economy growing?

- Why do inflation and unemployment occur?
- How may we assess the ability of the economy to generate economic welfare for its citizens?

The starting point is to measure the size of the economy by using the concept of national income.

National income is measured in order to assess the performance of an economy over a period of time, usually a year. This, in turn, will give some idea of changes in living standards and enable international comparisons to be made.

The definition of national income is:

*the total value of the goods and services produced by a country's resources over a year.*

Given the scale of economic activity in a modern economy, the accounting needed to measure national income is very complex. Measurement is done in three ways:

- by national output
- by national income
- by national expenditure.

When goods and services are produced, people receive incomes, and thus in theory the addition of the prices of all the goods and services should equal the sum of all the income of the population. Similarly, those figures should equate with the total amount of spending by the population on goods and services. However, numerous adjustments have to be made when calculating by each method.

National income can be used for a variety of purposes. In particular, when we wish to measure

- the *productivity* of an economy the appropriate measure of national income is gross domestic product (GDP);
- the *standard of living* in an economy the appropriate measure is gross national product (GNP).

In a closed economy with no economic relations with the rest of the world, the measures of GDP and GNP would be identical; in an open economy with international flows of goods, services and payments, they may differ.

## Gross domestic product (GDP)

This term is often referred to by economists because it shows the value of the output produced in an economy during one year. If it increases in real terms, then there has been economic growth.

If we take all the domestic spending and adjust for trade as in Table 4.1, we can calculate GDP at market prices. However, because the government interferes in the market system through indirect taxes and subsidies, this does not show the real cost of these goods and services (factor cost). So, indirect taxes are deducted and subsidies added. Thus GDP at market prices is adjusted to give the valuation of GDP at factor cost.

## Gross national product (GNP)

This term refers to the value of the output produced (and incomes earned) by all British residents in a year. To calculate this, the following must be added/deducted to the figure for GDP for a country.

**Table 4.1**  UK GDP by expenditure method 2,007

|  | £ million |
|---|---|
| Household consumption | 858,827 |
| Expenditure of non-profit institutions | 34,587 |
| Government expenditure | 296,900 |
| Gross domestic fixed capital formation | 249,238 |
| Change in inventories | 7,901 |
| Other | 374 |
| Total | 1,447,827 |
| Exports | 368,337 |
| Gross final expenditure | 1,816,164 |
| Minus total imports | 415,817 |
| Statistical discrepancy | 695 |
| GDP at market prices | 1,401,042 |

*Source*: ONS

- Income (profits, rents, interest) earned by domestic companies and individuals abroad and remitted back to the home country (added).
- Income (profits, rents, interest) earned by overseas companies and individuals operating in the home country and remitted back to their countries of origin reduces GNP (deducted).

## Capital consumption

Each year the nation's capital assets suffer wear and tear, and thus lose value, as they are used to produce goods and services. The deduction for this depreciation is termed *capital consumption*. It is deducted from GNP to get national income or net national product as it is sometimes termed.

Gross capital formation refers to new investment. Thus the difference between gross capital formation (total new investment) and capital consumption (depreciation) gives net investment during the year. The higher this figure, the greater is the future productive potential of the economy.

Some economists feel that the traditional emphasis on the acquisition and depreciation of physical assets is too narrow.

- The productive resources of any economy include the skills of its workers although the great difficulty of measurement makes such inclusions impractical and unlikely.
- Depletion of national assets is not included in the national income accounts. If there are social costs such as pollution resulting from production, natural assets like clear air and clean rivers may be diminished and become increasingly scarce. A valuation of such an amenity loss and resource depletion could be added to capital consumption.
- When irreplaceable resources, such as fossil fuels, are consumed in production this weakens the economy for the future. Hence, some economists have suggested that a deduction from national income should be made, in the same way as for depreciation of capital equipment. Hence some measure of sustainable national income might be derived.

## 4.1.2   National income calculation

The three methods used to calculate national income are described below.

### The expenditure method

This calculation adds together the spending on:

- consumption and investment goods and services by final consumers, businesses and the government;
- on current final output (not, for example second hand goods);
- changes in stocks, with additions to stocks being treated as spending by the firms holding them;
- exports of goods and services minus imports of goods and services.

There are two main technical problems with this method:

- transfer payments, such as income support, pensions, etc., are deleted from government spending because they are a transfer from taxpayers to recipients via the government;
- taxes and subsidies distort market prices and need to be allowed for; thus indirect taxes are deducted and subsidies added so that the true prices of output are determined.

### Usefulness of the expenditure method

- The expenditure method is useful for detecting changing trends in consumption and investment. Thus, it could reveal any changes between the shares of public sector and private sector, or between current and capital spending.
- However, some economists feel that certain public expenditure on administration, policing, environmental repair and defence inflate the real value of national income. This spending may be just making good the degradation of the environment and preventing the misuse of resources rather than increasing the amount of final output. Thus, this method may overestimate national output.

### The income method

In this method, the incomes received by the owners of resources (factors of production) are totaled.

- The main groups are:
    - income from employment (wages and salaries)
    - income from self-employment
    - trading profits of private sector companies
    - trading surpluses of public sector industries
- The sum of incomes gives GDP at factor cost. If indirect taxes and subsidies are allowed for this figure becomes GDP at market prices. Direct taxes can be ignored as they do not affect the market price of output.

The income method is illustrated in Table 4.2.

**Table 4.2** UK GDP by income method 2,007

|  | £ million |
| --- | --- |
| Compensation of employees | 744,857 |
| Surpluses of Corporations | 309,159 |
| Other incomes | 178,009 |
| Gross value added (incomes) at factor cost | 1,232,025 |
| Taxes – subsidies | 168,183 |
| Statistical discrepancy | 834 |
| GDP at market prices | 1,401,042 |

*Source*: ONS

## Usefulness of the income method

The income method is useful in showing the changes in share of income between different factors of production. For example, the 1980s have shown an increasing share attributable to self-employment. However, as the latter is a significant contributor to the black economy, total domestic income may have become underestimated.

## The output method

In this calculation, the value of the production from each industrial sector is ascertained and added.

- To avoid double counting, we take only the value added at each stage of production not the gross value of output at each stage. Alternatively we could measure the gross value of final output only. Either method will produce the same figure.
- The prices of some goods and services have to be imputed since they have no market prices. These are mainly services provided free of charge by the state and paid for out of taxation such as education, defence and policing. The value of these is usually based on the cost of producing them. The weakness of this method is that rising costs show up as increased output whether or not the service has improved.

## Usefulness of the output method

The output method shows the changing shares of the primary, secondary and tertiary sectors in an economy. For instance, the industrialisation of East Asian countries in recent years is illustrated by the fall in the relative contribution of primary activities to the total and the rise in industry and manufacturing.

However, there are weaknesses with this method:

- it excludes output produced but not sold on the market such as DIY, housework and other self-provided goods;
- increased leisure time resulting from improved technology does not show up in the output statistics;
- it is difficult to reflect improved quality of output in the data.

Thus the output method may underestimate or overestimate the real output of the economy.

## 4.1.3 The use of national income statistics

The difficulties of measurement and the discrepancies between the three different methods mean that the national income figure is really just a sophisticated estimate. In addition, in order to make valid comparisons, it requires further adjustments for inflation and population changes. Therefore, the most useful figure is probably real national income per head. Variations in this statistic give a general idea of changes in living standards, both through the years and between the countries.

### Comparisons over time

National income data can be used to compare living standards in one country over time. An increase in real national income per head would normally indicate a rise in living standards. However, there are some difficulties with this sort of comparison.

- Allowance has to be made for inflation over the period of comparison. Thus the required figure is the change in *real* national income per capita rather than the change in *nominal* national income per capita.
- The distribution of national income may have changed so that although *average* per capita income may have risen, the incomes of some members of society may not have risen or may, indeed, have fallen.
- The uses to which income is put may have changed. Thus if taxation has risen to finance increased defence expenditure, rising per capita income may not mean a rising standard of living.

Despite the qualifications which need to be made to national income calculations, it is universally agreed that the most people in developed economies are better off in terms of real income, personal assets and leisure time than in earlier decades. There may be concern regarding the pace of life, the environment and social standards but, financially, life for most people is now much improved compared with the inter-war years and the immediate post-war years.

However, it is clearly the case that this improvement has varied a great deal from one country to another. Within Europe comparisons have shown that United Kingdom per capita income, although rising at about 2 per cent a year for much of the last 50 years, fell relative to that of many other European economies. However, in the last decade United Kingdom performance has greatly improved and per capita income has risen faster than in many OECD economies. Likewise, poor growth performance in many developing economies can be contrasted to the rapid growth in income in such countries as China and India in recent years.

### Comparisons between countries

There are many problems when making such comparisons of economic development and growth between countries. There are two underlying differences which affect all others.

- Cultural differences mean that the way of life will place different values on different goods and services. For example, if barter, subsistence and mutual help are part of the culture then the official figures may understate the true level of output per head.
- The accuracy of the data will vary in quality and quantity. For instance, items included in one economy may not be included in another country's calculations. The integrity of the officials and the resources devoted to collection will determine the efficiency of the statistics.

- National data has to be converted into a common currency (usually the US$) for comparisons to be made. The resulting figure depends on the exchange rate used to convert the national data into US$. If the country's exchange rate is overvalued (undervalued) it will tend to exaggerate (underestimate) its national income in $ terms.

There are many other factors which make comparing living standards through a comparison of GDP figures problematic.

- Climatic and geographical differences affect what is needed and what is produced; in warm climates, less output of energy for heating is required. Thus lower national income in these economies does not necessarily mean lower economic welfare.
- Political factors may affect the structure of output. The end of the cold war led to lower defence spending in many countries thus releasing resources to produce output that generates consumer welfare. For example, the United Kingdom has recently engaged in a large-scale programme of public expenditure on health, education and transport.
- Social indicators of the quality of life do not feature directly in national income statistics. Social problems, such as crime or pollution, may even lead to the need for expenditures to deal with these social costs, thus producing an apparent increase in welfare as national income rises.

It is clear that making international comparisons of national income is fraught with difficulty. Technical adjustments are made for the variations in price levels between economies and changes in exchange rates against the standard of currency (the dollar) which is used. These adjustments facilitate more accurate comparison but the use of the mathematical mean (average) rather than the median can produce unrepresentative results (e.g. Kuwait has one of the highest average national incomes but most of its population receive less than what would be considered as low wages in Britain). This arises because of the high concentration of income in a few hands and the unevenness of income distribution.

All of the above problems and qualifications have led to comparisons using selected items which feature in most economies, such as major consumer durables (e.g. cars, telephones), divorce rates, doctors, stress-related illnesses and participants in higher education. These can be calculated per head and used for relative measurement. Although this method lacks precision, arguably it indicates the quality of life better than the bare national income data.

## Business use of national income data

National income data is of particular use to governments in formulating economic policy and to business when making strategic business choices. For businesses, especially large businesses operating in more than one country, national income data is helpful in making several types of strategic decision.

- *Sales and production strategy.* If a business knows that prospective rate of growth of income in its markets and the income elasticity of demand (see Chapter 2), it can predict its potential sales growth in those markets.
- *New markets.* Data on growth of income in different countries helps businesses to identify potential new markets. Many international businesses clearly see that rapid economic growth in China will make it a major future market for a wide range of both consumers and capital goods.

- *Location decisions.* National income data may also help businesses to choose appropriate locations for production facilities. Businesses prefer to locate in prosperous and dynamic countries. However other data indicating the *competitiveness* of particular locations including costs, taxation levels, the exchange rate, may be more significant in these decisions.

For governments, national income data is particularly important since sound policy making requires plentiful and accurate information about what is happening in the economy. Thus detailed national income data is essential. However effective economic policy making requires not only the national income data itself, but also an understanding of the factors and processes which determine the level and growth of national income. These are analysed using the framework of the circular flow of income.

## 4.2 The determination of national income: the circular flow model

Note: In the circular flow model there is extensive use of symbols to represent variables in the model. The most important of these are as follows:

| | |
|---|---|
| Y | national income |
| C | consumption |
| S | savings |
| I | investment |
| T | taxation |
| G | government expenditure |
| X | exports |
| M | imports |

Also note that the terms *companies* and *firms* are used interchangeably.

### 4.2.1 The circular flow model

The circular flow model refers to the movement of money resulting from economic transactions between different groups of people in an economy. Although the real economy is clearly greatly more complicated than this model, it does make it possible to illustrate the main links between different parts of the economy.

A simple model can be devised to show the income flows. It assumes:

- a two-sector economy of firms and households
- there is no government and no overseas sector
- furthermore, all income is spent on consumption and all production is sold to the households.

In this model firms pay incomes to households who provide services (e.g. labour, entrepreneurship) to the firms. In turn households become the consumers of the firms' output. This in turn provides firms with the means to pay incomes to households. In effect the system is circular and the level of incomes and output would remain constant.

*Note:* In all of these models real things (goods, services and work) go in one direction, payment for these (consumption expenditure, wages) go in the opposite direction.

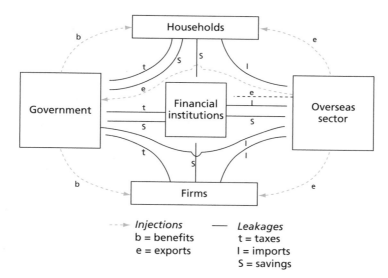

**Figure 4.1** Withdrawals and injections in a circular flow

Clearly more complex models can be devised (Figure 4.1).

- Households may save via financial institutions which may channel these savings to firms to finance investment.
- Governments tax incomes and may use these revenues either to purchase goods and services from the firms sector or to provide support incomes for certain households.
- International trade occurs. Exports will represent additional spending on the firm sector but imports will represent a diversion of spending away from the firm sector towards firms in other countries.

Therefore, when the simplifying assumptions are dropped and a more complex model is adopted, the circular flow becomes subject to *withdrawals* and *injections* out of and in to the circular flow of income.

- An injection (J) is any spending which is additional to the circular flow. It increases the level of income in the circular flow. The injections are:
  - business investment
  - government expenditure
  - exports.
- In contrast, a withdrawal (W) is some income which is not passed on as expenditure in the circular flow. It decreases the level of income in the circular flow. The withdrawals are:
  - savings
  - taxation
  - imports.

*Note*: Some textbooks refer to *withdrawals* as *leakages*. These terms have identical meanings.

## Equilibrium

An economy making full use of its resources will be moving towards a state of rest, or equilibrium. For equilibrium to be established in the circular flow, planned injections must equal planned withdrawals.

Equilibrium in national income is where

J (injections) = W (withdrawals)

Thus if:

- J > W, additions to the circular flow exceed withdrawals and so the level of national income will rise;
- J < W, additions to the circular flow are less than withdrawals so the level of national income will fall.

Thus the full condition for equilibrium in national income for an open economy is:

$$I + G + X = S + T + M$$

Where $I$ = investment
$G$ = government expenditure $\left.\right\}$ *injections*
$X$ = exports

And $S$ = savings
$T$ = taxation withdrawals $\left.\right\}$ *withdrawals*
$M$ = imports

It is not necessary that pairs of injections and withdrawals (such as imports and exports or taxation and government expenditure) are equal. Equilibrium only requires that the *sum* of injections is equal to the *sum* of withdrawals.

### 4.2.2 Consumption

The spending by people, or households on the circular flow model is termed *consumption*. The single most important determinant of the level of consumption is the level of income. This is true for both individuals and the economy as a whole. Thus the consumption function is written as:

$$C = f(Y)$$

(i.e. consumption is a function of national income.)

   Clearly since any income that is not spent on consumer goods is saved then it follows that:

$$S = f(Y)$$

and

$$Y = C + S$$

The consumption function is illustrated in Figure 4.2.

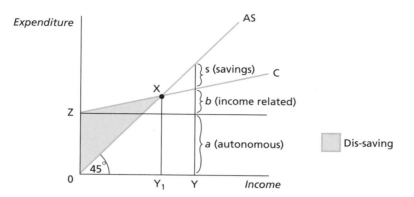

**Figure 4.2** The consumption function

The economist J.M. Keynes suggested that consumption can be seen to consist of two parts.

- *Autonomous* consumption does not vary with the level of income (denoted by *a* in Figure 4.2). For instance, someone with no income will need to consume goods and services in order to survive. This could be financed from savings. This action is known as *dis-saving*.
- *Non-autonomous* consumption varies with the level of income (denoted by *b* in Figure 4.2). Generally, as income rises so does consumption, with a tendency for a larger part of the extra income to be saved, rather than consumed, as a person becomes better off. The extent to which consumption changes with income is termed the *marginal propensity to consume (MPC)*.

The marginal propensity to consume is calculated by the formula:

$$\text{MPC} = \frac{\text{Change in consumption, } \Delta C}{\text{Change in income, } \Delta Y}$$

Thus, if a person's disposable income increases from \$100 to \$120 per week and her consumption increases from \$90 to \$105 per week, her MPC would be 0.75 (i.e. 15:20). The MPC varies considerably between economies, with some (e.g. Japan), having relatively low MPCs and some (e.g. the USA), having relatively high MPCs. Generally, it is assumed that the MPC is positive but likely to fall as income rises.

From these observations about autonomous and income-related consumption, Keynes devised an algebraic equation:

$$C = a + bY$$

This is again illustrated in Figure 4.2.

- The 45° line locates the points where income on the horizontal axis equals expenditure on the vertical axis.
- In Figure 4.2 at income Y a small proportion of income is saved. It is noticeable that if income were 0, there would be consumption of the autonomous amount funded by dis-saving.
- The triangle 0ZX shows that up to income level Y1, savings have to be utilised to finance consumption. However, beyond X, savings rise.

The slope of the consumption curve indicates the value of the marginal propensity to consume. If the MPC increased, the line CZ would be steeper. An increase in the MPC causes an increase in the average propensity to consume (APC). This term describes the proportion of disposable income which it is planned to consume. It is calculated by the formula:

$$APC = \frac{Consumption}{Income}$$

Thus, if a person spends $90 out of her disposable income of $100 then her APC is 0.9 (90/100). The APC for the British economy is positive and tends to fall as GDP rises. In Figure 4.2 the APC is more than 1.0 between 0 and Y1, equal to 1.0 at Y1 and less than 1.0 beyond Y1. In each case the MPC is lower than the APC.

In an economy, the consumption of goods and services is undertaken by households, companies and the government.

### Households

Factors influencing the level of household consumption are:

- *Income.* The Keynesian approach uses current income. Another possibility is that people's consumption is determined by their previous income or their expected future income.
- *Wealth.* At an individual level, an increase in wealth may raise MPC because less saving is needed. Conversely, at low income levels, wealth allows dis-saving, thereby pushing the APC above 1.0. In the economy as a whole, a more egalitarian wealth distribution is likely to raise consumption. The nature of wealth may also be significant; liquid wealth, such as savings under the bed, is likely to raise consumption, whereas illiquid wealth will probably have little effect on consumption.
- *Government policy.* By taxation and public spending, the government can influence the level (and pattern) of consumption. An increase in direct taxation lowers disposable incomes and thereby reduces the capacity for consumption. Alternatively, higher government spending, particularly on state benefits, raises incomes and stimulates consumption.
- *The cost and availability of credit.* The cheaper the cost (the rate of interest) and the greater the availability of credit, the more likely it is that consumption will occur. Credit is particularly influential when consumer durables are purchased. The United Kingdom has high levels of consumption financed by credit partly because of the wide range and sophistication of the credit instruments available.
- *Price expectations.* In certain circumstances, when price rises are anticipated, consumption might be brought forward. This temporarily raises MPC.

These factors can be described as 'objective' influences. In contrast, there are 'subjective' influences which determine individual behaviour, irrespective of the other factors. For instance, some cultures encourage high levels of savings (e.g. Japan). It is also usually argued that consumption by individuals in urban areas is higher than in rural areas.

### Companies

The consumption undertaken by companies is determined by very similar factors. Their income is mainly sales revenue and borrowing and it can be boosted from accumulated reserves. Government tax and spending policies will influence sales revenue while the rate of interest and credit availability will affect borrowing policies.

### Government

The government's consumption of goods and services is less determined by its income and more determined by need and political preference. Government expenditure can be divided into two categories:

- Transfer payments such as social security payments and pensions which are not normally counted as government consumption as this would involve double counting when the recipients (e.g. pensions) spent their pensions on consumer goods.
- Government consumption such as expenditure on salaries of government employees, and goods and services used in public services such as education, health and defence.

In virtually all economies households' spending on consumption accounts for the largest proportion, typically about two-thirds, of all domestic expenditure. The rest is split mainly between government consumption and investment.

## 4.2.3  Saving

Saving is defined as the amount of income not spent. It is therefore sometimes regarded as a residual; the amount of income left after consumption has been determined. Thus the factors determining saving are mainly the mirror image of the factors determining consumption.

Thus the factors influencing saving are as follows.

- *Income.* Both for the individual and the economy, the level of saving is determined mainly by income. The average propensity to save (APS) is the proportion of disposable income which is saved. It is calculated by saving divided by income. When the person in the earlier example consumed £90 of her £100 income, her APS was 0.1 (10/100). The APS added to the APC always equals unity (1.0) in the Keynesian model. The APS is negative (dis-saving) at low income levels. In Figure 4.2, the APS is negative up to Y1 and then positive and increasing.
- *Interest rates.* In theory, an increase in the rate of interest will mean that people need to save less in order to achieve a given target of income earned in interest. However, this income effect can be offset by the substitution effect. With higher interest rates, people might save more and spend less, as saving is now more attractive.
- *Inflation.* However, to rational consumers the money rate of interest is less important than the real interest rate (i.e. allowing for inflation). Even if the nominal rate of interest is high, a low real rate of interest might discourage savings. However, consumers might suffer from the *money illusion* and save more when nominal interest rates are high even if inflation reduces the real rate of interest.
- *Credit.* When credit is easily available consumers might acquire as much credit as they are saving; in effect there is no net saving. In some countries, notably the USA and the United Kingdom, the expansion of credit in recent years has meant that net household savings rates have fallen to historic lows.
- *Contractual savings.* Most household saving is contractual and regular such as payments into pension schemes. As the need to finance pensions increases, especially in developed economies with ageing economies, this form of saving is expected to increase.

Most saving is undertaken by households and the company sector. Governments save when they run budget surpluses and dis-save when they run budget deficits. The savings deficits of any one sector of the economy have to be financed by the saving of other sectors. Thus if the company sector plans to invest more than it is saving, it will have to borrow from other sectors which are net savers. This raises the question of what determines the level of investment in the economy.

### 4.2.4 Investment

Expenditure on investment covers:

- fixed capital formation (e.g. plant, machinery, roads, houses);
- the value of the physical increase in stocks of raw materials, work in progress and finished goods.

Investment is undertaken by the public sector and the private sector (the latter featuring firms and households) and it enhances the capacity of the economy.

- The capital stock of the economy is increased by the amount of net investment undertaken each year.
- Net investment is the difference between gross (total) investment and replacement investment (capital consumption), which accounts for the deterioration of the existing capital equipment stock.

In Figure 4.3, investment is shown as constant, being autonomously determined and not related to national income levels.

- Saving has been added as a separate function and equal to investment at the equilibrium level of national income $Y_e$.
- In the absence of a government sector, the curve C + I represents the total demand for goods and service. This is known as aggregate demand or aggregate monetary demand (AMD). The 45° can be regarded as indicating the ability of the economy to produce output: aggregate supply (AS).

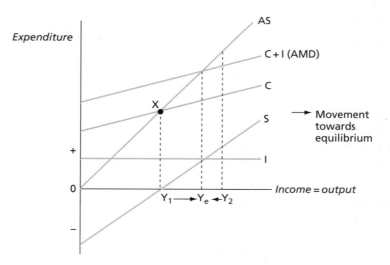

**Figure 4.3** Equilibrium national income

- The economy will be in equilibrium at $Y_e$ where aggregate demand and aggregate supply are equal.
- At $Y_1$ the economy would be in dis-equilibrium because the planned expenditure of firms and consumers (AMD) exceeds the planned output (AS).
- Equilibrium would be restored because the higher demand would produce higher output until the equilibrium position of $Y_e$ is reached.

At the equilibrium level of income $Y_e$, savings and investment are equal. In the absence of a government or international trade, saving is the only withdrawal and investment is the only injection. At $Y_1$, investment exceeds savings thus injections exceed withdrawals and national income rises to reach the equilibrium level of $Y_e$.

### The determinants of investment

The simple Keynesian model in Figure 4.3 has investment as a constant amount, which is clearly unrealistic. The general determinants of private investment by firms are:

- expectations about future profit flows; these expectations will be influenced by the anticipated revenue from the output of the investment compared with the anticipated costs of the investment.
- the current valuation which the firms place on the likely future profits, that is the opportunity cost of the investment.

Both of these determinants are incorporated in two very similar theories of investment discussed below.

### Discounted cash flow

A firm is concerned with the *net rate of return* from its investment. The main factors determining this are the expected revenue when the output is sold and the estimated operating costs. If the former does not exceed the latter, then the investment will not be undertaken.

The *rate of interest* is also crucial. If the funds to be used for investment could earn interest elsewhere, this interest is forgone when the investment is undertaken. Thus, the income stream which the investment generates needs to be reduced (discounted) to a present value (PV) so that the net return can be compared with the supply price of the investment. The cash flow which the investment generates is therefore discounted. If the present value of this discounted cash flow exceeds the supply price (current cost of the investment), then net present value is positive and the investment is likely to be profitable. Clearly the higher the rate of interest, the lower the present value of the investment. Details of the calculation of net present value can be found in Section 1.5.2.

### Marginal efficiency of capital

This investment theory is associated with Keynes. It differs from discounted cash flow in that the necessary rate of interest needed to make the present value of the income stream equal to the supply price is calculated. This rate of discount is termed the marginal efficiency of capital (MEC). If the MEC exceeds the current rate of interest then the investment will be profitable.

*The shape/slope of the MEC curve.* The marginal efficiency of capital can be represented diagrammatically. In Figure 4.4, at a high rate of interest the amount of investment is lower than at a low rate of interest, because MEC needs to be higher. This in turn means that expected returns on the investment need to be greater. The MEC is relatively interest

THE MACROECONOMIC CONTEXT OF BUSINESS

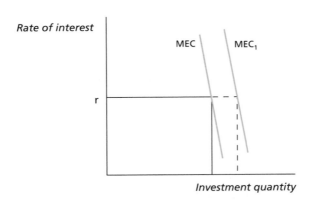

**Figure 4.4** The marginal efficiency of capital

inelastic in Figure 4.4, suggesting that the rate of interest is a relatively unimportant influence on investment decision-making. For instance, with long-term projects the rate of interest may vary frequently and so other factors will take precedence.

*Shifts in the MEC curve.* The expected yield probably carries more importance than the rate of interest. There are several factors which determine its value:

- *The state of business confidence.* If businesses are optimistic, they are likely to expect greater returns than if they are pessimistic. Thus changes in business confidence can push MEC to the right as shown in Figure 4.4.
- *The substitution of other factors.* If wages costs rise, then capital may be substituted thereby shifting MEC to the right. Similarly, if the cost of capital falls, then MEC will shift to the right, as the profitability of the project will increase.
- *Technological innovation.* If capital becomes more productive this is likely to raise the level of investment at any given rate of interest. This will also push MEC to the right.
- *Government policy.* Inconsistent and varying economic policies might increase business uncertainty and thereby deter investment. In contrast, reductions in corporation tax and improved tax allowances will increase the expected income stream and encourage investment. Also changes in interest rates will have direct effects on the profitability of investment.

## 4.2.5 The government and external sectors

The factors determining the level of government expenditure and taxation and the main influences on the balance of imports and exports will be discussed in later sections.

## 4.2.6 The accelerator

One of the features of the working of economies is that there may be important interactions between elements of the circular flow of income. One of these interactions is the way in which investment intentions may be affected by changes in the level of output and income in the economy. This is known as the *accelerator theory.*

Accelerator theory assumes that:

- firms will try to maintain a stable relationship between the amount of productive capital stock (e.g. machinery) and the expected volume of output/sales, this is known as the *capital/output ratio.*

- firms will replace worn out capital each year, this is known as *replacement investment.*
- total investment will be replacement investment plus additional investment to meet expected increases in demand/sales.

Thus if a firm replaces 10 per cent of its capital each year in the form of replacement capital but expects no growth in sales there will be no additional investment and so total investment will be equal to replacement investment. However, if in the following year the firm expects sales to rise in one year by 10 per cent, it would need to expand its total capital stock by 10 per cent in order to match productive capacity to expected sales. In this year total investment by the firm will therefore be equal to 10 per cent of its capital stock as replacement capital and 10 per cent of its capital stock as additional investment. Thus total investment expenditure will be double that of the previous year.

In this example the volume of investment is raised by expected changes in the level of income and thus expected sales. But the change in investment in this example is greater (100 per cent increase) than the change in income and sales (10 per cent). The same would work in reverse if sales were expected to fall. Thus change in income and sales produces a greater (*accelerated*) effect on investment spending.

### 4.2.7 The multiplier

This idea shows the change in national income resulting from a change in planned investment (in the simple model) or a change in government spending or a change in the overseas trade sector (in the five sector model of Figure 4.1). It looks at the effect of injections (less withdrawals) into the circular flow of income.

The simple Keynesian model featured earlier in this chapter can be extended to include a government sector and an overseas sector. Government spending (G) is usually added to consumption (C) and investment (I) to give aggregate monetary demand (AMD). Changes in injections, government expenditure, investment and exports may cause a more than proportional increase in national income. This is termed the *multiplier effect.*

Multiplier effects can occur in many ways. When any planned injection into the circular flow increases and other injections and withdrawals remain unchanged, then national income will lead to the use of more factors of production whose earnings will be spent, thereby adding to the income of others who may then spend more, and so on. . . . Thus an initial injection of additional expenditure in the circular flow will lead to a series of additional rounds of expenditure.

#### Determinants of the multiplier

*A simple economy*

The increase in national income caused by successive rounds of spending will not go on for ever since with each round some extra income will be lost to the circular flow through the operation of *withdrawals.* Thus each succeeding round of spending becomes smaller and smaller. If withdrawals were 20 per cent of income (e.g. a marginal propensity to save of 0.2) the increases in income in each round from an initial increase in spending of $100 would be:

|         |         |                                      |
|---------|---------|--------------------------------------|
| *Round 1* | *$100* |                                      |
| *Round 2* | *$80*  | *($100 minus $20 which is saved)*    |
| *Round 3* | *$64*  | *($80 minus $16 which is saved)*     |
| *Round 4* | *$51.2* | *($64 minus $12.8 which is saved)*   |

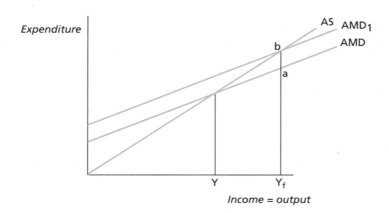

**Figure 4.5** The multiplier

In a simple economy the obvious withdrawal is saving. In this simple economy, with no government and no external sector, the value of the multiplier ($K$) is shown in the following equation.

$$K = \frac{1}{1 - \text{MPC}} = \frac{1}{\text{MPS}}$$

where    MPC    marginal propensity to consume
           MPS    marginal propensity to save.

If one assumed an MPC of 0.8 the multiplier would have a value of 5 and an increased injection of $10 m would increase total national income by $50 m. This is important for government policy making. If the economy was operating at below the full employment level of income (at $Y$ rather than at $Y_f$ in Figure 4.5), the government could increase its own expenditure to raise aggregate monetary demand from AMD to AMD1. As a result, the equilibrium national income would rise by a larger amount (from $Y$ to $Y_f$) through the operation of the multiplier.

*A real economy*

In a real economy, because of the existence of the government and an external sector, savings is not the only withdrawal. In this economy there are three withdrawals: savings, taxation and imports. Since withdrawals reduce the value of the multiplier, in the real world it will have a much lower value than that in the example above.

In the case of the economy with a government and an external sector, the value of the multiplier is now given as:

$$K = \frac{1}{\text{MPS} + \text{MRT} + \text{MPM}}$$

Where    MPS       marginal propensity to save
           MPT       marginal rate of taxation
           MPM       marginal propensity to import.

Thus if there is a high savings rate, a high marginal rate of taxation and an open economy with a high tendency to import, the value of the multiplier will be very low. For typical developed market economies the value of the multiplier is below 2.

## Policy making and the multiplier

It is clear that if a government wishes to engage in some form of *demand management* policy, that is using its levels of taxation and expenditure to influence the level of AMD and hence the level of national income, it will need to have some knowledge of the working of the multiplier and its value in their economy.

The government will also need to be aware that the value of the multiplier can vary not only over time as savings rates and the propensity to import changes, but also between government policy instruments.

- Expenditure tends to have a higher multiplier value than tax cuts since in the first round all public expenditure is 'spent' but some of the tax cuts may be saved.
- Some expenditure has immediate spending effects (e.g. increased pensions) whereas some (e.g. long-term investment projects) may only have their full effect over a period of years.
- Some economist (including monetarist and new classical economists) argue that the multiplier value of government expenditure is zero since an increase has to be financed via government borrowing from the private sector which 'crowds out' an equivalent amount of private expenditure.

## 4.3 The trade cycle and the problems of inflation and unemployment

The common economic issues facing all economies include the twin problems of inflation and unemployment. Much government economic policy effort is devoted to attempts to prevent either of these undesirable outcomes. In order to understand these economic policies it is first necessary to see how unemployment and inflation might arise in a market economy. The starting point for this understanding is the aggregate demand and aggregate supply model.

### 4.3.1 The aggregate demand and aggregate supply model

The circular flow model discussed in Section 4.2 showed how the total demand for goods and services in the economy was made up of several elements: consumption, investment, government expenditure and net exports (i.e. exports minus imports). Together these made up aggregate monetary demand or simply just aggregate demand (AD). However, an understanding of how the economy functions and why problems may occur cannot be explained solely in terms of the demand for goods and services; we also need to know about the ability of the economy to produce goods and services. This is known as aggregate supply (AS).

### Aggregate demand (AD)

In the circular flow model, AMD was related to the level of national income and the level of expenditure; in the aggregate demand and supply model, it is related to national income and to the price level. This makes possible a discussion of the origin of both unemployment and inflation. It is assumed that aggregate demand

- is made up of all components of expenditure in the economy, consumption, investment, government expenditure and net exports;

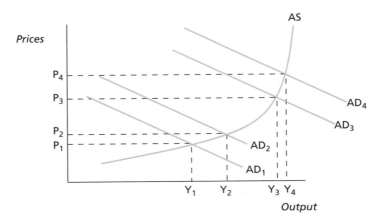

**Figure 4.6** The aggregate demand and supply model

- is inversely related to prices since a price fall would raise everyone's real (purchasing power) wealth and thus tend to raise spending;
- may shift if any one component (e.g. investment or exports) changes through the multiplier effect.

Thus the AD curve slopes down from left to right but may shift. This can be seen in Figure 4.6.

### Aggregate supply (AS)

The aggregate supply in an economy refers to the willingness and ability of producers in an economy, largely the business sector, to produce and offer for sale, goods and services. It is assumed that aggregate supply

- is the collective result of decisions made by millions of business producers, large and small to produce and sell goods and services;
- is positively related to the price level since, other things being equal, a rise in the price level will make sales more profitable and thus encourage businesses to expand output;
- is limited by the availability of resources (labour, capital, etc.) so that at full employment, output cannot be increased any further;
- can only shift in the long run as the result of a change in the costs of production or in the availability of factors of production.

Thus the AS curve slopes upward from left to right and does not shift in the short run. This is shown in Figure 4.6.

### The aggregate demand and aggregate supply model

In Figure 4.6, national equilibrium will be where the aggregate demand (AD) curve intersects with the aggregate supply (AS) curve; here the total demand for goods and services in the economy is equal to the total supply of goods and services in the economy. The particular value of this model is that it demonstrates the effect of changes in either aggregate demand or aggregate supply on both the level of national income and on the price level. Given the reasonable assumption that the level of employment in an economy in the short to medium run is a function of the level of national income, the model can show how inflation and unemployment might arise in an economy and how governments might respond to these problems.

## Changes in aggregate demand

*Example 1* Suppose that the economy is initially in equilibrium at a level of national income and employment denoted by $Y_1$. If there was an increase in aggregate demand from $AD_1$ to $AD_2$

- the new equilibrium would be at national income level $Y_2$;
- national income would have risen from $Y_1$ to $Y_2$ and unemployment would have fallen;
- the price level would have risen from $P_1$ to $P_2$.

In this case most of the effect of an increase in AD is felt in the form of rising income and employment and there is only a small inflationary impact. Thus in this case, if the government wished to reduce unemployment an expansion of AD by reducing taxes or by raising government expenditure would be an appropriate and effective policy.

*Example 2* Suppose that the economy is initially in equilibrium at a level of national income and employment denoted by $Y_3$. If there was an increase in aggregate demand from $AD_3$ to $AD_4$

- the new equilibrium would be at national income level $Y_4$;
- national income would have risen from $Y_3$ to $Y_4$ and unemployment would have fallen;
- the price level would have risen from $P_3$ to $P_4$.

In this case most of the effect of an increase in AD is felt in the form of a rise in the price level and there is only a small effect in raising national income and reducing unemployment. Thus in this case if the government attempted to further reduce unemployment by expanding AD the effect would be very small and the price would be a significant increase in inflationary pressure. Indeed, at this point the AS curve becomes very steep because the economy is approaching full employment; a more appropriate policy for government here might be to restrain AD by raising taxes and reducing government expenditure thus shifting aggregate demand from $AD_4$ to $AD_3$.

Of course, shifts in the AD curve may occur for reasons other than government policy. A recession, characterized by falling output and employment and reduced inflationary pressure will result from a leftward movement in the AD curve caused by, among other things,

- a fall in investment if business confidence is damaged;
- a fall in consumer expenditure if consumers lose confidence or if they reach the limits of their ability to finance extra credit;
- a fall in exports if there is a major loss of competitiveness or there is a recession in the country's major trading partners.

In 2009 this was indeed the experience of many developed economies, as declining consumer and business confidence led to falling aggregate demand and contracting national income. The result was a serious recession affecting much of the world economy.

Likewise, the economy may expand and experience a period of business boom characterised by rising output and employment and increasing inflationary pressures conditions if there is a rightward movement in the AD caused by, among other things,

- an investment boom if business is confident and profitable;
- a rapid rise in consumer expenditure if consumers are confident and have access to affordable credit;
- a rapid rise in exports if there is a major gain in competitiveness (e.g. from a depreciation of the currency) or there is a boom in the country's major trading partners.

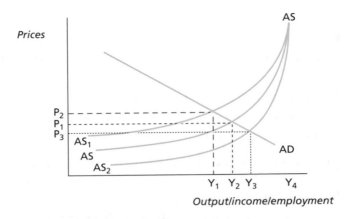

**Figure 4.7**   Changes in aggregate supply

## Changes in aggregate supply

It is also possible that, in the long run, the aggregate supply in the economy might change. This is shown in Figure 4.7 as shifts in the aggregate supply curve.

*Example 1* The economy might suffer from *supply-side shocks* which reduce the ability or willingness of productive businesses in the economy to produce and sell goods and services. If this occurred the AS would shift to the left, for example, from AS to $AS_1$. The result would be a rise in the price level from $P_1$ to $P_2$ and a fall in output from $Y_2$ to $Y_1$. This combination of falling output and rising inflation is sometimes referred to as *stagflation*. Such supply-side shocks might arise from:

- a major rise in energy and/or raw material prices such as the oil price rises in the 1970s and early 1980s;
- a major rise in labour costs; the problems of many of the European Union larger economies in past years may be partly the result of social and labour legislation significantly raising the cost of labour for businesses;
- a significant fall in productivity in businesses due to major technological problems; some fear that attempting to deal with global warming by emissions controls may have something of this effect on economies.

*Example 2* The economy might also experience a rightward shift in the AS curve such as from AS to $AS_2$. This would produce a highly beneficial result that national income and employment would expand from $Y_2$ to $Y_3$ and the price level would fall from $P_1$ to $P_3$. This might be seen as the opposite of stagflation. Such shifts to the right in the aggregate supply curve might arise from:

- favourable developments in the economy reducing costs such as falling energy and raw material prices or big productivity improvements from technological change;
- deliberate government *supply-side policies* designed to shift the AS curve to the right such as privatisation, business tax reductions or labour market reforms.

### Box 4.1   Oil, unemployment and inflation

The oil crises of the 1970s and governments' responses to it illustrate the aggregate demand and supply model well. The steep rise in oil prices was a supply-side shock to oil importing countries. Production costs across economies rose steeply and this was the equivalent of a sharp shift in the aggregate supply curve to the left; the consequence was a rise in unemployment and a sharp acceleration in the rate of inflation. Governments, fearful of the social and electoral consequences of high unemployment initially attempted to reduce unemployment by expansionary fiscal policy – in effect shifting the aggregate demand curve to the right. This reduced unemployment somewhat but resulted in a further sharp increase in inflation. Slow growth, unemployment and inflation were thus combined: stagflation had been born. By the 1990s some governments, notably in the United Kingdom and the USA accepted the importance of supply-side policy to shift the aggregate supply curve to the right. The result was a decade of steady growth and low unemployment without serious inflationary pressure.

However, in 2007/2008 upward pressure on energy and commodity prices, caused partly by the rapid growth of China and India and partly by the possible peaking of world oil output, threatened to lead to a repetition of the problems of the 1970s. The threat receded only when world recessionary forces led to major falls in oil and commodity prices.

## The trade cycle and government policy

Aggregate demand and supply analysis has shown how the trade cycle of recessions, recoveries and booms followed by further recession might occur and how government policy might be used to deal with these problems. Table 4.3 shows the typical features, causes and policy responses for the trade cycle in market economies.

Of course there might be a period of economic growth with all the features of a boom but without undue inflationary pressure, if the aggregate supply of the economy continually increases. The ability of some economies such as the United Kingdom and the USA to maintain steady growth with high levels of employment but without serious inflationary

**Table 4.3**  The trade cycle

| Stage of trade cycle | Features | Causes | Policy response |
|---|---|---|---|
| Recession | falling output/income, high and rising unemployment, reduced inflationary pressure, improving trade balance as imports fall | falling AD from lower levels of: consumer spending, investment, exports, government expenditure | raise AD by reducing taxation, raising public expenditure, lowering interest rates |
| Stagflation: special type of recession | falling output, income and employment, rising inflationary pressure | supply-side shocks reducing aggregate supply | supply-side policy to raise aggregate supply |
| Recovery | output and income begin to rise, unemployment begins to fall, only moderate inflationary pressure | returning confidence in business and consumer sectors, effect of government expansionary policy undertaken in recession | reduction in expansionary policy to prevent too strong a boom |
| Boom | high output and employment, rising inflationary pressure, deteriorating trade balance as imports rise | high and rising AD from higher levels of: consumer spending, investment, exports, government expenditure | reduce AD by raising taxation, reducing public expenditure, higher interest rates |

THE MACROECONOMIC CONTEXT OF BUSINESS

pressures in recent years may have been, at least partly, the result of supply-side reforms in these countries since the 1980s.

 ## Exercise 4.1

Answer the following questions based on the preceding information. You can check your answers below.

1. Name two withdrawals from the circular flow.
2. What is an injection into the circular flow?
3. When, in theory, is an economy in equilibrium?
4. What does the consumption function show?
5. What does the equation 'C = a + bY' mean?
6. Apart from households and firms, what else is a major consumer of goods and services?
7. Define net investment.
8. What does the accelerator theory show?
9. What does the multiplier show?
10. What is the formula for calculating the multiplier, $K$?

## Solutions

1. Withdrawals from the circular flow are savings, taxes and imports.
2. An injection into the circular flow is any additional expenditure that does not arise from the circular flow of income itself.
3. At equilibrium, injections and withdrawals are equal.
4. The consumption function shows how the level of consumption changes as the level of income changes.
5. This means that there is some consumption that is independent of the level of income (a) (autonomous consumption) and some which is a proportion of and determined by income received (bY).
6. There are two other major consumers of goods and services: the government and overseas consumers (via exports).
7. Net investment is the volume of investment in capital goods over and above that required to replace worn-out capital, that is depreciation.
8. The accelerator theory shows that changes in consumption expenditure may induce much larger proportional changes in investment expenditure and thereby contribute to the trade cycle.
9. The multiplier shows that an increase in expenditure (e.g. investment, government expenditure or exports) will produce a much larger increase in total income and expenditure through successive rounds of spending.
10. The multiplier can be calculated as $K = 1/(1 - \text{MPC})$ where MPC is the marginal propensity to consume.

## 4.4 The objectives of government economic policy: inflation and unemployment

### 4.4.1 Causes of inflation

Inflation can be explained in various ways. The three main causes usually identified are discussed below.

## Demand-pull inflation

This term is used when increases in aggregate demand pull up prices because supply is constant or very inelastic. Supply may have been constrained by a lack of capacity in the economy, or insufficient trained labour, or lack of capital investment.

The underlying causes of significant increases in demand may be:

- *Fiscal.* If a government relaxes its fiscal stance and/or runs a large budget deficit, then total demand in the economy is stimulated. For example, a cut in income tax rates will increase spending power, thereby raising AMD, and have a multiplier effect on the economy. This will stimulate employment, but if supply is relatively inelastic only some of the extra spending will be translated into output and most of the effect will be in rising prices. Increases in government spending, other things being equal, have a similar effect.
- *Changes in monetary conditions.* When extra credit is available to consumers, spending on goods and services will also increase, with the same likely effects on output and prices. The credit may be made available by the banks and other financial institutions primarily, but the growth of store credit cards in recent years has added a new source of consumer credit. In contrast, the rise in interest rates in 2006/2007 and the difficult credit conditions arising from problems in the US sub-prime mortgage market, was expected to eventually lead to a decline in demand pull inflationary pressures.

## Cost-push inflation

Cost push inflation occurs when production costs rise as a result of factors independent of the level of aggregate demand in the economy. These factors are referred to as *exogenous* (from outside the system) rather than *endogenous* (from inside the system). Such exogenous factors leading to cost push inflation may include:

- Increased trade union power leading to wage rises occurring irrespective of the demand for labour.
- Rises in indirect taxes, such as VAT, where much of the burden of the tax is passed onto consumers in the form of higher prices.
- Rising prices of imported energy and raw materials, especially for open economies with a high dependence on such imports.
- Depreciation of the currency (a fall in the exchange rate) which raises the price of imports in terms of the domestic currency.

It should be noted that some economists, notably *monetarists*, deny that cost push inflation can ever occur; for them, all inflation is a monetary phenomenon caused by excessive demand when the money supply expands too rapidly.

## Quantity theory of money

Demand pull and cost push were essentially Keynesian explanations of inflation. However, monetarists reject the idea of cost-push inflation, believing that inflation is caused by increases in the *money supply* leading to excess demand for goods and services. In their view, changes in the money supply affect prices but not output and employment, except in the short run.

Monetarism is based on the *quantity theory of money.* The volume of expenditure in an economy over a period of time can be identified in two ways.

1. It is the medium of exchange used to buy the output produced ($M$) multiplied by its velocity of circulation ($V$). The velocity of circulation measures the average number of times that the money is used each year.
2. Also, the volume of expenditure is calculated on real value of national income ($Y$) multiplied by the average price of each sale ($P$).

This can be written as $MV = PY$ since national expenditure must be equal to national income. The significance of this depends on the assumptions made by monetarist economists. These are:

- $V$ is constant and/or predictable. $V$ is not determined by money supply and it is unchanging in the short run;
- $Y$ is constant as total output is fixed in the short run, at full employment.

Given these assumptions, $V$ and $Y$ are constants and thus the quantity theory can be rewritten as:

$$P = f(m)$$

That is, any changes in the supply of money ($M$) will lead to changes in the level of prices ($P$); if the money supply increases, inflation will be the result.

In contrast, Keynesians do not accept that the velocity of circulation ($V$) is fixed, or that the level of real national income ($Y$) is fixed, even in the short run. Thus, for Keynesians, the relationship between the money supply and inflation is more complex.

## 4.4.2 The effects of inflation

If the rate of inflation is low then the effects may be beneficial to an economy. Business people are encouraged by fairly stable prices and the prospect of higher profits. However, there is some argument about whether getting inflation below 3 per cent to, say, zero is worth the economic pain (of, say, higher unemployment). There is agreement, though, that inflation above about 5 per cent is harmful – worse still if it is accelerating. The main arguments are that such inflation:

- *Distorts consumer behaviour.* People may bring forward purchases because they fear higher prices later. This can cause hoarding and so destabilise markets.
- *Redistributes income.* People on fixed incomes or those lacking bargaining power will become relatively worse off, as their purchasing power falls. This is unfair.
- *Redistributes wealth.* The real value of debts and financial assets is eroded by inflation. Thus wealth is redistributed away from those with net financial assets towards those with debts.
- *Affects wage bargainers.* Trade unionists on behalf of labour may submit higher claims at times of high inflation, particularly if previously they had underestimated the future rise in prices. If employers accept such claims this may precipitate a wage-price spiral which exacerbates the inflation problem.
- *Undermines business confidence.* Wide fluctuations in inflation make it difficult for entrepreneurs to predict the economic future and accurately calculate prices and investment returns. This uncertainty handicaps planning and production.
- *Weakens the external competitive position.* If a country's inflation exceeds its competitors then it makes exports less attractive (assuming unchanged exchange rates) and imports more competitive. This could mean a bigger trade deficit.

It is thus clear that the disadvantages of inflation, especially if it is rapid and/or unpredictable, outweigh any benefits that might occur. Thus governments almost always have the prevention of inflation as a major policy objective.

### 4.4.3 The causes of unemployment

Although it is the cause of unemployment that is closely linked to the characteristics of unemployment, it is useful to distinguish between *types* of unemployment and the *causes* of unemployment. The main types of unemployment are as follows.

#### Types of unemployment

##### Seasonal unemployment

Some occupations experience large fluctuations in demand for their service during a year.

- For instance, agricultural labourers will be needed less in the winter months, whereas ski instructors will not be required much in the summer.
- Such seasonal unemployment is less of an economic problem nowadays because of changes in employment legislation, the increased use of part-time staff and improved storage and freezing facilities which enable production in many industries to be continuous.
- The published unemployment statistics are seasonally adjusted to reduce the impact of seasonal unemployment and school leaving dates.

##### Frictional (search) unemployment

There is sometimes a transition period between a worker leaving one job and starting another.

- This indicates the imperfections in the labour market, such as lack of knowledge of available job opportunities, the geographical immobility of labour and the mismatch between the requirements of the employers and the available skills of the unemployed.
- If the unemployed are successful in searching for jobs, then unfilled vacancies will fall and frictional unemployment will decline. A relatively small and unchanging number of vacancies in the an economy indicates that there is little frictional unemployment at present.

##### Structural unemployment

When there are significant long-term changes in the pattern of demand and techniques of supply in an economy, then unemployment occurs in many parts of the labour market. If those becoming unemployed lack the skills to take up the job vacancies, because the industrial structure has changed, then the average duration of unemployment increases and temporary frictional unemployment becomes permanent structural unemployment. Structural unemployment may result from:

- *A fall in demand for a good or service* (e.g. the use of plastic instead of steel has reduced the demand for steel workers permanently). The wholesale decline in heavy industry in Europe and the United States (de-industrialisation) has created much of this type of unemployment. As some of these industries were localised in particular areas, the unemployment may be regionally concentrated and regional unemployment arises
- *Changes in production methods.* The installation of capital equipment may cause less demand for labour which, without retraining, will remain unemployed. For instance,

new technology used in printing produced unemployment, even though the industry was expanding. This has been termed *technological unemployment* because the and has largely affected manufacturing industry, with the service industries remaining largely unscathed because of the personal attention often needed. For instance, the impact of information technology on the United Kingdom financial services industry was to expand business by 8 per cent annually in 1975–85 and increase employment by 2 per cent annually. This indicated labour saving but not to the detriment of employment.

### Cyclical unemployment (demand deficient unemployment)

The trade cycle creates variations in demand in the economy. Assuming that the demand for goods/services and the demand for labour are positively related, a boom in the economy will probably lower unemployment while a slump will raise unemployment.

- These changes will probably affect most industries, and they occur in cycles. Hence the words 'general' and 'cyclical' have been used to describe the extra unemployment occurring in a slump or recession such as those of the 1930s and 1980s.
- Keynes used the phrase 'demand deficient unemployment' to explain the same phenomenon because he argued that the cause was insufficient aggregate demand and that extra demand could be created by a government through deficit budgeting.

Some economies are susceptible to cyclical unemployment because they are open economies and dependent on world trade. Thus a decline in world trade, as occurred in 1979–80, adversely affected exports with domestic unemployment repercussions. In this way recessions in other one part of the world may be communicated to other economies.

### Voluntary unemployment (real wage unemployment)

This unemployment has been defined following the work of the monetarist school of economics. It is said to occur when people are unwilling to work at existing wage rates. Some argue that relatively high levels of income support deter the unemployed from seeking jobs because the gain in income may be marginal. In contrast, workers are involuntarily unemployed when they would be willing to accept a job but there are no vacancies for what they can do.

## Causes of unemployment

### Demand deficiency

Lack of demand for goods and services causes workers to be laid off. Usually unemployment follows a fall in economic activity, with a lag of 12–18 months. A fall in aggregate demand below the level required for full employment may result from a fall in:

- *Consumer expenditure.* Unemployment in Japan in recent decades has been blamed on the unwillingness of Japanese consumers to increase their consumption levels, preferring to maintain very high savings ratios.
- *Business investment.* A decline in business confidence might lead to lower investment thus reducing aggregate monetary demand.
- *Exports.* Net exports may decline if there is a loss of competitiveness or if there is a world recession. The great depression of the 1930s had its origins in the USA but was communicated to the rest of the world via declining exports to the USA.
- *Government expenditure.* Attempts to reduce in government expenditure in the 1980s probably made the recession in the United Kingdom worse and unemployment higher.

In 2008/2009, faced with severe deflationary pressures leading to rising unemployment, many countries adopted expansionary fiscal and monetary policies in order to reduce the extent of demand deficient unemployment.

### Structural change

Structural change in economies occurs all the time. However sometimes this change is particularly rapid and thus structural unemployment is likely to arise. This may occur because of:

- *Rapid technological change.* If there are major technological changes which have widespread effects, such as the advent of stream power in the 19th century and the impact of the computer at the end of the 20th century, the demand for labour may change radically leaving significant groups unemployed.
- *Shifts in world industry.* Major changes in the structure of world industry may occur. The rapid growth of manufacturing in Asian economies, especially China and India, is threatening to generate structural unemployment in Europe and North America where such activity declines in the face of cheap imports.

Of course, structural change is rarely permanent; as some industries decline, others develop to take their place. Thus in Western economies the growth of service activities has helped to cushion the effect on employment of the decline of older manufacturing industry.

### Supply-side problems

Problems on the supply side of the economy may cause unemployment. If there is a shift in the aggregate supply (AS) curve to the left, national income will be in equilibrium at a lower level implying a higher rate of unemployment. The most important supply-side factors in this context are those operating in the labour market. Any feature of the labour market which raises the cost of employing workers may result in unemployment.

- *Trade unions.* It is argued that strong trade unions can cause unemployment by pushing for and obtaining wage rises for their members, they may reduce the willingness of their employers to replace people who leave and/or to take on new recruits. Also by resisting improvements in efficiency, trade unions might contribute to rising costs and prices which produce lower sales and less employment. The maintenance of established working practices, rigid demarcation and closed shops have been cited as barriers put up by trade unions to protect the short-term interests of their members. These barriers create imperfections in the labour market and are claimed to be detrimental to employment in the long run.
- *Labour market regulation.* Labour laws especially concerning the rights of workers in terms of conditions of employment, redundancy, working hours, sickness and holiday entitlements may raise the cost of employing workers.
- *Social security systems.* Generous social security benefits for the unemployed may encourage voluntary unemployment. In extreme cases there may a 'poverty trap' where some workers are better off being unemployed than working in low paid jobs.

It is possible that shifts in the aggregate supply (AS) curve to the left causing unemployment may arise from factors other than the labour market. For open economies, import prices may be a source of unemployment. An example of this is energy prices. A steep rise in energy prices would raise production costs generally in the economy thus shifting the AS curve to the left and leading to unemployment. Figure 4.8 shows a fairly consistent relationship between oil prices and unemployment in OECD economies over the last 40 years.

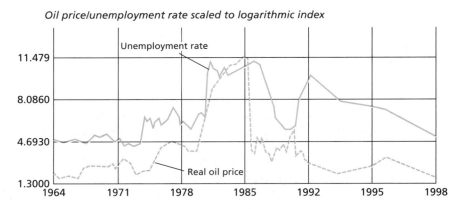

**Figure 4.8** Oil and unemployment

## 4.4.4 The effects of unemployment

There are economic, social, financial and political costs of unemployment.

- *Economic* resources are not being fully used and the opportunity cost of unemployment is the goods and services not produced as a result. Long-term economic capacity might be damaged as unemployed labour loses skills and is unable to acquire new skills and experience.
- *Financial* costs arise for the government and hence the taxpayer. The unemployed pay less in tax and have to be supported by state benefits.
- *Social* costs arise out of the impact on the unemployed themselves. The unemployed tend to experience more mental and physical health problems and there is a clear link between the level of unemployment and the level of crime.

## 4.4.5 The relationship between inflation and unemployment

### The Phillips curve

It is generally believed that unemployment and inflation are linked. Phillips correlated changes in United Kingdom money wages and the level of unemployment. The relationships suggested that when unemployment was 2.5 per cent, the rate of change in money wages would be non-inflationary. As wages accounted for 70 per cent of production costs and it was assumed that cost-plus pricing was adopted, it was concluded that prices and unemployment were also correlated. If an economy was run at a 2.5 per cent level of unemployment, it was suggested that the general price level would be stabilised. Thus the Phillips curve is normally shown as a relationship between the level of unemployment and the rate of inflation (Figure 4.9).

Thus the Phillips curve seemed to show a stable relationship between inflation and unemployment. This means that

- the lower the rate of unemployment, the higher the rate of inflation;
- the higher the rate of unemployment, the lower the rate of inflation;
- there was a trade off between employment and price stability;
- governments could not simultaneously achieve price stability and full employment.

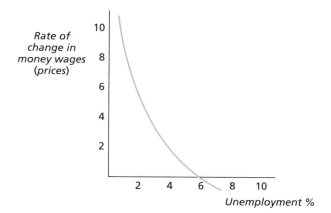

**Figure 4.9** The Phillips curve

The Phillips curve was neutral between the cost-push and demand-pull theories of inflation and between the Keynesian and monetarist schools of thought. It only showed a link between wage inflation and unemployment levels and did not necessarily specify causation.

- The demand-pull theorists interpreted low unemployment as an indication of excess demand which served to 'pull' up wages in the labour market.
- The proponents of cost-push inflation saw a low level of unemployment as a measure of trade union strength, enabling them to 'push' up wages when employers were vulnerable because wage costs could be passed on as higher prices in the buoyant economy.

For a government, the Phillips curve seems to offer the option of lower unemployment and higher inflation or higher unemployment and lower inflation. This gave policy makers a choice, but still meant that one major economic objective could not be fulfilled. Price stability and full employment appeared to be mutually exclusive.

## Development of the Phillips curve

By the time the Phillips curve had become established, 1970, the inverse relationship between unemployment and inflation began to break down. Monetarists were not surprised, as they had argued that the trade-off was at best temporary. As unemployment grew at higher rates of inflation (stagflation), Keynesian demand management was discredited. However, in the 1980s, the trade-off reappeared but at a higher absolute level. In effect, the Phillips curve appeared to have shifted to the right.

Several explanations have been put forward to explain this.

- *Structural unemployment.* The growth of structural and voluntary unemployment meant that there could be high pressure of demand for labour even if the unemployment figures suggested otherwise. This would mean a higher level of unemployment for each level of inflation.
- *Increased trade union power.* This would suggest that trade unions were able to secure higher wage increases at any given level of unemployment, thus generating higher inflation.
- *Cost pressures.* External cost rises such as that resulting from the oil price rises in the early and late 1970s would cause a higher rate of inflation at every level of unemployment. Administered prices in uncompetitive markets would contribute to this process.

Both of these arguments would suggest that the Phillips curve had moved outwards to the right as shown in Figure 4.10. Thus the employment/inflation trade-off still existed

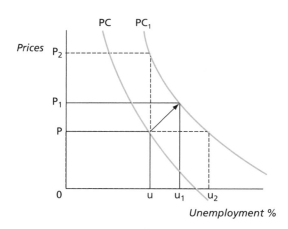

**Figure 4.10**   A shift in the Phillips curve

but that the inflation price of full employment had greatly risen. Cost-push pressures shift PC to PC$_1$.

- At an unemployment level of U$_1$ the rate of inflation will now be P$_1$.
- If the government expanded aggregate demand to reduce unemployment to U, the resulting rate of inflation would rise to P$_2$ – higher than the P rate of inflation when the economy was on the original Phillips curve, PC.

This appears to be the experience of many economies during 1970 and 1980s. However, in the last decade or so, some economies (e.g. the USA and the UK) have been able to combine low inflation with falling unemployment. This suggests that the Phillips curve has moved back to the left. This may be the result of:

- the effects of the *supply side policies* adopted in many countries from mid 1980s onwards;
- declining trade union power and militancy;
- a reduction in structural unemployment as structural change slows down;
- a temporary fall in real energy prices down to 2005.

### The role of expectations

An alternative approach to the Phillips curve incorporates price and/or wage expectations into the inflationary process. This approach claims that the negative relationship between inflation and unemployment is not permanent and that the long-run Phillips curve is vertical. Thus, there are no long-run trade-offs. Essentially the expectations distort the economic process, by influencing the behaviour of its economic agents. The expectations-augmented Phillips curve was devised by Friedman to show that the effect of expectations could be a long period of unemployment above the natural rate where demand and supply for labour is equal. Also, this would be the cost of irresponsible government intervention in the market which attempted to keep unemployment unnaturally low, by such means as Keynesian demand management policies.

Figure 4.11 explains the process. In this diagram each of the PE curves shows a differing expectation of inflation by workers. They are short-run Phillips curves. PC is the long-run Phillips curve.

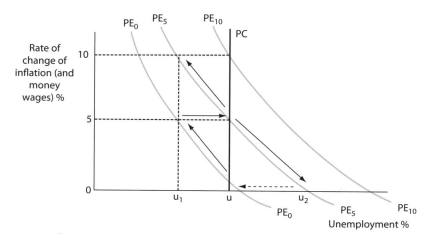

**Figure 4.11**   The expectations-augmented Phillips curve

- If the government attempts to reduce unemployment below the natural rate to $u_1$, when there is no inflation ($PE_0$), the increase in general demand needed will create excess demand in the labour market, causing 5 per cent wage inflation.
- It is assumed that wage inflation becomes price inflation of 5 per cent. This eventually changes price expectations from no inflation ($PE_0$) to 5 per cent inflation ($PE_5$) and shifts the Phillips curve to the right.
- This means that wage and price inflation are now higher at any given rate of unemployment. For instance, the natural rate of unemployment, $u$, can only be obtained at 5 per cent inflation now because of the expectations aroused.

Where does this leave government policy? The concept of the vertical Phillips curve appears to have removed much of the choice governments used to believe that they had over the balance between inflation and unemployment. No government could accept a situation in which the rate of inflation was continually accelerating since this would ultimately lead to hyper-inflation. At the very least governments would have to accept a level of unemployment equal to the natural rate of unemployment since at this level, the rate of inflation would at least be stable. Thus in policy terms, the natural rate of unemployment was also the non-accelerating inflation rate of unemployment or NAIRU.

### NAIRU

The non-accelerating inflation rate of unemployment (NAIRU) has evolved from the expectations-augmented Phillips curve.

- NAIRU is that level of unemployment where there is no tendency for inflation to accelerate or decelerate; the rate of inflation will stabilise.
- NAIRU is effectively the natural rate of unemployment; in Figure 4.11 NAIRU would be at $u$.
- This rate of unemployment may change over time and may give a clue as to why United Kingdom and USA unemployment rose in the 1980s and then fell again from the mid-1990s.

There is much evidence to suggest that the natural rate of unemployment/NAIRU rose in most countries during the 1970s and 1980s. This appeared to be especially marked in the

United Kingdom where it rose from 4.0 per cent in the period 1971–75 to 9.2 per cent in 1981–86. Among the reasons suggested for this are:

- increased structural unemployment where unemployed workers are effectively removed from the labour market;
- increased frictional and voluntary unemployment;
- the emergence of serious supply-side problems, with many workers effectively excluded from the labour market because of poor education and skills, low occupational and geographical mobility and discouragement among the long-term unemployed.

The result of this was that high levels of unemployment were inevitable as governments attempted to reduce rates of inflation. In terms of Figure 4.11, the natural rate of unemployment had risen ($u$ had moved to the right) and governments had to accept unemployment above this level as the price of slowing inflation.

However, from the early 1990s the USA and the United Kingdom experienced both falling unemployment and falling inflation. In terms of NAIRU, it appeared that the natural rate of unemployment was now falling and thus lower rates of inflation were becoming compatible with lower levels of unemployment. This fall in the natural rate is ascribed to such factors as:

- generally weaker wage pressure in labour markets as trade union membership and power declined;
- the effects of supply-side policies in improving the operation of the labour market, especially reductions in entitlement to unemployment payments;
- reductions in structural unemployment as the effects of the decline of old manufacturing industries faded away;
- improvements in the education and skills of the labour force;
- the development of more flexible working arrangements, especially the growth of part-time employment.

Conversely, the slow pace of reform of labour markets in most EU economies and the attempts to further regulate labour relations such as the introduction of a maximum working week, may have a major contributor to the slower fall in unemployment in many EU economies.

 **Exercise 4.2**

Answer the following questions based on the preceding information. You can check your answers below.

1. What could be the underlying causes of demand-pull inflation?
2. In cost-push inflation, cost rises are 'exogenous'. What does that mean?
3. What is the quantity theory of money?
4. Suggest four effects of inflation.
5. List three important types of unemployment.
6. Specify three costs of unemployment.
7. What does the Phillips curve show?
8. How did Keynesians attempt to reduce unemployment?
9. What is NAIRU?
10. In 'new' macroeconomic models, what effect will an increase in aggregate supply have on prices and unemployment?

**Solutions**

1. The principal cause is aggregate monetary demand exceeding the supply of goods and services at current prices. This could result from increases in injections into the circular flow when the economy is at or near full employment.

2. Exogenous cost rises are those that occur from outside of the economic system and are not the result of excessive aggregate demand. These could include increases in import prices or wage increases due to trade union pressure rather than the demand for labour.

3. The quantity theory of money claims that there is a stable link between the stock of money in the economy and the level of prices; if the money stock (supply) increases, this will raise the price level at some future date.

4. Inflation may: reduce the international competitiveness of the trade sector of an economy; shift wealth from the holders of financial assets to the holders of debts; discourage savings as the value of savings decreases; distort consumer expenditure as consumers attempt to anticipate price changes.

5. The main types of unemployment are: structural, frictional, cyclical, seasonal and voluntary.

6. The costs of unemployment include the loss of output, the loss of tax income to the government, the loss of income to the unemployed and damage to the unemployeds' skills and health.

7. The Phillips curve shows the relationship between the level of unemployment and the rate of inflation.

8. Keynesians believe that unemployment is the result of demand deficiency, and advocate the use of the government budget to increase aggregate demand by raising public expenditure and reducing taxation.

9. NAIRU is the non-accelerating inflation rate of unemployment – the rate of unemployment at which the current rate of inflation will have no tendency to change.

10. An increase in aggregate supply will reduce the price level and reduce the level of unemployment.

## 4.5 Economic growth and external balance

In addition to the objectives of full employment and price stability, most governments also wish their economies to achieve:

- economic growth
- external balance.

### 4.5.1 Economic growth

Policies to promote economic growth are difficult to design and difficult to implement for three main reasons.

1. Economists are less sure about the process of economic growth and why some economies grow faster than others, than most economic processes. Some of the factors affecting economic growth may be non-economic and thus not readily understandable using standard economic analysis.

2. Because the factors influencing economic growth may be non-economic as well as economic, it is not easy to see how governments can design economic policies to promote the rate of economic growth in their countries.

3. Economic growth is a very long-term process and may therefore need long-term policies, consistently applied over long periods of time. Few governments have such long time perspectives. Moreover, changes in governments in the medium term may mean a change of emphasis in economic objectives and a change of economic policies.

The record of recent economic growth, the factors that determine the rate of economic growth and policies to promote a higher rate of economic growth are discussed in more detail in Section 5.1 of the next chapter.

### 4.5.2 External balance

In addition to the main economic objectives of full employment, price stability and economic growth, governments have to concern themselves with the issue of external balance. External balance refers to the international payments and receipts made by and received by the residents of a country.

- *Receipts* come from exports of goods and services and inflows of capital.
- *Payments* arise from imports of goods and services and outflows of capital.

The balance of payments accounts are conventionally divided into:

- the *current account* which is the balance of imports and exports of goods and services;
- the *capital account* which is the balance of inflows and outflows of capital for the acquisition of certain types of fixed assets and for government transactions (e.g. foreign aid);
- the *financial account* which is the balance of inflows and outflows for the sales/purchasing of assets such as shares and bank deposits.

Since the accounts contain all international transactions, the balance of payments accounts *as a whole* always balance. However, there may be surpluses or deficits in each of the sub-accounts. Thus:

- a *deficit* on the *current account* would have to be matched (*financed*) by a *surplus* on the capital or financial accounts;
- a *surplus* on the *current account* would have to be matched (*financed*) by a *deficit* on the capital or financial account.

There would appear, therefore, to be no particular problem with respect to the balance of payments for a country. The problem arises when there is a persistent problem on the current account that must be financed on the capital or financial accounts.

- A persistent *surplus* can be financed although there may be an increase in the domestic money supply as the net inflow of foreign currency is converted into domestic currency.
- It may not be possible to finance a persistent *deficit* for ever because of the nature of the financing process.

Let us suppose that a country is running a persistent deficit on its current account – its trade in goods and services with the rest of the world. Let us also suppose that the capital account is in balance. This means that the deficit must be financed on the financial account. This can be done in a variety of ways:

- *assets* could be sold to foreigners, for example the sales of shares in domestic companies or the sale of shares in foreign companies owned by residents;

- *liabilities* could be increased, for example foreign funds could be attracted into bank accounts in the country or borrowing from foreign banks and international institutions could be undertaken either by domestic financial institutions or by the central bank;
- *reserves* of foreign currency held by the central bank could be run down.

It should be noted that a balance of payments current account deficit cannot be financed by the government through its own budget; the government accounts are quite separate and not concerned with external payments and receipts.

Thus a current account deficit can be financed by a combination of selling assets to foreigners, acquiring liabilities from foreigners or by running down reserves of foreign exchange. None of these can be done indefinitely since reserves and assets would eventually be exhausted and liabilities cannot be built up for ever without a loss of international confidence which would lead to foreigners being unwilling to lend any further funds to that country.

It becomes clear from this that governments need to conduct economic policy in such a way as to achieve two objectives should a balance of payments current account deficit arise. First is the need *to finance* the imbalance in the short to medium run and, secondly, to *correct* the imbalance in the long run.

## Financing the deficit

In order to finance a deficit on the current account of the balance of payments, a country needs to attract capital and financial inflows into that country. It might attempt to do this by:

- creating a favourable business environment to encourage multinational companies to invest in the country and locate production there. This inflow of capital would appear as a credit on the capital or financial accounts. It was claimed that the large inflow of such capital into the United Kingdom economy in the 1990s compared to other EU economies was the result of a more 'business friendly' environment. However such flows are not likely to be large and will only occur over a long period.
- encouraging a flow of international mobile liquid funds into the country's banking system by maintaining an attractive level of interest rates. If the return on such funds is higher than in other countries, there is likely to be a net inflow of such funds. This is likely to be the main means of funding a current account deficit.

For most countries then the means of financing a significant current account deficit is to conduct monetary policy so that interest rates are relatively high compared with financial centres in other countries. The problem that arises is that monetary policy is now being determined by an external requirement and not by the needs of the domestic economy. It is possible that the domestic economy may be in recession in which case the appropriate monetary policy would be *lower* interest rates, but interest rates have to be *raised* in order to attract in and retain foreign funds to finance an external imbalance. The severity of the recession in the United Kingdom in the early 1990s was partly the result of the government having to raise interest rates, rather than reduce them, because of external balance of payments problems.

## Correcting the deficit

In the longer run therefore, the need is to correct the imbalance on the balance of payment current account. This can be done in a variety of ways and the appropriate policy method depends on the reasons for the imbalance on the current account in the first place. Two broad possibilities exist.

- *Expenditure reduction*: If the government adopts a deflationary policy it can reduce the level of AMD in the economy. Since this reduces total expenditure and as imports are, in the short to medium run, a function of the level of expenditure, the level of imports tends to fall. This approach is most appropriate when the source of the problem is excess AMD and the economy has a high ratio of imports to GDP. Since much of the fall in expenditure will fall on domestic expenditure, the cost of this approach is a lower level of economic activity and higher unemployment.
- *Expenditure switching*: If the rate of exchange for the currency is reduced (devaluation or depreciation) the foreign exchange price of exports falls and the domestic price of imports rises. This encourages overseas consumers to switch to the country's exports and domestic consumers to switch away from imports to domestically produced alternatives. This approach is most appropriate when the source of the problem is a loss of international competitiveness. The cost of this approach is a fall in living standards as imports become more expensive and a rise in costs for businesses using imported inputs in their production processes.

A more detailed discussion of the balance of payments issues can be found in Section 5.5.

## 4.6 Government economic policy

In order to achieve the objectives of full employment, price stability, economic growth and external balance, governments have a range of policy instruments available to them. These policy instruments generally fall into one of the three categories:

1. monetary policy
2. fiscal policy
3. supply-side policy.

### 4.6.1 Monetary policy

Monetary policy is concerned with managing the monetary environment in order to influence the decisions of economic agents including consumers, investors and businesses. It can do this by affecting either the *availability of* credit or the *price* of credit. The main feature of monetary policy is the policy of changing interest rates since they are the price of credit.

#### A central rate of interest

It is clear that there is no such thing as the rate of interest because there are many rates of interest, which reflect varying risk. However, there has always been a central rate around which the others vary and to which governments have paid great attention. This has usually been the rate at which the central bank would lend to the money market, based on the treasury bill rates.

In the case of the United Kingdom, the government in 1997 established a Monetary Policy Committee at the Bank of England. It gave the seven members, including five external experts, the power to decide the central rate of interest in the United Kingdom.

- The committee has a target rate of inflation of 2.0 per cent.
- Should the rate of inflation vary from this target by 1 per cent or more, the Bank of England is required to provide a written explanation to the Chancellor of the Exchequer.

- It is generally assumed that this would be most likely to occur if the rate of inflation exceeded the 2.0 per cent target. However, by 2001 it was clear that inflation was undershooting the target and it was just as likely that the Bank of England would have to explain why the rate of inflation had fallen by 1 per cent below the target. Nonetheless, by 2008 the expected situation had occurred with the rate of inflation exceeding the target of 2%.

In the EU, the European Central Bank manages monetary policy for the eurozone and a similar process operates with the central bank being given an inflation target. Even in those countries where a formal target does not exist, central banks are required to regard the rate of inflation as the main policy target for monetary policy and to conduct interest rate policy accordingly.

### Real interest rates

The real interest rate puts interest rates in the context of inflation. It shows the interest rate, allowing for inflation.

- When the nominal rate of interest is higher than the rate of inflation there is a positive real rate. This means that borrowers are losing in real terms but savers are gaining.
- Conversely, when the rate of inflation exceeds the nominal rate of interest there is a negative real rate of interest. In such a case, borrowers gain and savers lose.

For decision-making by individuals and businesses, it is the real rate of interest which is the important variable.

### The effects of interest rate changes

Changes in interest rates affect the economy in many ways. The following consequences are the main effects of an *increase* in interest rates:

- *Spending falls.* Expenditure by consumers will be reduced. This occurs because the higher interest rates raise the cost of credit and deter spending. If we take incomes as fairly stable in the short term, higher interest payments on credit cards/mortgages, etc. leave less income for spending on consumer goods and services.
- *Investment falls.* A rise in interest rates will reduce the net return to investment and thus discourage businesses from undertaking new investment projects.
- *Asset values fall.* The market value of financial assets will drop, because of the inverse relationship between bonds and the rate of interest explained. This, in turn, will reduce many people's wealth. It is likely that they will react to maintain the value of their total wealth and so may save, thereby further reducing expenditure in the economy.

The total effect of these consequences of a rise in interest rates is to *deflate* the economy, that is to reduce aggregate demand and thereby lower inflationary pressures but at the cost of reducing the level of economic activity and raising unemployment.

In addition to these domestic effects there may be some external effects of a rise in interest rates.

- *Foreign funds are attracted into the country.* A rise in interest rates will encourage overseas financial businesses to deposit money in domestic banking institutions because the rate of return has increased, relative to that in other countries.
- *The exchange rate rises.* The inflow of foreign funds raises demand for the currency and so pushes up the exchange rate. This has the benefit of lowering import prices and thereby

bearing down on domestic inflation. However, it makes exports more expensive and possibly harder to sell. The longer-term effect on the balance of payments could be beneficial or harmful depending on the elasticity of demand and supply for traded goods.

The overall effect – and in most cases its intended effect – of a rise in interest rates is to reduce the inflationary pressures in the economy.

Clearly businesses will be affected both directly and indirectly by changes in interest rates. These effects fall into three categories.

- Costs are affected by changes in interest rates. Some of the costs of a business, such as the cost of credit and the cost of stockholding, are directly determined by the rate of interest the business has to pay.
- Investment decisions are influenced by expected net returns. The rate of interest is the cost of acquiring external investment funds, or the opportunity cost of using internal funds; a change in interest rates will therefore affect the profitability of investment projects.
- Sales revenue is affected by changes in interest rates. The volume of sales will decrease if interest rates rise: this is partly because this will generate deflationary pressure in the economy and partly because some sales, for example consumer durable goods, are often based on credit.

Of course, the reverse would happen if interest rates were to be *reduced*. This would be a reflationary policy and appropriate when inflationary pressures are weak and the economy is experiencing low levels of output and high unemployment. In this case lower interest rates would reduce business costs, raise the profitability of investment projects and thus encourage investment, and raise sales revenue as consumes have access to cheaper credit. Thus the thrust of monetary policy affects the economy as a whole and impacts in many ways on the businesses that make up the economy.

## The development of monetary policy

Monetary policy is concerned with the supply and price (interest rate) of money in the economy. Its primary objective is to limit inflation and thereby maintain the value of money:

- a loose monetary policy (of low interest rates) leads to a lot of borrowing (and thus spending) which will cause inflation, higher output and employment and possibly an external trade deficit;
- a tight monetary policy (of high interest rates) may slow down demand and reduce inflationary pressure but output may fall and cause unemployment.

Monetary policy has occupied a gradually more important place in economic management in the post-war period. In the period through to the early 1970s monetary conditions were seen mainly as a by-product of other policies. However, the relaxation of direct controls (on hire purchase) and the ending of fixed exchange rates led to closer consideration of monetary policy in many countries.

In the case of the United Kingdom monetary policy has developed through several stages since the early 1980s.

- *1980–86 tracking the money supply.* During this period the government sought to control the money supply in the United Kingdom and gradually reduce inflation and inflation expectations.

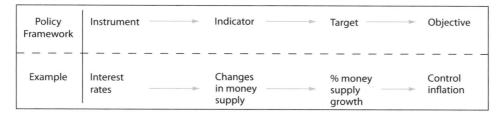

**Figure 4.12** From policy instrument to economic objective

- *1986–92 tracking exchange rates.* Governments came to believe that the exchange rate for sterling was a good indicator of monetary conditions in the United Kingdom and therefore keeping a stable exchange rate would ensure a stable monetary environment for the economy.
- *1993–97 tracking broad money.* Having abandoned exchange rate targeting and the narrow measures of money supply, broad money, M4, became the important indicator and target for monetary policy.
- *1997–2008 tracking inflation.* From 1997 the rate of inflation itself became the focus and direct target for monetary policy.

Thus the nature of monetary policy, in terms of the targets and indicators used, has changed. The control of monetary policy has also changed. Also, the government has given the Bank a degree of independence in conducting monetary policy. The Bank has an inflation target (2.0 per cent) and the Bank's Monetary Policy Committee is free to make interest rate decisions in the light of that target.

Figure 4.12 shows the links in the chain between policy instruments and economic objectives. Thus the ultimate objective and target for monetary policy is the rate of inflation. If indicators, such as money supply figures or retail sales data, suggest that the rate of inflation will differ from its target (currently 2.0 per cent), action, such as altering interest rates or the growth in the supply of money, is called for. If this policy is successful it will ultimately be revealed in the behaviour of the objective, the rate of inflation.

### The limitations of monetary policy

A central bank faces four main problems in applying monetary policy:

- First, the Bank lacks sufficient detailed, up-to-date information on the economy in general and money supply in particular. For instance, general economic information is received after the event in many cases and is often based on estimates. In particular, money supply is difficult to measure, as the government's changes of target measure indicate. Further uncertainty is created by the fact that there is a time lag between the initiation of a policy and its fruition, by which time the original problem may have been overcome anyway.
- A second problem is that the banks dislike close supervision. The history of monetary policy in many countries shows that they were not averse to evading the central bank's restraints.
- Third, central banks over-vigorous control may stifle the initiative of the banks and hinder their profit-maximising ethos. As the central bank wants an efficient and profitable banking sector, it cannot go very far in enforcing credit restraint without undermining the banks' ability to make profits.

THE MACROECONOMIC CONTEXT OF BUSINESS

- Conflicting objectives are the fourth constraint on central bank activities. A change in interest rates has effects on both the domestic economy and on external factors such as the exchange rate. What is required by the domestic economy may conflict with that need for external equilibrium.

The issues surrounding the operation of monetary policy are illustrated in Box 4.2.

---

### Box 4.2 Monetary policy or fiscal policy?

For much of the post-war period (1945–1979), the UK government used fiscal policy, the manipulation of government expenditure and taxation via the budget as the primary means of managing the economy. This reflected the dominance of the Keynesian model of how the economy functions.

However, by the late 1970s the growth of unemployment, along with accelerating inflation ('stagflation'), saw the apparent failure of the Keynesian approach to economic management. This, and the development of the monetarist model, encouraged a shift in policy: after 1979 monetary policy became the dominant instrument of policy. Budgetary policy was no longer concerned with Keynesian demand management, but with supply side policies of encouraging work and effort by attempting to reduce the disincentive effects of the taxation system. Steady growth, low unemployment and low inflation from 1995 onwards seemed to validate this change of approach.

But in 2008 the world changed again. Faced with a near collapse of the banking system in many countries and the onset of a severe recession, governments began to doubt whether monetary policy would be enough. The experience of Japan in the 1990s was that even very low interest rates (below 1%) would not necessarily be enough to expand aggregate demand sufficiently to pull the economy out of a long drawn out recession. Many governments, fearing that major reductions in interest rates would not work strongly enough or quickly enough, began to adopt major fiscal boosts to their economies through tax cuts and public expenditure increases.

It looked like the Keynesian model was back in business.

---

### 4.6.2 Fiscal policy: taxation and spending

There are many aims to taxation and their priority varies with the political complexion of the government. However, all governments are agreed on the need to raise revenue. Originally this income was used to wage war, but today the bulk of it goes on more socially desirable expenditure such as education, health and social services. The different types of taxation used in the UK are shown in Figure 4.13. It should be noted that in the UK social security taxes are referred to as 'national insurance contributions'.

Taxation can be used to:

- *Change markets.* Certain potentially harmful goods, such as cigarettes and alcohol, may be heavily taxed, thereby lowering the quantity demanded and reducing consumption levels. Over 75 per cent of the price of cigarettes goes in tax; and at times higher taxes on petrol have been used to deter consumption and induce energy conservation also.
- *Influence the level of aggregate monetary demand.* AMD can be reduced by raising taxation and can be raised by reducing taxation.

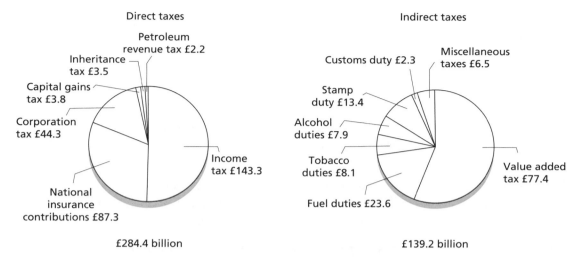

**Figure 4.13**   UK central government taxation revenue 2006/2007
*Source:* ONS

- *Finance the provision of public and merit goods.* The collective provision of certain public goods, such as defence, paid for from taxation revenue, enables it to be given free to everyone. Similarly, the zero price provision of a merit good such as education provides access to everyone, when market-priced supply might lead to under-consumption by many, which society might consider to be undesirable.
- *Change the distribution of income and wealth.* Direct taxes and especially progressive direct taxes fall most heavily on upper groups while indirect taxes and regressive taxes in general fall most heavily on lower income groups. Changing the balance between different taxes can thus alter income distribution.

## Principles of taxation

Adam Smith outlined four canons of taxation and these are still appropriate at present. These four principles are as follows.

1. *Certainty.* If people know what is expected of them in terms of what, when, how and where to pay, then the system operates efficiently and evasion is minimised.
2. *Convenience.* The PAYE system in the United Kingdom operates on this basis and the payment of local authority tax by monthly instalments has developed for this reason.
3. *Equitable.* They should be fairly based on an individual's ability to pay. Equality of sacrifice is often subject to conflicting interpretations, but it is usually agreed that a progressive element to income tax is fair in that the better off can bear a higher tax burden more easily than those on low incomes.
4. *Economy.* Taxes should be cheap to collect.

Since Smith's day, other principles have been added. These include:

- *Efficiency.* A tax needs to achieve its objective efficiently and not undermine other aims and taxes. For instance, if the basic rate of tax is reduced to encourage effort but taxpayers substitute more leisure, then it is not operating efficiently.
- *Flexibility of a tax.* A tax needs to be capable of variation in order to fit with changes in economic management.

## Types of taxation

Taxes can be classified in several ways:

- What is taxed? The three main categories are:

| *Income* | *Expenditure* | *Capital* |
|---|---|---|
| Income tax | VAT | Inheritance tax |
| Corporation tax | Excise duties | Capital gains tax |
| National insurance | Customs duties | |

However, there are also taxes on property ownership (e.g. council tax in the United Kingdom), car use (motor vehicle licence duty), television use (licence fee), a firm's payroll (employers' social security taxes), and oil royalties (petroleum revenue tax).

- Who is levying the tax? Most taxes are imposed by central government but some local government authorities are given the power to raise taxes.
- Who is paying the tax? Usually a distinction is made between direct and indirect taxes. With a direct tax the person receiving the income pays the tax to the authorities, for example income tax. In contrast, most taxes on expenditure are termed indirect, because the purchaser who benefits from the consumption is charged, usually in the purchase price, but the actual tax revenue is remitted, for convenience, by the seller to the authorities. Although the seller pays in the nominal sense he/she may be able to pass on the burden of the tax to the purchaser through a higher price.
- What percentage of income is paid in tax? – at various income levels. The main categories here are:
  - *progressive.* A larger percentage of income is paid in tax as income rises, e.g. income tax (above a certain minimum).
  - *regressive.* A smaller percentage of income is paid in tax as income rises, e.g. VAT (on most goods and services).
  - *proportional.* The same percentage of income is paid in tax at all income levels.

Thus, with a progressive tax the average rate of taxation rises with income, whereas with a regressive tax the average rate falls. The average rate of tax is constant with a proportional tax. The marginal rate of taxation (percentage of extra $1 income paid in tax) also varies between these different types of tax. The marginal rate is higher than the average rate with a progressive tax but lower with a regressive tax as income rises. The two rates are equal for a proportional tax.

---

### Box 4.3 Policy differences in taxation

Although the Conservative Party sees a more limited role for taxation funding, it subscribes to the above functions in agreement with the Labour Party. However, there is less agreement over issues of income and wealth distribution. Between 1979 and 1997 Conservative governments reduced the basic rate of income tax from 33 per cent to 23 per cent, and the highest rate from 83 per cent to 40 per cent, while increasing VAT, a regressive tax, from 8.5 per cent to 17.5 per cent. This redistributed income from the poor to the rich, but was justified by the desire to increase incentives and encourage investment. Since 1997 the Labour government has further reduced the standard rate of income tax to 20%, but has also introduced a range of tax and expenditure changes that redistributed income towards lower-income groups. These changes have included the introduction of a system of family tax credit and a significant rise in child benefit. In the 2002 budget the government also announced a significant extension of national insurance charges which became effective in April 2003. These were mainly designed to raise revenue to pay for the large increases in expenditure on health and education announced in 2002.

Finally, in 2008 the government announced extensive tax changes to take effect from 2010 onwards including a new higher rate of tax of 45% to be paid on taxable incomes over £150,000.

## Incidence and burden of taxation

The incidence of a tax occurs in two ways.

- The formal *incidence* refers to the person or organisation who is required to remit the tax to the government, for example retailers paying VAT or sales tax.
- The real incidence refers to the person on whom the *burden* of the tax falls, for example the customer on whom most of the burden of VAT falls. The ability of a producer to pass on the burden of an indirect on to the customer depends on the price elasticity of demand.

Expenditure taxes, such as VAT and sales taxes, distort prices and quantity supplied. Such taxes shift a producer's supply curve to the left as shown in Figure 4.14

- At each price the producer is now prepared to supply less because part of his sales income goes in tax to the government.
- The supply schedule shows that at $2 price, before tax, fifteen units were supplied; but since the tax was levied ($1 per unit) only ten were marketed.
- The supplier's total revenue before tax was $30 but now it is only $10 (20–10 tax)
- In order to achieve net revenue of $30, the supplier needs to produce fifteen units at $3 (45 – 15 tax – 30). In the diagram, the vertical distance (*ab*) between the two supply curves shows the tax per unit.

The original equilibrium was $3 and twenty units. The imposition of the tax has caused a contraction in the quantity demanded to seventeen units and a price rise to $3.30. This

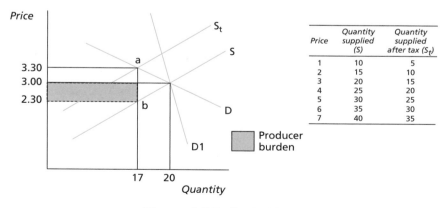

**Figure 4.14** Tax incidence

occurred because of the elasticity of demand. A more inelastic demand curve, $D_1$, would cause a smaller fall in quantity demanded and a higher market price.

The only circumstance in which the supplier can shift all of the incidence onto the consumer is when the demand for the product is completely price inelastic. In most circumstances the burden will be shared. In Figure 4.14 the consumer pays an extra 30 cents. On each sale, the supplier has to pay $1 to the government and so really bears 70 cents of the tax. Thus, the more elastic the demand curve is, the greater the incidence of the tax borne by the producer.

## Tax yield

### Direct taxes

The government is particularly concerned with the yield from taxation, both in total and per individual tax. It is probably easier to calculate the yield from changes in direct taxes, particularly those on income, than from changes in indirect taxes. However, higher income tax rates may lead to evasion and tax avoidance schemes. It has been argued that the growing black economy has resulted from higher taxes, and such activities obviously mean a loss of government revenue. Also, citizens may substitute leisure for work because they dislike the marginal tax rate on their earnings and this may slightly lower the tax yield. In recent years it has been argued that lower rates of taxation, especially of income tax, may actually raise the total tax yield. This is based on Laffer curve analysis which suggests that there is an optimum rate of tax for maximising total revenue. If taxes go above this level, tax revenues will fall. This suggests a strong case for reducing tax rates.

Five main arguments have been used to justify the reduced payment of income tax:

- High levels of income tax are a disincentive to work. For instance, in the United Kingdom in 1986 the marginal rate of tax and national insurance combined was 39 per cent on most incomes between £95 and £300 per week, and this deterred people from overtime working. It also acted as a disincentive to the self-employed and small companies, who faced higher marginal tax rates. In Figure 4.15, when the tax rate exceeds $C$ total government revenue falls because workers substitute leisure. Thus it could be argued that the tax is no longer efficient. So a tax cut from $D$ to $C$ would actually increase tax yield by £3 m (23–20). Similarly, taxes could be reduced from $D$ to $B$ without any negative impact on tax revenues. Furthermore, it was claimed that in America in 1981–83 such a policy had raised extra revenue. However, critics have argued that it is virtually impossible to separate out the effects of a cut in tax

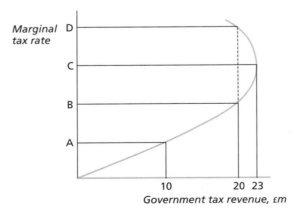

**Figure 4.15** Income tax rates and government revenue

rates from other economic things that are going on at the same time. Furthermore, the 'disincentive to work' argument takes a narrow view of worker motivation. Also, there is really no satisfactory way of measuring work effort, because the number of working hours fails to capture variables such as dedication, loyalty, drive, pride and long-term career choice.

- In the 1970s Britain experienced a 'brain drain' when well-qualified and well-paid (by British standards) professionals, such as doctors, golfers, etc., emigrated, particularly to the USA. One explanation given was the high rates of income tax, with a top marginal rate of 83 per cent. This exodus meant that British investment in human resources had been wasted.
- High tax rates mean that fewer funds are available for investment. It was claimed that people on high incomes invested their savings.
- Reductions in tax liability may lead to lower wage claims, and thus dampen inflation. This may occur because the tax reductions raise the workers' net disposable income and so they do not seek such high future wage claims, in their attempt to keep better off.
- Lower direct taxes would reduce the poverty trap, encouraging unemployed workers to accept low paid employment as the post tax income would now be higher.

However, the evidence to support these claims is rather mixed and the long term consequences of reduced direct taxation are not entirely clear.

### Indirect taxes

The effect on yield of taxation on goods and services depends on consumer preferences, demand elasticities and time. When a good has price inelastic demand, then sales will not fall by much and tax will be collected. However, if the good has high price elasticity of demand then demand will fall steeply when the price rises as result of the imposition of a tax. This effect would become stronger in the long run and the total revenue gained would be greatly reduced. For this reason the heaviest indirect taxes are typically levied on those goods with very low price elasticities of demand. These goods include tobacco and cigarettes, alcohol and petrol.

### The conduct of fiscal policy

A government's fiscal policy is concerned with the balance between its income and spending and the effects which changes in the balance might have on the economy.

- The difference between central government income and expenditure is termed the *budget deficit* or *budget surplus*.
- However, the balance between the income and spending of the whole of the public sector is nowadays more significant and is termed *public sector borrowing*.
- The current term for government borrowing in the UK is *public sector net borrowing* (PSNB). Previously, the terms *public sector borrowing requirement* (PSBR) and *public sector net cash requirement* (PSNCR) had been used. All three terms can be regarded as effectively interchangeable.

The PSNB incorporates the borrowing of central government, public corporations and local authorities. Much of the central government's borrowing is used to subsidise public corporations through specific grants and local authorities through support grants.

The government budget may be in:

- *Deficit* where the flow of government expenditure exceeds the flow of its taxation income.
- *Surplus* where the flow of government expenditure is less than the flow of its taxation income.

A budget deficit (surplus) should not be confused with a trade deficit (surplus). Both are important sets of accounts, but the latter refers to the balance of payments between a country and its trading partners. A budget deficit shows where the flow of government expenditure exceeds the flow of its tax income.

The PSNB is the difference between two large accounting totals. It is a cash concept which quickly and fairly accurately measures actual money flows. Thus it gives reliable and timely information for economic decision-making. PSNB projections, which are generally less accurate, are given annually, from November since 1993.

A budget deficit may occur for three main reasons.

- In recessions, tax yields fall and public expenditure on social security for the unemployed rise. This can be seen in many countries in the early 1980s and especially in the recession of 1990–1993 and also that of 2008–2009. As the economy grows the reverse happens and the budget moves into surplus as can be seen from the period 1998–2001.
- Governments might run a budget deficit to increase aggregate demand in the economy as part of a reflationary policy to reduce unemployment.
- Governments might wish to undertake significant amounts of public expenditure (e.g on health and education in the United Kingdom in recent years) and finance some of this through borrowing rather than taxation provided that this borrowing is not believed to be excessive or permanent.

### The problem of government borrowing

When governments run budget deficits and borrow to finance those deficits a distinction can be made between two elements in those deficits:

- a *cyclical* element in which the deficit arises as a result of the downswing phase of the trade cycle and will decrease or even turn into a surplus in the upswing phase of the trade cycle;
- a *structural* element in which the deficit is the result of a permanent imbalance between expenditure and taxation and will not be affected by the trade cycle.

A cyclical deficit is much less concern since over the whole trade cycle, budget deficits would be broadly balanced by budget surpluses. However, a structural deficit implies continuous borrowing by governments and an increasing total debt ('national debt') owed by the government. There are some reasons to believe that many countries are facing pressures are tending to increase public expenditure on a long-term basis and hence threatened the emergence of structural budget deficits.

These pressures include:

- *an ageing population* which increases public expenditure on health care for the elderly and on state pensions;
- *inflation* in the prices of public sector goods and services which are mainly labour intensive and thus tend to show the fastest rate of inflation;
- *spending commitments* for public and merit goods especially social welfare, education and health, which are difficult to decrease in the ace of voter opposition;
- *tax changes* as it is always politically much easier to reduce taxes than to raise them thus making raising more tax revenue problematic.

Thus many governments are faced with the problem of financing budget deficits. The ways in which this might be done can be distinguished by:

- *from whom* the government borrows; this might be the non-bank private sector such as pension funds or individual households;

- *the type of liability* the government issues where the main distinction is between different degrees of liquidity of those liabilities. Long term government securities (in the United Kingdom, 'gilts') are the principal liabilities of governments.

For most governments the PSNB arising from the budget deficit is mainly financed by the sale of long-term government debt to the private (non-bank) sector of the economy. This is likely to have some effects on the economy but the nature of those effects is subject to some debate among economists.

- Some, mainly Keynesians, believe that the effects are *real* in that a budget deficit financed in this way will tend to affect the real variables in the economy, raising output and employment via the effect of the deficit on aggregate demand.
- Others, including monetarists and new classical economists, believe that the effects are *monetary* in that government borrowing injects liquid assets into the economy thus boosting the money supply and casing inflation. Moreover, government borrowing may push up interest rates thus reducing private spending. This reduction in private spending will offset the government expenditure financed by borrowing – a process known as 'crowding out'.

The problems of financing budget deficits and the potential problems arising from the need to service (pay interest on) the national debt have led governments across the world to adopt policies designed to control the level of government borrowing. In the European Union, a condition of joining the single currency (euro) was a maximum size of national debt and of current government borrowing in relation to the national income of the country concerned. Once a country has joined the single currency and adopted the euro, it is obliged to keep control of its government borrowing via the 'stability pact' which specifies maximum amounts that governments can borrow. In the United Kingdom since 1997 the government has adopted *the golden rule* for government finances.

This rule states that

- over the whole trade cycle, government current expenditure on goods, services and transfer payments should not exceed its taxation income;
- only government investment expenditure may be financed by government borrowing;
- the overall burden of public debt should not go above sustainable levels, generally taken to mean equal to 40 per cent of GDP.

However, the effect of the recession in the UK from 2008 onwards forced the government to effectively abandon this golden rule. This is discussed in Box 4.4.

---

**Box 4.4   Budgetary rules under pressure?**

The serious recession in the UK which developed from 2008 onwards had a two-fold effect on the government budget. In the autumn of 2008 the government predicted that the effect of the recession would be to greatly increase the size of its budget deficit. This was inevitable as the recession would reduce tax revenues as output and incomes fell, and would raise expenditure on unemployment payments. The effect would be a budget deficit in 2009/2010 and subsequent years so large that it would effectively break all three fiscal rules.

However, the problem did not stop there. The government felt that in order to limit the severity of the recession, it would need to inject extra spending into the economy in order to raise aggregate demand. The government therefore proposed to accelerate some public investment programmes and reduce some tax rates in the following year. The biggest of these tax cuts was a temporary reduction in VAT from 17.5% to 15%. This would make the budget deficit even bigger.

The overall result was that the government predicted that its borrowing would peak at £118b in 2009/2010 (equivalent to 8% of GDP). The government was thus forced to adopt much looser 'temporary operating rules' for its budgetary policy.

### 4.6.3 Supply side policy

Monetary policy and fiscal are primarily concerned with influencing the level of aggregate monetary demand in the economy. In terms of the aggregate demand and supply model (see Figure 4.6) these policies are aimed to shift the AD curve to the right when the problem is unemployment and to the left when the problem is inflation. However, concern over the effectiveness of such policies, has led to a shift of emphasis towards *supply side policies.*

The object of supply side policy is to shift the aggregate supply curve to the right. In terms of the aggregate demand and supply model, this would have effect of raising national income and lowering unemployment at the same time as reducing inflationary pressures in the economy. In effect such policies, if effective, would shift the Phillips curve to left thus reducing the natural rate of unemployment: price stability could be achieved with lower rates of unemployment.

Supply side policy typically consists of a wide range of measures the most important of which are:

- shifting taxation away from direct to indirect taxation and reducing marginal rates of taxation to encourage work and enterprise;
- reducing social security payments and tailoring them to encourage the unemployed to seek employment;
- an emphasis on vocational education and training to improve work skills in the labour force;
- reducing the power of trade unions and employee organisations to limit entry into occupations and to raise wages above equilibrium levels;
- deregulation and privatisation to encourage enterprise and risk-taking.

In the longer run such policies appear to have been successful. In the USA and the UK where such policies have been most widely adopted, both unemployment and inflationary pressures fell significantly in the 1990s and into the current decade.

However, supply side policies have had other, less desirable consequences. The most significant of these have been:

- making the taxation system much more regressive: in the UK the proportion of income paid in tax by the poorest 20% of the population is higher than that paid by the richest 20%;
- a more unequal distribution of income;
- a greater degree of uncertainty for workers in the labour market and with less employment protection;
- a fall in the relative (and sometimes absolute) standard of living of many who are dependent on social security payments.

## 4.6.4 Debates over economic policy

### Keynesians and monetarists

There are major and continuing debates over the way in which economies function and therefore over the way in which economic policy should be conducted. The most important debate is between those economists who can be broadly called 'monetarists' and those who are broadly 'Keynesian'.

The monetarists, like the classical economists who preceded Keynes, believe that

- real and monetary forces are separate. The market forces of demand and supply determine the level of output and relative prices, but money influences the overall price level.
- unemployment is largely voluntary, caused by workers pricing themselves out of jobs and by trade union activity.
- inflation is created by the government through the excessive supply of money in the economy.
- fiscal policy is only important for its contribution towards the level of government spending, which they seek to minimise, and its impact on money supply.
- full employment and growth are best promoted by supply-side policies to 'free up' markets.

In contrast, Keynesians, whose beliefs have their origins in the work of the economist J.M. Keynes in the 1930s,

- reject the quantity theory of money and maintain that money is a vital link between markets and because money may be stored, the level of demand may be insufficient to maintain full employment.
- argue that involuntary unemployment may arise, where workers would accept a job for which they are qualified at the current wage but are unable to find such a job.
- believe that in such circumstances the government has a positive role to play in stimulating aggregate demand in order to reduce unemployment.
- argue that excess demand in an economy at full employment causes inflation.
- accept a more interventionist role for governments with. active fiscal policy to manage aggregate demand

Although there appear to be serious differences between monetarist and Keynesian approaches to economic policy, in practice governments of both persuasions were often aiming at the same objectives and working within similar constraints. The result has been some convergence of views and, by the late 1990s, the emergence of something approaching a new consensus in the conduct of economic policy. Whether this consensus survives the strains and stresses that will arise as governments struggle with the effects of the recent banking crisis and the current recession remains to be seen.

### Objectives of economic policy

A useful illustration of the economy's performance and the success of economic policy is the 'economic diamond' showing the main economic objectives of governments. Although the priority among the objectives varies with the government's values and political motives the following four objectives are typical of most governments:

- *Price stability.* A low annual rate of inflation.
- *Full employment.*
- *External balance* implying no long-term tendency for balance of payments current acount deficits.
- *Economic growth* as measured by the annual rise in GDP.

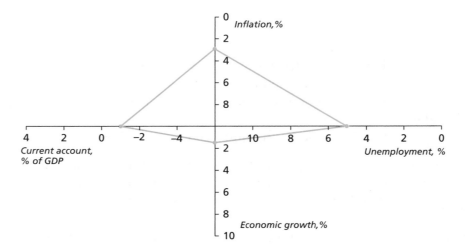

**Figure 4.16**  The economic diamond

In effect, the bigger the diamond is, the better the performance of the economy and the more successful economic policy might be judged. The economic diamond is illustrated in Figure 4.16.

Of course the conduct of economic policy by any government in a market economy is constrained by many factors, most of which are outside of the control of governments.

The most important of these constraints are:

- *previous policies* which cannot be abandoned or altered by new governments since there has to be a degree of continuity in policy to ensure a reasonably stable economic environment in which individuals and businesses can work.
- *information* which is always limited and imperfect and limits the value of economic predictions upon which economic policy making must be based.
- *time lags* between the design and implementation of economic policy and the point at which they start to have an effect on the economy.
- *political limitations* which constrain what is possible and acceptable to the electorate and may condition what governments are prepared to do.

## 4.7  Chapter summary

So far this chapter has discussed various features of the macroeconomic environment in which businesses operate. It has developed three main sets of related ideas and principles. These are as follows:

- an *economic model* of how the economy as a whole functions – the circular flow model which provides an explanation of the main economic processes in an economy and a framework for considering economic problems and issues of economic policy.
- an emphasis on *aggregate demand and aggregate supply* for analysing problems and questions related to the economy as a whole.
- a discussion of *macroeconomic problems* such as unemployment and inflation, and the ways in which governments might use *fiscal, monetary and supply-side policy* in approaching these problems.

# Revision Questions

4

This section contains examination-standard questions and solutions relevant to the content of Chapter 4. You should use these questions for examination practice and revision.

## Question 1 Multiple-choice selection

**1.1** GNP (gross national product) at factor cost may be best defined as:

(A) the total of goods and services produced within an economy over a given period of time.
(B) the total expenditure of consumers on domestically produced goods and services.
(C) all income received by residents in a country in return for factor services provided domestically and abroad.
(D) the value of total output produced domestically plus net property income from abroad, minus capital consumption.

**1.2** Structural unemployment is best defined as that caused by:

(A) the long-term decline of particular industries.
(B) the trade cycle.
(C) an insufficient level of aggregate demand.
(D) seasonal variations in demand for particular goods and services.

**1.3** Which one of the following would cause a fall in the level of aggregate demand in an economy?

(A) A decrease in government expenditure.
(B) A fall in the propensity to save.
(C) A fall in the level of imports.
(D) A decrease in the level of income tax.

**1.4** The PSNB (public sector net borrowing) is:

(A) the accumulated debts of the government.
(B) the total amount borrowed by all members of the public.
(C) the amount borrowed by the government and public authorities in a given period.
(D) the amount borrowed to finance a balance of payments deficit.

**1.5**   A progressive tax is one where the tax payment:

(A) rises as income increases.
(B) falls as income increases.
(C) is a constant proportion of income.
(D) rises at a faster rate than income increases.

**1.6**   According to the advocates of supply-side economics, which one of the following measures is most likely to reduce unemployment in an economy?

(A) Increasing labour retraining schemes.
(B) Increasing public sector investment.
(C) Increasing unemployment benefits.
(D) Decreasing the money supply.

**1.7**   The *crowding-out effect* refers to:

(A) low wages leading workers to leave an industry.
(B) firms wishing to locate production away from congested areas.
(C) public expenditure displacing private expenditure.
(D) increased rates of taxation leading to lower total tax revenue.

**1.8**   In an aggregate demand and supply diagram, if the aggregate supply curve shifted to the left, the consequences would be:

(A) national income and the price level would both fall.
(B) national income and the price level would both rise.
(C) national income would fall and the price level would rise.
(D) national income would rise and the price level would fall.

## ? Question 2

The following data refer to the principal sources of taxation revenue for the government of a developed economy

*Government tax revenue: main tax sources as a percentage of total tax revenue*

|  | 200X | 200Y |
|---|---|---|
|  | % | % |
| 1. Income taxes | 34.1 | 30.0 |
| 2. Social security taxes | 19.2 | 20.0 |
| 3. Corporation tax | 6.8 | 7.9 |
| 4. Value added tax | 14.7 | 22.9 |
| 5. Excise duties | 15.9 | 14.3 |
| 6. Other expenditure taxes* | 7.7 | 3.7 |
| 7. Capital gains tax | 0.9 | 0.6 |
| 8. Inheritance tax | 0.7 | 0.6 |

*includes stamp duty and motor vehicle duties

## Requirements

Using *both* your knowledge of economic theory *and* material contained in the table:

(a)  State whether each of the following is a direct tax or an indirect tax:

    (i)  income tax;
    (ii)  corporation tax;
    (iii)  value added tax;
    (iv)  excise duties;
    (v)  social security taxes. **(5 marks)**

(b)  State whether each of the following statements is true or false.

    (i)  Between 200X and 200Y the burden of taxation this economy shifted from indirect towards direct taxation.
    (ii)  Retailers cannot pass all of an indirect tax onto the customer.
    (iii)  Most tax revenue is gained when indirect taxes are levied on goods with high price elasticity of demand.
    (iv)  Taxes will have act as a disincentive if the income effect outweighs the substitution effect.
    (v)  Indirect taxes are likely to more regressive than direct taxes. **(5 marks)**

**(Total marks = 10)**

## ? Question 3

The following data refer to an economy over a period of 13 years.
  Consider the data and answer the following questions:

| Year | Rate of growth of GDP[1] % | Govt. borrowing[2] $bn | Balance of payments[3] $bn |
|------|------|------|------|
| 1994 | −2.0 | +11.8 | +2.6 |
| 1995 | −1.1 | +10.5 | +6.7 |
| 1996 | +1.7 | +4.8 | +4.6 |
| 1997 | +3.7 | +11.5 | +3.5 |
| 1998 | +2.0 | +10.3 | +1.4 |
| 1999 | +4.0 | +7.4 | +2.2 |
| 2000 | +4.0 | +2.5 | −0.9 |
| 2001 | +4.6 | −1.4 | −5.0 |
| 2002 | +4.9 | −11.9 | −16.5 |
| 2003 | +2.2 | −9.3 | −22.5 |
| 2004 | +0.6 | −2.1 | −18.2 |
| 2005 | −2.3 | +7.7 | −7.6 |
| 2006 | −0.5 | +28.9 | −8.5 |

1.  Annual rate of growth of gross domestic product (GDP)
2.  Government borrowing (PSNB) '+' denotes net borrowing, '−' denotes repayment of previous debt.
3.  Balance of payments, current account: '+' denotes surplus, '−' denotes deficit.

## Requirements

Using *both* your knowledge of economic theory *and* the data contained in the table:

(a)  With respect to the data in the above table, identify 2 years of economic recession in this economy and state whether in a recession: **(2 marks)**

   (i) government borrowing increases or decreases;
   (ii) the current account of the balance of payments moves towards deficit or surplus. **(2 marks)**

(b)  State whether, other things being equal, the following would increase or decrease the level of government borrowing (the PSNB) or have no effect:

   (i) a rise in exports;
   (ii) a fall in unemployment. **(2 marks)**

(c)  State whether each of the following is *true* or *false*.

   (i) A current account deficit must be financed by a surplus on the capital and financial accounts.
   (ii) If the government has a budget deficit it must borrow from abroad to finance it.
   (iii) The national debt is the amount of money owed by the government to other countries.
   (iv) The government budget acts as an automatic stabiliser in the trade cycle.

**(4 marks)**
**(Total marks = 10)**

# Solutions to Revision Questions

4

The answers given below indicate what might reasonably be expected of a candidate, under examination conditions, in order to obtain a good pass mark. It should be noted that there is a high level of objective testing in the examination. The multiple-choice questions have only one answer, as do of the subquestions in the data-response questions.

## ☑ Solution 1

**1.1**  Solution: (C)

GNP is a measure of all incomes received by residents. (A) is incorrect since it refers to domestic output and incomes, (B) is incorrect since it ignores incomes spent on imports and (D) is incorrect since it considers depreciation (capital consumption) and is a measure of net, not gross, national product.

**1.2**  Solution: (A)

(D) is incorrect since it clearly refers to seasonal unemployment. (B) and (C) refer to unemployment caused by a lack of aggregate demand; this would cause unemployment in the economy as a whole. Structural unemployment is that which occurs irrespective of the overall level of demand and affects only certain industries.

**1.3**  Solution: (A)

(D) would increase consumer incomes and therefore demand. (B) would mean consumers spending a higher proportion of their income. (C) would imply an increase in demand for home-produced goods. A is correct because government expenditure is one component of aggregate demand.

**1.4**  Solution: (C)

The PSNB refers to borrowing by the governments and other public sector authorities when their expenditure exceeds their income. (B) and (D) are incorrect since the first refers to private borrowing and the second to the balance of payments, not the government budget. (A) is incorrect: this is the accumulation of previous borrowing, not the current level of borrowing.

**1.5** Solution: (D)

B refers to a regressive tax and (C) refers to a proportional tax. (A) is insufficient since the tax payment could rise with regressive and proportional taxes. (D) is correct since it identifies a progressive tax as one where the proportion of income taken in tax rises.

**1.6** Solution: (A)

Supply-side theorists believe unemployment is the result of problems with the supply of labour. (B) and (D) are concerned with aggregate demand and the demand for labour, and are therefore incorrect. (C) is incorrect since supply-side theorists believe that generous unemployment benefits encourage unemployment.

**1.7** Solution: (C)

The crowding-out effects refers to the process by which an increase in public expenditure may be offset by a fall in private expenditure. If the public expenditure is financed by taxation, private expenditure will fall. If it is financed by borrowing, interest rates are likely to increase, thus discouraging private expenditure.

**1.8** Solution: (C)

On the aggregate supply and aggregate demand diagram AS/AD the horizontal axis is national income and the vertical axis is the price level. If the AS curves shifts to the left then, national income must fall. Since the AD curve is normally sloped down left to right the new AS curve will intersect is a higher point. Thus the price level will rise.

 **Solution 2**

(a)  (i) direct tax
(ii) direct tax
(iii) indirect tax
(iv) indirect tax
(v) direct tax

(b)  (i) *False.* The burden of taxation shifted towards indirect taxation.
(ii) *True.* A retailer can only pass on all of a tax onto customers if the demand for the good is perfectly price inelastic.
(iii) *False.* Most revenue is gained from taxing goods with very low price elasticity since consumers continue to buy even when the price has risen such as in the case of tobacco, petrol and alcohol.
(iv) *False.* A rise in taxation makes people take more leisure because of the substitution effect but to take less because of the income effect. Only if the substitution effect is strongest is there a net disincentive effect.
(v) *True.* Indirect taxes are unrelated to income and therefore tend to be strongly regressive.

**Solution 3**

(a)   The years of recession are 1994, 1995, 2005 and 2006 and in a recession
   (i)  government borrowing would *increase*.
   (ii)  the balance of payments current account would move towards a *surplus*.

(b)   (i)  A rise in exports would have *no direct effect* on the government budget and therefore on government borrowing.
   (ii)  A fall in unemployment would lead to *lower* government borrowing as expenditure on unemployment pay fell and tax receipts rose.

(c)   (i)  *True*. The balance of payments always balances so a deficit (surplus) on one account is always matched by a surplus (deficit) on the other.
   (ii)  *False*. If the government has a budget deficit is must borrow but it can do this domestically as well as internationally.
   (iii)  *False*. Most government borrowing is done domestically so the bulk of the national debt is debt owed by the government to individuals and organisations in its own country.
   (iv)  *True*. In a recession taxes fall and expenditure rises thus limiting the recession; the reverse occurs in a boom period.

5

# The Macroeconomic Context of Business: The International Economy

# The Macroeconomic Context of Business: The International Economy

## LEARNING OUTCOMES

This chapter is concerned with the wider macroeconomics context within which business operates. It discusses the process of economic growth in the world economy and the factors which affect the rate of economic growth. With respect to the international economy, the focus is upon international trade and its consequences for business and the financial arrangements which make international trade possible. Issues related to the international economy, globalisation, exchange rate systems and national and international policy towards the international economy are reviewed.

After completing this chapter you should be able to:

▶ identify the conditions and policies necessary for economic growth in traditional, industrial and post-industrial societies, and the potential consequences of such growth;

▶ identify the role of the foreign exchange market and the factors influencing it, in setting exchange rates and in helping organisations finance international trade and investment;

▶ explain the concept of the balance of payments and its implications for business and government policy;

▶ identify the main elements of national policy with respect to trade, including protectionism, trade agreements and trading blocs;

▶ explain the concept and consequences of globalisation for business and national economies;

▶ identify the major institutions promoting global trade and development, and their respective roles.

# 5.1 Economic growth

## 5.1.1 Economic growth

In its strictest sense economic growth, is taken to mean the growth of productive potential for the economy. However, the usual definition of economic growth is an increase in real gross national product (GNP).

Economic growth has been given high priority as a policy objective, because if the growth of output exceeds the growth of population, per capita income will rise, that is, the standard of living will rise. In the longer term, the compound effect on output of a constant rate of growth is impressive. For example, if output grows every year by 2 per cent, GDP will double in approximately 36 years; but if the growth of output can be increased to 3 per cent each year, output will double in approximately 24 years.

## 5.1.2 Record of economic growth

Rates of economic growth vary from country to country.

Table 5.1 shows that the highest rates of growth are associated with newly industrialised countries such as China and India. By comparison the UK had a poorer growth record although this has shown considerable improvement in the last decade.

But one is not just concerned with long-term economic growth but also with short-term fluctuations in an economy's growth rate. Thus economic growth in the United Kingdom over the last 50 years has been as high as 7 per cent and also been negative on three occasions, as seen in Figure 5.1. In 2008 economic growth fell, with a recession,

**Table 5.1** Economic growth (average percentage per annum)

| Growth | Japan | UK | USA | EU (15) | China | India |
|---|---|---|---|---|---|---|
| 1970–1979 | 4.3 | 2.0 | 2.8 | 3.2 | 7.0 | 3.6 |
| 1980–1989 | 4.0 | 2.4 | 2.5 | 2.2 | 7.8 | 5.5 |
| 1990–1999 | 1.9 | 1.6 | 2.1 | 1.9 | 3.9 | 5.6 |
| 2000–2006 | 1.6 | 2.8 | 2.8 | 1.7 | 9.5 | 6.8 |

*Source:* International Monetary Fund

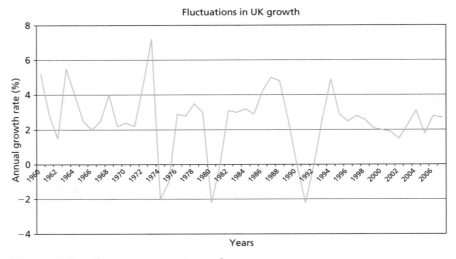

**Figure 5.1** Fluctuations in UK growth

*Source:* Economic Trends

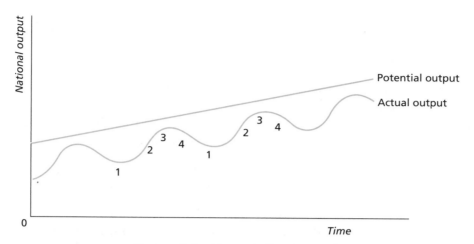

**Figure 5.2**   The trade/business cycle

defined as negative economic growth over two consecutive quarters, being recorded in the UK and most of the EU.

The fluctuations in short-term economic growth can be related to the trade or business cycle. Economies can experience high levels of economic growth which are referred to as booms. In other years economies can experience a slowdown in economic growth. In the United Kingdom, if negative economic growth occurs for more that two quarters, it is officially called a recession.

The stages of the business cycle are shown in Figure 5.2.

- *The trough* (1). This is the bottom of the cycle when the level of economic output is at its lowest.
- *The recovery* (2). Here economic growth is at its fastest as it picks up from the lowest level of output in the trough.
- *The peak* (3). Here economic output has risen to its highest level and the gap between actual and potential output has narrowed. Economic growth, however, has slowed down and may have even stopped.
- *The downturn* (4). At this stage there is a decline in economic growth, which if it leads to an actual fall in the level of output, can mean the economy could enter a recession.

### 5.1.3   Factors influencing economic growth

The growth potential of an economy is dependent upon two things:

- The amount of economic resources. The more factors of production there are, in the form of land, labour, enterprise and capital, the greater the potential for economic growth.
- The productivity of these factors of production.

Improvements in productivity are important for economic growth as it will not only increase output from a given stock of factors of production but it will also improve the competitiveness of an economy. *Productivity* is the amount of output produced per unit of input. As a result higher rates of productivity would lower unit costs of production for a firm, leading to greater competitiveness. The firm could, therefore, expect to gain sales in domestic and international markets. Lower costs could enable a firm to lower its prices, thereby expanding the market, and encourage it to raise its levels of investment. This in turn would expand productive potential and lead to still higher productivity which in turn can produce a virtuous circle of economic growth. Productivity growth is, therefore, clearly an important ingredient in achieving a higher rate of economic growth in an economy.

Capital can play a major part in economic growth.

- The greater the capital/output ratio, the higher the productivity of labour. The greater the levels of investment, the faster will be the growth in the capital stock.
- The higher the quality of capital, the more advanced will be the technology progress. This will occur when machinery is updated and when investment in research and development is high.

Labour also influences economic growth via its quantity and quality.

- Demographic factors such as the size and gender/age composition of the population determine the size of the work force. *The participation rate* measures the proportion of any age group which makes itself available for work. The greater this is, the greater the size of the working population.
- Education and training are likely to make a work force more adaptable and enterprising. This in turn will improve mobility of labour and raise its productivity.

### 5.1.4 Policies to promote economic growth

Due to the importance of economic growth in raising standards of living, governments have always taken an interest in policies to promote it. A necessary condition is that levels of *aggregate monetary demand* are kept sufficiently high to see that existing productive capacity is fully used and that firms are encouraged to expand potential production by further investment.

- Governments can use fiscal and monetary policy to keep aggregate monetary demand close to its full employment level.
- Tax rates can be cut and interest rates lowered to encourage consumer and investment spending.

Doubts exist regarding the success of such policies. The preferred route in the United Kingdom is to use fiscal and monetary policy so as to control inflation and reduce uncertainty in government economic policy rather than as a way of stimulating aggregate monetary demand. Government policy tries to create favourable economic conditions for firms to thrive, thereby raising economic growth.

However government policies will also seek to encourage *aggregate supply* in order to expand production in the economy. In the United Kingdom this has been linked to a recognition that productivity in the United Kingdom is lower than in other developed economies. Figure 5.3 shows productivity as measured by output per worker is 13 per cent below that in Germany, 20 per cent lower than in France and 18 per cent below that in the United States.

Supply-side policies attempt to increase the total quantity of factors of production especially capital as well as raise levels of productivity. Such policies can be market driven or interventionist in nature. *Market driven* policies seek to create as free a market as possible within which private enterprise and entrepreneurial activity can thrive. Such policies aim to reduce the role of government in the economy and place a greater emphasis on the role of the individual in driving economic activity.

- Thus privatisation of government industries, e.g. electricity, gas and water in the United Kingdom, and deregulation, as with the London Stock Exchange in 1986, have been introduced.

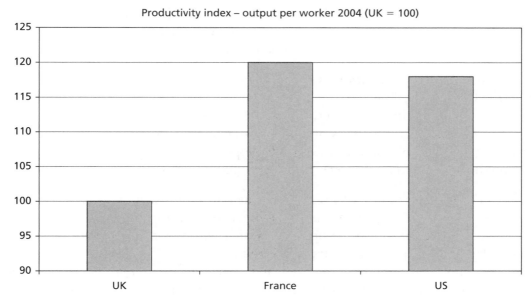

**Figure 5.3** Productivity index – output per worker 2004 (UK = 100)
*Source*: ONS

- Similarly an internal market was introduced in several public services notably the National Health Service. The intention was to generate competition in sectors previously devoid of it and hence raise efficiency.
- The dependency culture was also attacked by reducing welfare payments for the unemployed and making it more difficult to qualify for such benefits. This should expand the numbers seeking work as people cannot so readily rely on State benefits for support, thus raising the supply of labour, one of the factors of production.

Supply-side policies also seek to offer greater incentives in the economy. Marginal rates of taxation can be cut for workers and firms.

- This should encourage workers to work harder and longer hours as they will retain a greater amount of their earnings.
- It might also encourage previously non-active persons, such as housewives, to enter the labour market as the opportunity costs of not doing so has now risen.
- Consequently the amount of labour as well as its productivity could rise as income tax rates are reduced, thus raising economic growth.
- Cuts in business tax would raise the level of retained profits, providing more funds for firms to reinvest in the business and thus raising the capital stock in the economy.

Finally, market driven policies will seek to reduce the amount of controls in the economy. This could involve regulations which include unnecessary restrictions on business activity, for example, licensing laws, or the amount of bureaucratic form-filling required from small firms.

- In the United Kingdom retail restrictions have been lifted so that shops can open seven days a week and the licensing laws on the sale of alcohol liberalised.
- The VAT threshold on small firms has been raised while all foreign exchange controls were removed in 1979, thereby permitting the free inflow and outflow of capital.

- The powers of trade unions have also been reduced in the United Kingdom. These include enforced secret ballots before a union can call a strike, restrictions on secondary picketing and the outlawing of union closed shops.

The overall impact of these measures has been the liberalisation of labour and capital markets in the United Kingdom.

However not all firms and entrepreneurs automatically thrive in a free market. Consequently supply-side policies are often *interventionist* in order to promote further economic growth in an economy. In most developed economies governments support the infrastructure to give firms a stronger foundation from which to conduct their businesses.

- This can take the form of modernisation of the transport system, such as the motorway network, which will enhance the distribution networks of firms.
- Education and training may be upgraded which will provide firms with potentially a more adaptable and productive supply of labour.
- The government may sponsor research and development in universities in order to provide an economy with an advantage in respect of leading edge technologies.
- In the United Kingdom the government recognises the importance of small and medium size firms to the economy. It provides them with assistance in the form of market information, advice on exporting, management training, technical assistance as well as tax concessions. Thus there are many ways in which inventionist policies of government can strengthen the position of firms in a market economy and enhance economic growth.

### 5.1.5 Sustainable economic growth

A strongly expressed view is that by failing to take the environmental impact of economic growth into account, conventional measures of GNP do not provide an accurate indication of *sustainable economic welfare*, that is the flow of goods and services an economy can generate without reducing its future economic capacity.

GNP, therefore, needs to be adjusted by omitting:

- *Defensive expenditure.* For example, some double glazing may be installed to reduce the noise from increased use of lorries needed to move goods around the country.
- *Environmental depreciation of natural resources.* Finite mineral resources can only be used once in the growth process. Their contribution is included in GNP at their current market value. However, the exhaustion of such finite resources impacts negatively on future sustainable growth.
- *Pollution damage incurs costs.* For example, water companies have to install treatment plants to cleanse drinking water due to the intensive use of nitrates and fertilisers by farmers which then runs off the land into water catchment areas.
- *An Index of Sustainable Economic Welfare (ISEW) provides an alternative measure of economic growth.* It subtracts from GNP defensive expenditures, depreciation of environmental and physical capital, as well as the costs involved in overcoming pollution. This produces a clear distinction between conventional measures of economic growth and sustainable economic welfare. Whereas for the United Kingdom 1996–2005, average annual growth in real GNP was 2 percent per year, the ISEW showed only a 0.5 per cent annual growth.

# 5.2  Globalisation

## 5.2.1  Context

International trade has existed ever since economies had goods to trade. Such trade was, however, limited and the study of economics, while acknowledging international trade, concentrated on domestic economic matters. Over the last fifty years, dramatic increases in the volumes of goods and services traded internationally and of currency bought and sold in the foreign exchange markets have led people to see the world in terms of the *global economy*.

The global economy refers to an open economy where the ratio of exports to output forms a significant proportion of economic activity. The overwhelming majority of economies are more open today than forty years ago. Figure 5.4 shows the growth in export shares between 1960 and 2005. Most countries trade internationally at least 20 per cent of their output. Surprisingly, given the size of its trade surplus, Japan exports only 13.5 per cent of what it produces while the United Kingdom exports 31 per cent.

The growth of world trade has been expanding more rapidly than world output. Figures from the World Trade Organisation (WTO) show that for the period 1975–2005, world GDP grew annually at 2.9 per cent while world trade grew annually at 4.5 per cent. As world trade has been increasing so too has the importance of regional trade arrangements. Regional trading blocs are particularly important in Western Europe, North America and East Asia. Intra-regional trade accounts for over 50 per cent of total exports in the European Union (EU) and in the North American Free Trade Agreement (NAFTA).

Neighbouring countries have always traded with each other but the tendency in recent years has been to make such arrangements more formal. Regional trading agreements can take several forms.

- *Free trade areas* agree to reduce or abolish trade restrictions between member countries while allowing members to impose their own separate trade restrictions against non-members.

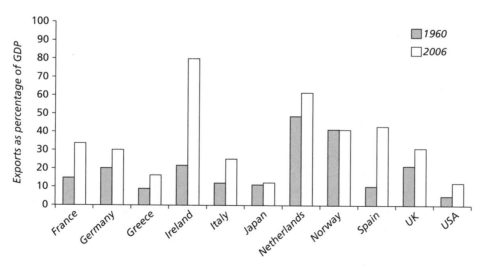

**Figure 5.4**  Trade ratios: exports as a percentage of GDP

*Source*: IMF

- *Custom unions* encourage free trade among members but erect a *common external tariff on imports* from non-member countries.
- *Common markets* are similar to custom unions but include *the free movement of factors of production* as well as trade.
- *Economic unions* take the development of a common market even further by encouraging the harmonisation of national economic policies, such as competition policy, financial regulations, product standards.

The best known regional trading bloc is probably the EU. It came into being in January 1993 having taken the place of its predecessor the European Economic Community (EEC) which had been founded in January 1958. In 2008 it has 27 members and a population of approximately 500 million. This represents only 7 per cent of the world's population but accounts for over a fifth of global imports and exports. It has its own central bank, its own currency, the *euro,* and its own budget. It is by far the most advanced example of an economic union in the global economy.

Arguments abound regarding the effects of regional trading blocs.

- Their supporters say that they encourage *trade creation by harmonizing economic policies* and standards within member countries and reducing prices as trade restrictions are removed.
- Opponents state that they lead to *trade diversion.* Member countries buy within the regional trading bloc when cheaper sources are available outside.
- Common external tariffs can encourage a regional fortress mentality which can lead to conflicts between different regional trading blocs. For example, NAFTA has complained over the EU's agricultural imports while the EU has complained over NAFTA's restrictions on steel imports.
- The fear is that regional trading blocs could lead to the development of protectionism worldwide at a time when the WTO is seeking to create free trade.

## 5.2.2 Foreign exchange market transactions

Globalisation is not restricted to international trade in goods and services. It also includes transactions on the foreign exchange markets. In April 2007 on an average trading day in the foreign exchange markets, currency valued at $3.2 billion was traded, a figure which has doubled since 2001. Most of this trading finances international capital flows rather than trade in goods and services.

Given the magnitude of these figures, one can clearly see why the global economy forms an integral part of the economic environment. An important agent in this global economy is the multinational or transnational corporation (MNC/TNC).

## 5.2.3 Multinational corporations

### Definitions

A multinational corporation is one which owns or controls production or service facilities in more than one country. A corporation does not become multinational merely by trading internationally, for example, by exporting its products from its home country.

MNCs can be ranked according to the amount of foreign assets they control. When ranked in this way the United States accounts for six of the ten largest MNCs. Such MNCs are mainly found in the petroleum, automotive and electronics/computing sectors.

Alternatively MNCs can be ranked according to a transnationality index. This is a composite index that is calculated as the average of the following ratios: foreign assets/total assets; foreign sales/total sales; foreign employment/total employment. This index gives a different ranking to the one based solely on foreign assets. It is a better indicator of the extent to which a corporation operates outside its home country.

Many firms with a high ranking in this index come from smaller countries with a restricted domestic market and it is dominated by European Union countries.

### Size of MNCs

The United Nations estimated that in 2002 there were approximately 64,000 MNCs with around 866,000 affiliates located abroad. Their sales revenues are equivalent to about 31 per cent of world GDP and a third of the world's largest economic units are MNCs rather than nation states. MNCs account for around 30 per cent of GDP in the United Kingdom and almost half of manufacturing employment. Foreign MNCs operating in the United Kingdom account for 23 per cent of output and 11 per cent of all employment. The United Kingdom is a major recipient of inward direct foreign investment (DFI). For example, in recent years 30 per cent of all Japanese DFI in the European Union has been in the United Kingdom. Likewise the United Kingdom is a major provider of outward DFI. United Kingdom home-based MNCs were the providers of 14 per cent of all DFI in 2004 despite representing only 2 per cent of all MNCs. Thus the United Kingdom is very much part of the globalisation process.

### Explanation of MNC activity

There are several advantages for a corporation in establishing a production base overseas rather than trading with foreign companies.

- *Costs* can be reduced if cheaper production facilities are available in other countries. This is especially applicable in the manufacturing sector due to the abundance of cheap, high-quality labour in developing countries.
- *Expand sales* by entering new markets. MNCs have gradually switched from exporting to a foreign market to establishing sales outlet and finally a production facility. By producing overseas the MNC can avoid the costs of transporting its product and also bypass any tariffs or quotas.
- *Secure supply* by vertical integration backwards. Oil companies, such as BP and Shell, can gain access to the gas and oil resources they need.
- An *organisational structure* to manage the operations is necessary if potential advantages are to be realised. The MNC must be able to exploit those assets internal to the corporation, including human capital, financial resources, marketing and managerial skills. This process has been made possible by the use of divisional corporate structures based on product and/or geographic characteristics which have helped the management of complex global corporations.
- Advances in *new technologies* have made it easier to conduct business across national frontiers. The spread of IT-based communications systems alongside cheaper air travel have improved communications. The globalisation of consumer markets via media and popular culture have opened world markets to MNCs.

### Impact of MNCs

Any assessment of the impact of MNCs on national economies will need to consider various costs and benefits.

THE MACROECONOMIC CONTEXT OF BUSINESS

- First, DFI by an MNC should improve economic welfare as capital is transferred to economies where the marginal rate of return on capital is highest. However, MNCs may finance overseas investment by raising the capital on the local capital market. In such cases inward investment may merely displace domestic investment that would otherwise have taken place.

- The involvement of an MNC in a foreign economy may often promote *technology transfer* which will be of benefit to the recipient economy. New technologies may be introduced without the research and development costs and the learning time which would other wise have been needed.

- Similarly local producers can copy the superior processes and organisational patterns of the MNCs. The latter may also establish direct linkages with domestic suppliers which raise the productivity of the local producers.

- However, technology transfer may only be at a low level. The MNC may only use the recipient economy as an assembly base using basic technology. Many working practices successful in an MNC's home economy may not readily transfer to another economy with different cultural traditions.

- MNCs will also impinge on the macro variables of an economy. The *balance of payments* will gain from inflows of DFI but will suffer when profits from the investment are remitted back to the home economy of the MNC. *Employment* can also be provided by MNC activity. Direct employment in the MNC's subsidiary can be supplemented by further employment in local suppliers to the MNC's operations.

- However, the employment effects can be weakened if the MNC displaces existing domestic firms. Furthermore MNCs' operations are mobile and they could well choose to locate in another economy if it proved advantageous to do so.

- Finally, MNCs can affect a government's taxation and expenditure. MNCs are notorious for being able to reduce their tax liabilities by means of *transfer pricing*. Where intra-corporation trade takes place, internal prices are set to minimise profits in economies with the highest tax rates. On the other hand, a government often has to offer grants and subsidies to MNCs in order to attract them to their economy.

Consequently the impact of the MNCs on national economies can be profound. To what extent national economies benefit from their relationships with MNCs is uncertain. The growth of globalisation seems unstoppable and with it their power to influence international trade.

## 5.3 International trade

### 5.3.1 The benefits

Britain is a trading nation, because of its location and history. International trade is necessary when a nation such as Britain specialises, so that its surpluses can be exchanged for the excess output of other countries. In theory, free trade between nations is desirable, but often in practice various forms of protection are used.

- *Specialisation* benefits world trade, because it enables different nations with differing skills and resources to gain the rewards from the division of labour. In theory, nations specialise in the production of goods for which they have a natural advantage. For instance, Saudi Arabia extracts oil, Argentina rears beef and Britain provides financial services. Specialisation usually enables an industry to benefit from large-scale production and make the maximum use of resources.

- The *economies of scale* which can be obtained are determined by the size of the market. As international trade opens up new markets, it facilitates economies of scale. Such efficiency has benefits for the trading economies because it should produce lower prices and better products, leading to improvements in general living standards.
- *Competition* should be fostered by world trade, particularly free trade. A domestic market which is controlled by a monopolist might be subject to a foreign competitor. Alternatively, the market of a few complacent home suppliers might be revitalised by the entry of foreign firms (e.g. Japanese and American companies in British consumer goods industries).
- *Lower prices* and *greater choice* should be available to consumers. The increased choice which results from international competition is particularly evident in the British car industry. However, it must be noted that these benefits perhaps need to be set against the loss of employment in domestic industries.

## 5.3.2 The theory

The *theory of comparative advantage* was devised by David Ricardo to demonstrate the gains from specialisation and free trade. The theory requires the following simplifying assumptions:

- two trading economies each producing the same two goods;
- the factors of production in each economy are perfectly mobile;
- there are no trade barriers and no transport costs;
- the state of technology is unchanged.

The 'before' section of Table 5.2 shows the output of each economy when resources are allocated equally between the production of each good. However, as A is more efficient at producing $Y$ and B is more efficient at making $X$, then specialisation by A in $Y$ and B in $X$ leads to increased total world output. This has been achieved without the use of more resources and represents increased efficiency. Both nations will benefit if trade takes place. For instance, A could trade $80Y$ for $40X$ produced by B. This would give A $120Y$ and $40X$, while B would have $140X$ and $80Y$ – so both nations would gain, although B perhaps more so at this exchange rate.

In the above case, each nation had an *absolute advantage* in the production of one good and specialisation and trade was fairly obvious. However, Ricardo showed that even where one nation had an absolute advantage in producing both of the goods, specialisation could still be mutually beneficial. The principle of *comparative advantage* explains this.

As depicted in Table 5.3 country A is more efficient in producing both $X$ and $Y$. However, B is relatively better (less worse) at producing $X$. If A and B then specialise where

**Table 5.2** Specialisation and absolute advantage

| | Production | | | |
|---|---|---|---|---|
| | Annual output before specialization | | Annual output after specialization | |
| Country | X | Y | X | Y |
| A | 30 | 100 | 0 | 200 |
| B | 90 | 40 | 180 | 0 |
| | 120 | 140 | 180 | 200 |

each has a comparative advantage, A produces $160Y$ and B produces $180X$. The total output of goods is raised but there are now fewer $X$ than before. Therefore, if A devotes one-fifth of its resources to the production of $X$ and four-fifths of its resources to making $Y$, then the total output of both goods is increased, as shown in the 'after' section of Table 5.3.

If the opportunity cost ratios were identical in A and B, and B could produce $72Y$, then nothing would be gained by specialisation and trade. The principle of comparative advantage relies on each country having different opportunity cost ratios. If the production possibility frontier is drawn for each country and the two lines are parallel, then speciaisation and trade will not be mutually beneficial. However, in practice, economies of scale could occur with specialisation, thereby changing the opportunity cost ratios and facilitating trading gains.

Several conditions are necessary for international trade. In addition to transport and peace, *exchange rates* need to be established. Each country needs to determine a price for its exports, and this usually reflects the cost of resources used. Thus in Table 5.3 country A uses fewer resources in producing each $X$ than each $Y$, and we would expect $X$ to be cheaper (approximately four-fifths of $Y$'s price as four-fifths of resource is required). Conversely, in country B, $Y$'s are very expensive, needing a lot of resources for their production (nine times what is needed for $X$). Thus domestic prices reflect opportunity cost ratios.

The domestic prices section of Table 5.4 gives monetary values to the goods produced, showing that $X$ is priced at £100 in country A and $40 in country B, and $Y$ is priced at £125 and $360. This gives price ratios of £1 = $0.40 for $X$ and £1 = $2.88 for $Y$. As long as the exchange rate falls within these limits, trade will occur because both economies can gain. If the exchange rate were £1 = $1.50, then country A could import $X$ for £26.66 (price $40 in country B = £26.66 when exported to A at this exchange rate) as shown in the 'price to import' section of Table 5.4. This price is cheaper than the domestic price and a clear gain if country A imports it from B. At the exchange rate of £1= $1.50, A might import $80X$, because with specialised production it has fewer $X$ and more $Y$. With the £2,133.33 which country B receives for selling these $80X$, it could buy $25Y$ (at £83.33 each) because it has not produced any $Y$, because of specializing in the production of $X$s.

**Table 5.3** Comparative advantage

| | Production | | | |
|---|---|---|---|---|
| | **Annual output before specialization** | | **Annual output after specialization** | |
| **Country** | **X** | **Y** | **X** | **Y** |
| A | 100 | 80 | 40 | 128 |
| B | 90 | 10 | 180 | 0 |
| | 190 | 90 | 220 | 128 |

**Table 5.4** Prices in free trade

| | **Domestic prices** | | **Price to import at £1 = $1.50** | |
|---|---|---|---|---|
| **Country** | **X** | **Y** | **X** | **Y** |
| A, £ | 100 | 125 | 26.66 | 83.33 |
| B, $ | 40 | 360 | 150 | 187.50 |

**Table 5.5** Consumption after exchange

| Country | X | Y |
|---------|-----|-----|
| A | 120 | 103 |
| B | 100 | 25 |

Table 5.5 illustrates the final consumption after exchange and shows that both A and B now each have more *X* and more *Y*.

The theoretical gains from free trade based on comparative advantage forms the basis of why GATT and the WTO have sought to dismantle restrictions on trade.

### Terms of trade

International trade is influenced by changes in *relative prices*. The terms of trade show such price changes, which result from either changes in *domestic prices* or changes in the *exchange rate* or both. For instance, in Table 5.5, if country A became more efficient in producing *Y* and its price fell to £100 and the exchange rate fell to £1 = $1.25, then B could import *Y*s for $125, rather than $187.5.

The terms of trade indicate the relationship between the *average price* of a nation's exports and the average price of its imports. In each case the average price is *weighted* according to the volume of trade in the different goods and it is expressed through an index number.

The *measurement* formula is

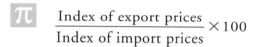

$$\frac{\text{Index of export prices}}{\text{Index of import prices}} \times 100$$

This ratio is taken as 100 in the base year. Britain's terms of trade index was 96.8 in 1996 (2003 = 100) but had risen to 100.6 in 2005.

- A rise in the ratio is described as an *improvement* because export prices are rising faster than import prices and this means that fewer exports need to be sold to pay for each import.
- However, this supposedly favourable movement in the terms of trade indicates a worsening of the *competitive position*. As export prices rise, the quantity demanded will probably fall (depending on the elasticity of demand), while cheaper imports may mean a loss of market share for home producers, and possible unemployment.

However, the terms of trade are only a guide to competitiveness because they only measure visible trade (i.e. trade in goods). Trade in services is not included, while non-price factors, such as the quality of products, are not evaluated in the index.

### 5.3.3 Practical limitations

The advantages which can be gained from specialisation and international trade may be limited in practice by many of the following:

- *Factor immobility.* Free trade theory assumed that factors were perfectly mobile, thereby enabling resources to be shifted between different sectors of production. In the real world, factors tend to be fairly immobile in the short run, and over longer periods in some industries, for instance, coal. However, improved technology has lowered factor costs and thereby facilitated more international trading.

- *Transport costs.* The simplifying assumption of no transport costs is clearly unrealistic. Although the production of certain bulky intermediate goods, such as cement, may be cheaper abroad, the distribution costs are so great that domestic suppliers still have a stranglehold over the market. Interestingly, coal imports into Britain increased only when the miners' strike of 1984–85 curtailed domestic production and made importing viable to coal users, when previously it had been uneconomic. However, generally transport costs in world trade are falling, thereby stimulating trade.

- *The size of the market.* Specialisation and the resultant possible economies of scale are only justified if the production can be sold. No longer can any individual European country support a commercial or military aircraft building industry from the size of its own domestic market. Consequently pan European production facilities have been established to produce the A380 Airbus and the Euro fighter.

  As the standard of living improves around the world so the sizes of markets grow. Generally, the development of new products, particularly in fields such as microelectronics, encourages world trade, as it creates new markets.

- *Government policies.* Governments may install barriers to trade for political, economic and social reasons. For example the United Kingdom prohibits trade with Zimbabwe and restricts arm sales to certain countries. The methods of trade restriction used are outlined in the next section.

### 5.3.4 Trade protection

#### The reasons for protection

- *To protect employment.* The free trade theory assumes that factors of production are mobile, but in reality they are not so. Therefore, if a nation with an absolute or comparative advantage successfully exports a good (e.g. Chinese textiles) thereby causing redundancies in a recipient nation (e.g. Britain), workers may become unemployed. The de-industrialisation of the British economy has created extensive localised unemployment because many of the redundant are not adaptable to the alternative service sector. In addition, there are insufficient jobs in the 'new' industries. For instance, the decline of the textile industry caused the British government to support the multi-fibre agreement (since 1975), which has restricted the import of cheap textiles into Europe so that jobs can be, at best, maintained or, at worst, only gradually shed.

- *To help an infant (sunrise) industry.* The classic argument for protection is that new industries require help during their infancy because of the high initial costs and lack of economies of scale. If this help was not provided and they had to face competition from fully developed similar industries, it is claimed that these industries might not survive. Import controls might enable a new industry to build a solid domestic base and benefit from economies of scale before embarking upon international competition. India uses a range of tariffs and controls to enable its domestic firms to become firmly established in its rapidly developing economy.

- *To prevent unfair competition.* A government may justify protection by reference to the trading policies of its competitor nations. For instance, certain third-world producers try to sell fake British goods in Britain. These imitations break the copyright and patent laws in purporting to be of British origin, and are justifiably banned. Another unfair practice, which is not illegal, is dumping. This involves selling exports at artificially low prices, in order to gain a start in foreign markets. For instance, Japanese excavators were sold for export at 45 per cent of the production cost. The losses abroad were subsidised by profits at home. Furthermore, the larger output, because of increasing exports, enabled economies of scale to be attained and unit costs lowered.

  Unfair trading can be more subtle than either of the above two varieties. Governments often subsidise their industries to enable them to compete in world markets, and Britain is not without its critics for giving such help to farming. Clearly, it is very difficult to decide objectively what constitutes 'fair trading'.

- *To protect the balance of payments.* One remedy suggested for persistent balance of payments deficit is the use of import controls. Britain has a high marginal propensity to import, which means imports grow more than proportionately as the domestic economy expands. The result is that frequent payments deficits have caused deflationary domestic policies, which inhibited domestic investment and weakened British industry. In addition, the rise in imports has reduced the market share of British firms, thereby making them less viable and less optimistic.

- *To raise revenue.* Protective tariffs will raise revenue for the Exchequer if such duties are levied on goods with inelastic demand.

- *To maintain security.* Essential products may be produced at home even when foreign goods may be more efficient, for example, defence equipment.

## Arguments against protection

- *Inefficiency is encouraged.* If British firms are protected from competition they may settle for their existing market share and profits. Such complacency will discourage innovation and risk-taking. New technology may not be introduced and overmanning may persist. The protected industry (e.g. the textiles industry) may lobby to make temporary help permanent.

- *Resources are misallocated.* By maintaining existing patterns of trade, resources do not move from declining industries, which are protected, to expanding industries. In addition, protection for one industry (e.g. steel) may adversely affect another (e.g. buyers of steel) because unit costs are raised.

- *The cost of living is raised.* Protection will probably raise prices and so domestic consumers have to pay higher prices for (the taxed) imported goods or for (the protected) home-produced goods.

- *Welfare gains will be lost.* The welfare gains resulting from specialisation-trade-exchange will be restricted if exchange is proscribed by protective measures. Ironically, it may be because a nation feels that it is not gaining enough of the global increase in welfare that it imposes trade restrictions. These restrictions may reduce consumer choice and increase the cost of living.

- *Retaliation may occur.* Protection by one nation may provoke its trading partners to take similar action, and this will reduce the volume of world trade with the attendant consequences outlined above. This may weaken confidence, as the internationally accepted rules for trading are weakened when governments take unilateral action.

## The methods of protection

- *Tariffs.* The most common import control is the tariff. This tax may be *ad valorem* – a given percentage of the import price – or *specific* (a set amount per item). It is sensible to levy tariffs on imports with an elastic demand if the objective is to reduce the volume of imports (e.g. the 33 per cent tariff on Japanese excavators in 1986). However, if a tariff is imposed in order to raise revenue, then goods with inelastic demand should be chosen. Tariffs, therefore, act on the price of goods/services.
- *Quotas.* In contrast, quotas are restrictions on the *quantity* of imports. The World Trade Organisation has tried to stop quotas, although it does permit exceptions for nations with severe balance of payments difficulties. A more acceptable and modern type of protection which aims to limit the amount of a certain good being imported is the *Voluntary Export Restraint Agreement* (VERA). In 1991 the EC applied a VERA to the Japanese car industry, which was supposed to have halted its exports to Europe when sales of Japanese cars exceeded 16 per cent of the market.
- *Hidden restrictions.* Also, there are hidden import restrictions and procedures which can be utilised to subtly undermine foreign competition. *Administrative devices* include complicated forms, special testing regulation and safety certification, unusual product specification and the specialisation of customs posts. For instance, the colour of yellow Trebor Refreshers had to be modified for sale in Japan because they were considered an optical health danger. Such devices may frustrate exporters and thereby protect domestic producers from imports. They are a relatively modern development in world trading and have accelerated since 1973. For example, in 1989 the EU banned hormone-fed meat from America for health and safety reasons and continues to discourage the introduction of genetically modified seeds for farming.

  In addition, the British government like others has used official persuasion to exclude imports; for example Ford Motor Company reduced the imports out of its European factories from 50 to 30 per cent of its United Kingdom sales because of government pleas. *Public procurement* can also be used to assist domestic firms. Government departments may deliberately buy goods from British firms even though they may not be the 'best on the market' (e.g. computer software for the Inland Revenue in 1993).
- *Subsidies.* As well as restricting imports, governments often *encourage exports* by various means. The systematic use of *export credits* and official support for export deals by departments is increasingly becoming part of Britain's trading strategy. Such measures make exporting cheaper and easier; a theme which is furthered by the government-sponsored international promotions and exhibitions.

  However, the most blatant help given to exporters is the direct subsidy, for example, the subsidies given by both national governments and the European Commission to European steel firms. This is outlawed by the WTO and so done in more subtle ways nowadays. For instance, VAT on exports is refunded by the British Government to the producers. Similarly, some European governments subsidise domestic producers. For example, Germany gives subsidies on electricity which indirectly helps German manufacturers' costs of production.

International friction has increased because of the expansion of protectionism. There is friction between governments (e.g. between countries of the EU over beef and livestock movements), and between governments and trading blocs. The EU is often in dispute with the United States over steel and agriculture exports and with Japan over many manufactured goods.

## Box 5.1   The Doha round drags on

In the summer of 2007 the main players in the WTO's current round of trade negotiations, the United States, the European Union, Brazil and India met to hammer out an agreement that would allow the Doha round to progress. The principal points at issue were agricultural protection and subsidies in the rich, developed economies and tariffs on industrial goods in developing economies.

Since it appeared that neither side would get all that they wanted from the Doha round, there was some talk of compromise and more modest ambitions. The United States appeared willing to reduce somewhat its subsidies to agriculture, but there was a fear among US farmers that current prosperity might not be permanent and continued protection was essential. In the EU opposition to serious reductions in the protection given to agriculture by the Common Agricultural Policy remained strong, especially from France and Poland. Meanwhile, Brazil suggested that it was willing to accept a maximum tariff of 30% that it could impose on imports industrial goods, but this was nearly double that envisaged by the developed economies.

However in 2008 the talks collapsed with no agreement being reached. In December Pascal Lamy, the director general of the WTO considered calling trade ministers together in the hope of concluding the deal. But the worsening economic environment and the onset of recession in many countries makes it unlikely that many countries would agree to reduce their protectionism in the near future.

## 5.3.5   World trade organisation

The World Trade Organisation (WTO) is the only global international organisation dealing with the rules of trade between nations. It replaced the General Agreement on Tariffs and Trade (GATT) on 1 January 1995, and 151 countries are members. At its heart are the WTO agreements, negotiated and signed by the bulk of the world's nations and ratified in their parliaments. The goal is to help producers of goods and services, exporters and importers conduct their business.

The major functions of the WTO are:

- Administer WTO trade agreements
- Provide a forum for trade negotiations
- Handle trade disputes
- Monitor national trade policies
- Provide technical assistance and training for developing countries.

In December 2005, ministers from the WTO's 151 member governments met in Hong Kong. After difficult negotiations certain outcomes were agreed:

- To end export subsidies in agriculture by 2013.
- An acceleration in ending export subsidies in cotton by the end of 2006.
- Cotton exports from least developed countries will be allowed into developed countries without tariffs or quotas from 2007.

The WTO has examined more than 300 cases of unfair trading practices and has the power to enforce binding arbitration on its members.

The G8 also has a role in supporting the international economy. It constitutes the heads of state or government of the major industrial democracies who meet annually to deal with major economic and political issues facing their domestic societies and the international community. Its members are the United States, Britain, France, Germany, Italy, Japan, Canada and Russia. The host of the 2008 G8 summit is Japan. The G8 has developed a network of supporting ministerial meetings, for example finance, which allow ministers to meet regularly throughout the year to continue the work set out at each summit.

The G8 summit has consistently dealt with:

- Macroeconomic management
- International trade
- Energy issues
- Development issues and relationships with developing countries
- Issues of international concern such as terrorism and organised crime.

The G8 does not have any formal resources or powers as is the case with other international organisations such as the WTO.

However, it provides a forum for the most powerful nations to discuss complex international issues and to develop the personal relations that help them respond in effective collective fashion to sudden crises or shocks. The summit also gives direction to the international community by setting priorities, defining new issues and providing guidance to established international organisations.

 ## Exercise 5.1

Answer the following questions based on the preceding information. You can check your answers below.

1. International trade is based on which principle?
2. What is the difference between absolute advantage and comparative advantage?
3. Why are exchange rates important?
4. What are the terms of trade?
5. What factors inhibit international trade?
6. Give three arguments for trade protection policies.
7. What is a VERA?
8. What does the WTO attempt to do?
9. Why have some companies become multinational in structure?
10. How can multinational companies benefit national economies?

 ## Solutions

1. International trade is theoretically based on the theory of comparative advantage.
2. Absolute advantage occurs where one country is much better than another at producing one good (but much worse at producing a second good). However, a country with a comparative advantage is one which is much better at producing two (or more goods) but by different amounts.
3. Exchange rates facilitate pricing and this enables international comparisons to be made.
4. The terms of trade refers to the average price of exports compared with the average price of imports.
5. International trade is inhibited by transport costs, the immobility of factors, market size and protective policies.

6. Protection is used to protect employment, help infant industries, prevent unfair competition and help the balance of payments.
7. Voluntary export restraint agreement.
8. The WTO tries to reduce tariff barriers and other protective measures.
9. To reduce costs and expand markets and sales. This has been helped by the development of appropriate organisational structures and technologies.
10. Direct foreign investment can boost: domestic capital fund; technology transfer; improvement in production processes and organisational structures; employment gains.

## 5.4 Foreign exchange

### 5.4.1 Exchange rates

The exchange rate of a currency is a *price*. It is the external value of a currency expressed in another currency, for example, £1 = $1.60. A more complex measure expresses the value in terms of a *weighted average* of exchange rates as an index number. These are currencies of a nation's main trading partners in manufactured goods and collected in a representative basket. This is known as the *effective* exchange rate and shows the relative importance of the country as a competitor in export markets. Britain's effective exchange rate has fluctuated since the new indexing in 1985. A fall in the index shows an overall relative depreciation of a currency. Thus in January 1997 it was 92.4 (January 2005 – 100) but had risen to 104.3 in August 2007.

The exchange of currencies is vital for trade in goods and services. British firms selling abroad will require foreign buyers to exchange their currency into sterling to facilitate payment. Similarly, British importers will need to pay out in foreign currencies. Also, when funds are transferred between people in different countries, foreign exchange is required. Today, the sale and purchase of currencies for trading purposes is dwarfed by the *lending* and *borrowing* of funds.

### 5.4.2 The foreign exchange market

This market enables companies, fund managers, banks and others to buy and sell foreign currencies. Capital flows arising from trade, investment, loans and speculative dealing create a large demand for foreign currency, particularly sterling, US dollars and euros and typically deals worth £400 billion are traded daily in London, the world's largest foreign exchange centre. London benefits from its geographical location, favourable time intervals (with the United States and the Far East in particular) and the variety of business generated there – insurance, commodities, banking, Eurobonds, etc.

Foreign exchange trading may be *spot* or *forward*.

- Spot transactions are undertaken almost immediately and settled within two days.
- However, forward buying involves a future delivery date from three months onward. Banks and brokers, on behalf of their clients, operate in the forward market to protect the anticipated flows of foreign currency from exchange rate volatility.

The forward price of a currency is normally higher (at a premium) or lower (at a discount) than the spot rate. Such premiums (or discounts) reflect interest rate differentials between currencies and expectations of currency depreciations and appreciations.

As the foreign exchange market has grown, so other instruments such as futures and options have been developed to protect foreign exchange commitments. Currency futures involve the trading of forward transactions other than for currencies themselves, while currency options enable buyers (at a premium paid to the writer of the option, usually a bank) to guarantee a buying (or selling) price for a currency at a future specified date.

### 5.4.3 Exchange rate systems

The world economy has experienced different exchange rate mechanisms. In the nineteenth and twentieth centuries, the gold standard was used, where exchange rates were fixed in terms of gold. A managed exchange rate system was established at Bretton Woods (United States) in 1944. This established exchange rates between economies but allowed a 1 per cent band either side of its parity. This system ended in 1972 when the pound sterling was allowed to float and other currencies soon followed.

#### Floating exchange rates

Exchange rates that float are flexible and free to fluctuate in the light of changes which take place in demand and supply. Such exchange rates are examples of nearly perfect markets.

(a) *Theory*. The simple theory assumes that a currency is only demanded and supplied for *trading* purposes, and that the curves are *elastic*. The demand curve for a currency shows the amount that traders wish to buy at various rates of exchange. This demand is higher at low exchange rates, in the normal way.

- The demand for pounds is a *derived* demand, reflecting the demand for British exports. A fall in the exchange rate will increase the competitiveness of exports and thereby raise the demand for pounds, assuming elastic demand for exports.
- In contrast, the *supply* of pounds represents the demand for British *imports*. This is because pounds are needed to buy the foreign currencies required to pay for the imports.

In Figure 5.5, a fall in the demand for British exports causes a shift to $D_1$. This shift causes a fall in the exchange rate to $P_1$, assuming that the demand for British imports remains unchanged. $P_1 Q_1$ would be a new equilibrium position at which the demand for pounds and the supply of pounds are equal. If pounds are bought and sold just for trading purposes, exchange rate equilibrium also produces balance of payments

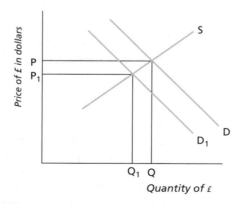

**Figure 5.5** Floating exchange rate

equilibrium. Nevertheless, changes in the non-price competitiveness of British goods and other countries' goods will cause disequilibrium. However, unimpeded floating exchange rates theoretically restore equilibrium automatically.

(b) *Practice.* The exchange rates, which have floated since 1972, are subject to influences other than trade.

Deposits of money can be transferred from one currency to another at short notice. This clearly affects the demand for, and supply of, currencies. The main factors influencing such transfers of what has been called 'hot money' are:

- relative interest rates – if the differential between nations changes, then capital tends to move towards the nation whose interest rate offers the most lucrative return;
- expectations – if the holders of 'hot money' expect a currency to appreciate, they will deposit money in that country, as the appreciation will raise the exchange value of the deposits;
- inflation – countries with relatively high rates will find their currency less attractive to depositors because its value is depreciating more than that of other countries.

Often, currencies are bought and sold for *speculative* motives. Speculators are interested in short-term capital gains. For instance, if a currency is backed by significant national assets, such as oil reserves, and sustained in attractiveness by high interest rates, it could be much demanded. This might override the demand for a currency for trading purposes and produce an exchange rate which does not reflect trading conditions. If this persists and the currency is higher than the underlying economic circumstances warrant, then it might be deemed *overvalued*. Thus, the simple theory does not apply in practice, as market forces can be distorted and exaggerated.

Furthermore, in the real world the demand and supply elasticities for goods and services, as well as currencies, are not perfectly elastic. A foreign exchange rate will tend to be unstable when the supply curve is more elastic than the demand curve. Thus, only in theory are floating exchange rates inherently self-stabilising.

### Dirty floating

Governments often intervene in the foreign exchange markets in order to maintain or achieve an *exchange rate target*. The purpose of this normally is to make a country's exports more competitive, by lowering the exchange rate, or to assist in the control of inflation. The central bank will be instructed to:

- Buy or sell the currency to raise or lower the exchange rate.
- Alter interest rates to encourage the buying or selling of the currency. For example, a raising of interest rates should encourage speculators to deposit more funds in that country. The subsequent rise in demand for the currency should cause a rise in the exchange rate.

### 5.4.4 Arguments for floating rates

(a) In theory, the floating rate *automatically adjusts* a balance of payments disequilibrium. This was explained above. The self-correcting mechanism means that policies, such as deflation, to rectify a balance of payments deficit will not need to be implemented. This gives a government greater freedom to pursue domestic policies.

- However, it can be countered that demand and supply inelasticities, the activities of speculators and the behaviour of government prevent this adjustment from occurring in the real world. The rise of 30 per cent in the value of the pound sterling in the decade to 2007 was evidence, for opponents of floating exchange rates, that the self-correcting mechanism does not always work as during this period the United Kingdom experienced persistent deficits in the current account of its balance of payments with ensuing damage to its industrial base and international competitiveness.
- In addition, it can be argued that the freedom leads to reckless *irresponsibility*. A government may assume that a floating exchange rate will solve an inflation problem and so not pursue necessary domestic policies, which maintenance of a fixed exchange rate might have forced on them, thereby worsening the inflation problem.

(b) Less *speculation* will occur because a currency can appreciate or depreciate, whereas under a fixed rate regime currency changes were nearly always devaluations. This meant that speculators, who sold a currency which had been devalued, could not lose and could only gain.

For instance, someone holding £1,000 at £1 = $1.80 moves into dollars, securing $1800 (assuming no transaction costs). If sterling is devalued to £1 = $1.40 the dollar holding is now worth £1286 if the switch back into sterling is made in order to secure a capital gain. Conversely, if sterling is not devalued, the switch back into sterling is still worth £1,000 with no loss made.

(c) A more efficient allocation of resources is secured if exchange rates reflect changed economic conditions. It is argued that floating rates will reflect changes in demand and supply, and that they are more *sensitive* and respond quickly to underlying economic trends. This might enable the theory of comparative advantage to be operative. As floating rates change daily, they are more subtle but probably at the cost of greater volatility.

Fluctuations in exchange rates can cause *uncertainty*. This could deter trade, as contracts with fixed prices become more risky as exchange rate appreciation will cut profit margins. However, to some extent this problem can be offset by buying a currency in the forward market.

(d) A large supply of *reserves* is unnecessary in a floating system because the automatic adjustment of a balance of payments deficit (or surplus) is achieved by an exchange rate depreciation (or appreciation). In theory, reserves will be automatically maintained and so domestic policy changes such as interest rate increases will not be needed to keep the exchange rate up.

### 5.4.5 Exchange rate changes

*Long-term theory*

There are three main theories which attempt to explain the underlying reasons why exchange rates change over time:

(a) *Purchasing power parity* (PPP). This theory maintains that exchange rates will tend towards the point at which their *international purchasing power* is equal. Thus, if one country's inflation increases 5 per cent more than another's in one year, the former's exchange rate would depreciate by 5 per cent. This would restore the former country's international purchasing power in theory.

However, there are several problems with the use of this theory:

- *Inflation measurement.* the usual measure (RPI) includes goods and services (e.g. housing) which are not internationally traded, and indirect taxes which only change domestic prices. This limits its usefulness. As an alternative measure of competitiveness unit wage costs have been suggested. However, unless they are taken just for manufactured goods, allowances will need to be made for non-tradeable goods and services and public sector employment.

- *Base year.* this choice is arbitrary, unless some very unrealistic assumptions are made about exchange rate equilibrium and inflation stability.

- *Capital movements.* Exchange rates, since the 1980s particularly, have reflected the perceptions and expectations of international financiers, rather than the real trading between economies. The massive transactions of currency relating to borrowing exceed those connected with trade by at least 20 times (some estimates give 100 times), and so it could be argued that exchange rates do not indicate real changes in a nation's competitiveness. The massive rise of sterling from $1.75 to $2.50 in six months of 1980 was against a background of dwindling manufactured exports and rising domestic inflation.

- *Empirical evidence.* If PPP holds true then the 'real exchange rate', which is the nominal rate adjusted for differential inflation, should remain roughly constant. At worst, it should tend towards a long-run equilibrium, and be less volatile than the nominal rate. Research by both Williamson and Morgan Guaranty, using different base years, shows Britain's real exchange rate persistently well above 100 since 1977, peaking around 150 in late 1980 and plummeting to 115 in 1985, that is significantly overvalued.

(b) *The Keynesian approach.* Keynesians do not see exchange rates as automatically adjusting. They believe that the 'real exchange rate' can be in *disequilibrium* for years. There is not a PPP equilibrium in the short or medium term because:

- prices may be very slow to adjust to changes in nominal exchange rates (because of the inflexibility of wages in the labour market);

- interest rates have a distorting effect on the nominal exchange rate. High interest rates can be used to keep up the external value of the currency. This might enable a government's anti-inflation strategy to succeed;

- speculators can distort market forces. If they see a price steadily falling, they sell, and it takes a shock to reverse the trend. In recent years, speculation has destabilised the foreign exchange market by following the trend rather than reversing it. The continued overvaluation of the dollar in 1985–86, which was attributable to high interest rates, fat profits and an economic boom, was only undermined by concerted intervention in the market by several major governments, bringing a fall in the dollar in Autumn 1986.

(c) *Monetarist theory.* Changes in exchange rates reflect changes in domestic money supply conditions (based on the quantity theory of money view of inflation). Thus, if Britain increases its monetary growth by 20 per cent and Japan keeps its growth unchanged, sterling will depreciate against the yen. This means that exchange rates will modify so that home goods are priced at the world equilibrium price. If not, British consumers will buy imports, unless trade is restricted, and eventually force down domestic prices.

Economic growth, by absorbing some of the monetary expansion, will tend to keep the exchange rate up. It will also encourage a currency to appreciate because international financiers will behave *rationally* (expecting the appreciation) and bring about the appreciation by buying the currency. Thus, supposedly rational factors will determine the exchange rate.

As in other matters, monetarists do not believe in government meddling. However, if a monetarist government has a policy rule of slow money supply growth, then the associated policy of high interest rates to deter the demand for money will probably cause the exchange rate to rise. Interestingly, this might bring about lower inflation, as an appreciating exchange rate reduced import prices. In general, the monetarists believe in the exchange rate, like other prices, being determined by *market forces*. To them, the exchange rate is 'just another price'.

### Short-/medium-term factors

The demand and supply of currencies is determined by several economic forces, and some other elements

- *Relative inflation rates.* Nations with comparatively high inflation are likely to find their currencies in less demand, other things being equal, because funds transferred will lose their real value more quickly.
- *Trade flows.* Countries with balance of payments deficits are more likely to suffer depreciating currency because supply of their currency will exceed its demand.
- *Investment flows.* If foreign investment is attracted to an economy (perhaps by its internal conditions, e.g. low wage costs) then this will stimulate demand for its currency.
- *Economic prospects.* If the economic forecasts for an economy are bullish, then this will attract footloose international funds, raising demand and enhancing the exchange rate.
- *Speculators' judgment.* As 95 per cent of demand is from market makers and dealers, rather than trade customers, if they perceive that a currency is overvalued they will sell, thereby lowering its rate. Often they react to political as well as economic news which is unexpected, because anticipated events will have already been 'discounted'.
- *Technical analysis.* Sometimes the charts of banks and brokers indicate future movements of a currency are likely, given the underlying assumption that price movements follow broadly predictable patterns. Such predictions may influence demand.

---

### Box 5.2   The development of the euro

The euro has been in operation for a decade. Early after its inception the euro weakened a great deal against the dollar and sterling, but has since recovered. Initially this tended to reflect the dollar's weakness rather than any underlying strength of the euro, but in recent years the success of the eurozone and stability of the euro have contributed to its strengthening exchange rate. Moreover, in long term, the impact of the euro could be far reaching.

As goods and services are priced in euros, consumers will be able to *compare prices* across Europe and greater price convergence can be expected.

The single currency will lead to the elimination of transactions costs in switching from one currency to another and will remove *exchange rate risks* for trade within the eurozone. As a result, intra-EU trade, with all its benefits, should expand.

Moreover all of this will *increase competition* within the EU and may encourage cross-country mergers as companies seek to operate across the EU.

This is not to say that problems do not exist. The need for economic convergence within the eurozone is crucial if one currency, and therefore one monetary policy conducted by the European Central Bank is to be effective.

## 5.4.6 European central bank

The primary objective of the European Central Bank (ECB) is to maintain stability within the euro area. This can bring it into conflict with Article 2 of the Treaty on European Union which seeks to maintain a high level of employment and sustainable non-inflationary growth. The basic tasks of the ECB are to:

- Implement the monetary policy of the euro area. In effect this means the operation of interest rates to check inflation;
- Conduct foreign exchange operations;
- Hold and manage the official foreign reserves of euro area countries;
- Promote smooth operation of payment systems;
- Oversee and issue banknotes within the euro area.

# 5.5 The balance of payments

## 5.5.1 The accounts

The balance of payments is an account showing the financial transactions of one nation with the rest of the world over a period of time. The statistics are calculated monthly and analysed on quarterly and annual bases. The official figures are often revised. This results from the use of estimates and the problems of information gathering. Clearly these accounts are difficult to assemble and *revisions* sometimes occur years later. For instance, the overseas earnings of the Lloyd's insurance syndicate can only be an estimate until Lloyd's accounts are published, and these cover three-year trading periods.

Trend changes in the balance of payments can be a useful indicator to the government. For example, the deterioration in Britain's non-oil visible trade balance caused by deindustrialisation is clear in the accounts. However, they are a lagging indicator and as such of limited value for immediate policy action.

The balance of payments accounts have been organised in various ways at different times. Presently, they are divided into three accounts: current, capital and financial.

### The current account

This is composed of two parts.

(a) *Visible trade.* This is trade in goods. Exports by Britain are shown as credits (e.g. machinery sold to Saudi Arabia); while imports are debits (e.g. French perfume sold in Britain). The difference between the totals is known as the balance of trade.

Historically, Britain has run a deficit on visible trade, with the imports of food and raw materials outweighing the exports of manufactured goods. However, in 1980–82 visible trade moved into surplus because of the earnings of North Sea oil and gas. If the non-oil trade balance was calculated for the period, though, only four quarters showed a surplus. From 1983 visible trade returned to deficit and this has increased with the effects of de-industrialisation, as shown in Table 5.6.

(b) *Invisible trade.* Invisible trade includes trade in services, investment income and transfers of money between individuals and national bodies. The trade in services is shown. The income earned from the sale of British services abroad is known as an invisible export (e.g. consultancy fees paid to a British firm for advice on a Saudi Arabian building project).

THE MACROECONOMIC CONTEXT OF BUSINESS

**Table 5.6** Britain's visible balance 1996–2006

|  | Exports £m | Imports £m | Visible balance £m |
|---|---|---|---|
| 1996 | 167,403 | 180,489 | −13,086 |
| 1999 | 267,845 | 195,217 | −27,372 |
| 2003 | 187,846 | 235,136 | −47,290 |
| 2006 | 245,105 | 328,736 | −83,631 |

*Source*: ONS

**Table 5.7** Britain's trade in services 1996–2006

|  | Invisible balance £m |
|---|---|
| 1996 | +11,204 |
| 1999 | +13,597 |
| 2003 | +19,162 |
| 2006 | +29,194 |

*Source*: ONS

In contrast, invisible imports arise when British citizens spend money on foreign services (e.g. a British tourist to Texas pays for accommodation). The invisible account can be considered in three sectors:

- *Interest, profits and dividends* (IPD). This sector shows substantial surpluses (£22 billion in 2006). Investment income is made up of interest, profits and dividends earned by British institutions, from the activities of the overseas branches of British-based companies and from the holding by Britons of overseas (paper) assets. These earnings are likely to grow because, since 1979, with the abolition of exchange controls and the portfolio investment of the North Sea oil surpluses, British overseas investment by the private sector has increased. Some critics felt that it would be a once-and-for-all adjustment in institutional portfolios, but the expertise acquired by fund managers appears to have stimulated increasing capital outflows.
- *Services.* These have earned a large invisible surplus in most years. The financial services of the City of London dominate this sector, with the earnings of solicitors, brokers, merchants, bankers and commodity traders having a net credit of £25 billion in 2006, although transport and travel have a net debit over of £18 billion.
- *Transfers.* Transfers by both private individuals and the government tend to be outward on balance, with the government's share being larger and being spent on embassies, military bases and contributions to international organisations, including the EU. This sector produced a debit of over £12 billion in 2006.

### Current account balance

This combines the visible and invisible trade, as shown in Table 5.8. Generally a surplus balance is a good sign, and can indicate a prosperous and expanding economy. Britain's current account was in surplus in the early 1980s but has been in deficit ever since.

A deficit (surplus) on the current account will be balanced by a surplus (deficit), that is a net inflow (outflow) on the combined capital and financial accounts. However, as changes

**Table 5.8** Britain's current account 1996–2006

|  | Visibles £m | Invisibles £m | Current account balance £m | %GDP |
|---|---|---|---|---|
| 1996 | −13,086 | +6,703 | −6,717 | −0.9 |
| 1999 | −27,372 | +5,655 | −21,717 | −2.4 |
| 2003 | −47,290 | +32,369 | −14,921 | −1.3 |
| 2006 | −83,361 | +35,580 | −47,781 | −3.7 |

*Source*: ONS

**Table 5.9** Capital and financial account (net transactions)

|  | 1996 | 2003 | 2006 |
|---|---|---|---|
| Capital Balance | 1,260 | 1,466 | 678 |
| Financial account |  |  |  |
| Direct Investment | −5,952 | −24,113 | 7,395 |
| Portfolio investment | −16,764 | 58,955 | −40,733 |
| Other investment | 24,054 | −10,493 | 52,110 |
| Reserve assets | 510 | 1,559 | 426 |
| Net financial transaction | 2,811 | 20,507 | 26,647 |
| Balancing items | 2,646 | −7,052 | 20,456 |

*Note*: These accounts do not exactly balance because of the exclusion of some minor items and different basis for calculation of some items.

*Source*: ONS

in the current account affect national income, a deficit means a decrease in spending power (and a net withdrawal from the circular flow), which is *deflationary*.

### The capital and financial accounts

These accounts show transactions in Britain's external assets and liabilities, as shown in Table 5.9. It records *capital and financial movements* by firms, individuals and governments. It also includes the *balancing item*. A positive balancing item indicates unrecorded net exports, while a negative total shows unrecorded net imports. Since 1988 Britain had some unusually high balancing items. The figure arises because of the errors and omissions which occur in the collection of such detailed and numerous statistics based on enormous numbers of international transactions.

The movement of funds into Britain (external liabilities) is indicated by positive numbers, whereas outflows of funds are marked with a minus sign (−). This is the acquisition of external assets. For example, the investment by Toyota in British car plants would be an inflow under the direct investment category. Conversely, if a British bank buys shares in a French company this would be included in the portfolio investment overseas by United Kingdom residents' section. An 'investment' such as the latter will benefit the balance of payments in the long run as it generates invisible income for the current account. However, it has been argued that it harms the British economy because resources are used overseas and so a leakage from the circular flow is created.

In contrast, net inward investment benefits the balance of payments in the short run because less official financing is needed. It also adds to the circular flow and stimulates domestic economic activity in terms of employment and ancillary production. However, it may eventually be detrimental to the balance of payments because profits from the investment will be remitted abroad and become invisible imports, while the goods produced may supplant British goods in the home market.

The short-term capital movements in the account are the changes in foreign currency and sterling holdings. Such transfers of 'hot money' tend to be volatile and unpredictable, fluctuating with interest rate changes and exchange rate variations. The 'other' category includes the official resources, private sector transactions with banks, trade credit and inter-government loans. It was calculated that £15 billion of resources were used on 'Black Wednesday' in September 1992 to buy sterling in order to try to keep it in the ERM. When devaluation by about 20 per cent did occur, a £3 billion loss in the value of the reserves was sustained.

## 5.5.2 Disequilibrium

Although the balance of payments accounts always balance for technical reasons, economists are concerned with the component parts of the structure. Persistent imbalances in certain sections, such as the visible trade and the current account, indicate *fundamental disequilibrium* and induce governments to undertake policy action to create/restore equilibrium. For instance, a persistent balance of payments current account deficit may be covered by substantial capital inflows or by a decrease in official reserves. The former may be achieved by higher interest rates for a short period of time, while the latter similarly cannot be undertaken indefinitely. However, this temporary expediency may have damaging consequences for the economy, such as higher debt repayments, lower investment and a higher exchange rate. Thus, remedial action to deal with a balance of payments problem may constrain policies which are designed to achieve other economic objectives, that is economic growth via lower interest rates.

Disequilibrium occurs when the balance of payments on current account is persistently imbalanced over several years. In the case of Britain this occurred in the 1970s, when deficits frequently arose. However, in the early 1980s there were annual surpluses, mainly because of North Sea oil. Since 1985 the problem of persistent deficit has returned alarmingly.

In 2006 the deficit was 3.7 per cent of GDP. A deficit demonstrates the uncompetitiveness of British trade. In Britain's case, as we have seen visible trade in goods suffers a comparative disadvantage, while the service sector with invisible surpluses seems to indicate a comparative advantage.

### Causes

(a) *Import penetration.* This can arise from imports taking larger shares of static markets or from imports maintaining their shares of expanding markets. In Britain's case both occurred and most sectors of industry experienced substantial import penetration, mainly from Europe and Japan. For instance, 7 per cent of vehicles bought in Britain came from abroad in 1970, but by 2006 this had reached 70 per cent. These figures show the increased competitiveness of foreign suppliers.

Import penetration has increased for many reasons.

- The income elasticity of demand for manufactured goods is high in the United Kingdom, around +3 compared to +2 in Germany. The income elasticity of demand for all imports is +1.8. This become particularly important as Britain has large consumption expenditure as a proportion of GDP. The consumer boom in the late 1990s and early 21st century was, therefore, largely supported by imports.

- For many goods lower unit costs in the United Kingdom's trading partners have made imports more competitive than domestic substitutes.
- The periodic overvaluation of sterling, for example in 2004–2007 reduced the sterling price of imports in the United Kingdom market.
- Some United Kingdom producers have lacked competitiveness in non-price factors such as design, reliability, delivery and pre and after sales service.

(b) *Export performance.* The other main obvious symptom of Britain's current account deficits was the relatively poor export performance. British exports needed to grow disproportionately faster than those of rivals because of Britain's high importing propensity. However, the factors determining British exports are similar to those affecting the demand for imports.

- First, the willingness and ability of domestic producers to supply abroad. For instance, a growing home market and a lack of surplus capacity will inhibit exporting and lead to concentration on home sales.
- Second, the price competitiveness of British exports. Unfortunately, the short-run price elasticity of demand for British exports has been calculated as less than 0.5.
- Third, the *income elasticity of demand* in foreign markets. This is much lower than in Britain because other trading economies are less open and their firms tend to have more surplus capacity which can be quickly utilised to raise output for domestic consumption.

Specific underlying problems with Britain's exports seem to be insufficient investment in new technology, inadequate management and a lack of quality products. Despite productivity improvements, Britain's overall productivity still lags still lags behind other G8 countries with output per man hour worked being significantly higher in France and the USA. Furthermore a report, *Made in Britain* (IBM London Business School), reckoned that only 2 per cent of United Kingdom factories are world class and that at least 40 per cent are beyond hope. There is a big failure to invest in research and development. British companies spend 1.5 per cent of sales revenue on this, compared with 4.6 per cent by the world's 200 largest companies.

Manufacturing is highly important to Britain's current account, with around 54 per cent of its export earnings in 2006 coming from trade in manufactures. Since the 1970s the rate of growth of manufacturing exports has been well below that for manufacturing imports. As a consequence Britain's share of world manufacturing exports fell from 17 per cent in 1960 to 3.7 per cent in 2006. Some reckon that foreign-owned 'transplants' into Britain (e.g. Toyota and other Japanese car makers) will act to bring British component makers up to the quality and delivery standards of our main trading rivals. However competition from newly industrialised countries may make this difficult to achieve. In 2005 Chinese manufacturing exports were twice as large as those of Britain.

Britain's structural *disequilibrium* in its balance of payments is due to a high demand for imports alongside a weak export performance in manufacturing products.

## 5.5.3 Policies

Many policies have been advocated to restore a balance of payments account to equilibrium, usually when deficits have been a regular feature and there is evidence of fundamental disequilibrium.

## Depreciation of the exchange rate

Prior to 1972, when there was a system of fixed exchange rates, a reduction in the exchange rate was termed a *devaluation*.

- This was undertaken in 1967 when the pounds was devalued from $2.80 to $2.40. The objective was to make British goods more competitive by lowering an overvalued exchange rate which had kept prices artificially high.
- For instance, prior to devaluation a British export priced at £5 would sell in America for $14; but when the exchange rate was lowered to $2.40, it would sell for $12, thus becoming more price-competitive.
- Conversely, an American export at $56 would sell in Britain at £20 before the 1967 devaluation and at £23.33 afterwards. Thus British imports would become dearer and less competitive.

However, since 1972 exchange rates have for the most part floated, and a depreciation refers to a *downward float*.

- Thus in autumn 2008, the £ fell from $2.00 to $1.50 before recovering. This had a similar effect, making British exports cheaper and British imports dearer.
- Floating exchange rates are less under government influence and they are sup-posedly determined by market forces.
- However, governments do intervene, by instructing their central banks to buy or sell the currency as necessary. Such action has been termed *dirty floating*. For example, in late 1986 the Bank of England borrowed heavily to buy pounds to maintain the value of sterling.

In addition, a government can influence the exchange rate by general and specific pol-icies. It can seek to persuade the market that it is pursuing economically acceptable policies in order to retain faith in the currency and keep the rate up. Alternatively, it can more spe-cifically manipulate interest rates in order to artificially influence the international demand for the currency. An increase in interest rates tends to raise demand and thus the exchange rate appreciates. In September 1986, the Bank of England's extra purchasing of sterling on the foreign exchanges was insufficient to cause the value of sterling to appreciate and so the Chancellor of the Exchequer acted to raise interest rates by 1 per cent to thwart the downward pressure on the pound. In this case the exchange rate was maintained because a fall was not desired. The primary economic objective at the time was control of inflation, and it was feared that a lower exchange rate would raise the cost of living, via more expen-sive imports, and reduce real incomes. The Treasury model maintains that any gains from depreciating sterling turn into later losses as higher domestic costs feed through.

Usually, though, the objective behind depreciation and devaluation has been to induce *expenditure-switching* by consumers. This occurs in two ways:

- dearer imports hopefully lead British consumers to buy British goods instead,
- while cheaper exports cause foreign consumers to purchase British exports rather than foreign products.

The effectiveness of such an expenditure-switching policy is largely dependent upon the price elasticities of demand for imports and exports.

- The British balance of payments will benefit from devaluation only if the amount spent on imports is exceeded by the amount received from exports.
- This occurs if the sum of the import and export elasticities exceeds unity (1).

For instance, if the demand for British exports is elastic, the lower price will bring about an increase in the total revenue from exports. Conversely, if the demand for foreign imports is elastic, then their higher price will cause a fall in total spending on imports.

However, the elasticities approach proposed by Marshall–Lerner has been heavily criticised.

- It is very simple in that it assumes that goods are bought solely on the basis of *relative prices* (ignoring design, delivery, etc.).
- In addition, it assumes that *income effects* are non-existent or that income elasticities are zero for all goods.
- Further, by looking at just the demand side, the Marshall–Lerner approach ignores supply. It assumes that supply is infinitely elastic so that increases in the quantity of exports demanded can be immediately fulfilled. Britain's lack of spare capacity makes that assumption unrealistic.
- In the first quarter after the 1992 devaluation (ERM exit), exporters responded to the new competitive advantage by boosting export prices 6 per cent while export volume rose by only 0.5 per cent (thus suggesting that supply is most *inelastic*).

Therefore, the elasticities approach is very simplistic.

It is also non-operational, because of the enormous difficulties of calculating the elasticity values. Estimates of the price elasticities for British goods vary between forecasting bodies and for different time periods. However, generally the price elasticity for British exports is low, being 0.5, but increasing to above 1.0 after 16 quarters in most models. As the price elasticity of imports is also low, and possibly around 0.4, it is clear that the Marshall–Lerner condition is unlikely to be achieved (as the total elasticity is less than 1.0). This conclusion undermines the devaluation/depreciation policy. Ironically, it suggests that appreciation would be better, because if combined elasticities are less than 1.0, a higher valued exchange rate will raise foreign exchange receipts by more than it increases import payments.

Even if elasticities are favourable, a depreciation/devaluation will not immediately benefit a balance of payments in practice.

- There is an initial worsening of the current account because volumes are fixed and prices adjust automatically.
- However, eventually demand and supply become more elastic and so consumption and production patterns change, creating an improvement in the accounts.
- This tendency for the balance of payments to deteriorate initially following depreciation and subsequently to improve has been termed the *'J'-curve effect*, as illustrated in Figure 5.6.

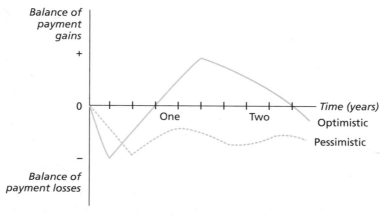

**Figure 5.6**  Possible 'J'-curve effect

The exact shape of the 'J'-curve depends upon the assumptions made. In Figure 5.6 the optimistic 'J'-curve shows that after nine months the balance of payments gains from devaluation and that this benefit may continue for another six quarters, yielding a net surplus. The pessimistic curve has a wholly negative effect, because it assumes inelastic supply and rising domestic inflation. Furthermore, there is some evidence that, following a depreciation, British exporters maintain their foreign exchange price (i.e. raise their prices measured in sterling) rather than lowering them; this raises their short-run profits at the expense of long-run sales growth.

### Deflation

An effective, but generally undesirable, policy used to return a balance of payments deficit to equilibrium has been domestic deflation to induce *expenditure-reduction* by consumers.

- The government, through either tight fiscal or restrictive monetary policy, curbs demand at home.
- The balance of payments is improved because the growth of import demand is weakened and domestic suppliers, facing a static home market, might switch resources towards export markets in order to fully utilise capacity.
- Additional gains from government deflationary policies can be to weaken trade union bargaining power through the fear of unemployment and by restraining production costs help to reduce inflation.

Although deflation improves the current account of the balance of payments, it has unfortunate costs for the economy.

- The tightening of fiscal policy, by either tax increases or expenditure cuts, and the restrictions on money supply, both reduce the demand for goods.
- Less demand means less supply and so unemployment rises.
- The general effect is to constrain the rate of economic growth, by depressing business optimism, lowering investment and under-utilizing resources.

Deflation is often used in conjunction with depreciation (devaluation) of the currency to improve the current account of the balance of payments.

### Import controls

These have the effect of causing expenditure switching rather than expenditure reduction. *Quotas* prevent the purchase of imports, while *tariffs* raise import prices and possibly lower outgoings (assuming elastic demand for imports). The advantage gained from implementation will probably only be temporary because the basic weakness of price uncompetitiveness has not been changed. The likelihood would be that a fundamental disequilibrium would return once the import controls were lifted.

In Britain's case, wide-ranging import controls are not a realistic option. As a member of the WTO Britain has disavowed such a policy, while membership of the EU obviates such a unilateral action. There is also the danger of retaliation by our trading partners, with the consequent diminution in world trade.

### Supply-side policies

These were policies which attempt to improve the efficiency of the supply base of the economy. By freeing up markets, increasing incentives, deregulating and removing the dead hand of the state from economic activity, it is claimed that the economy can be revitalised and achieve non-inflationary economic growth. The intention is to transform attitudes and behaviour so that British competitiveness re-emerges. Although the renaissance of any economy cannot happen overnight, the British economy has managed a period of sustained economic growth for a period 1995–2007. However there is little evidence that this has brought about any permanent improvement in the balance of payments.

## 5.5.4 International financial organisations

**The International Monetary Fund (IMF)** was created in 1945 to help promote the health of the world economy. It is governed by and accountable to the governments of the 185 countries that make up its near-global membership.

Its main responsibilities are to:

- promote international monetary co-operation;
- facilitate the expansion and balanced growth of international trade;
- promote exchange rate stability;
- assist in the establishment of a multilateral system of payments;
- support members experiencing balance of payments difficulties.

To enable it to carry out these roles the IMF:

- conducts in depth appraisal of each member country's economic situation;
- provides technical assistance and advice on fiscal and monetary policy, banking and financial system supervision and regulation and statistics;
- provides financial assistance. In 2006, $28 billion was on loan to 74 countries. Some of these loans are used to reduce poverty, for example by the Heavily Indebted Poor Countries (HIPC) initiative.

**The World Bank** is a vital source of financial and technical assistance to developing countries. It is owned by 185 member countries who make subscriptions to enable it to function. It supports two development institutions. The International Bank for Reconstruction and Development (IBRD) which focuses on middle income and creditworthy poor countries; and the International Development Association (IDA) which deals with the world's poorest countries.

The mission of the World Bank is to work with partner countries to alleviate poverty.
It does this by a variety of means:

- Providing loans and grants on favourable terms. These can be used to improve infrastructure or for economic and social development projects.

    Each borrower's project proposal is assessed to ensure that the project is economically, financially, socially and environmentally sound. During negotiations the World Bank may make the loans and/or grants conditional on the borrower country making changes in the management of its own economy. Such interference in domestic economic policy making has attracted criticism of the World Bank.
- Analytical and advisory services.

## Exercise 5.2

Answer the following questions based on the preceding information. You can check your answers below.

1. Name one invisible earning.
2. What do the capital and financial accounts show?
3. What is 'hot money'?

4. What has caused Britain's balance of payments current account deficit?
5. What is the difference between devaluation and depreciation of the exchange rate?
6. How could a fall in the exchange rate help an economy?
7. What does the 'J'-curve show?
8. How can deflation help the balance of payments deficit?

##  Solutions

1. A dividend from an overseas share.
2. The capital and financial accounts show changes in a country's external assets and liabilities.
3. 'Hot money' refers to short-term capital movements of currencies by international financiers/speculators.
4. Britain's current account deficit has been caused by a lack of competitiveness (for many reasons) in trade.
5. A devaluation occurs when a fixed exchange rate is lowered, whereas depreciation refers to a floating exchange rate which is moving downwards.
6. A fall in the exchange rate could help an economy by reducing the price of exports (and increasing the price of imports) and thereby increasing sales, which might lead to increased employment and greater export earnings (if demand is price elastic).
7. The 'J' curve shows the effect of a currency depreciation on the current account, in particular, that the initial effect is likely to be a deterioration in that account.
8. Deflation can help the balance of payments by suppressing domestic demand for imports and by releasing goods for export (if home sales are stagnant).

## 5.6 Chapter summary

In this chapter the analysis of economic processes and economic decisions has been extended to the international economy. Most economies are now *open economies* where there are significant movements of goods, services and factors of production, especially capital, across national borders. These movements raise a range of important issues. These have been discussed in this chapter and the focus has been on:

- the process of economic growth in the international economy; the factors which influence the rate of growth and policies towards growth.
- the globalisation process and the forces contributing to globalisation, especially the multi-national company.
- the process of international trade in goods and services, and the theoretical explanations of trade and its economic benefits; the institutions of international trade, especially the World Trade Organisation, and issues of trade policy.
- the operation of foreign exchange markets and the determination of exchange rates under different exchange rate regimes; the impact of changes in exchange rates on businesses and economies.
- the balance of payments accounts; the structure of the balance of payments accounts, balance of payments problems and policies towards managing the balance of payments.

# Revision Questions

You should use these questions for practice and revision for the content of this chapter. The first question contains a selection of multiple-choice subquestions; questions 2 and 3 are data-response questions.

## Question 1 Multiple-choice selection

1.1   A country is said to have a comparative advantage in the production of a good when:

(A)  it can produce more of it than any other country.
(B)  it has captured a larger share of the world market than any other country.
(C)  it can produce it at a lower opportunity cost than its trading partners.
(D)  its costs of production for the good are lower than in other countries.

1.2   The existence of international trade is best explained by the fact that countries:

(A)  use different currencies.
(B)  have different economic systems.
(C)  have different endowments of factors of production.
(D)  have specialised in different goods and services.

1.3   Which of the following might cause a country's exports to fall?

(A)  A fall in the exchange rate for that country's currency.
(B)  A reduction in other countries' tariff barriers.
(C)  A decrease in the marginal propensity to import in other countries.
(D)  A rise in that country's imports.

1.4   The current account of the balance of payments includes all of the following items except which *one*?

(A)  The inflow of capital investment by multinational companies.
(B)  Exports of manufactured goods.
(C)  Interest payments on overseas debts.
(D)  Expenditure in a country by overseas visitors.

1.5   The main objective of the WTO is:

(A)  to raise living standards in developing countries.
(B)  to minimise barriers to international trade.

(C) to harmonise tariffs.

(D) to eliminate customs unions.

**1.6** The main advantage of a system of flexible (floating) exchange rates is that it:

(A) provides certainty for international traders.

(B) provides automatic correction of balance of payments deficits.

(C) reduces international transactions costs.

(D) provides policy discipline for governments.

**1.7** Which of the following would normally result from an increase (appreciation) in a country's exchange rate?

(i) A fall in the country's rate of inflation.

(ii) A rise in the volume of its exports.

(iii) An improvement in its terms of trade.

(iv) A surplus on its current account.

(A) (i), (ii) and (iii) only.

(B) (ii), (iii) and (iv) only.

(C) (i) and (iii) only.

(D) (ii) and (iv) only.

**1.8** If a country has a *floating (flexible)* exchange rate, which one of the following would lead to a fall (depreciation) in the rate of exchange for its currency?

(A) A rise in capital inflows into the economy.

(B) An increase in the country's exports.

(C) An increase in the country's imports.

(D) A fall in the country's rate of inflation.

## ? Question 2 Balance of payments

The following data refer to a country's balance of payments:

|   |   | $m |
|---|---|---:|
| 1. | Exports | 65,500 |
| 2. | Interest, profits and dividends (net) | +1,080 |
| 3. | Services (net) | +2,400 |
| 4. | Imports | 63,200 |
| 5. | Current transfers | −1,810 |
| 6. | Increase in external assets (net) | 30,830 |
| 7. | Increase in external liabilities (net) | 28,570 |
| 8. | Balancing item | 1,710 |

### Requirements

Using *both* your knowledge of economic theory *and* the material contained in the table:

(a) From the table calculate the following:

(i) the visible trade balance;

(ii) the invisible trade balance;

(iii) the current account balance;

(iv) the net capital outflow. **(4 marks)**

(b) State whether each of the following is *true* or *false*:

(i) The value of the balancing item is determined by the extent to which total currency inflows and outflows differ.

(ii) Current account surpluses have to be financed by capital and financial accounts deficits.

(iii) The 'J'-curve shows that the short-term effect of a depreciation in the currency is that the current account moves towards surplus.

(iv) Capital flows are counted in the capital and financial accounts but interest payments on that capital are counted in the current account.

(v) The balance of payments accounts always balance to zero.

(vi) If a country has a freely floating exchange rate system, imbalances on the current account will not occur. **(6 marks)**

**(Total marks = 10)**

## ? Question 3

The following passage is based on a newspaper article published in February 1997, and discusses the effects of the rise in the sterling exchange rate in 1996:

'United Kingdom companies are expressing alarm at the strength of sterling after seeing the rising exchange rate choke off their exports' the CBI (Confederation of British Industry) said yesterday as the pound sterling rose to DM2.7070 in late trading.

The CBI said that demand for exports had levelled off for the first time since the autumn of 1993, with optimism and order books hit by the 9 per cent appreciation of sterling in the final three months of 1996. According to the CBI survey, prices were regarded as more of a constraint on exports than at any time since October 1989. The picture which emerged was of weakening export orders balanced by the strength of domestic demand for United Kingdom-produced consumer goods.

The CBI said that the decision on whether the government should raise interest rates was 'finely balanced'. Any rise in interest rates to prevent the very rapid recovery from recession leading to excessive inflation was likely to further strengthen sterling and have an adverse effect on exporters' order books.

However, the prospects of a rise in interest rates to slow inflation were lessened by the latest figures for the growth of the money supply. They showed that broad money growth fell from an annual rate of 10.8 per cent in November to 9.6 per cent in December. However, these were still well above the government's target for the growth of the money supply. In response, a Government source pointed out that the rise in sterling itself would act to reduce the rate of inflation through its effects on costs and on the level of aggregate demand.

### Requirements

Using *both* your knowledge of economic *theory and* material contained in the above passage:

(a) State whether, other things being equal, the effect of each of the following would be to raise the exchange rate for a currency, lower the exchange rate or leave the exchange rate unaffected.

(i) A rise in interest rates in the country.

(ii) A rise in the rate of inflation in a country.

(iii) A surplus on the current account of the balance of payments.

(iv) A government budget deficit.

(v) An increase in the export of capital from the country.                                    **(5 marks)**

(b) State whether each of the following is *true* or *false*:

   (i) A rise in the exchange rate tends to reduce the domestic rate of inflation.

   (ii) A rise in the exchange rate tends to reduce domestic unemployment.

   (iii) A rise in the exchange rate tends to worsen the terms of trade.

   (iv) A rise in the exchange rate tends to worsen the balance of trade.

   (v) A rise in the exchange rate tends to raise domestic living standards.        **(5 marks)**

**(Total marks = 10)**

# Solutions to Revision Questions

5

## ✓ Solution 1

**1.1**   Solution: (C)

The comparative cost theory is concerned with costs, not the level of output. A and B are therefore incorrect. The theory also stresses that trade is based on relative or opportunity cost, not absolute cost. C, not D, is therefore the correct answer.

**1.2**   Solution: (C)

The existence of different currencies is irrelevant, as is the fact that countries may have different economic systems. Trade occurs because of comparative advantage and this arises mainly because different countries have different endowments of land, labour and capital. Specialisation is not the reason for international trade, but the consequence of it.

**1.3**   Solution: (C)

A fall in the exchange rate (depreciation or devaluation) or a fall in barriers to trade will be likely to lead to increases in a country's exports. A rise in a country's imports will have no direct effect on its exports, but may indirectly raise them, since it will have increased the level of incomes in trading partners. However, if the propensity to import in the country's trading partners falls, exports would decline.

**1.4**   Solution: (A)

Exports of goods clearly appears in the balance of trade element of the current account. Interest payments and tourist expenditure appear on the invisible items section of the current account. The movement of capital by multinational companies, however, is recorded on the financial account.

**1.5**   Solution: (B)

The WTO is an organisation concerned with trade agreements and associated matters, and seeks a reduction in barriers to trade. The minimalisation of trade barriers is its primary aim. The WTO may see the others as desirable, but they are not its direct concerns.

**1.6**   Solution: (B)

A and B are benefits of a fixed exchange rate system since the exchange rate remains fixed and domestic economic policy is constrained by this. Response C is incorrect since transaction costs occur whenever foreign exchange is bought or sold, irrespective of the exchange rate regime. The correct solution is B since a deficit would lead to a fall in the exchange rate, which would improve the country's competitiveness and thus correct the deficit.

**1.7** Solution: (C)

A rise in the exchange rate will raise export prices; exports will fall and the current account will move towards deficit. However, import prices will fall, dampening domestic inflation. Also, since import prices will have fallen and export prices risen, the terms of trade, the ratio of import and export prices, will have improved.

**1.8** Solution: (C)

The exchange rate will rise if the demand for the currency increases; this will result from increased inward capital flows and increased exports, especially if lower inflation increases the demand for exports. Increased imports however will increase the supply of the currency to pay for them; the currency will therefore depreciate.

## ✓ Solution 2

(a) (all in $m)
- (i) +2,300
- (ii) +1,670
- (iii) +3,970
- (iv) −2,260

(b) (i) *False*

Total currency inflows and outflows are always equal; the balancing item is the amount by which these flows have been miscounted.

(ii) *True*

All surpluses and deficits on the current account must be offset ('financed') on the capital and financial accounts.

(iii) *False*

The 'J'-curve shows that in the short run the effect of a depreciation is to shift the current account toward a deficit; only in the long run does the account move towards a surplus.

(iv) *True*

The capital account is concerned with the sale and acquisition of capital assets, but any income, such as interest or profits, appears in the current account.

(v) *True*

The balance of payments are a set of double entry accounts and therefore always balance.

(vi) *False*

A floating exchange rate system cannot guarantee a competitive rate and so a currency may become overvalued or undervalued.

**Solution 3**

(a)   (i)  Raise

    (ii)  Lower

   (iii)  Raise

   (iv)  No effect

    (v)  Lower

(b)   (i)  *True*

       A rise in the exchange rate reduces the domestic price of imports.

   (ii)  *False*

       A rising exchange rate reduces exports and raises imports, thus increasing domestic unemployment.

  (iii)  *False*

       The terms of trade are a measure of the relative prices of imports and exports; a rising exchange rate raises export prices and reduces import prices.

  (iv)  *True*

       As export prices rise, total exports tend to fall, but the opposite occurs for imports, thus worsening the trade balance.

   (v)  *True*

       The rise in exchange rate reduces import prices and thus raises the purchasing power of domestic incomes.

# Preparing for the Assessment

# Preparing for the Assessment

This chapter is intended for use when you are ready to start revising for your assessment. It contains:

- a summary of useful revision techniques;
- details of the format of the assessment;
- a bank of assessment-standard revision questions and suggested solutions. These solutions are of a length and level of detail that a competent student might be expected to produce in an assessment.

## Revision technique

### Planning

The first thing to say about revision is that it is an addition to your initial studies, not a substitute for them. In other words, do not coast along early in your course in the hope of catching up during the revision phase. On the contrary, you should be studying and revising concurrently from the outset. At the end of each week, and at the end of each month, get into the habit of summarizing the material you have covered to refresh your memory of it.

As with your initial studies, planning is important to maximise the value of your revision work. You need to balance the demands of study, professional work, family life and other commitments. To make this work, you will need to think carefully about how to make best use of your time.

Begin as before by comparing the estimated hours you will need to devote to revision with the hours available to you in the weeks leading up to the assessment. Prepare a written schedule setting out the areas you intend to cover during particular weeks, and break that down further into topics for each day's revision. To help focus on the key areas try to establish:

- which areas you are weakest in, so that you can concentrate on the topics where effort is particularly needed;
- which areas are especially significant for the assessment – the topics that are tested frequently.

Don't forget the need for relaxation, and for family commitments. Sustained intellectual effort is only possible for limited periods, and must be broken up at intervals by lighter activities. And don't continue your revision timetable right up to the moment when you enter for the assessment: you should aim to stop work a day or even two days before the assessment. Beyond this point the most you should attempt is an occasional brief look at your notes to refresh your memory.

## Getting down to work

By the time you begin your revision you should already have settled into a fixed work pattern: a regular time of day for doing the work, a particular location where you sit, particular equipment that you assemble before you begin and so on. If this is not already a matter of routine for you, think carefully about it now in the last vital weeks before the exam.

You should have notes summarizing the main points of each topic you have covered. Begin each session by reading through the relevant notes and trying to commit the important points to memory.

Usually this will be just your starting point. Unless the area is one where you already feel very confident, you will need to track back from your notes to the relevant chapter(s) in the *Study System*. This will refresh your memory on points not covered by your notes and fill in the detail that inevitably gets lost in the process of summarisation.

When you think you have understood and memorised the main principles and techniques, attempt an assessment-standard question. At this stage of your studies you should normally be expecting to complete such questions in something close to the actual time allocation allowed in the exam. After completing your effort, check the solution provided and add to your notes any extra points it reveals.

## Tips for the final revision phase

As the assessment looms closer, consider the following list of techniques and make use of those that work for you:

- Summarise your notes into more concise form, perhaps on index cards that you can carry with you for revision on the way to work.
- Go through your notes with a highlighter pen, marking key concepts and definitions.
- Summarise the main points in a key area by producing a wordlist, mind map or other mnemonic device.
- In areas that you find difficult, rework questions that you have already attempted, and compare your answers in detail with those provided in the *Learning System*.

## Format of the assessment

The assessment for Economics for Business is a two hour computer-based assessment comprising 75 compulsory questions. There will be no choice and all questions should be attempted if time permits. CIMA are continuously developing the question styles within the CBA system and you are advised to try the on-line website demo, to both gain familiarity with the assessment software and examine the latest style of questions being used.

In broad terms, the entire syllabus will be covered in each assessment. Please note that the weightings of the syllabus and of the assessment are not exactly reflected in the space allocated to the various topics in this book.

The current weightings for the syllabus sections are:

- The goals and decisions of organisations – 20 per cent
- The market system and the competitive process – 30 per cent
- The financial system – 20 per cent
- The macroeconomic context of business – 30 per cent.

# Revision Questions

| Learning Outcomes | Question number |
|---|---|
| **The goals and decisions of organizations** | |
| (i) Distinguish the goals of profit-seeking organisations, not-for-profit organisations and governmental organisations. | 1 |
| (ii) Compute the point of profit maximisation for a single product firm in the short run. | 3, 6, 9 |
| (iii) Distinguish the likely behaviour of a firm's unit costs in the short run and in the long run. | 2, 7 |
| (iv) Illustrate the effects of long-run cost behaviour on prices, the size of the organisation and the number of competitors in the industry. | 8 |
| (v) Illustrate shareholder wealth, the variables affecting shareholder's wealth and its application in management decision-making. | 5, 12 |
| (vi) Identify stakeholders and their likely impact on the goals of not-for-profit organisations and the decisions of the management of nor-for-profit organisations. | 10 |
| (vii) Distinguish between the potential objectives of management and those of shareholders, and the effects of this principal–agent problem on decisions concerning price, output and growth of the firm. | 4 |
| (viii) Describe the main mechanisms to improve corporate governance in profit-seeking organisations. | 11 |
| **The market system and the competitive process** | |
| (i) Identify the equilibrium price in a product or factor markets likely to result from specified changes in conditions of demand or supply. | 13, 16, 20, 21 |
| (ii) Calculate the price elasticity of demand and the price elasticity of supply. | 22, 26, 30 |
| (iii) Identify the effects of price elasticity of demand on a firm's revenues following a change in prices. | 14, 23 |
| (iv) Describe market concentration and the factors giving rise to differing levels of concentration between markets. | 18, 28 |
| (v) Describe market failures, their effects on prices, efficiency of market operation and economic welfare, and the likely responses of government to these. | 17, 27 |

**265**

| | | |
|---|---|---|
| (vi) | Distinguish the nature of competition in different market structures. | 15, 19, 25 |
| (vii) | Identify the impacts of different forms of competition on prices and profitability. | 24, 29 |

**The financial system**

| | | |
|---|---|---|
| (i) | Identify the factors leading to liquidity surpluses and deficits in the short, medium and long run in households, firms and governments. | 34 |
| (ii) | Explain the role of various financial assets, markets and institutions in assisting organisations to manage their liquidity position and to provide an economic return to holders of liquidity. | 31, 32, 33, 39, 42 |
| (iii) | Identify the role of insurance markets in the facilitation of the economic transfer and bearing of risk for households, firms and governments. | 36, 41 |
| (iv) | Identify the role of the foreign exchange market and the factors influencing it, in setting exchange rates and in helping organisations finance international trade and investment. | 37, 40 |
| (v) | Explain the role of national and international governmental organisations in regulating and influencing the financial system, and the likely impact of their policy instruments on businesses. | 35, 38 |

**The macroeconomic context of business**

| | | |
|---|---|---|
| (i) | Explain macroeconomic phenomena, including growth, inflation, unemployment, demand management and supply-side policies. | 44, 45, 50, 60 |
| (ii) | Explain the main measures and indicators of a country's economic performance and the problems of using these to assess the wealth and commercial potential of a country. | 47, 59 |
| (iii) | Identify the stages of the trade cycle, its causes and consequences, and discuss the business impacts of potential policy responses of government to each stage. | 46, 51, 60 |
| (iv) | Explain the main principles of public finance (i.e. deficit financing, forms of taxation) and macroeconomic policy. | 43, 56 |
| (v) | Explain the concept of the balance of payments and its implications for business and for government policy. | 53, 54 |
| (vi) | Identify the main elements of national policy with respect to trade, including protectionism, trade agreements and trading blocks. | 55, 59 |
| (vii) | Identify the conditions and policies necessary for economic growth in traditional, industrial and post-industrial societies, and the potential consequences of such growth. | 48, 57 |
| (viii) | Explain the concept and consequences of globalisation for businesses and national economies. | 50, 58 |
| (ix) | Identify the major institutions promoting global trade and development, and their respective roles. | 52 |

## The goals and decisions of organisations

 **Question 1**

The term 'opportunity cost' means:

(A) the difference between the cost of a good and its price.
(B) a special sale of goods below their cost of production.
(C) a change in costs resulting from a shift in the production possibility frontier.
(D) the value of goods that are forgone in order to produce something else.

**(2 marks)**

 **Question 2**

The fall in a firm's short-run average total cost with an increase in production would be due to which of the following?

(A) The greater divisibility of fixed costs.
(B) Diminishing returns to a fixed factor.
(C) Economies of scale.
(D) Diseconomies of scale.

**(2 marks)**

 **Question 3**

According to the traditional theory of the firm, the equilibrium position for all firms will be where:

(A) revenue is maximised.
(B) output is maximised.
(C) profits are maximised.
(D) costs are minimised.

**(2 marks)**

 **Question 4**

The pursuit of profit will ensure that business organisations are efficient provided that:

(A) they operate in competitive markets.
(B) they produce at the profit-maximizing level of output.
(C) prices are set where demand and supply are equal.
(D) excess profits are reinvested in the businesses.

**(2 marks)**

**Question 5**

Other things being equal, all of the following would lead to a rise in share prices except which *one?*

(A)  A rise in interest rates.
(B)  A reduction in corporation tax.
(C)  A rise in company profits.
(D)  A decline in the number of new share issues.

**(2 marks)**

 **Question 6**

The following data refer to the cost and revenue schedules of a business:

| Quantity sold | Price £ | Total cost £ |
|---|---|---|
| 0 | – | 12 |
| 1 | 16 | 20 |
| 2 | 14 | 25 |
| 3 | 12 | 30 |
| 4 | 10 | 34 |
| 5 | 8 | 45 |
| 6 | 6 | 66 |
| 7 | 4 | 110 |

(a)  Calculate for each level of sales:
   (i)  the marginal revenue;
   (ii)  the marginal cost.

**(2 marks)**

(b)  Calculate:
   (i)  the price elasticity of demand for a price rise from £10 to £12;
   (ii)  the profit maximizing level of sales and the total profits made at this point.

**(2 marks)**

 **Question 7**

Identify the correct word or phrase in the following to complete each of the following statements.

 (i)  Internal economies of scale can only be obtained when the *industry/company/market* increases in size.
(ii)  Diseconomies of scale occur when the business becomes *inefficient/technically out-dated/too large* and, inconsequence, costs begin to rise.
(iii)  External economies of scale reduce the costs of all firms when *suppliers become more efficient/the industry becomes larger/social costs of production are reduced.*
(iv)  Technical economies of scale arise when a company is large enough to *adopt new technology/invest in research and development/produce on a large scale.*

**(4 marks)**

**Question 8**

State whether each of the following statements is *true* or *false*.

| Statements | True | False |
|---|---|---|
| (i) Economies of scale act as a barrier to entry into an industry. | | |
| (ii) If there are significant economies of scale, the number of firms in the industry will tend to be small. | | |
| (iii) Diseconomies of scale cause the short-run average cost curve to rise. | | |
| (iv) If output rises at the same rate as average cost rises, this is called constant returns to scale. | | |

**(4 marks)**

 **Question 9**

| Output | Total revenue (£) | Total costs (£) |
|---|---|---|
| 0 | – | 110 |
| 1 | 50 | 140 |
| 2 | 100 | 162 |
| 3 | 150 | 175 |
| 4 | 200 | 180 |
| 5 | 250 | 185 |
| 6 | 300 | 194 |
| 7 | 350 | 219 |
| 8 | 400 | 269 |
| 9 | 450 | 325 |
| 10 | 500 | 425 |

The following data refer to the revenue and costs of a firm:

**Requirements**

Using *both* your knowledge of economic theory *and* the data given above:

(a) From the data above calculate:
    (i) marginal revenue for every level of output;     **(1 mark)**
    (ii) marginal cost for every level of output;     **(1 mark)**
    (iii) the firm's fixed costs.     **(1 mark)**

(b) Assuming that the firm is a profit maximiser, state:
    (i) the level of output the firm will aim to produce;     **(1 mark)**
    (ii) the total level of profit at this level of output.     **(1 mark)**
    **(Total marks = 5)**

## ? Question 10

Which of the following would be regarded as stakeholders in a not- for-profit organisation?

(i) Management
(ii) Employees
(iii) Suppliers
(iv) Customers
(v) Local community

(A) (i), and (iii) only.
(B) (i), (ii) and (iv) only.
(C) (iii), (iv) and (v) only.
(D) all of them.

**(2 marks)**

## ? Question 11

All of the following have been recommended in order to improve corporate Governance except one. Which *one* is the exception?

(A) The separation of the powers of chairman and chief executive.
(B) Limited contract for directors.
(C) Less use should be made of non-executive directors.
(D) Annual accounts should include a statement from auditors that the company is a 'going concern'. **(2 marks)**

## ? Question 12

A Company is planning to invest in a new project. The information about this project is as follows:

| | | |
|---|---|---|
| Capital cost of project | | $15000 |
| Expected life of the project | | 3 years |
| Scrap value of investment at end | | $5000 |
| Expected net income streams | Year 1 | $5000 |
| | Year 2 | $5000 |
| | Year 3 | $5000 |

You are required to:

(a) Calculate the discounted cash flow of the project assuming a discount rate of 10%.

**(2 marks)**

(b) Calculate the discounted cash flow of the project assuming that the income stream in the third year is reduced to $3000.

**(2 marks)**

(c) Calculate the net present value of the project for each case.

**(2 marks)**

## The market system and the competitive process

### ? Question 13

When the price of a good is held above the equilibrium price, the result will be:

(A) excess demand.
(B) a shortage of the good.
(C) a surplus of the good.
(D) an increase in demand.

**(2 marks)**

### ? Question 14

If the price of a good fell by 10 per cent and, as a result, total expenditure on the good fell by 10 per cent, the demand for the good would be described as:

(A) perfectly inelastic.
(B) perfectly elastic.
(C) unitary elastic.
(D) elastic.

**(2 marks)**

### ? Question 15

One of the characteristic features of oligopoly is that

(A) free entry of firms into the industry is always encouraged.
(B) the pricing policy of a firm is largely determined by the state.
(C) known consumers' preferences play no part in firms' policy decisions.
(D) the pricing policy of firms is influenced by that of rival firms.

**(2 marks)**

### ? Question 16

Which *one* of the following would not, of itself, cause a shift of the demand curve for a product? A change in:

(A) consumers' preferences.
(B) consumers' income.
(C) the price of the product.
(D) the prices of related products.

**(2 marks)**

## Question 17

If the social costs of producing a good exceeds its private cost, in order to improve resource allocation, the government should:

(A) provide the producers with a subsidy equal to the difference between private and social costs.
(B) impose an indirect tax equal to the difference between private and social costs of producing the good.
(C) tax the profits of the producers of the good at a higher rate than normal.
(D) pay a subsidy to all consumers of the product.

**(2 marks)**

## Question 18

A horizontal merger occurs when the merging firms are:

(A) in different stages of the production chain.
(B) major firms operating in the same region.
(C) producing different goods or services.
(D) producing the same goods or services.

**(2 marks)**

## Question 19

The kinked demand curve model of oligopolistic competition is used to explain:

(A) collusion between firms.
(B) price rigidity.
(C) price leadership.
(D) price competition.

**(2 marks)**

## Question 20

The following diagram represents the demand and supply for a particular good over a period of time:

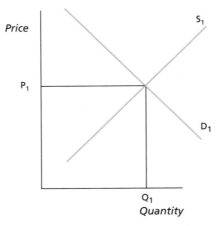

With respect to the diagram answer the following questions.

(i) Would the imposition of an indirect tax shift *the supply curve* or *the demand curve*?

(ii) Would the burden of tax be shifted most to consumers when the demand curve for the product was *price elastic* or *price inelastic*?

(iii) Would the government get the most tax revenue from imposing the tax if the demand for the product was *price elastic* or *price inelastic*?

(iv) Would the sales/output of the good fall most when the demand for the good was *price elastic* or *price inelastic*?

**(4 marks)**

## ? Question 21

If trade unions attempt to increase the wages of their members, the result is usually that for their members:

(A) wages rise and employment falls.
(B) wages and employment both rise.
(C) wages rise without affecting employment.
(D) wages fall but employment rises.

**(2 marks)**

## ? Question 22

The following passage is based on newspaper articles and refers to the market for coffee:

Supermarkets recently ended ten years of cheap coffee when some raised the price of their own brands of instant coffee by up to 12 per cent.

Reports of severe frost damage to Brazilian coffee plantations sent the open market price of coffee beans up from $3100 a ton to $4000 a ton – the highest price since 1986. Even before the frost damage, the price had been rising because many coffee farmers, discouraged by the previous low price of coffee, had moved away to other crops in the search for more profit.

The current price increases will end a golden age for coffee drinkers. From 1986 to 1993, the retail price of coffee had fallen by more than 15 per cent; given that these were years of rapid inflation, the real price of coffee fell even more steeply. The result was a boom in coffee drinking, and coffee sales in the United Kingdom exceeded those of tea. Rising coffee prices may now lead to a switch back to tea drinking. This happened in the 1970s when sharp rises in coffee prices encouraged many coffee drinkers to switch their consumption to tea.

### Requirements

Using *both* your knowledge of economic theory *and* information in the passage:

With reference to the concept of the price elasticity of demand,

(i) which one of the following is the correct measurement of the price elasticity of demand for coffee?

1. $\dfrac{\text{\% change in price of coffee}}{\text{\% change in the demand for coffee}}$

2.  $\dfrac{\text{change in the demand for coffee}}{\text{change in the price of coffee}}$

3.  $\dfrac{\text{\% change in the demand for coffee}}{\text{\% change in the price of coffee}}$

**(1 mark)**

(ii)  if the price elasticity of demand for coffee has a value of $-2$ would the demand be said to be
   1.  price elastic or
   2.  price inelastic or
   3.  of unitary elasticity?

**(1 mark)**

(iii)  if the demand for coffee was price inelastic, would the result of a shift in the supply of coffee to the left be,
   1.  a large fall in price and small fall in sales or
   2.  a large rise in price and large fall in sales or
   3.  a large rise in price and a small fall in sales or
   4.  a small rise in price and a large fall in sales or
   5.  a small fall in price and a large rise in sales?

**(2 marks)**

(iv)  if there was a high positive cross elasticity of demand between coffee and tea and the supply of tea was price inelastic, would the result of a rise in the price of coffee be
   1.  a small rise in the sales of tea and small rise in its price or
   2.  a large rise in the sales of tea and a large rise in its price or
   3.  a small rise in the sales of tea and a large rise in its price or
   4.  a large rise in sales of tea and small rise in its price?

**(2 marks)**

## ❓ Question 23

State whether each of the following statements is *true* or *false*.

| Statement | True | False |
| --- | --- | --- |
| (i)  A change in supply of a good will have the largest effect on price when the demand is price elastic. | | |
| (ii)  The cross elasticity of demand measures the relationship between the demand for one good and demand for another. | | |
| (iii)  If the cross elasticity of demand has a negative value, it shows that the two goods are complements. | | |
| (iv)  A change in the demand for a good will have no effect on the price if the supply of the good is perfectly price elastic. | | |

**(4 marks)**

# Question 24

The following diagram shows the cost and revenue curves for a monopoly firm selling its products in two separate markets:

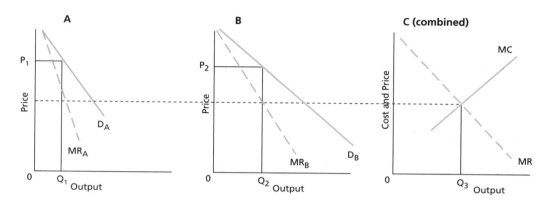

With the use of the diagram
  (i)   show the total output the firm will aim to produce;                                    **(1 mark)**
  (ii)  show the share of output allocated to each market;                                      **(1 mark)**
  (iii) identify the price that the firm will charge in each market.                            **(1 mark)**

 # Question 25

All of the following are examples of anti-competitive behaviour by manufacturing companies except which one?

(A)  Price-fixing agreements.
(B)  Minimum price contracts with retailers.
(C)  Exclusive contracts with retailers.
(D)  The heavy use of advertising.

                                                                                               **(2 marks)**

# Question 26

The following data refers to the supply and demand for a product.

| Price ($) | Quantity demanded | Quantity supplied |
|-----------|-------------------|-------------------|
| 8         | 130               | 80                |
| 9         | 120               | 95                |
| 10        | 100               | 100               |
| 11        | 90                | 105               |

Using the data, calculate for this product:
  (i)   the price elasticity of demand for a fall in price from $10 to $9.
  (ii)  the price elasticity of supply for a rise in price from $10 to $11.
  (iii) calculate the change in total revenue for the seller of the product if the price fell from $10 to $9.

                                                                                               **(3 marks)**

**Question 27**

If the price of producing a good involves net social costs greater than the private costs then:

(A) the private sector will produce less than the socially optimal level of output.
(B) the private sector will not produce the goods because it would not be profitable to do so.
(C) the government could improve resource allocation by imposing a tax on the good.
(D) a subsidy should be paid to the private sector to offset the extra costs.

**(2 marks)**

 **Question 28**

All of the following would tend to increase the degree of competition in a market except one. Which *one* is the exception?

(A) An increase in the number of firms in the market.
(B) Significant economies of scale in the industry.
(C) An increase in consumer knowledge and awareness of the product.
(D) A reduction in barriers to entry into the industry.

**(2 marks)**

 **Question 29**

Railway companies offering off-peak services at lower prices than for peak services must ensure that, in the short run, these lower prices cover at least

(A) the variable cost of providing the service.
(B) overhead costs.
(C) the fixed costs of production.
(D) the average cost of providing the service.

**(2 marks)**

 **Question 30**

State whether each of the following statements is *true* or *false*.

| Statement | True | False |
|---|---|---|
| (i) If the supply of a good decreases, its price will rise and the demand curve for the product will shift to the left. | | |
| (ii) The supply of a good is described as price inelastic if a fall in price leads to a smaller proportionate fall in the quantity supplied. | | |
| (iii) If a tax is imposed on a good, the burden of the tax shifted to consumers will be greatest when the demand for the good is price inelastic. | | |
| (iv) If the demand for a good has a price elasticity of $-1$ then a 10% fall in price will lead to a 10% fall in demand. | | |

**(4 marks)**

## The Financial system

### [?] Question 31

Venture capital is best described as:

(A) investment funds provided for established companies.
(B) short-term investment in Eurocurrency markets.
(C) capital funds that are highly mobile between financial centres.
(D) equity finance in high-risk enterprises.

**(2 marks)**

### [?] Question 32

Which *one* of the following can be used by governments to finance a budget deficit?

(A) A rise in direct taxation.
(B) The sale of public assets.
(C) An increase in interest rates.
(D) An issue of government savings certificates.

**(2 marks)**

### [?] Question 33

Financial institutions are said to provide financial intermediation. This is best defined as providing:

(A) a means of payment by cheques.
(B) financial advice to business customers.
(C) an efficient means of linking net savers with net borrowers.
(D) a service for the purchase and sale of foreign exchange.

**(2 marks)**

### [?] Question 34

State whether each of the following statements is *true* or *false*.

| Statement | True | False |
|---|---|---|
| (i) Governments will have a financial deficit if the country's imports exceed exports. | | |
| (ii) Companies need financial intermediaries if their receipts exceed their payments. | | |
| (iii) Governments can finance their budget deficits by raising taxation. | | |
| (iv) An overdraft is a means for individuals to meet short-term lack of liquidity. | | |

**(4 marks)**

## Question 35

Which *one* of the following is not a function of a central bank?

(A) Management of the National Debt.
(B) Holder of the foreign exchange reserves.
(C) The conduct of fiscal policy.
(D) Lender of the last resort.

**(2 marks)**

## Question 36

Of the following risks, which *one* cannot be insured against by a business?

(A) Injury or illness of employees.
(B) Loss of sales because of a downturn in trade.
(C) Theft of company assets.
(D) Legal action taken against the company by a customer.

**(2 marks)**

## Question 37

For each of the following events, state whether the direct effect on a country with a flexible exchange rate would be to lead to a rise (appreciation) or fall (depreciation) in the country's exchange rate or to leave the exchange rate unaffected.

| Event | Rise in the exchange rate | Fall in the exchange rate | Leave the exchange rate unaffected |
|---|---|---|---|
| (i) A rise in interest rates in the country. | | | |
| (ii) A rise in the demand for imports in the country. | | | |
| (iii) A significant short term fall in share prices in the country. | | | |
| (iv) Purchase of foreign exchange by the country's central bank. | | | |

**(4 marks)**

## Question 38

All of the following would result from a rise in interest rates except one. Which *one* is the exception?

(A) Business investment would tend to fall.
(B) Share prices would tend to fall.
(C) Sales of consumer good would tend to fall.
(D) Government revenue would tend to rise.

**(2 marks)**

## ? Question 39

For each of the following financial instruments state whether they are money market (M) or capital market (C) instruments.

  (i)  Treasury bills
 (ii)  Certificates of deposit
(iii)  Corporate bonds
 (iv)  Mortgages
  (v)  Bills of exchange

**(4 marks)**

## ? Question 40

Which *one* of the following would *not* result from the United Kingdom joining the single European currency (the Euro)?

(A)  International transactions costs would rise.
(B)  Exchange rate uncertainty would be reduced.
(C)  The United Kingdom could no longer operate an independent monetary policy.
(D)  There would be increased price transparency between the United Kingdom and other EU countries.

**(2 marks)**

## ? Question 41

State whether each of the following statements is *true* or *false*.

| Statement | True | False |
|---|---|---|
| (i)  A insurance broker undertakes the task of underwriting but not reinsurance. | | |
| (ii)  Reinsurance occurs when an insurer shares the risk and the premiums with other insurers. | | |
| (iii)  Insurers will not insure against events they know will occur. | | |

**(3 marks)**

## ? Question 42

If in the short run a business's receipts exceed its payments it can finance this financial shortfall by all of the following except one. Which *one* is the exception?

(A)  Using its cash reserves.
(B)  Issuing shares.
(C)  A bank overdraft.
(D)  A bill of exchange.

**(2 marks)**

## The macroeconomic context of business

 **Question 43**

Which *one* of the following is likely to result from an increase in the size of the public sector net borrowing?

(A) A decrease in the level of inflation.
(B) A reduction in the level of taxation.
(C) A rise in the price of shares.
(D) A rise in the rate of interest.

**(2 marks)**

 **Question 44**

Which *one* of the following is a withdrawal from the circular flow of income?

(A) Investment.
(B) Exports.
(C) Taxation.
(D) Profits.

**(2 marks)**

 **Question 45**

The following diagram shows the relationship between income and expenditure for an economy:

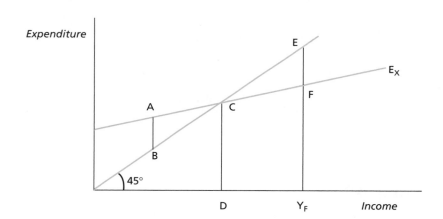

With reference to the diagram, state what are the following:
  (i) two components of the expenditure curve;                    **(2 marks)**
 (ii) the equilibrium level of national income;                   **(1 mark)**
(iii) the deflationary gap.                                       **(1 mark)**

## Question 46

The upswing phase of the trade cycle normally leads to:

(A) A fall in structural unemployment.
(B) A reduction in inflationary pressure.
(C) The government budget moving towards a surplus.
(D) The current account of the balance of payments moving towards a surplus.

**(2 marks)**

## Question 47

Which *one* of the following is a transfer payment in national income accounting?

(A) Salaries of university lecturers.
(B) Payments of examination entry fees.
(C) Payments for the purchase of textbooks.
(D) Educational grants and scholarships.

**(2 marks)**

## Question 48

The following diagram represents the production possibility frontiers (curves) for an economy:

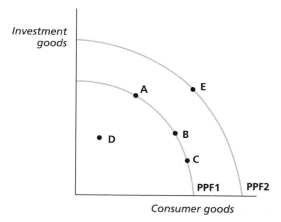

Identify the point on the diagram which corresponds to:

 (i) less than full employment of available resources;
 (ii) a bias in production towards consumer goods;
(iii) a bias in production towards investment goods;
(iv) economic growth compared to point A.

**(4 marks)**

## Question 49

The theory of the natural rate of unemployment says that:

(A) there is no inflation–unemployment trade-off in the long run.
(B) the short-run Phillips curve is steeper than the long-run Phillips curve.
(C) there will always be some workers seeking employment who cannot find jobs.
(D) there is always some frictional unemployment in an economy.

**(2 marks)**

**Question 50**

A multinational / transnational company is one which:

(A) exports goods to more than one country.
(B) buys many of its inputs from overseas countries.
(C) has shareholders in many countries.
(D) has production facilities in more than one country.

**(2 marks)**

 **Question 51**

The following diagram shows the aggregate demand curve (AD) and the aggregate supply curve (AS) for an economy:

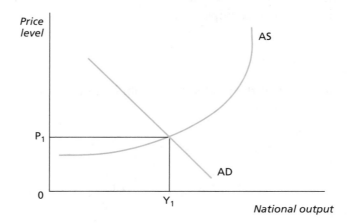

With reference to the diagram show what would happen to national output if there were:

(i) a negative supply shock;
(ii) a positive supply shock;
(iii) an expansionary fiscal policy;
(iv) a deflationary monetary policy.

**(4 marks)**

 **Question 52**

The World Trade Organisation (WTO) has all of the following functions except which *one*?

(A) Establishing rules for the conduct of international trade.
(B) Providing short-term capital to finance trade for low income countries.
(C) Providing a forum negotiating reductions in trade barriers.
(D) Settling trade disputes between member countries.

**(2 marks)**

## Question 53

The following data refers to a country's balance of payments accounts, measured in billions of dollars.

| | Credits $ billion | Debits $ billion |
|---|---|---|
| Trade in goods | 164 | 184 |
| Trade in services | 60 | 48 |
| Investment income | 105 | 95 |
| Transfers | 15 | 22 |
| Direct investment abroad | | 40 |
| Inward direct investment | 29 | |
| Portfolio investment (assets) | | 31 |
| Portfolio investment (liabilities) | 37 | |
| Other investments | 44 | 16 |

Calculate the country's:

(i) balance of trade;
(ii) balance on current account;
(iii) net flow of foreign direct investment;
(iv) adjusting item to balance the accounts.

**(4 marks)**

## Question 54

All of the following are included as invisible items on the current account of the balance of payments except which *one*?

(A) Flows of profits from assets held overseas.
(B) Inflows of overseas investment.
(C) Expenditure by foreign tourists within the country.
(D) Interest payments received from bank accounts held in other countries.

**(2 marks)**

## Question 55

The European Union has all the following features except which *one*?

(A) The absence of barriers to trade between all member states.
(B) The absence of barriers to the movement of capital between member states.
(C) Common rates of indirect taxation.
(D) A common external tariff.

**(2 marks)**

**Question 56**

State whether each of the following statements is *true* or *false*.

| Statement | True | False |
|---|---|---|
| (i)   The heaviest indirect taxes tend to be on goods with a high price elasticity of demand. | | |
| (ii)  An indirect tax is one where the incidence and the burden of the tax fall on different persons. | | |
| (iii) Indirect taxes on goods are desirable since the burden of the tax falls on the foreign producer. | | |
| (iv)  Direct taxes are preferred to indirect taxes because they are always progressive. | | |

**(4 marks)**

 **Question 57**

All of the following would be likely to restrict long-term economic growth except which *one?*

(A)  Increasing cost of energy as oil reserves decrease.
(B)  The scarcity of natural resources and raw materials.
(C)  Environmental damage caused by both production and consumption.
(D)  Increasing openness of economies to international trade.

**(2 marks)**

 **Question 58**

All of the following are features of globalisation except one. Which *one* is the exception?

(A)  Rising trade ratios.
(B)  Increased international capital flows.
(C)  Improved terms of trade for all countries.
(D)  Reduced barriers to international factor movements.

**(2 marks)**

## Question 59

State whether each of the following statements is *true* or *false*.

| Statement | True | False |
|---|---|---|
| (i) If a country imposes trade barriers on its imports, that country's economic welfare will be reduced. | | |
| (ii) An advantage of flexible exchange rate regimes is that uncertainty is reduced for business. | | |
| (iii) An advantage of fixed exchange rate regimes is that they make trade deficits less likely to occur. | | |
| (iv) Free trade enables a country to re-allocate its resource to more productive uses. | | |

**(2 marks)**

## Question 60

The following refers to the Japanese economy in the 1990s:

**Table 1**   Gross domestic product (1996)

| | Billions Yen | % of total |
|---|---|---|
| 1. Private consumption expenditure | 299,440 | 59.8 |
| 2. Domestic fixed capital formation | 148,190 | 29.6 |
| 3. Government consumption expenditure | 48,969 | 9.6 |
| 4. Stockbuilding | 1,058 | 0.2 |
| 5. Exports | 49,589 | 9.9 |
| 6. Imports | −46,900 | −9.1 |
| **Gross domestic product** | 500,355 | 100.0 |

**Table 2**   Growth rates of GDP components (% per annum)

| | GDP | | Investment | Government expenditure | Exports |
|---|---|---|---|---|---|
| 1990 | 4.8 | 4.4 | 8.8 | 4.3 | 5.7 |
| 1991 | 3.8 | 2.3 | 2.8 | 3.8 | −0.9 |
| 1992 | 1.0 | 2.2 | −2.0 | 2.8 | −0.3 |
| 1993 | 0.3 | 1.7 | −2.8 | 2.9 | −7.3 |
| 1994 | 0.6 | 2.5 | −2.4 | 2.0 | 0.3 |
| 1995 | 1.4 | 2.1 | 0.2 | 4.6 | 2.8 |
| 1996 | 3.6 | 3.0 | 8.3 | 2.9 | 9.2 |

(i)  From Table 1 identify the three injections into the circular flow.  **(3 marks)**

(ii)  State whether slow GDP growth would be expected to raise, lower or be of no effect on each of the following:

- the level of employment;
- the government budget surplus;
- the level of imports.  **(3 marks)**

# Solutions to Revision Questions

 **Solution 1**

Solution (D)

Opportunity costs arise from the scarcity of resources. When an economy is fully employed, the output of one good can only be increased by decreasing the output of another. Thus the real, or opportunity, cost of a good is the value of the foregone production.

 **Solution 2**

Solution (A)

Economies and diseconomies of scale refer to the long-run cost curve, hence (C) and (D) are incorrect. Diminishing returns is the short-run process which leads to rising costs. Short-run average costs thus fall initially because fixed costs are spread over a larger output.

 **Solution 3**

Solution (C)

The theory of the firm states that firms are profit maximisers. Thus, to be in equilibrium, where the firm would have no incentive to raise or lower output, the firm would have to be at the profit maximising level of output.

 **Solution 4**

Solution (A)

(B) and (C) are the conditions necessary for profit maximisation to take place and (D) refers to the use of profits whether the firm is efficient or not. The necessary condition for the pursuit of profits to lead to efficiency is competition; when competition is restricted firms may make profits without being efficient.

## Solution 5

Solution (A)

The price of shares is determined by demand and supply. (B) and (C) would raise the demand for shares and (D) would reduce the supply. However, a rise in interest rates would reduce the demand for shares as alternative investments have become more attractive.

 ## Solution 6

(a)

| Quantity | Total revenue £ | Marginal revenue £ | Total cost £ | Marginal cost £ |
|---|---|---|---|---|
| 0 | 0 | 0 | 12 | 12 |
| 1 | 16 | 16 | 20 | 8 |
| 2 | 28 | 12 | 25 | 5 |
| 3 | 36 | 8 | 30 | 5 |
| 4 | 40 | 4 | 34 | 4 |
| 5 | 40 | 0 | 45 | 11 |
| 6 | 36 | −4 | 66 | 21 |
| 7 | 28 | −8 | 110 | 44 |

(b)　(i)　Price elasticity of demand is $\dfrac{\%\ \text{change in demand}}{\%\ \text{change in price}}$

Thus $\dfrac{-25\%}{+20\%} = -1.25$

(ii)　Profit maximizing point is where MC = MR
This is at output level 4.
Total profit at this point is total revenue − total cost.
This is £40 − £34 = £6.

## Solution 7

(i) *Company*. Internal economies arise from the advantages of large scale production within the business.

(ii) *Too large*. Diseconomies of scale occur when a business becomes too big, the others can occur in a business of any size.

(iii) *The industry becomes larger*. External economies occur when the industry is large (such as specialised supporting firms), the others could occur irrespective of the size of the industry.

(iv) *Produce on a large scale*. Technical economies arise out of more efficient use of existing technology as the business becomes bigger. The others could occur at any size of business.

**Solution 8**

Statement whether each of the following statements is *true* or *false*.

| Statement | True | False |
|---|---|---|
| (i) Economies of scale act as a barrier to entry into an industry | X | |
| (ii) If there are significant economies of scale, the number of firms in the industry will tend to be small. | X | |
| (iii) Diseconomies of scale cause the short-run average cost curve to rise. | | X |
| (iv) If output rises at the same rate as average cost rises, this is called constant returns to scale. | | X |

(i) Economies of scale will give a cost advantage to existing firms thus making it difficult for new firms to enter an industry.

(ii) Economies of scale will favour large firms thus smaller firms will go out of business, reducing the number in the industry.

(iii) Diseconomies of scale affect the long-run average cost curve not the short-run cost curve.

(iv) Constant returns to scale occur when total costs and total output rise at the same rate thus keeping average costs constant.

 **Solution 9**

| Output | Total revenue TR | Marginal revenue $TR_n - TR_{n-1}$ | Total costs TC | Marginal costs $TC_n - TC_{n-1}$ | Total profit TR-TC |
|---|---|---|---|---|---|
| 0 | | | 110 | | |
| 1 | 50 | 50 | 140 | 30 | −90 |
| 2 | 100 | 50 | 162 | 22 | −62 |
| 3 | 150 | 50 | 175 | 13 | −25 |
| 4 | 200 | 50 | 180 | 5 | 20 |
| 5 | 250 | 50 | 185 | 5 | 65 |
| 6 | 300 | 50 | 194 | 9 | 106 |
| 7 | 350 | 50 | 219 | 25 | 131 |
| 8 | 400 | 50 | 269 | 50 | 131 |
| 9 | 450 | 50 | 325 | 56 | 125 |
| 10 | 500 | 50 | 425 | 100 | 75 |

(a)  (i) The firm's marginal revenue is given in the table above.

(ii) The firm's marginal cost is given in the table above.

(iii) The firm's fixed costs are £110.

(b) (i) The firm will maximise profits where marginal cost and marginal revenue are equal; this is at output level 8.

(ii) Total profit at this level of output will be the difference between total costs and total revenue; this is £131.

(Note: profits are also maximised at an output of 7 although MC and MR are not equal; this is the result of dealing in proportionally large changes in units of output rather than very small changes.)

 ## Solution 10

Solution (D)

Anyone with an interest in the behaviour of a business, whether profit seeking or not, is a stakeholder in that business. All of these may have a legitimate interest in the business.

 ## Solution 11

Solution (C)

All of the others have been recommended by various bodies such as the Greenbury Committee. The Committee also recommended greater, not less, use of non-executive directors.

 ## Solution 12

(a) the calculation for the net present value is to discount each years income thus

Thus discounted cash flow of the project is $16191

| Year 1 | $5000/(1.1) = $4545.45 |
| Year 2 | $5000/(1.1)^2 = $4132.23 |
| Year 3 | $10000/(1.1)^3 = $7513.15 |

(b) the calculation now becomes

Thus the discounted cash flow of the project is $14688

| Year 1 | $5000/(1.1) = $4545.45 |
| Year 2 | $5000/(1.1)^2 = $4132.23 |
| Year 3 | $8000/(1.1)^3 = $6010.52 |

(c) The NPV of the project

| First case: | $16,191 − $15,000 = $1191 |
| Second case: | $14,688 − $15,000 = −$312 |

 ## Solution 13

Solution (C)

The equilibrium price is where demand and supply are equal. If the price is forced above this level, it will lead to an extension of supply and a contraction of demand and a surplus would exist in the market.

## Solution 14

Solution (A)

If a reduction in the price of 10% resulted in a fall in total revenue of 10%, then, since revenue is equal to price multiplied by the quantity sold, the quantity sold must have stayed the same. This implies that the price has no effect on the quantity demanded: the demand is perfectly inelastic.

 ## Solution 15

Solution (D)

The essential feature of oligopoly is that of interdependence: the effects of policy decisions are crucially affected by the reaction of rival firms. Thus pricing decisions must always take into account how rival firms are likely to react to reductions or rises in price.

 ## Solution 16

Solution (C)

Responses (A), (B) and (D) all refer to conditions of demand which affect the position of the demand curve. Response (C) refers to the price of the good itself; a change in this would lead to a movement along the demand curve, not a shift in the curve itself.

 ## Solution 17

Solution (B)

Efficient resource allocation requires that prices reflect costs. Prices will only reflect private costs since social costs are those not incurred by the producers. To correct this, the government should impose an indirect tax equal to the difference between private and social costs.

 ## Solution 18

Solution (D)

A horizontal merger is one between firms producing similar goods at the same stage of production. (A) is an example of vertical integration and (C) is a conglomerate merger. (B) might be a merger of any sort.

 ## Solution 19

Solution (B)

The kinked demand curve shows that, under conditions of oligopoly, price competition may be dangerous and reduce the firm's revenue; hence there is a preference for avoiding price changes and to concentrate on non-price competition.

## Solution 20

(i) An indirect tax shifts *supply curve.*

(ii) The burden of tax would be shifted most to consumers when the demand curve for the product was *price inelastic.*

(iii) If the demand for the product was *price inelastic.*

(iv) Sales/output of the good would fall most when the demand for the good was *price elastic.*

 ## Solution 21

Solution (A)

If trade unions secure a wage increase for their members, employment is likely to fall since the demand curve for labour like any other demand curve slopes downwards. A rise in price of labour (wages) will thus lead to a contraction in the demand for labour and decrease employment.

 ## Solution 22

(i) 3. $\dfrac{\%\ \text{change in the demand for coffee}}{\%\ \text{change in the price of coffee}}$.

(ii) 1. price elastic.

(iii) 3. a large rise in price and a small fall in sales.

(iv) 3. a small rise in the sales of tea and a large rise in its price.

 ## Solution 23

| Statement | True | False |
|---|---|---|
| (i) A change in supply of a good will have the largest effect on price when the demand is price elastic. | | X |
| (ii) The cross elasticity of demand measures the relationship between the demand for one good and the demand for another. | | X |
| (iii) If the cross elasticity of demand has a negative value, it shows that the two goods are complements. | X | |
| (iv) A change in the demand for a good will have no effect on the price if the supply of the good is perfectly price elastic. | X | |

**Solution 24**

The firm will:

(i) produce a total output of $Q_3$ in part C of the diagram since here the combined marginal revenue is equal to the marginal cost of production;

(ii) sell in each market an amount where the marginal cost of production is equal to the marginal revenue in that market, that is $Q_2$ in the market B and $Q_1$ in market A;

(iii) charge a price determined by the demand for the product in each market, that is $P_2$ in market B and $P_1$ in market A.

 **Solution 25**

Solution (D)

All of the first three are attempts to limit competition in one way or another. However, (D), the use of advertising, is not since advertising is one form of competition and is particularly important in some markets, especially oligopolies.

 **Solution 26**

(i) $\text{PED} = \dfrac{\% \text{ change in demand}}{\% \text{ change in price}}$ thus $\dfrac{+20\%}{-10\%}$ hence $\text{PED} = -2$

(ii) $\text{PES} = \dfrac{\% \text{ change in supply}}{\% \text{ change in price}}$ thus $\dfrac{+5\%}{+10\%}$ hence $\text{PES} = +0.5$

(iii) Revenue at \$10 is $\$10 \times 100 = \$1000$
$\$9$ is $\$9 \times 120 = \$1080$ thus change in revenue is +\$80

 **Solution 27**

Solution (C)

If there are positive net social costs, private producers who do not pay these additional costs will tend to overproduce the good or service. To correct this the government can reduce demand by making the price more closely reflect total costs. It can do this by imposing a tax on the product.

 **Solution 28**

Solution (B)

(A) and (D) would increase competition by raising the number of firms in the market. (C) would increase competition because it would raise consumer awareness of competing products. However, (B) would give a cost advantage to the larger firms and erect a barrier to entry; the number of firms will fall and competition will decrease.

 **Solution 29**

Solution (A)

Since, in the short run, the business will have to pay fixed costs whatever the level of output, the minimum they must cover is the additional variable costs of the service. Any income above this will go towards paying the fixed cost that must be met anyway.

# Solution 30

| Statement | True | False |
|---|---|---|
| (i) If the supply of a good decreases, its price will rise and the demand curve for the product will shift to the left. | | X |
| (ii) The supply of a good is described as price inelastic if a fall in price leads to a smaller proportionate fall in the quantity supplied. | X | |
| (iii) If a tax is imposed on a good, the burden of the tax shifted to consumers will be greatest when the demand for the good is price inelastic. | X | |
| (iv) If the demand for a good has a price elasticity of $-1$ then a 10% fall in price will lead to a 10% fall in demand. | | X |

 # Solution 31

Solution (D)

Venture capital is that invested in new and high-risk enterprises by buying shares in those businesses.

 # Solution 32

Solution (D)

A budget deficit is the difference between government expenditure and its income from taxation; this deficit must be financed by borrowing. Only (D) represents this borrowing. (A) and (B) would reduce the deficit and (C) has no direct relevance.

 # Solution 33

Solution (C)

The other three are services provided by typical commercial banks, but not by all financial institutions. But (C) is the core function of financial intermediation performed by all financial institutions.

# Solution 34

| Statement | True | False |
|---|---|---|
| (i) Governments will have a financial deficit if the country's imports exceed exports. | | X |
| (ii) Companies need financial intermediaries if their receipts exceed their payments. | X | |
| (iii) Governments can finance their budget deficits by raising taxation. | | X |
| (iv) An overdraft is a means for individuals to meet short-term lack of liquidity. | X | |

 # Solution 35

Solution (C)

Fiscal policy is concerned with the government budget and the balance of taxation and public expenditure. This is the responsibility of the government, not the central bank.

 # Solution 36

Solution (B)

Insurance can only be obtained for risks that are predictable, not likely to affect all those insured simultaneously and can be measured. A fall in sales in a trade downturn cannot be predicted and might affect all firms. Moreover, the fall in sales might be the result of a wide range of factors.

 # Solution 37

| Event | Rise in the exchange rate | Fall in the exchange rate | Leave the exchange rate unaffected |
|---|---|---|---|
| (i) A rise in interest rates in the country. | X | | |
| (ii) A rise in the demand for imports in the country. | | X | |
| (iii) A significant short-term fall in share prices in the country. | | | X |
| (iv) Purchase of foreign exchange by the country's central bank. | | X | |

## Solution 38

Solution (D)

Government revenue is not directly affected by interest rates. Indeed, since the government has a net debt ('the national debt') its expenditure would rise rather than its revenue. This is because with higher interest rates, the cost of servicing the national debt would increase.

 ## Solution 39

|       |                        |                |
| ----- | ---------------------- | -------------- |
| (i)   | Treasury bills         | M money market |
| (ii)  | Certificates of deposit | M money market |
| (iii) | Corporate bonds        | C capital market |
| (iv)  | Mortgages              | C capital market |
| (v)   | Bills of exchange      | M money market |

 ## Solution 40

Solution (A)

The benefit of a single currency would include reduced exchange rate uncertainty (there are no exchange rates within the eurozone) and because no currency would be exchanged on intra-European trade, transactions costs would fall, not rise.

## Solution 41

| Statement | True | False |
| --------- | ---- | ----- |
| (i) A insurance broker undertakes the task of underwriting but not reinsurance. | | X |
| (ii) Reinsurance occurs when an insurer shares the risk and the premiums with the other insurers. | X | |
| (iii) Insurers will not insure against events they know it will occur. | | X |

 ## Solution 42

Solution (B)

The other three are all means of acquiring short-term liquidity to meet a short-term shortfall in finances. However, issuing shares is means of raising long-term finance typically for investment purposes.

## Solution 43

Solution (D)

Increased borrowing by the government is likely to lead to a rise in interest rates. This, in turn, will normally depress share prices. Moreover, increased borrowing tends to inject expenditure into the economy, thus raising the rate of inflation.

 ## Solution 44

Solution (C)

A withdrawal from the circular flow is a process that removes expenditure from the circular flow. Investment and exports add expenditure to the flow and are, therefore, injections. Profit is form of income and is neither an injection nor a withdrawal.

 ## Solution 45

(i) Any two of the following:
   Investment expenditure
   Government expenditure
   Net exports.
(ii) Point C at income level D (i.e. where income and expenditure are equal).
(iii) Gap EF (i.e. the level of expenditure is less than the level of income).

 ## Solution 46

Solution (C)

In the upswing phase of the trade cycle aggregate demand rises. This increases inflationary pressure ('demand pull inflation') and pulls in extra imports worsening the balance of payments. Cyclical unemployment will tend to fall but not structural unemployment which is caused by long term not cyclic factors. However, the increase in income raises tax revenue and the fall in unemployment reduces government expenditure. The government budget moves towards surplus.

 ## Solution 47

Solution (D)

All of the other are payments in return for an economic good or service. However, educational grants and scholarships are transfers between taxpayers and students and are not in return for an economic goods or service.

 ## Solution 48

(i) D this is inside the production possibility frontier.
(ii) C this is close to the horizontal axis and far from the vertical axis.
(iii) A this is close to the vertical axis and far from the horizontal axis.
(iv) E this is a move to a higher possibility frontier where more of all goods can be produced.

**Solution 49**

Solution (A)

The natural rate of unemployment is where the demand and supply for labour are equal and is known as the vertical long-run Phillips curve. Attempts to reduce unemployment below this level merely led to higher inflation. Responses (C) and (D) are true statements, but have nothing to do with the natural rate hypothesis.

 **Solution 50**

Solution (D)

Transnational companies (also known as multinational companies) may have all of the characteristics listed here. But the defining feature of such companies is that they produce their good or service in more than one country. A company producing in just one country may have all three of the other characteristics.

 **Solution 51**

(i) National output would *fall* as the AS curve would move to the left.
(ii) National output would *rise* as the AS curve would move to the right.
(iii) National output would *rise* as the AD curve would move to the right.
(iv) National output would *fall* as the AD curve would move to the left.

 **Solution 52**

Solution (B)

The WTO's main functions are to promote free trade, resolve trade disputes and provide a framework of trade rules. However, it has no financing function. This is left to the other international bodies such as the IMF and the World Bank.

 **Solution 53**

| | | |
|---|---|---|
| (i) | −$20 billion | Trade in goods, credits minus debits ($164–$184). |
| (ii) | −$5 billion | All trade in goods and services, credits and debits for trade in goods, trade in services, investment income and transfers. |
| (iii) | −$11 billion | Direct investment abroad minus inward direct investment. |
| (iv) | −$18 billion | All credit minus all debits. |

 **Solution 54**

Solution (B)

Responses (A), (C) and (D) are all payments for economic services received. All would thus appear on the current account as invisible items. However, the flows of investment are flows of capital and therefore appear on the capital account.

# Solution 55
Solution (C)

The EU is a common market and thus has no internal barriers to the movement of either goods, services or factors of production. It also maintains a common external tariff, but indirect taxes, for example, VAT still vary from one member state to another. The Single European Market project is designed to progressively reduce these tax differences.

 # Solution 56

| Statement | True | False |
|---|---|---|
| (i) The heaviest indirect taxes tend to be on goods with a high price elasticity of demand. | | X |
| (ii) An indirect tax is one where the incidence and the burden of the tax fall on different persons. | X | |
| (iii) Indirect taxes on imports are desirable since the burden of the tax falls on the foreign producer. | | X |
| (iv) Direct taxes are preferred to indirect taxes because they are always progressive. | | X |

 # Solution 57
Solution (D)

Increase output requires extra energy and raw materials. So a shortage of either would constrain the rate of economic growth. Also, environmental damage from pollution may become unacceptable (e.g. global warming) and thus places limits on output. Increased trade does none of these things and generally tend to raise productivity and hence economic growth.

 # Solution 58
Solution (C)

All of the others are features of globalisation but (C) cannot happen. The terms of trade measure the relationship between the prices of exports and imports. If they improve for one trading partner, they must, by definition, deteriorate for the other trading partner.

**Solution 59**

| Statement | True | False |
|---|---|---|
| (i) If a country imposes trade barriers on its imports, that country's economic welfare will be reduced. | X | |
| (ii) An advantage of flexible exchange rate regimes is that uncertainty is reduced for business. | | X |
| (iii) Advantage of fixed exchange rate regimes is that they make trade deficits less likely to occur. | | X |
| (iv) Free trade enables a country to re-allocate its resource to more productive uses. | X | |

 **Solution 60**

(i) The three injections are:
- Domestic fixed capital formation
- Government consumption expenditure
- Exports.

(ii) Slow GDP growth would be expected to:
- *Lower* the level of employment
- *Reduce* the government budget surplus
- *Lower* the level of imports.

Mock Assessment 1

# Mock Assessment 1

Instructions: attempt all 75 questions

Time allowed 2 hours

Do not turn the page until you are ready to attempt the assessment under timed conditions

**Mock Assessment 1 – Questions**

 ## Question 1

Which *one* of the following would lead directly to an outward shift in a country's production possibility frontier?

(A) A rise in the population of working age.
(B) A fall in unemployment.
(C) An increase in outward migration.
(D) A rise in the school leaving age.

**(2 marks)**

## Question 2

The cost of one good or service measured in terms of what must be sacrificed to obtain it is called:

(A) real cost.
(B) potential cost.
(C) opportunity cost.
(D) social cost.

**(2 marks)**

 ## Question 3

The following financial data refers to a company.

| | | |
|---|---|---|
| Capital employed | 1.1.06 | $900000 |
| Capital employed | 31.12.06 | $1100000 |
| Gross profits for year ending | 31.12.06 | 105000 |
| Interest payments year ending | 31.12.06 | 20000 |
| Tax paid on profits year ending | 31.12.06 | 15000 |

What is the value of the rate of return on capital for this company?

**(2 marks)**

## Question 4

All of the following are essential features of a market economy except which *one?*

(A) Private ownership of productive resources.
(B) Allocation of resources by the price mechanism.
(C) Absence of entry and exit barriers to and from industries.
(D) Prices determined by market forces.

**(2 marks)**

## Question 5

Consider the following data for business:

| Output | Fixed Cost | Total Variable Cost | Marginal Revenue |
|--------|-----------|---------------------|------------------|
| 10 | $100 | $150 | $12 |
| 11 | $100 | $164 | $12 |
| 12 | $100 | $176 | $12 |
| 13 | $100 | $199 | $12 |
| 14 | $100 | $236 | $12 |
| 15 | $100 | $275 | $12 |

From this data you are required to calculate for this business:

(A) the average cost of production at output level 10.
(B) the marginal cost of production at output level 11.
(C) the optimum level of output for this business.
(D) the profit maximising level of output for this business.

**(4 marks)**

## Question 6

A business will maximise profits only if it produces where:

(A) average cost = marginal revenue.
(B) marginal cost = marginal revenue.
(C) average cost = average revenue.
(D) marginal cost = average revenue.

**(2 marks)**

## Question 7

Consider the following data for a proposed investment project.

| | |
|---|---|
| Capital cost of the project | $7000 |
| Life of the investment | 3 years |
| Scrap value of the capital at end of Year 3 | $500 |
| Income generated by the project | |
| Year 1 | $2000 |
| Year 2 | $3000 |
| Year 3 | $2000 |

From this data you are required to calculate:

(a) The discounted cash flow for the project assuming a discount rate of 10%

**(2 marks)**

(b) Is this project profitable for the company    yes/no

**(2 marks)**

(c) The net present value for the project assuming a discount rate of 6% and a final scrap value of $1000

**(2 marks)**

## Question 8

The price earnings ratio is measured by:

(A) Dividing earnings per share by the market price of the share.
(B) Dividing the current market price of the share by the earnings per share.
(C) Dividing the earnings per share by the rate of discount.
(D) Dividing the current market price of the share by total profits.

**(2 marks)**

 ## Question 9

All of the following would be expected to raise share values except which *one*?

(A) An announcement of higher than expected profits.
(B) A reduction in corporation tax.
(C) A rise in interest rates.
(D) A rise in share prices on overseas stock markets.

**(2 marks)**

 ## Question 10

The ... (i) ........ in a company are all those who have an interest in the strategy and behaviour of the ... (ii) ........ Their interest may not always coincide with those of the ... (iii) ........ who are principally interested in ... (iv) ........ The task of .... (v) ........ is to attempt to reconcile these conflicting interests.

Read the above passage and indicate where each of the following words should be placed in the passage.

(A) Management
(B) Shareholders
(C) Stakeholders
(D) Company
(E) Profits

**(5 marks)**

 ## Question 11

State whether each of the following statements about limited liability companies are true or false.

| Statement | True | False |
|---|---|---|
| (i) Shareholders are not liable for the debts of the company. | | |
| (ii) Owners always exercise day-to-day decision-making authority. | | |
| (iii) Owners share in the profits of the company, but not necessarily in proportion to the number of shares that they own. | | |

**(3 marks)**

# ? **Question 12**

The principal–agent problem refers to:

(A) situations where a company's selling agents are not meeting the company's main sales targets.
(B) problems arising when a principal delegates authority to an agent but cannot ensure the agent will always act in his/her interest.
(C) cases where companies lack knowledge of particular markets and have to seek agents to act of their behalf.
(D) the power a large company may exert over suppliers when it is the dominant buyer of that suppliers output.

**(2 marks)**

# ? **Question 13**

For each of the following economic processes, indicate whether the effect on the *short-run average cost* for a firm would be to raise the cost curve, lower the cost curve or to leave the cost curve unaffected.

| Economic process | Raise curve | Lower curve | Leave curve unaffected |
| --- | --- | --- | --- |
| A rise in wage costs | | | |
| Increase opportunities for economies of scale. | | | |
| A fall in the price of raw materials | | | |
| A shift in the demand curve to the left | | | |

**(4 marks)**

# ? **Question 14**

Indicate whether each of the following statements is *true* or *false*.

| Statement | True | False |
| --- | --- | --- |
| The law of diminishing returns shows how long-run cost tends to rise as if the scale of output becomes too great | | |
| A firm's short-run cost curve is always U shaped; the long cost curve may or may not be | | |
| For most firms technological change is one of the most important economies of scale | | |
| Economies of scale act as barrier to entry to industries. | | |

**(4 marks)**

# Question 15

Indicate whether each of the following are typical characteristics of an oligopoly market (yes/no).

| Characteristic | Yes | No |
| --- | --- | --- |
| A large number of small firms | | |
| A preference for non-price competition over price competition | | |
| Interdependence of decision-making | | |
| Ease of entry and exit to and from the industry. | | |

**(4 marks)**

 # Question 16

State whether each of the following statements is *true* or *false*.

| Statement | True | False |
| --- | --- | --- |
| Collusion is more likely in oligopoly markets than in other markets | | |
| If there are economies of scale, a monopoly firm may charge lower prices than equivalent firms facing competition | | |
| Oligopolistic firms can never achieve lower long-run costs than could competitive firms in the same industry | | |
| Oligopolistic firms can make excess profits but only in the short run. | | |

**(4 marks)**

 # Question 17

If a business currently sells 10,000 units of its product per month at $10 per unit and the demand for its product has a price elasticity of −2.5, a rise in the price of the product to $11 will:

(A) raise total revenue by $7,250.
(B) reduce total revenue by $17,500.
(C) reduce total revenue by $25,000.
(D) raise total revenue by $37,500.

**(2 marks)**

**Question 18**

In the kinked demand curve model of oligopoly, the kink in the firm's demand curve is due to the firm's belief that competitors will:

(A)  set a price at the kink of the demand curve.
(B)  will match all price increases and price reductions.
(C)  will match any price increases, but not any price reductions.
(D)  will match any price reductions, but not any price increases.

**(2 marks)**

 **Question 19**

Which *one* of the following is a natural barrier to the entry of new firms into an industry?

(A)  Large initial capital costs.
(B)  The issuing of patents.
(C)  A government awarded franchise.
(D)  The licensing of professions.

**(2 marks)**

 **Question 20**

The following data refers to an industry consisting of 8 companies.

| Company | Sales | Market Share |
|---------|-------|--------------|
| No 1 | 1200 | |
| No 2 | 800 | |
| No 3 | 600 | |
| No 4 | 600 | |
| No 5 | 500 | |
| No 6 | 500 | |
| No 7 | 450 | |
| No 8 | 350 | |
| The four-firm concentration ratio | | |

You are required to calculate:

(a)  the market shares for each company.
(b)  the four-firm concentration ratio for this industry.

**(3 marks)**

 **Question 21**

If the market supply curve for a good is inelastic, an increase in demand will:

(A)  Raise total sales proportionately more than it will raise the market price.
(B)  Raise total sales proportionately less than it will raise the market price.
(C)  Raise the market price but leave total sales unaffected.
(D)  Raise total sales but leave the market price unchanged.

**(2 marks)**

## Question 22

Mergers between businesses engaged in the same stage of production of a similar good or service are known as:

(A)  Horizontal mergers.
(B)  Conglomerate mergers.
(C)  Vertical mergers.
(D)  Cross mergers.

**(2 marks)**

## Question 23

A good which is characterised by both rivalry and excludability is called:

(A)  a public good.
(B)  a private good.
(C)  a government good.
(D)  an external good.

**(2 marks)**

## Question 24

The burden of an indirect tax on a good will fall more heavily on the producer when:

(A)  demand for the good is price elastic.
(B)  demand for the good is price inelastic.
(C)  demand for the good has unit elasticity.
(D)  supply of the good is price elastic.

**(2 marks)**

## Question 25

In practice a monopoly may have its market power limited by all of the following except which *one*?

(A)  Countervailing power from its customers.
(B)  The market may be contestable.
(C)  There may be close substitutes for the good.
(D)  The firm's long-run average cost curve may be falling.

**(2 marks)**

## Question 26

The following is a list of possible sources of market failure.

  (i)  Externalities
 (ii)  Monopoly power
(iii)  Public goods and services
 (iv)  Merit goods
  (v)  Monopsony power
 (vi)  Lack of knowledge

For each of the following cases, indicate which one of the above sources of market failure matches the case given:

(A) Businesses fail to properly train their employees because they fear that they will move to other firms after their training.

(B) There is a failure to provide efficient street cleaning services because it is impossible for the service providers to ensure that all who benefited from the services paid for them.

(C) Employers pay their workers wages which are below their productivity – their marginal revenue product.

(D) A company's marginal revenue is not equal to the price of the good it produces and it therefore does not equate price with marginal cost.

**(2 marks)**

## Question 27

Which *one* of the following is the best example of a merit good?

(A) Street lighting.
(B) A national defence force.
(C) Company cars for top sales executives.
(D) A system of public libraries.

**(2 marks)**

## Question 28

There are three types of mergers

(i) Horizontal mergers
(ii) Vertical mergers
(iii) Conglomerate mergers

Match the following reasons for a merger with the appropriate type of merger listed above.

(A) To increase monopoly power and control over the market.
(B) To ensure control over supplies of raw materials and components.
(C) To secure economies of scale.
(D) To reduce risk by diversifying the range of products sold and the range of markets.

**(4 marks)**

## Question 29

State whether the following statements about the privatisation of state industries are true or false.

| Statement | True | False |
|---|---|---|
| (i) Privatisation increases the commercial pressure on the business to make a profit. | | |
| (ii) Privatisation ensures the business faces competition and so encourages greater efficiency. | | |
| (iii) Privatisation is a means of solving the principal–agent problem. | | |
| (iv) Privatisation is likely to make the business more responsive to needs of its customers. | | |

**(4 marks)**

**Question 30**

Which of the following are features of monopolistic competition?

 (i) Large numbers of producers in the industry.
 (ii) Differentiated products.
 (iii) Companies producing at less than optimum output.
 (iv) Monopoly profits in the long run.

(A) (i), (iii) and (iv) only.
(B) (ii), (iii) and (iv).
(C) (i), (ii) and (iii) only.
(D) (i), (ii) and (iv) only.

**(2 marks)**

 **Question 31**

The cobweb theorem:

(A) shows that, without intervention some agricultural prices will fall continuously over time.
(B) explains why some agricultural prices are characterised by instability from one year to another.
(C) shows that when some agricultural prices are disturbed, prices steadily return to their equilibrium level.
(D) the imposition of minimum prices in agricultural products always lead to unsold surpluses.

**(2 marks)**

 **Question 32**

The following diagram shows the cost and revenue curves for a monopoly firm. The firm is producing at output level Q1.

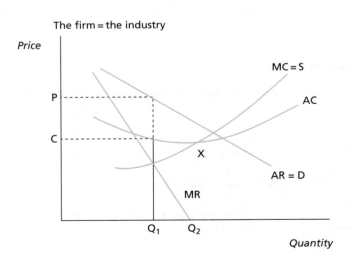

You are required to:

(a) State whether the firm is producing at, above or below the optimum level of output.                                                                 at/above/below

(b) State whether the firm is producing at, above or below the profit maximising level of output.                                                       at/above/below

(c) Identify the abnormal (monopoly) profits the firm is currently earning.

**(3 marks)**

## ? Question 33

The necessary conditions for a firm to be able to practice price discrimination are:

 (i)  The firm must be a price setter.
 (ii)  The markets must be kept separate.
(iii)  The price elasticity of demand must be different in each market.
(iv)  Customers in each market must not be aware of the prices changed in other markets.

(A)  (i), (ii) and (iii) only.
(B)  (i), (ii) and (iv) only.
(C)  (ii), (iii) and (iv) only.
(D)  all of them.

**(2 marks)**

## ? Question 34

If an indirect tax is imposed on a good or service:

(A)  The price will rise by an amount equal to the tax.
(B)  The producer decides on how much of the tax to pass on to the customer.
(C)  The price rise will be smaller the greater is the price elasticity of demand.
(D)  The price rise will be greater the smaller is the price elasticity of supply.

**(2 marks)**

## ? Question 35

All of the following are examples of where externalities are likely to occur except which *one*?

(A)  A business providing training schemes for its employees.
(B)  Government expenditure on vaccination programmes for infectious diseases.
(C)  Attending a concert given by a government funded orchestra.
(D)  Private motorists driving cars in city centres.

**(2 marks)**

## ? Question 36

Whenever government intervention prevents prices from reaching their equilibrium level, the result will always include all of the following except which *one*?

(A)  Shortages or surpluses.
(B)  Demand and supply not equal.
(C)  Reduced profits for producers.
(D)  Resources not allocated by price.

**(2 marks)**

## Question 37

A rise in the price of a good accompanied by a fall in the quantity sold would result from

(A) a decrease in supply.
(B) an increase in demand.
(C) a decrease in demand.
(D) an increase in supply.

**(2 marks)**

## Question 38

If the demand curve for Good A shifts to the left when the price of Good B rises, we may conclude that

(A) the goods are substitutes.
(B) Good A is an inferior good.
(C) the goods are complements.
(D) the demand for Good A is price elastic.

**(2 marks)**

## Question 39

The introduction of a national minimum wage will lead a business to reduce its number of employees most when

(A) the demand for its final product is price elastic.
(B) wage costs are a small proportion of total costs.
(C) there is a low degree of substitutability between capital and labour.
(D) the supply of substitute factors of production is price inelastic.

**(2 marks)**

## Question 40

The following is a list of different types of market structure.

- Perfect competition
- Monopolistic competition
- Oligopoly
- Monopoly

Match to each of the following situations the market structure that is being described.

| Situation | Market Structure |
| --- | --- |
| (i) In the long run, abnormal profits are competed away by the entry of new firms and for each firm output will be the optimum level of output. | |
| (ii) The behaviour of any one firm is conditioned by how it expects its competitors to react to its price and output decisions. | |

**(2 marks)**

## Question 41

Which one of the following is not a characteristic of not-for-profit organisations?

(A) They need efficient and effective management.
(B) They make financial surpluses and deficits.
(C) They have a range of stakeholders.
(D) The absence of any principal–agent problem.

**(2 marks)**

## Question 42

In order to finance an excess of expenditure over taxation receipts, a government could:

(A) reduce its current expenditure.
(B) issue government bonds.
(C) raise income tax.
(D) run an overdraft on its account with the World Bank.

**(2 marks)**

## Question 43

A business could use all of the following to finance a lack of synchronisation in its short-term payments and receipts except which *one*?

(A) a bank overdraft.
(B) trade credit.
(C) its cash reserves.
(D) a hire purchase agreement.

**(2 marks)**

## Question 44

A risk that an organisation may not be able to realise its assets to meet a commitment associated with financial instruments is known as:

(A) credit risk.
(B) liquidity risk.
(C) interest rate risk.
(D) currency risk.

**(2 marks)**

## Question 45

State whether each of the following financial instruments appearing on a commercial bank's balance sheet is an asset or liability for the bank.

| Instrument | Asset | Liability |
| --- | --- | --- |
| Advances | | |
| Money at call with discount houses | | |
| Deposit accounts | | |
| Shareholder capital | | |

**(4 marks)**

## Question 46

If banks are required to keep a reserve assets ratio of 10% and also wish to keep a margin of liquid reserves of 10%, by how much would deposits ultimately rise by if they acquire an additional $1000 of reserve assets?

(A) $10000
(B) $5000
(C) $1000
(D) $500

**(2 marks)**

 ## Question 47

If a commercial banks reallocates some of its assets from less profitable to more profitable ones,

(A) the bank's liquidity will be increased.
(B) the safety of the bank's assets will be increased.
(C) the bank's liquidity will be decreased.
(D) the liquidity and safety of the bank's assets will be unaffected.

**(2 marks)**

 ## Question 48

Which of the following statements about the relationship between bond prices and bond yields is true?

(A) They vary positively.
(B) They vary inversely.
(C) They vary inversely or positively depending on business conditions.
(D) They are not related.

**(2 marks)**

 ## Question 49

Read the following passage.

A business will need to insure itself against a range of risks. It can do so by employing a ........(i)... to seek out the most appropriate insurance policies. If the risks involved are very large the insurance company......(ii)...... the risk may engage in ... (iii)...... the risk with other companies.

You are required to indicate which of the following words should placed in each of the gaps in the passage.

(a) Broker
(b) General insurance company
(c) Reinsuring
(d) Underwriting
(e) Assuring

**(3 marks)**

## ? Question 50

Under a regime of flexible exchange rates, which one of the following would lead to a rise in the exchange rate for a country's currency?

(A) a shift in the country's balance of payments current account towards a surplus.
(B) a rise in interest rates in other countries.
(C) an increasing balance of trade deficit.
(D) the central bank buying foreign exchange on the foreign exchange market.

**(2 marks)**

## ? Question 51

Exchange rates are determined by supply and demand for currencies in the foreign exchange market. State whether each of the following would be part of the supply of a country's currency or part of the demand for that country's currency.

| Statement | Supply | Demand |
| --- | --- | --- |
| Payments for imports into the country. | | |
| Inflows of capital into the country. | | |
| Purchases of foreign currency by the country's central bank. | | |

**(2 marks)**

## ? Question 52

Each of the following is a source of funds for capital investment for business except one. Which *one* is the exception?

(A) Commercial banks.
(B) Internally generated funds.
(C) The stock market
(D) The central bank.

**(2 marks)**

## ? Question 53

The linking of net savers with net borrowers is known as:

(A) the savings function.
(B) financial intermediation.
(C) financial regulation.
(D) a store of value.

**(2 marks)**

## Question 54

If a consumer price index rises, it shows that

(A) the value of the currency has increased.
(B) real consumer income has fallen.
(C) all prices in the economy have risen.
(D) the purchasing power of money has decreased.

**(2 marks)**

 ## Question 55

The main function of the money market is to

(A) enable businesses and governments to obtain liquidity.
(B) encourage saving.
(C) permit the efficient buying and selling of shares.
(D) deal in credit instruments of more than one year maturity.

**(2 marks)**

 ## Question 56

The effects of low real interest rates include all of the following except which *one*?

(A) Credit based sales will tend to be high.
(B) Nominal costs of borrowing will always be low.
(C) Business activity will tend to increase.
(D) Investment will be encouraged.

**(2 marks)**

 ## Question 57

Which *one* of the following would cause the value of the multiplier to fall?

(A) A fall in the level of government expenditure.
(B) A rise in the marginal propensity to consume.
(C) A fall in business investment.
(D) A rise in the marginal propensity to save.

**(2 marks)**

 ## Question 58

The recession phase of the trade cycle will normally be accompanied by all of the following except which *one*?

(A) A rise in the rate of inflation.
(B) A fall in the level of national output.
(C) An improvement in the trade balance.
(D) A rise in the level of unemployment.

**(2 marks)**

## Question 59

According to the new classical school, in order to manage the economy governments should:

(A) use active fiscal and monetary policy.
(B) adopt a *laissez faire* approach and leave everything to market forces.
(C) announce monetary rules to control inflation, and liberalise product and factor markets.
(D) use only monetary policy to increase output and employment.

**(2 marks)**

## Question 60

The following is a list of types of unemployment.

> Structural unemployment
> Cyclical unemployment
> Real wage (classical) unemployment
> Frictional unemployment
> Seasonal unemployment.

Match the above types of unemployment to the following definitions.

| Definition of unemployment | Type of unemployment |
| --- | --- |
| (i) Unemployment that occurs in particular industries and arises from long-term changes in the patterns of demand and supply. | |
| (ii) Unemployment associated with industries or regions where the demand for labour and wage rates regularly rise and fall over the year. | |

**(2 marks)**

## Question 61

All of the following will lead to a fall in the level of economic activity in an economy except which *one*?

(A) A rise in cyclical unemployment.
(B) A fall in business investment.
(C) A decrease in government expenditure.
(D) A rise in interest rates.

**(2 marks)**

## Question 62

The best measure of the standard of living in a country is

(A)  gross domestic product per capita.
(B)  per capita personal consumption.
(C)  gross national product per capita.
(D)  personal disposable income.

**(2 marks)**

 ## Question 63

Supply-side policy is designed to

(A)  raise the level of aggregate monetary demand in the economy.
(B)  manage the money supply in the economy.
(C)  improve the ability of the economy to produce goods and services.
(D)  reduce unemployment by limiting the supply of labour.

**(2 marks)**

## Question 64

Indicate whether each of the following taxes are direct taxes or indirect taxes.

| Type of tax | Direct | Indirect |
| --- | --- | --- |
| Income tax | | |
| Value added tax | | |
| Corporation tax | | |
| National insurance (social security tax) | | |

**(4 marks)**

## Question 65

International trade is best explained by the fact that:

(A)  all countries have an absolute advantage in the production of something.
(B)  all countries have specialised in the production of certain goods and services.
(C)  no country has an absolute advantage in the production of all goods and services.
(D)  all countries have a comparative advantage in the production of something.

**(2 marks)**

## ? Question 66

The following diagram shows the aggregate demand curve (AD) and the aggregate supply curve (AS) for an economy:

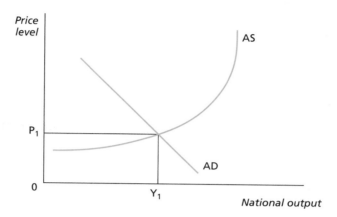

With reference to the diagram:

A ............. supply shock would shift the ............... curve to the left and cause the rate of inflation to increase. However the level of ............... would fall. A(n) ............... fiscal policy would shift the ............... curve to the right leading to a ............... in both the level of national output and the rate of inflation.

Use the following words and phrases to full in the gaps in the above passage.

> positive
> aggregate demand
> rise
> expansionary
> negative
> deflationary
> aggregate supply
> inflation
> national output
> fall

**(6 marks)**

## ? Question 67

All of the following will encourage the process of the globalisation of production except which *one*?

(A) Reductions in international transport costs.
(B) Higher levels of tariffs.
(C) Reduced barriers to international capital movements.
(D) Increased similarity in demand patterns between countries.

**(2 marks)**

**Question 68**

Intra-industry trade occurs when a country:

(A) exports and imports different products.
(B) exports and imports the same products.
(C) imports materials to be used by its domestic industry.
(D) exports materials for use in industries in other countries.

**(2 marks)**

 **Question 69**

Which *one* of the following shows the lowest degree of international mobility?

(A) Unskilled labour.
(B) Financial capital.
(C) Technical knowledge.
(D) Management.

**(2 marks)**

 **Question 70**

Identify which of the following statements about the balance of payments is true and which is false.

| Statement | True | False |
|---|---|---|
| (i) A deficit on a country's balance of payments current account can be financed by a surplus of invisible earnings. | | |
| (ii) Flows of profits and interest on capital appear in the Capital Account. | | |
| (iii) Flexible exchange rate systems should, in principle, prevent persistent current account imbalances. | | |
| (iv) Current account deficits tend to worsen in periods of rapid economic growth. | | |

**(4 marks)**

 **Question 71**

A fall in the exchange rate for a country's currency will improve the balance of payments current account if:

(A) the price elasticity of demand for imports is greater than for exports.
(B) the price elasticity of demand for exports is greater than for imports.
(C) the sum of the price elasticities for imports and exports is less than one.
(D) the sum of the price elasticities for imports and exports is greater than one.

**(2 marks)**

## Question 72

All of the following are benefits which all countries gain when adopting a single currency such as the Euro, except which *one*?

(A)  Reduced transactions costs.
(B)  Increased price transparency.
(C)  Lower interest rates.
(D)  Reduced exchange rate uncertainity.

**(2 marks)**

## Question 73

For each of the following events, indicate whether the direct effect of each on an economy would raise inflation, reduce inflation or leave the rate of inflation unaffected. Assume that the economy is close to full employment.

| Event | Raise inflation | Lower inflation | Leave inflation unchanged |
|---|---|---|---|
| (i)   A rise (appreciation) in the exchange for the country's currency. | | | |
| (ii)  A significant increase in the money supply. | | | |
| (iii) The removal of house prices from the consumer price index. | | | |
| (iv)  A rise in business expectations leading to an increase in investment. | | | |

**(4 marks)**

## Question 74

Compared to a fixed exchange rate system, an economy will benefit from a flexible exchange rate system because:

(A)  it enables businesses to vary their export prices.
(B)  governments will not have to deflate the economy when balance of payments deficits occur.
(C)  it reduces the cost of acquiring foreign exchange.
(D)  it ensures that businesses never become uncompetitive in international markets.

**(2 marks)**

**Question 75**

All of the following statements are true except which *one*?

(A) Import quotas tend to reduce prices.
(B) Trade protection tends to reduce consumer choice.
(C) Trade protection tends to reduce exports.
(D) Tariffs tend to reduce competition.

**(2 marks)**

## ☑ Mock Assessment 1 – Solutions

## ☑ Solution 1

A

## ☑ Solution 2

C

## ☑ Solution 3

10.5%

## ☑ Solution 4

C

## ☑ Solution 5

(a) $25
(b) $14
(c) 12 or 13
(d) 12

## ☑ Solution 6

B

## ☑ Solution 7

(a) $6176
(b) No
(c) $76

## ☑ Solution 8

B

## ☑ Solution 9

C

## ☑ Solution 10

The *stakeholders* in a company are all those who have an interest in the strategy and behaviour of the *company*. Their interest may not always coincide with those of the *shareholders* who are principally interested in *profits*. The task of *management* is to attempt to reconcile these conflicting interests.

## ☑ Solution 11

| Statement | True | False |
|---|---|---|
| (i) Shareholders are not liable for the debts of the company. | X | |
| (ii) Owners always exercise day-to-day decision-making authority. | | X |
| (iii) Owners share in the profits of the company, but not necessarily in proportion to the number of shares that they own. | | X |

**Solution 12**

B

 **Solution 13**

| Economic process | Raise curve | Lower curve | Leave curve unaffected |
|---|---|---|---|
| A rise in wage costs. | X | | |
| Increase opportunities for economies of scale. | | | X |
| A fall in the price of raw materials. | | X | |
| A shift in the demand curve to the left. | | | X |

 **Solution 14**

| Statements | True | False |
|---|---|---|
| The law of diminishing returns shows how long-run cost tends to rise as if the scale of output becomes too great | | X |
| A firm's short-run cost curve is always U shaped; the long cost curve may or may not be | X | |
| For most firms technological change is one of the most important economies of scale | | X |
| Economies of scale act as barrier to entry to industries. | X | |

 **Solution 15**

| Characteristics | Yes | No |
|---|---|---|
| A large number of small firms. | | X |
| A preference for non-price competition over price competition | X | |
| Interdependence of decision-making | X | |
| Ease of entry and exit to and from the industry | | X |

## Solution 16

| Statement | True | False |
|---|---|---|
| Collusion is more likely in oligopoly markets than in other markets | X | |
| If there are economies of scale, a monopoly firm may charge lower prices than equivalent firms facing competition | X | |
| Oligopolistic firms can never achieve lower long-run costs than could competitive firms in the same industry | | X |
| Oligopolistic firms can make excess profits but only in the short run. | | X |

 ## Solution 17

B

 ## Solution 18

D

 ## Solution 19

A

## Solution 20

| Company | Sales | Market Share (in %) |
|---|---|---|
| No 1 | 1200 | 24 |
| No 2 | 800 | 16 |
| No 3 | 600 | 12 |
| No 4 | 600 | 12 |
| No 5 | 500 | 10 |
| No 6 | 500 | 10 |
| No 7 | 450 | 9 |
| No 8 | 350 | 7 |
| The four-firm concentration ratio | 64% | |

 ## Solution 21

B

 ## Solution 22

A

 ## Solution 23

B

## ☑ Solution 24

A

## ☑ Solution 25

D

## ☑ Solution 26

(a)   (i)   Externalities
(b)   (iii)  Public goods and services
(c)   (v)   Monopsony power
(d)   (ii)  Monopoly power

## ☑ Solution 27

D

## ☑ Solution 28

(a)   (i)   Horizontal merger
(b)   (ii)  Vertical merger
(c)   (i)   Horizontal merger
(d)   (iii)  Conglomerate merger

## ☑ Solution 29

| Statements | True | False |
|---|---|---|
| (i) Privatisation increases the commercial pressure on the business to make a profit. | X | |
| (ii) Privatisation ensures the business faces competition and so encourages greater efficiency. | | X |
| (iii) Privatisation is a means of solving the principal–agent problem. | | X |
| (iv) Privatisation is likely to make the business more responsive to needs of its customers. | X | |

## ☑ Solution 30

C

## ☑ Solution 31

B

## ☑ Solution 32

(a)  Below the optimum output.
(b)  At the profit maximising level.
(c)  Area PC – Q1

## Solution 33
A

## Solution 34
C

## Solution 35
C

## Solution 36
C

## Solution 37
A

## Solution 38
C

## Solution 39
A

## Solution 40

| Situations | Market Structure |
|---|---|
| (i) In the long run, abnormal profits are competed away by the entry of new firms and for each firm output will be the optimum level of output. | *Perfect competition* |
| (ii) The behaviour of any one firm is conditioned by how it expects its competitors to react to its price and output decisions. | *Oligopoly* |

## Solution 41
D

## Solution 42
B

## Solution 43
D

## Solution 44
B

**Solution 45**

| Instrument | Asset | Liability |
|---|---|---|
| Advances | X | |
| Money at call with discount houses | X | |
| Deposit accounts | | X |
| Shareholder capital. | | X |

 **Solution 46**

B

 **Solution 47**

C

 **Solution 48**

B

 **Solution 49**

A business will need to insure itself against a range of risks. It can do so by employing a *broker* to seek out the most appropriate insurance policies. If the risks involved are very large the insurance company *underwriting* the risk may engage in *reinsuring* the risk with other companies.

 **Solution 50**

A

 **Solution 51**

| Statement | Supply | Demand |
|---|---|---|
| Payments for imports into the country. | X | |
| Inflows of capital into the country. | | X |
| Purchases of foreign currency by the country's central bank. | X | |

 **Solution 52**

D

 **Solution 53**

B

 **Solution 54**

D

 **Solution 55**

A

## ✓ Solution 56

B

## ✓ Solution 57

D

## ✓ Solution 58

A

## ✓ Solution 59

C

## ✓ Solution 60

| Definition of unemployment | Type of unemployment |
|---|---|
| (i) Unemployment that occurs in particular industries and arises from long-term changes in the patterns of demand and supply. | *Structural unemployment* |
| (ii) Unemployment associated with industries or regions where the demand for labour and wage rates regularly rise and fall over the year. | *Seasonal unemployment* |

## ✓ Solution 61

A

## ✓ Solution 62

B

## ✓ Solution 63

C

## ✓ Solution 64

| Type of tax | Direct | Indirect |
|---|---|---|
| Income tax | X | |
| Value added tax | | X |
| Corporation tax | X | |
| National insurance (social security tax) | X | |

## ✓ Solution 65

D

## ✓ Solution 66

A *negative* supply shock would shift the *aggregate supply* curve to the left and cause the rate of inflation to increase. However the level of *national output* would fall. An *expansionary* fiscal policy would shift the *aggregate demand* curve to the right leading to a *rise* in both the level of national output and the rate of inflation.

☑ **Solution 67**

B

☑ **Solution 68**

B

☑ **Solution 69**

A

☑ **Solution 70**

| Statement | True | False |
|---|---|---|
| (i) A deficit on a country's balance of payments current account can be financed by a surplus of invisible earnings. | | X |
| (ii) Flows of profits and interest on capital appear in the Capital Account. | | X |
| (iii) Flexible exchange rate systems should, in principle, prevent persistent current account imbalances. | X | |
| (iv) Current account deficits tend to worsen in periods of rapid economic growth. | X | |

☑ **Solution 71**

D

☑ **Solution 72**

C

☑ **Solution 73**

| Event | Raise inflation | Lower inflation | Leave inflation unchanged |
|---|---|---|---|
| (i) A rise (appreciation) in the exchange for the country's currency. | | X | |
| (ii) A significant increase in the money supply. | X | | |
| (iii) The removal of house prices from the consumer price index. | | | X |
| (iv) A rise in business expectations leading to an increase in investment. | X | | |

☑ **Solution 74**

B

☑ **Solution 75**

A

Mock Assessment 2

# Mock Assessment 2

**Paper CO4**

**Fundamentals of Business Economics**

Instructions: attempt all 75 questions

Time allowed 2 hours

Do not turn the page until you are ready to attempt the assessment under timed conditions

**Mock Assessment 2 – Questions**

## Question 1

All of the following are profit-seeking organisations except one. Which *one* is the exception?

(A)  Private limited companies.
(B)  Public corporations.
(C)  Partnerships.
(D)  Sole traders.

**(2 marks)**

## Question 2

The concept of opportunity cost can be shown on a production possibility frontier diagram as:

(A)  an outward movement of the production possibility frontier.
(B)  a movement from inside the production possibility frontier to the frontier.
(C)  a movement along the production possibility frontier.
(D)  an inward shift of the production possibility frontier.

**(2 marks)**

## Question 3

Public goods are produced in the public sector because:

(A)  they are characterised by non-excludability and non-exclusivity.
(B)  of the high initial capital costs their production involves.
(C)  they are examples of natural monopolies.
(D)  their production and consumption involves significant external social benefits.

**(2 marks)**

## Question 4

Indicate whether each of the following statements is *true* or *false*.

| Statements | True | False |
| --- | --- | --- |
| The marginal cost curve cuts the average cost curve at its lowest point. | | |
| Profits are maximised only where marginal revenue and average cost are equal. | | |
| Optimum output is where average costs are lowest. | | |
| The short-run average cost curve for firms eventually rises because of operation of diseconomies of scale. | | |

**(4 marks)**

**Question 5**

Variable cost is best defined as:

(A) the cost of labour and materials.
(B) costs which change over time.
(C) the change in total costs when output is raised by one unit.
(D) costs which vary with the level of output.

**(2 marks)**

 **Question 6**

For each of the following events indicate whether the effect would normally be to raise a company's share price, lower its share price or leave its share price unchanged.

| Events | Raise share price | Lower share price | Leave share price unchanged |
|---|---|---|---|
| A reduction in corporation tax | | | |
| An issue of additional shares in the company | | | |
| A fall in interest rates | | | |
| A high price-earnings ratio | | | |

**(4 marks)**

 **Question 7**

Consider the following data for a business:

| Output/Sales | Price |
|---|---|
| 10 | $100 |
| 11 | $95 |
| 12 | $90 |
| 13 | $85 |
| 14 | $80 |

From this data you are required to calculate for this business:

(A) the average revenue at output level 13.
(B) the marginal revenue when output is raised from 11 to 12 units.
(C) the price elasticity of demand for a price fall from $100 to $95.

**(3 marks)**

**Question 8**

Consider the following data for a company's proposed investment project.

| | |
|---|---|
| Capital cost of the project | $6000 |
| Life of the investment | 3 years |
| Scrap value of the capital equipment at end of Year 3 | $1000 |

Income generated by the project at end of each year

| Year 1 | ($1000) |
| Year 2 | $4000 |
| Year 3 | $3000 |

From this data you are required to calculate:

(A)  The discounted cash flow for the project assuming a discount rate of 10%.

**(2 marks)**

(B)  Whether the company should undertake the project? Yes/No

**(1 mark)**

(C)  The net present value for the project if the discount rate was 5%.

**(2 marks)**

## ? Question 9

The following data refers to a company.

| Capital employed | 01.01.07 | $1.4 m |
| Capital employed | 31.12.07 | $1.8 m |
| Gross profits for year ending | 31.12.07 | $0.4 m |
| Corporation tax paid for year ending | 31.12.07 | $0.10 m |
| Interest payments for year ending | 31.12.07 | $0.05 m |

What is the value of the rate of return on capital for this company?

**(2 marks)**

## ? Question 10

State whether each of the following is an appropriate measure of the short-run performance or the long-run performance of a business.

| Measures | Short run | Long run |
| --- | --- | --- |
| Net present value | | |
| Rate of return on capital employed | | |
| Earnings per share | | |

**(3 marks)**

## ? Question 11

Assuming a discount rate of 5% the present value of $10.000 to be received in one year's time is:

(A)  $10500
(B)  $10050
(C)  $9524
(D)  $6667

**(2 marks)**

## Question 12

An example of the principal–agent problem in business is where principals, such as ..........., delegate control to agents, such as .......... The problem is one of devising methods to ensure that agents act in the best interest of the principals. Managerial reward systems which link pay and bonuses to the improvement in .......... is one such method.

Read the above passage and indicate which of the following words should be placed in each of the gaps in the passage.

(A) Management.
(B) Stakeholders.
(C) Shareholder wealth.
(D) Shareholders.
(E) Efficiency.

**(3 marks)**

## Question 13

Which of the following groups are stakeholders in a particular business?

(i) Employees.
(ii) Shareholders.
(iii) Management.
(iv) Customers.
(v) Suppliers.

(A) (i), (ii) and (iii) only.
(B) (i), (ii), (iii) and (iv) only.
(C) (ii) and (iii) only.
(D) all of them.

**(2 marks)**

## Question 14

All of the following statements about earnings per share (EPS) are true except which *one*?

(A) It is relatively easy to calculate.
(B) It is a useful measure of the change in shareholder wealth.
(C) It is normally calculated on an annual basis.
(D) It can be used to calculate the price-earnings ratio.

**(2 marks)**

## Question 15

Economies of scale could occur in the long run for all of the following reasons except one. Which *one* is the exception?

(A) Bulk buying by big companies.
(B) Long-run improvements in technology in large firms.

(C) Cheaper long-term finance for large companies.

(D) Mass production technology adopted by large-scale producers.

**(2 marks)**

## ? Question 16

Indicate whether each of the following statements about a market economy is *true* or *false*.

| Statements | True | False |
| --- | --- | --- |
| The price mechanism is the only means for allocating scarce resources. | | |
| The public sector is smaller than the private sector. | | |
| Market prices fully reflect all production costs. | | |
| Prices convey important information for both producers and consumers. | | |

**(4 marks)**

## ? Question 17

If a business is facing a demand for its product which is price inelastic, which one of the following would occur if that business raised the price of its product?

(A) Sales volume would fall and total revenue would fall.

(B) Sales volume would stay the same and total revenue would rise.

(C) Sales volume would fall and total revenue would stay the same.

(D) Sales volume would fall and total revenue would rise.

**(2 marks)**

## ? Question 18

The price elasticity of supply of a good is a measure of the relationship between:

(A) the price of a good and the quantity supplied.

(B) the volume of supply and changes in demand for the good.

(C) a change in price of the good and the change in the quantity supplied.

(D) a change in the cost of producing a good and the quantity supplied.

**(2 marks)**

## ? Question 19

A business has current sales of 10,000 units per month at a unit price of $24. It reduces its price to $21.60 and finds that its monthly sales rise to 11,500 units. Calculate the price elasticity of demand for this product.

**(1 mark)**

## Question 20

A producer has a price inelastic supply curve for its product. State whether each of the following effects would occur (yes/no) if the firm experienced an increase in demand for its product.

| Effects | Yes | No |
| --- | --- | --- |
| Sales volume would increase. | | |
| The volume of supply would increase. | | |
| The equilibrium price would rise. | | |
| In the short run, unit production costs would increase. | | |

**(4 marks)**

## Question 21

If the government imposed a price for a good that was above the equilibrium price, the consequence would be:

(A)  a contraction of demand, an increase in supply and a market surplus.
(B)  a decrease in demand, an extension of supply and a market surplus.
(C)  a contraction in demand, an extension in supply and a market surplus.
(D)  a rise in supply, a fall in demand and a market shortage.

**(2 marks)**

## Question 22

State whether each of the following statements is *true* or *false*.

| Statements | True | False |
| --- | --- | --- |
| If the demand curve for Good A shifts to the right when the price of Good B falls we can conclude that A and B are substitute goods. | | |
| If the demand for a good is price inelastic, a fall in its price will leave sales volume unchanged and total revenue reduced. | | |
| The more price inelastic is the demand for a good, the greater is the proportion of any indirect tax levied on it that can be passed onto the consumer. | | |
| An indirect tax imposed upon a good which has negative externalities will improve resource allocation. | | |

**(4 marks)**

## ❓ **Question 23**

For firms in monopolistic competition, excess profits cannot be earned in the long run because:

(A) all firms are producing similar, undifferentiated goods.
(B) there is a very large number of firms in the industry.
(C) perfect knowledge ensures that customers always buy from the firm with the lowest price.
(D) there are no significant barriers to entry into the industry.

**(2 marks)**

## ❓ **Question 24**

The following diagram shows the cost and revenue curves for a firm in an oligopolistic market.

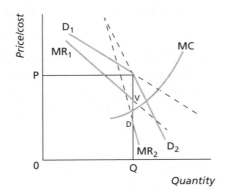

With reference to the diagram, state whether each of the following statements is true or false.

| Statements | True | False |
| --- | --- | --- |
| If the firm were to raise its price, it would expect its total revenue to fall. | | |
| If the firm were to lower its price, it would expect its total revenue to rise. | | |
| The kink in the firm's demand curve is the result of the firm's expectations about the reaction of its rivals to changes in its price. | | |
| Because of the kink in the demand curve the firm could increase profits by raising output above Q. | | |

**(4 marks)**

## ❓ **Question 25**

Which *one* of the following would act as a barrier to enter into an industry?

(A) A falling long-run average cost curve.
(B) A U-shaped short-run average cost curve for all firms.
(C) The existence of external economies of scale.
(D) Constant returns to scale in the industry.

**(2 marks)**

## Question 26

The output of merit goods is likely to be less than the social optimum because:

(A)  firms cannot ensure that all consumers pay the full price of the good or service.
(B)  the consumption of the good involves positive externalities.
(C)  the goods are necessities but are too expensive for some low-income groups.
(D)  the consumption of the good or service by one person does not preclude its consumption by others.

**(2 marks)**

## Question 27

Match the following company mergers with the merger type indicated below.

| Company merger | Merger type |
| --- | --- |
| A steel producer merges with a producer of iron ore. | |
| A car producer merges with a producer of commercial vans. | |
| A financial services company merges with a travel company. | |
| A brewing company merges with a chain of inns and bars. | |

(A)  A horizontal merger.
(B)  A backward vertical merger.
(C)  A forward vertical merger.
(D)  A conglomerate merger.

**(4 marks)**

## Question 28

All of the following are arguments in favour of a policy of privatisation except one. Which *one* is the exception? Privatisation:

(A)  will reduce X inefficiency because competition is always increased.
(B)  encourages efficiency because it introduces the profit motive.
(C)  forces businesses to respond more to consumer preferences.
(D)  raises useful short-term funds for the government.

**(2 marks)**

## Question 29

If a government imposes a maximum price for a good that is below the equilibrium price, the resulting market shortage will be greatest when:

(A)  the demand is price elastic and the supply is price inelastic.
(B)  the demand is price elastic and the supply is price elastic.
(C)  the demand is price inelastic and the supply is price elastic.
(D)  the demand is price inelastic and the supply is price inelastic.

**(2 marks)**

## Question 30

In an oligopoly market, there is a heavy dependence on advertising and marketing because:

(A) oligopoly is characterised by product differentiation.
(B) advertising and marketing are the only effective barriers to entry for firms.
(C) the small number of firms ensures that price competition often leads to losses for all firms.
(D) in oligopoly one firm's pricing policy affects the sales of other firms.

**(2 marks)**

## Question 31

Match the following situations to the definitions given below:

| Situations | Definition |
| --- | --- |
| The emission of dangerous fumes from car exhausts. | |
| Pollution caused by the production of consumer electrical goods. | |
| Premature death of consumers of tobacco. | |
| Improved health among consumers of low fat food products. | |

### Definitions

(A) Positive externality in consumption.
(B) Negative externality in consumption.
(C) Negative externality in production.
(D) None of the above.

**(4 marks)**

## Question 32

All of the following would lead to a high price elasticity of demand for a good except one. Which *one* is the exception?

(A) The good has a large number of substitutes.
(B) Consumers spend a large proportion of income of the good.
(C) It refers to a long time period.
(D) It has numerous complementary goods.

**(2 marks)**

## ? **Question 33**

Indicate whether each of the following statements about not-for-profit organisations is *true* or *false*.

| Statements | True | False |
| --- | --- | --- |
| Because they only operate in non-competitive markets, X-inefficiency is greater than that for profit-seeking organisations. | | |
| The absence of shareholders means that the principal–agent problem has no impact on them. | | |
| They need to avoid losses in the long run. | | |
| They operate in both the public and the private sectors of the economy. | | |

**(4 marks)**

## ? **Question 34**

Which *one* of the following would cause the supply curve for a good to shift to the left?

(A) The introduction of a new substitute product for the good.
(B) A rise in wage rates for workers employed in making the good.
(C) A fall in the price of raw materials used in its production.
(D) The abolition of a government-imposed minimum price for the good.

**(2 marks)**

## ? **Question 35**

If an industry is characterised by a high concentration ratio it means that

(A) The industry's main customers are mainly located in one region.
(B) Most of the output of the industry is sold to a few large customers.
(C) The bulk of the industry's output is produced by a small number of firms.
(D) Each firm in the industry specialises in a narrow range of products or markets.

**(2 marks)**

## ? **Question 36**

All of the following are conditions of demand for a good except one. Which *one* is the exception?

(A) The price of the good.
(B) Consumers preferences and tastes.
(C) The income of consumers.
(D) The number and price of complementary goods.

**(2 marks)**

# Question 37

As a result of poor harvest, the ……. (i) of coffee was significantly reduced and the supply curve shifted to the ……. (ii). Because the demand for coffee had a ……. (iii) price elasticity of demand, the result was a very steep rise in its price.

Read the above passage and indicate which of the following words should be placed in the gaps in the passage.

(A) supply.
(B) demand.
(C) high.
(D) low.
(E) left.
(F) right.

**(3 marks)**

 # Question 38

All of the following statements about a monopoly firm in the long run are correct except one. Which *one* is the exception?

(A) It will tend to produce at less that optimum output.
(B) It will earn abnormal profits.
(C) It will not necessarily have a U-shaped average cost curve.
(D) It will tend to produce at less than the equilibrium output.

**(2 marks)**

 # Question 39

All of the following are functions of money except one. Which *one* is the exception?

(A) A store of value.
(B) A medium of exchange.
(C) A unit of account.
(D) A means of financial intermediation.

**(2 marks)**

# Question 40

Indicate whether each of the following statements is *true* or *false*.

| Statements | True | False |
| --- | --- | --- |
| A government could finance a budget deficit by raising taxation. | | |
| The principal function of financial institutions is financial intermediation. | | |
| 'Liquidity' refers to the ease with which assets can be converted into cash. | | |
| The nominal value of a bond shows the amount a bond is currently worth. | | |

**(4 marks)**

## Question 41

In their role as financial intermediaries, banks fulfil all of the following functions except one. Which *one* is the exception?

(A) Financial synchronisation.
(B) Risk reduction.
(C) Aggregation.
(D) Maturity transformation.

(**2 marks**)

## Question 42

A bond has the following features.

| | |
|---|---|
| Nominal value | £1000 |
| Coupon rate | 4% |
| Current market value | £1050 |

Calculate the running yield for this bond.

(**2 marks**)

## Question 43

For each of the following sources of finance for a business, state whether they are appropriate to meet lack of financial synchronisation in the *short term*, the *medium* term or the *long term*.

| Sources of Finance | Short term | Medium term | Long term |
|---|---|---|---|
| Trade credit for a business | | | |
| Equity capital | | | |
| Hire purchase | | | |
| Bank overdraft | | | |

(**4 marks**)

## Question 44

If a bank had total assets of $100 b and was operating with a 10% reserve assets ratio, by how much would its total assets change in the long run if its reserve assets rose by $2 b but the monetary authorities required banks to raise their reserve assets ratio to 12.5%?

(A) Rise by $4 b
(B) Fall by $4 b
(C) Rise by £2 b
(D) Fall by £2.5 b

(**2 marks**)

## Question 45

All of the following would tend to raise the exchange rate (appreciate) for a country's currency except one. Which *one* is the exception?

(A) A fall in the volume of imports.
(B) A rise in foreign investment in the country.
(C) A fall in domestic interest rates.
(D) A rise in the country's invisible earnings.

(**2 marks**)

 ## Question 46

Which *one* of the following is an advantage for a country adopting a flexible exchange rate regime?

(A) It provides certainty for organisations engaging in international trade.
(B) It eliminates transactions costs.
(C) It reduces the need for central banks to keep reserves of foreign exchange.
(D) Monetary policy can be used to manage the exchange rate for the currency.

(**2 marks**)

 ## Question 47

Insurance companies undertake reinsurance because it:

(A) is a means of spreading risks.
(B) enables them charge higher premiums.
(C) helps them to avoid taking on more risky insurance contracts.
(D) enables them to invest the premium income at a higher rate of return.

(**2 marks**)

 ## Question 48

Indicate whether each of the following statements is *true* or *false*.

| Statements | True | False |
| --- | --- | --- |
| For a bank, its most liquid assets tend to be the least profitable. | | |
| Certificates of deposit are tradable financial instruments. | | |
| Bills of exchange are risky financial instruments because there is no guarantor. | | |
| Bond prices and bond yields vary positively. | | |

(**4 marks**)

**Question 49**

All of the following are functions of a central bank except one. Which *one* is the exception?

(A) Acting as lender of the last resort.
(B) Providing finance for long-term investment projects.
(C) Acting as banker for the government.
(D) Managing the country's foreign exchange reserves.

**(2 marks)**

 **Question 50**

Indicate whether each of the following financial instruments is used in the *money market* or the *capital market*.

| Instruments | Money market | Capital market |
| --- | --- | --- |
| Mortgage | | |
| Bill of Exchange | | |
| Certificates of Deposit | | |
| Gilt-edged Stock | | |

**(4 marks)**

 **Question 51**

If the exchange rate for a country's currency were to rise (appreciate), would the following prices *rise, fall* or remain *unchanged* as a direct result?

| Price | Rise | Fall | Remain unchanged |
| --- | --- | --- | --- |
| Domestic price of imported goods. | | | |
| Foreign price of imported goods. | | | |
| Domestic price of exported goods. | | | |
| Foreign price of exported goods. | | | |

**(4 marks)**

 **Question 52**

Which of the following risks can a business insure itself against?

 (i) Bad debts.
 (ii) Public liability.
(iii) Consequential loss.
(iv) Employers liability.

(A) (i), (ii) and (iii) only.
(B) (ii), (iii) and (iv) only.
(C) (ii) and (iv) only.
(D) all of them.

**(2 marks)**

## ? Question 53

Show what you would expect to happen to the following economic indicators in the boom phase of the trade cycle in the economy.

| Indicators | Rise | Fall | Remain unchanged |
|---|---|---|---|
| The rate of inflation. | | | |
| The rate of unemployment. | | | |
| A deficit on the balance of trade. | | | |
| A surplus on the government's budget. | | | |
| The underlying long-term rate of economic growth. | | | |

**(5 marks)**

## ? Question 54

According to the Keynesian view, the economy:

(A) will always tend to settle at a full employment equilibrium.
(B) will always tend to settle at an equilibrium with high unemployment.
(C) may settle at an equilibrium with any level of unemployment.
(D) will not settle at any equilibrium.

**(2 marks)**

## ? Question 55

In order to calculate gross national product (GNP) for a country it is necessary to take gross domestic product (GDP) and:

(A) add the value of exports and subtract the value of imports.
(B) add net property income from abroad.
(C) add subsidies and subtract indirect taxes.
(D) subtract the value of exports and add the value of imports.

**(2 marks)**

## ? Question 56

Indicate whether each of the following components is an *injection*, a *withdrawal (leakage)* or *neither* in the circular flow model of the economy.

| Components | Injection | Withdrawal | Neither |
| --- | --- | --- | --- |
| Taxation | | | |
| Exports | | | |
| Consumption | | | |
| Investment | | | |

**(4 marks)**

## ? Question 57

An economy has a marginal propensity to consume of 0.8. If the government raises public expenditure by $100 m, by how much will national income ultimately rise as a result?

**(2 marks)**

## ? Question 58

The accelerator theory argues that the level of business investment is determined by:

(A)  changes in the rate of interest.
(B)  the level of consumer income.
(C)  swings in business optimism and pessimism.
(D)  changes in the level of demand for goods and services.

**(2 marks)**

## ? Question 59

Inflation has all of the following effects except one. Which *one* is the exception?

(A)  It shifts wealth from debtors to creditors.
(B)  It reduces a country's international competitiveness.
(C)  It reduces the real income of those on fixed incomes.
(D)  It raises government tax revenue.

**(2 marks)**

## ? Question 60

The following is a list of types of unemployment.

> Cyclical unemployment
> Structural unemployment
> Frictional unemployment
> Real wage unemployment

Match the above types of unemployment to the appropriate policy response below.

| Policy | Type of unemployment |
|---|---|
| A policy of retraining and education. | |
| Adopting an expansionary monetary policy. | |
| Reducing the power of trade unions and professional bodies. | |
| Improving the information flows at job centres. | |

**(4 marks)**

 ## Question 61

The Phillips curve showed a:

(A) negative relationship between inflation and wage rates.
(B) positive relationship between inflation and unemployment.
(C) negative relationship between inflation and unemployment.
(D) negative relationship between unemployment and economic growth.

**(2 marks)**

 ## Question 62

All of the following are direct taxes except one. Which *one* is the exception?

(A) Income tax.
(B) National insurance (social security tax).
(C) Corporation tax.
(D) Value added tax.

**(2 marks)**

 ## Question 63

The following diagram represents aggregate demand in an economy.

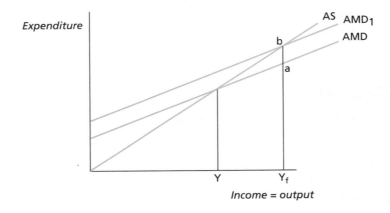

(i) From the following list, identify which *one* is the correct list of components of aggregate demand.

(A) $C + G + I + X + M$
(B) $C + G + T + I$
(C) $C + G + I + X - M$
(D) $G + I + X$

**(2 marks)**

(ii) If the government wished to shift the aggregate demand curve from AMD to $AMD_1$, which of the following measures would be appropriate?

(i) A reduction in taxation.
(ii) A rise in interest rates.
(iii) A depreciation of the exchange rate.
(iv) An increase in public expenditure.

(A) (i), (ii) and (iii) only.
(B) (i), (iii) and (iv) only.
(C) (ii), (iii) and (iv) only.
(D) (i), (ii) and (iv) only.

**(2 marks)**

(iii) State the term given to the distance ab on the diagram when $Y_f$ is the full employment level of national income.

**(2 marks)**

## ? Question 64

If the government were to adopt a restrictive monetary policy, all the following would result except one. Which *one* is the exception?

(A) Business investment would tend to decline.
(B) Private saving rates would tend to rise.
(C) Demand for goods, especially durable goods, would tend to decline.
(D) On foreign exchange markets the currency would tend to depreciate.

**(2 marks)**

## ? Question 65

Indicate whether each of the following statements is *true* or *false*.

| Statements | True | False |
| --- | --- | --- |
| Supply policies are designed to shift a country's aggregate supply curve to the left. | | |
| Monetarists believe that control of the money supply is the only effective means of preventing inflation. | | |
| Keynesians recommend budget deficits as a means of reducing unemployment. | | |

**(3 marks)**

**Question 66**

A progressive tax is best defined as one where:

(A) the amount of tax paid rises as income rises.
(B) the proportion of income paid in tax rises as income rises.
(C) the lower the level of income, the lower the amount of tax paid.
(D) there are higher tax bands applicable to higher income levels.

**(2 marks)**

 **Question 67**

Economic growth is best defined as:

(A) A rise in gross domestic product.
(B) A shift in the economy closer to its production possibility frontier.
(C) An outward movement of a country's production possibility frontier.
(D) A rise in per capita gross national income.

**(2 marks)**

 **Question 68**

If a government adopted an expansionary fiscal policy it would:

(A) lower taxes, lower public expenditure and maintain government borrowing.
(B) lower taxes, raise public spending and increase government borrowing.
(C) raise public expenditure and finance this through a rise in taxation.
(D) reduce government borrowing in order to ease credit conditions for the private sector.

**(2 marks)**

 **Question 69**

All of the following are features of the globalisation process except one. Which *one* is the exception?

(A) An expanding role for multinational companies.
(B) A reduction in artificial barriers to international trade.
(C) Increasing international factor mobility.
(D) A decline in the importance of international specialisation.

**(2 marks)**

## Question 70

Indicate for each of the following transactions whether they would be entered into the current account or the capital and financial account of the balance of payments for a country.

| Transactions | Current account | Capital/Financial account |
|---|---|---|
| Payment for a foreign holiday taken by a resident of the country. | | |
| A deposit of funds by a foreigner into a bank account in the country. | | |
| Receipt of interest from a bank account in another country. | | |
| A rise in the country's foreign exchange reserves. | | |

**(4 marks)**

## Question 71

If a group of countries adopt free trade between themselves, establish a common external tariff and allow free movement of factors of production between member states, this is called:

(A)  a common market.
(B)  an economic union.
(C)  a customs union.
(D)  a free trade area.

**(2 marks)**

## Question 72

The law of comparative advantage (cost) states that

(A)  all countries benefit from trade, provided they specialise in one main good or service.
(B)  countries gain most from trade when they have absolute advantage in producing their export good.
(C)  all countries gain from trade, provided they specialise in producing those goods whose opportunity cost is lowest.
(D)  countries will gain most from trade by exporting the goods and services in which they have specialised.

**(2 marks)**

**Question 73**

Indicate whether each of the following statements is *true* or *false*.

| Statements | True | False |
|---|---|---|
| Tariff barriers always reduce the economic welfare of the country imposing them. | | |
| Taxes on expensive imports are a useful way of reducing domestic inflationary pressure. | | |
| The main purpose of tariffs is to enable domestic producers to charge higher prices. | | |
| The main benefit of forming a free trade area is that it encourages international specialisation between member states. | | |

**(4 marks)**

 **Question 74**

Providing investment finance for development projects is the main function of:

(A) The International Monetary Fund.
(B) The World Trade Organisation.
(C) The World Bank.
(D) The European Central Bank.

**(2 marks)**

 **Question 75**

All of the following could be used by a government attempting to reduce the country's balance of payments current account deficit except one. Which *one* is the exception?

(A) A deflationary fiscal policy.
(B) An appreciation in the currency.
(C) A rise in interest rates and restrictions on credit.
(D) The imposition of exchange controls.

**(2 marks)**

## ✓ Mock Assessment 2 – Solutions

### ✓ Solution 1

B

### ✓ Solution 2

C

### ✓ Solution 3

A

### ✓ Solution 4

| Statements | True | False |
|---|---|---|
| The marginal cost curve cuts the average cost curve at its lowest point. | X | |
| Profits are maximised only where marginal revenue and average cost are equal. | | X |
| Optimum output is where average costs are lowest. | X | |
| The short-run average cost curve for firms eventually rises because of operation of diseconomies of scale. | | X |

### ✓ Solution 5

D

### ✓ Solution 6

| Event | Raise share price | Lower share price | Leave share price unchanged |
|---|---|---|---|
| A reduction in corporation tax | X | | |
| An issue of additional shares in the company | | X | |
| A fall in interest rates | X | | |
| A high price-earnings ratio | | | X |

### ✓ Solution 7

(a) $85

(b) $35

(c) −2

## Solution 8

(a) $5402
(b) No
(c) $131

 ## Solution 9

25%

 ## Solution 10

| Measures | Short run | Long run |
|---|---|---|
| Net present value | | X |
| Rate of return on capital employed | X | |
| Earnings per share | X | |

 ## Solution 11

C

 ## Solution 12

An example of the principal–agent problem in business is where principals, such as *shareholders*, delegate control to agents, such as *management*. The problem is one of devising methods to ensure that agents act in the best interest of the principals. Managerial reward systems which link pay and bonuses to the improvement in *shareholder value* is one such method.

 ## Solution 13

D

 ## Solution 14

B

 ## Solution 15

B

 ## Solution 16

| Statements | True | False |
|---|---|---|
| The price mechanism is the only means for allocating scarce resources. | | X |
| The public sector is smaller than the private sector. | X | |
| Market prices fully reflect all production costs. | | X |
| Prices convey important information for both producers and consumers. | X | |

## ✅ Solution 17

D

## ✅ Solution 18

C

## ✅ Solution 19

−1.5

## ✅ Solution 20

| Effects | Yes | No |
|---|---|---|
| Sales volume would increase. | X | |
| The volume of supply would increase. | | X |
| The equilibrium price would rise. | X | |
| In the short run, unit production costs would increase. | X | |

## ✅ Solution 21

C

## ✅ Solution 22

| Statements | True | False |
|---|---|---|
| If the demand curve for Good A shifts to the right when the price of Good B falls we can conclude that A and B are substitute goods. | | X |
| If the demand for a good is price inelastic, a fall in its price will leave sales volume unchanged and total revenue reduced. | | X |
| The more price inelastic is the demand for a good, the greater is the proportion of any indirect tax levied on it that can be passed onto the consumer. | X | |
| An indirect tax impose upon a good which has negative externalities will improve resource allocation. | X | |

## ✅ Solution 23

D

MOCK ASSESSMENT 2

 **Solution 24**

| Statements | True | False |
|---|---|---|
| If the firm were to raise its price, it would expect its total revenue to fall. | X | |
| If the firm were to lower its price, it would expect its total revenue to rise. | | X |
| The kink in the firm's demand curve is the result of the firm's expectations about the reaction of its rivals to changes in its price. | X | |
| Because of the kink in the demand curve the firm could increase profits by raising output above Q. | | X |

 **Solution 25**

A

 **Solution 26**

B

 **Solution 27**

| Company merger | Merger type |
|---|---|
| A steel producer merges with a producer of iron ore. | B |
| A car producer merges with a producer of commercial vans. | A |
| A financial services company merges with a travel company. | D |
| A brewing company merges with a chain of inns and bars. | C |

 **Solution 28**

A

 **Solution 29**

B

 **Solution 30**

C

 **Solution 31**

| Situations | Definition |
|---|---|
| The emission of dangerous fumes from car exhausts. | B |
| Pollution caused by the production of consumer electrical goods. | C |
| Premature death of consumers of tobacco. | D |
| Improved health among consumers of low fat food products. | D |

**Solution 32**

D

 **Solution 33**

| Statements | True | False |
|---|---|---|
| Because they only operate in non-competitive markets, X-inefficiency is greater than that for profit-seeking organisations. | | X |
| The absence of shareholders means that the principal–agent problem has no impact on them. | | X |
| They need to avoid losses in the long run. | X | |
| They operate in both the public and the private sectors of the economy. | X | |

 **Solution 34**

B

 **Solution 35**

C

 **Solution 36**

A

 **Solution 37**

As a result of poor harvest the *supply* of coffee was significantly reduced and the supply curve shifted to the *left*. Because the demand for coffee had a *low* price elasticity of demand, the result was a very steep rise in its price.

 **Solution 38**

D

 **Solution 39**

D

 **Solution 40**

| Statements | True | False |
|---|---|---|
| A government could finance a budget deficit by raising taxation. | | X |
| The principal function of financial institutions is financial intermediation. | X | |
| 'Liquidity' refers to the ease with which assets can be converted into cash. | X | |
| The nominal value of a bond shows the amount a bond is currently worth. | | X |

**Solution 41**

A

 **Solution 42**

3.81%

 **Solution 43**

| Sources of Finance | Short term | Medium term | Long term |
|---|---|---|---|
| Trade credit for a business | X | | |
| Equity capital | | | X |
| Hire purchase | | X | |
| Bank overdraft | X | | |

 **Solution 44**

B

 **Solution 45**

C

 **Solution 46**

C

 **Solution 47**

A

 **Solution 48**

| Statements | True | False |
|---|---|---|
| For a bank, its most liquid assets tend to be the least profitable. | X | |
| Certificates of deposit are tradable financial instruments. | X | |
| Bills of exchange are risky financial instruments because there is no guarantor. | | X |
| Bond prices and bond yields vary positively. | | X |

 **Solution 49**

B

 **Solution 50**

| Instruments | Money market | Capital market |
|---|---|---|
| Mortgage | | X |
| Bill of Exchange | X | |
| Certificates of Deposit | X | |
| Gilt-edged Stock | | X |

## Solution 51

| Price | Rise | Fall | Remain unchanged |
|---|---|---|---|
| Domestic price of imported goods. | | X | |
| Foreign price of imported goods. | | | X |
| Domestic price of exported goods. | | | X |
| Foreign price of exported goods. | X | | |

 ## Solution 52

D

 ## Solution 53

| Indicators | Rise | Fall | Remain unchanged |
|---|---|---|---|
| The rate of inflation. | X | | |
| The rate of unemployment. | | X | |
| A deficit on the balance of trade. | X | | |
| A surplus on the government's budget. | X | | |
| The underlying long-term rate of economic growth. | | | X |

 ## Solution 54

C

 ## Solution 55

B

 ## Solution 56

| Components | Injection | Withdrawal | Neither |
|---|---|---|---|
| Taxation | | X | |
| Exports | X | | |
| Consumption | | | X |
| Investment | X | | |

 ## Solution 57

$500 m

 ## Solution 58

D

 ## Solution 59

A

# Solution 60

| Policy | Type of Unemployment |
|---|---|
| A policy of retraining and education. | *Structural unemployment* |
| Adopting an expansionary monetary policy. | *Cyclical unemployment* |
| Reducing the power of trade unions and professional bodies. | *Real wage unemployment* |
| Improving the information flows at job centres. | *Frictional unemployment* |

 # Solution 61

C

 # Solution 62

D

 # Solution 63

(i)  C
(ii)  B
(iii)  Deflationary gap

 # Solution 64

D

 # Solution 65

| Statements | True | False |
|---|---|---|
| Supply-side policies are designed to shift a country's aggregate supply curve to the left. | | X |
| Monetarists believe that control of the money supply is the only effective means of preventing inflation. | X | |
| Keynesians recommend budget deficits as a means of reducing unemployment. | X | |

 # Solution 66

B

 # Solution 67

C

 # Solution 68

B

# Solution 69

D

# Solution 70

| Transactions | Current account | Capital/Financial account |
|---|---|---|
| Payment for a foreign holiday taken by a resident of the country. | X | |
| A deposit of funds by a foreigner into a bank account in the country. | | X |
| Receipt of interest from a bank account in another country. | X | |
| A rise in the country's foreign exchange reserves. | | X |

 # Solution 71

A

 # Solution 72

C

 # Solution 73

| Statements | True | False |
|---|---|---|
| Tariff barriers always reduce the economic welfare of the country imposing them. | X | |
| Taxes on expensive imports are a useful way of reducing domestic inflationary pressure. | | X |
| The main purpose of tariffs is to enable domestic producers to charge higher prices. | X | |
| The main benefit of forming a free trade area is that it encourages international specialisation between member states. | X | |

 # Solution 74

C

# Solution 75

B

Index

# Index